CONTINUING PROFESSIONAL EDUCATION IN TRANSITION

Visions for the Professions and New Strategies for Lifelong Learning

Edited by
William H. Young

Foreword by
Ronald M. Cervero

KRIEGER PUBLISHING COMPANY
MALABAR, FLORIDA
1998

Original Edition 1998

Printed and Published by
KRIEGER PUBLISHING COMPANY
KRIEGER DRIVE
MALABAR, FLORIDA 32950

Copyright © 1998 by Krieger Publishing Company

FROM A DECLARATION OF PRINCIPLES JOINTLY ADOPTED BY A COMMITTEE OF THE AMERICAN BAR ASSOCIATION AND A COMMITTEE OF PUBLISHERS:

This Publication is designed to provide accurate and authoritative information in regard to the subject matter covered. It is sold with the understanding that the publisher is not engaged in rendering legal, accounting, or other professional service. If legal advice or other expert assistance is required, the services of a competent professional person should be sought.

Library of Congress Cataloging-in-Publication Data

Continuing professional education in transition: visions for the professions and new
    strategies for lifelong learning / edited by William H. Young; foreword by Ronald
    M. Cervero.–original ed.
        p.   cm.
    Includes bibliographical references and index.
    ISBN 0-89464-997-3 (hard: alk. paper)
    1. Professional education–United States.   2. Continuing education–United
States.   I. Young, William H., 1943-
LC1072.C56C662   1998
374′.973–dc21   97-25897
                                                                            CIP

10 9 8 7 6 5 4 3 2

DEDICATION

This book is for my continuing professional education colleagues at Penn State, University of Illinois and Northern Illinois University. I have been fortunate to have worked with talented and humane continuing educators who took a sincere interest in me and my professional growth. I will be forever grateful.

Second, I wish to dedicate this book to the family members, partners and significant others who created and encouraged the authors and yours truly to finish this book. Specifically, I have chosen to honor the memory of my mother and father, Helen Grace Young and William H. Young, Jr. and my favorite little companion, friend and son, Douglas Bryan Young. Thanks, Mom and Dad, for the little things and the self-confidence necessary to live a full life, and thank you, Doug, for giving me a renewed life worth living and the time to work at home to finish this book.

DEDICATED TO MY SON

DOUGLAS BRYAN YOUNG

AND

TO THE MEMORY OF MY PARENTS

HELEN GRACE YOUNG

AND

WILLIAM H. YOUNG, JR.

CONTINUING PROFESSIONAL EDUCATION IN TRANSITION

Visions for the Professions and
New Strategies for Lifelong Learning

Part II. The Role of Continuing Professional Education in Resolving Critical Issues Facing Selected Professions

Contents

FOREWORD
Ronald M. Cervero

Whenever I speak to groups of professionals about the kind of continuing education that they experience, I use a picture painted in words by Philip Nowlen (1988). He said that the most frequently encountered form of continuing professional education is one where "a single instructor lectures and lectures and lectures fairly large groups of business and professional people, who sit for long hours in an audiovisual twilight, making never-to-be-read notes at rows of narrow tables covered with green baize and appointed with fat binders and sweating pitchers of ice water" (p. 23). This picture is as universally recognizable to the members of my audiences in any profession as it is criticized for being largely ineffective in improving the performance of these same professionals. Yet we get stuck when we try to imagine a similarly recognizable picture of continuing education that is effective in today's complex world. I believe that one reason for this lack of a unifying picture of effective continuing education is that the professions are in a transitional stage of experimenting with many different purposes, forms, and institutional locations for the delivery of continuing education. Given this situation, then, it is no accident that this book was written because its central theme is that continuing professional education is in transition.

In order to see the importance of this transition, I would like to sketch a brief history of continuing education for the professions. Until about 30 years ago little systematic thought was given to the organization of systems of continuing education. It was believed that the three to five years of preservice training was sufficient for a lifetime of work. However, with the rapid social changes and technological innovations of the past quarter century, the need for continuing education is nearly universally accepted today. The systems that have been built up in most professions may be characterized as (1) devoted to updating practitioners about the newest developments, and (2) transmitted in a didactic fashion, (3) by a pluralistic group of providers, (4) which do not work together, and (5) which are almost entirely unconnected to the previous levels of professional education.

As the many chapters in this book indicate, however, there is much change occurring in all five of these dimensions. This is to be expected because, relatively speaking, systems of continuing education are in their infancy. By way of analogy, continuing education is in the same state of development as preservice education was at the beginning of this century. Medical education serves as a useful example on this point. In 1910, of the 155 medical schools in this country, only 16 expected that their incoming students would have any previous college work. It is clear that no one at that time would have predicted the structure of medical education today. Likewise, systems of continuing education will grow through this transitional period to achieve an equivalent coherence, size, and stature as the preservice stage of professional education.

This book is able to capture the dynamism of this transitional stage because its many authors are reporting what they see in their own part of the continuing education environment. They present a picture of rapidly changing practice settings across the professions, and thus, the need for a continuing education response that is up to the task of preparing professionals for this world. The first part of the book considers a number of very important dimensions of this changing environment including the racial and ethnic diversity of professionals; the impact of the technological developments on professional practice and, therefore, continuing education; and the need to move beyond simply the delivery of content to educating for empowerment, wellness, critical thinking, and entrepreneurship. The book's second section provides a very rich discussion of how continuing education is being used to resolve critical issues in the structure and practice of 12 different professions. This section is particularly useful because it shows the transition continuing education is going through with many real-life dilemmas and issues.

This book does not intend to offer a single answer to the question, "Now what?" However, by showing the terrain that must be trod, the book illuminates the environment in which we will seek to move beyond this transitional stage in building systems of continuing education for the professions.

REFERENCE

Nowlen, P. M. (1988). *A new approach to continuing education for business and the professions: The performance model.* New York: Macmillan.

INTRODUCTION
William H. Young

The authors and I have organized this book so the reader can utilize the content of any chapter as a stand-alone resource. Each chapter has its own message, its own uniqueness, and its own sense of importance. Together, the chapters do constitute a book with a single theme—continuing professional education in transition.

Professionals are being asked to perform more, learn more, and accept more responsibilities. At the same time, they are being retired, displaced, and outsourced. Organizations where professionals work are currently undergoing downsizing, rightsizing, and reengineering. The survival of the professions and the professional in America is in a state of transition; therefore, the education used to support these individuals, continuing professional education, is in transition, also.

The chapters begin with an attempt to define continuing professional education (CPE) within the context of adult and continuing education. We need to have a sense of where we have been before we can understand where we are and where we hope to go. In Chapter 1, Thomas Lifvendahl, argues that human resource development using principles and practices of continuing professional education needs to be placed into a new context in order to understand the present state and future direction of continuing professional education. Tom develops a schema designed to integrate the diversity of thinking and doing within the broad field of adult and continuing education by classifying current completed dissertations and other selected documents. He concludes with recommendations and observations for practitioners in the field.

Professionals pleased with their professional and personal growth and development are exhibiting qualities that other professionals do not seem to possess. First of all, leading edge professionals are mentally, physically, and emotionally well, are empowered, have critical thinking skills, and are entrepreneurial. These individuals work successfully in a variety of settings, have a strong knowledge of technology, have embraced diversity, and are committed to a systematic continuing professional education effort. The remaining chapters in the first section of this book explore these traits, qualities, competencies, and performance-based behaviors that are necessary for professional survival and success in the coming decades.

In Chapter 2 Michele Hamil reminds us that good health is the foundation block for the good life and for learning. The link between wellness and professional success has been receiving increasing attention in human resource development and continuing professional education. By considering the whole person, educators can improve programming and learning environments and help professionals and their organizations reach goals established within their mission and vision. Michele provides a practical guide to enhance individual and organizational quality of life by fostering a state of wellness that should be the foundation of a systematic continuing professional education effort.

Jane Flagello explores the role of continuing professional education as the catalyst to workplace empowerment in Chapter 3. Jane provides information on the changing nature of work and the need professionals have to participate in meaningful activities that make a difference. As the old paternalistic corporate, military, and higher education order declines and the implied employer-employee contracts are increasingly broken, more and more companies are faced with the harsh realities of survival in a changing economic and global landscape. The entitlement mentality must give way to one of professional responsibility and self-efficacy, and the role of continuing professional education in these changes will be increasingly important.

As a graduate of several professional schools, Arnold Bickham, in Chapter 4, tells us that professional schools do not spend enough time teaching or exposing individuals to critical thinking as students learn to be professionals. Liberal arts and other general education classes enrolling 75–1,000 students don't create environments conducive to critical thinking in any form. Arnold believes that every profession may want to examine itself, highlight those areas where critical thinking and continuing professional education are flourishing, and develop new strategies to infuse critical thinking into the other areas. Professionals need to know that critical thinking today is one of the more important skills and mindsets needed for survival and success. The two central activities of critical thinking are identifying and challenging assumptions and exploring alternative ways of thinking and acting about information and incidents appearing in life and in print. Several of my colleagues argue that critical thinking is almost never utilized as a content area or as a strategy in continuing professional education.

Once professionals leave their universities qualified to practice their profession, they find they must seek information outside those universities about how to actually implement their knowledge and skills in a business. Zira Smith, in Chapter 5, points out that most professionals learn how to operate their business enterprises by trial and error. Zira believes that continuing professional education personnel must develop programmatic responses via readily accessible self-employment information specifically geared to the kinds of business started by professionals. Small business development is one of the major growth areas for professional employment and for continuing professional education. Professional school leaders need to focus their attention on several of her conclusions in order to include entrepreneurship across the professional school curriculum.

Brenda Young, in Chapter 6, explores the unexamined assumption that if you give people enough information or a new technology, they will know what it means and know what to do with it, and that people will reason their way to the best use of something. However, when looking at the historical introduction to new tools, technology, or ideas, people seldom immediately recognize the significance of a transforming technology or idea, and may indeed reject it as a fad, foolhardy, or worse. Within Brenda's chapter, she warns us that educational leaders and their organizations must recognize that we are truly at a point of departure and for those institutions which do not recognize this transformation from the industrial age to the information age there may be a "Wait for Me! I'm your leader!" scenario. Educators must find ways to utilize the new communications technologies and the most significant changes centered around the timing of programs, the volume of information needed, and the decentralization of organizational communications which will bring about the democratization of technology.

In Chapter 7, Deborah and Michael Colky talk about one of the newest changes in the professional work environment. The virtual organization is an attempt to satisfy customer requirements by providing services and products around the clock and around the world while meeting the needs of employees for more balance in the lives of professionals. It is a way of organizing a business and it appears to be growing steadily. Deborah and Michael explore the role of continuing professional education in these new virtual organizations.

LaVerne Gyant briefly discusses the history of blacks and their participation in formal and informal continuing professional education in Chapter 8. This history provides insight as to why continuing professional education personnel have neglected diverse population issues in their programming. LaVerne provides strategies to improve and increase diverse populations' participation in CPE.

Chapter 9 concludes the first section of the book. I deal with the issue of creating administrative and political systematic continuing professional education efforts focusing on the mandatory continuing professional education dinosaur and the creation of new systematic efforts that educators must begin to embrace or become antiquated in providing CPE.

Part II focuses on issues directly affecting 12 of the professions. I had a difficult task in choosing which professions to include in this book. I started by including Law, Medicine, Engineering and the Clergy simply based upon the fact that most individuals include these professions in any discussion about continuing professional education. Second, the health professions as a group have been leaders in the development of formal continuing professional education activities for their members. Dietetics, Nursing, and Medicine represent these leading edge professions in creating systematic CPE for their members. The "helping" professions have been very active in continuing professional education; therefore, Social Work and K–12 Education appeared to be benchmark professions in this arena. The literature is filled with information about emerging professions. Organizations representing these professionals have been very creative and innovative in their ideas, approaches, and content used in continuing professional education. Real Estate, Policing, and Informations Systems Specialists represent the emerging professions. Finally, a book on continuing professional education would not be complete without including a discussion about Military Leadership CPE. The Military has provided systematic continuing professional education for its leaders since the Revolutionary War. Current efforts manifested for this group of professionals are also noteworthy. There were other professions considered, but it was necessary to keep this book to a manageable size. The issues discussed in the 12 representative professions cover the major current issues and the future directions of most professions. The interest and enthusiasm exhibited by the potential chapter authors also played a role in the final decisions of which to include when an either/or decision was necessary.

Katherine Pijanowski, in Chapter 10, provides a synthesis of information on continuing medical education in the United States. Kitty calls for the creation of a new continuing medical education paradigm that focuses on the improvement of patient care through the facilitation of change in medical practice. The physician as learner must be at the center of the educational planning process and must assume responsibility in a self-determined and self-regulating educational system.

In Chapter 11, Anne Devney presents evidence that nurses see continuing education as an essential means of acquiring new skills and knowledge, as well as updating skills previously learned to improve health care delivery. Anne believes that continuing education can serve as a survival strategy for those nurses who need to cross-train to improve their chances of job retention. Continuing professional educators are served well by Anne's efforts to explore the current and potential means by which this important profession seeks, implements, and expands its practicing knowledge and skills.

Social work, a profession known by its advocacy for society's poor and disenfranchised groups, is explored by Sandra Mills in Chapter 12. Sandra provides strategies for this profession's survival and the role of continuing professional education in its rebirth. The suggested role of continuing professional education in this profession's future is benchmark material.

As the technical demand and knowledge base continue to expand along with the institutional and public expectations of accountability, dietetics practitioners will be expected to communicate, formulate, and adhere to standards of practice well beyond those expected today. In Chapter 13, Janet Regan-Klich presents the critical issues facing the profession and provides CPE personnel with programming possibilities and with practitioners' expectations about the educational efforts.

Monty Winters tells us that the last quarter of the 20th century has not been kind to the office or profession of the clergy. In Chapter 14, Monty tells us that the directions and viability of continuing professional education for the ministry will lie not only in updating or enhancing the profession, but also will require transforming that education to fit with a changing church in an uncertain society. Those challenges that are unique to the heritage, goals, and focus of the minister form the substance of this chapter.

In Chapter 15, Daniel Cavallini talks about the significant changes in staff development in the school. Continuing professional education for the K–12 educators has moved from supplemental and perhaps remedial teacher training to an important vehicle for change in the modern school. A brief description of past practice is followed by current school problems and the utilization of continuing professional education as part of the solution.

A call for mandatory continuing legal education and the increased involvement of law school professors in the process of continuing legal education are two very important issues discussed by Patrick Waring in Chapter 16. Pat also looks critically at the contributions CPE personnel offer and reviews the influence of private companies, bar associations and, the judiciary in continuing legal education.

In Chapter 17, Thomas Arnold and Gene Scaramella provide continuing professional education personnel with a brief overview regarding the professionalization of the field of law enforcement by offering a rationale for determining whether policing can be viewed as a profession. Tom and Gene describe the current state of CPE relevant to policing; identify what they believe to be the major obstacles to effective CPE in policing; offer an informal opinion of whether a policy of mandatory CPE should be implemented; and finally, provide recommendations for more effective programming for this emerging profession.

Tony Latham, in Chapter 18, points out that individuals who serve in our armed forces are linked by one theme—their participation in continuing professional education. Participation is related to their individual duties and responsibilities, their roles as members of teams, and to the missions of their units. The vast majority of CPE personnel never participated in military service; therefore, a review of the military leadership continuing professional education system may help the reader to compare and contrast the military system of education with that of other professions. New roles for continuing professional educators outside the military may be possible given the needs for distance education and technology delivery of "just-in-time" education.

Margot Weinstein, in Chapter 19, discusses the history of real estate professionals in America and talks about the controversies, critical issues, trends, and visions in real estate continuing professional education for the 21st century. She makes a case for mandatory continuing professional education for this emerging profession. In order to deal with the rapid pace of change in their workplaces, communities, and social structures, real estate professionals are pursuing lifelong education in their professional associations, in colleges and universities, and within their employing agencies.

In Chapter 20, Richard Clehouse talks about reengineering the engineer, engineering and engineering education. Dick provides some answers concerning the possible change agent role that continuing professional education will play in resolving the critical issues facing engineering to retrofit the present workforce and script the future for the workplace 2005.

Information systems personnel are a discrete profession and David Branigan, in Chapter 21 describes the need for content-related CPE, talks about certification in the field and discusses the need for educational programs that go beyond the specific content-related material (soft skills) that are applied directly to the improvement of computer technology skills.

Finally, Chapter 22 provides a model for professional development that has been introduced in the K-12 education field that may be of value to other professions as well. Rita Clehouse documents her belief that a powerful transformation results from involvement with the National Board for Professional Teaching Standards Certification and these results last a lifetime.

In conclusion I make the case that learner-centered, just-in-time educational activity, which improves professional practice, must become the focus for all continuing professional education.

CONTRIBUTORS

Dr. Thomas Arnold is professor, criminal justice, College of Lake County, Grayslake, Illinois.

Dr. Arnold Bickham is a principal staff member and manager of the Workplace Literacy Institute, a nonprofit organization working with Chicago's inner-city literacy deficient population. In addition, he works in the Adult Learning Skills Program at Kennedy-King College, Chicago, Illinois. After receiving his M.D. degree from Meharry Medical College, Bickham practiced many years as a physician and administrator for two medical corporations. During those years, he found time to serve as the Illinois State Director for Prison Fellowship and completed an M.A. degree in Organizational Development at Loyola University in Chicago. His earlier education is diverse coming from Xavier University in Science, DePaul University in Public Administration and the University of Chicago's Executive MBA program.

Mr. David D. Branigan is assistant professor, computer information systems, DeVry Institute of Technology. He has been a practitioner of continuing education for information systems professionals for more than fifteen years. He has conducted technical seminars in database and applications development for customers at Intel, Cullinet and ACI; written and conducted seminars on CD-Rom authoring for Microtrends; hired and trained programmers as Systems Manager of Training for Marshall Field's Company; and directed and taught programming for El Valor Corporation's ProgramAble, and IBM sponsored computer career training program for persons with disabilities.

Dr. Daniel J. Cavallini is the Special Education Department chair, Zion-Benton Township High School, Zion, Illinois. He has thirty years of teaching experience in Indiana and Illinois public schools. Dr. Cavallini has taught many subjects in most K–12 grade levels mainly in social studies and special education. Critical reading of this author's chapter by Mr. Herb Ramlose, Zion-Benton Township High School English Department is gratefully acknowledged.

Dr. Ronald M. Cervero is professor, Department of Adult Education, The University of Georgia. Professor Cervero has published extensively in adult education, with particular emphasis in the areas of continuing education for the professions and program planning. His three books on the topic have won several national awards, including the 1989 Cyril O. Houle World Award for Literature in Adult Education (*Effective Continuing Education for Professionals,* Jossey-Bass). He has been invited to present his work at many national and international meetings . His recent book, *Planning Responsibly for Adult Education: A Guide to Negotiating Power and Interests* (Jossey-Bass), offers a theory of program planning practice. Ron has served in a variety of leadership positions including the editorship of *Adult Education Quarterly.* He has been a visiting faculty member at several Canadian and American Universities.

Mr. Richard Eugene Clehouse is a dean at the DuPage campus of De-Vry Institute of Technology for two programs: Electronics Technology and Telecommunications Management. He has been in this position for fourteen years. Richard has been an electronics teacher in both secondary education and community colleges, a plant manager for Quality Service Electronics, and a chief technical editor for Electronic Training Systems of California. His undergraduate and master's degrees were completed at Indiana State University. He is currently completing a doctorate degree in adult continuing education with a cognate in higher education.

Ms. Rita E. Clehouse, having taught grades kindergarten through college for 25 years, is one of the first National Board Certified Teachers (NBCT). Currently, she is teaching at risk students at The Phoenix Experience while working for educational improvement on a state and national level. As an NBCT, Rita mentors candidates for National Board Certification and pilots site assessments for Educational Testing Serivce (ETS). She is involved with interstate New Teacher Assessment and Support Consortium's (INTASC) project to develop and implement prototype performance assessments that will guide the licensing of teachers within thirteen states. Rita is also working with the Illinois State Board of Education's pilot mentoring program, professional development reassessments, and state goals and guidelines. Continually seeking her own improvement as a teacher, Rita shares her research on teaching and learning with audiences locally, nationally, and internationally. She is pursuing a doctorate degree in adult continuing education with cognates in curriculum, instruction and higher education.

Ms. Deborah Lavin Colky is a principal of Just Results, Inc., a research and training company located in Oak Park, Illinois. A professional in training and development for more than fifteen years, Deborah's background is in adult education and management. As an instructional designer and trainer, Deborah developed and facilitated training for a diverse list of clients, including Ameritech, American Medical Association, Allstate, Abbott Labs, Chicago Title and Trust and Suburban Propane. She received an award from Ameritech Cellular for her work on the Customer Service Improvement Project. Because of her belief that education can be a life-enriching experience, Ms. Colky is pursuing a doctorate in adult continuing education. In that capacity, she is involved in research on the role of education and training in the virtual organization. Deborah has a M.S.Ed. from Indiana University and a B.A. from St. Norbert College. She serves on the advisory board and is a faculty member of Roosevelt University's master's degree program in training and development.

Dr. Michael Colky is the president of Just Results, Inc., a research and training company located in Oak Park, Illinois. During the past fifteen years, Michael has been responsible for the development, administration, and implementation of research, education and training for diverse clientele including Suburban Propane, Ameritech, AT&T, The Mirage Hotel and Casino, Midas International and Federal Express. Michael began his professional career in the university environment where he served as an administrator of continuing education programs for adults. In this capacity, he was able to bridge the gap between academia and industry, and was much sought after as a speaker and consultant because of his success. Recently, his research has focused on the concept of the virtual organization. Dr. Colky has a Ph.D. from Loyola University, a M.S. Ed. from Indiana University, and a B.S. from the University of Illinois.

Dr. Anne M. Devney, Ed.D., R.N. is director, health services, College of Lake County, Grayslake, Illinois and Adjunct Faculty Member at College of Lake County, National-Louis University, College of St. Francis, and Northern Illinois University. She is a Commander, Nurse Corps, U. S. Navy (Retired).

Dr. Jane R. Flagello is a personal and professional coach with Direction Dynamics, Inc., Naperville, Illinois, a company dedicated to companioning successful and healthy adults along their journey as they create the life they truly want to be living. Direction Dynamics is a direct outgrowth of Dr. Flagello's dissertation research and study of adulthood and the challenges adults face now, at the dawn of the twenty-first century. Dr. Flagello is also a professor of management and leadership at DeVry Institute of Technology, DuPage Campus and a visiting lecturer at North Central College in Naperville, Illinois.

Dr. LaVerne Gyant is assistant professor, adult continuing education, Department of Leadership and Educational Policy Studies, College of Education and Assistant Director, Black Studies Center, Northern Illinois University.

Dr. Michele Hamil is the manager for Conference Planning and Services, Hoffman Estates Education Center, Northern Illinois University and has been involved in instructional design and management development for a large corporation. She is also currently working as an author and writer and is an adjunct faculty member at University of St. Francis and Benedictine University in the Chicagoland area.

Dr. Tony Latham is a retired colonel, United States Army and an assistant professor, Physical Therapy Department, Finch University of the Health Sciences, The Chicago Medical School.

Dr. Thomas A. Lifvendahl is curriculum director for the Division of Business and Management, Cardinal Stritch College. Tom's present research interests are focused on investigations of the philosophical and historical grounding of adult education. Dr. Lifvendahl has a varied background in secondary education, business management, and higher education.

Ms. Sandra J. Mills, MSW, ACSW, LCSW, is assistant professor, Social Work and Child, Family and Community Services, University of Illinois at Springfield and Manager of Government Affairs, National Association of Social Workers-Illinois Chapter.

Ms. Katherine Pijanowski, M.S.Ed., is the director of Program Development, Hospital Occupational Medicine. Kitty is the former assistant director of Education, American College of Occupational and

Enviromental Medicine where she organized and administered continuing medical education programs for member physicians.

Ms. Janet Regan-Klich has been a staff member at the American Dietetics Association and was clinical assistant professor, Department of Nutrition, College of the Associated Health Professors, University of Illinois, Chicago. She continues to be a practicing dietitian.

Mr. Gene Scaramella is the director, Office of Organized Crime Research, Office of International Criminal Justice and Adjunct Faculty Member, Department of Criminal Justice, University of Illinois at Chicago.

Dr. Zira J. Smith is the Regional Director of the Illinois Institute for Entrepreneurship Education.

Dr. Patrick J. S. Waring is currently developing the LL.M. in intellectual property law while serving as assistant professor, Department of Law, City University of Hong Kong. Pat comes to Hong Kong after completing the LL.M. degree at Columbia University in New York City. Previous to that, Dr. Waring completed both his J.D. and Ed.D. degrees at Northern Illinois University. While at Northern Illinois University, Pat worked with the Office of the General Counsel, the Department of Leadership and Educational Policy Studies, and the Department of Curriculum and Instruction. Pat has experience teaching at both the undergraduate and graduate education levels. His interests focus on legal education, law and the social sciences, the higher education law and intellectual property law.

Ms. Margot B. Weinstein is vice president of Kingston Group, Inc., a commercial real estate company located in Northbrook, Illinois. She has been a professional in the real estate field for thirty years in which she has worked in various training and leadership roles. Throughout her career, she has continued to pursue both formal and informal education. She received a baccalaureate degree with honors in 1992, a master's degree in 1994, a second master's degree in 1997, and is a degree candidate in a doctoral program of studies. She plans to write her dissertation on continuing professional education in the field of real estate. Ms. Weinstein is a member of the National Association of Realtors, The Illinois Association of Realtors, The American Association of Adult and Continuing Education, The American Psychological Association of Graduate Students, The American Association of University Women, and The American College Personnel Association.

Dr. Monty Winters is an ordained minister with over seventeen years of experience in pastoral and denominational leadership. Monty is an experienced program developer living in Tecumseh, Oklahoma. He consults with churches and mission agencies in designing innovative programs to educate and train church leaders and pastors.

Ms. Brenda G. Young, M.B.A., has worked as an account executive and marketing manager in the computer and telecommunications fields for many years. Her master's degree research centered on how people adapt to and adopt new technologies.

Dr. William H. Young is professor of adult continuing education, Department of Leadership and Educational Policy Studies, College of Education, Northern Illinois University. He has many years of continuing professional education experience working as an assistant dean for continuing medical education, a health science center director for continuing health professions education and as a dean of a college of continuing education.

Part I
Issues and Visions for the
Continuing Education
of Professionals

1

Visioning in Continuing Professional Education Via Paradigm Shifts in Research Activities: A Pragmatic Approach

Thomas A. Lifvendahl

INTRODUCTION

Adult Continuing Professional Education (ACPE) is a relatively new field of study whose movement toward becoming "a distinct field of practice is unmistakable" (Cervero in Meriam & Cunningham, 1989, p. 514). It has striven to define its practice along lines of inquiry that has led some writers to criticize the field's practitioners "as aid[ing] in bringing about flexibility [in application of learning recommendations] and responding to change, but not in directly bringing about this change" (Rose, 1996). ACPE, much less adult education, is also portrayed by some researchers as "merely a means to an end" (Rose, 1996) where an organizational objective can be met by simply employing specific methods in order to reach preferred ends. Thus, one can view ACPE as a "tool for transformation" that tends to emphasize individual growth and development at the expense of social change.

I believe that this critique creates a phenomenon that manifests itself repeatedly whenever one asks adult educators to specifically define adult continuing education in the professions. Generally, adult educators seem unable to come to consensus as to what ACPE "is." Jarvis (1990) stated that definition "is among the most problematic [issues] in the field" (p. 6). The intellectual basis for this situation, I believe, is exacerbated by the fact that many practitioners advocate seeking a single, all-encompassing definition of the field of ACPE.

ACPE is a field in rapid flux. In this chapter, I will argue that understanding the "true nature" of professional development mediated through ACPE requires a new analytical approach. I will further argue that the field consider adopting a philosophy capable of integrating the diversity of thinking and research modalities endemic in adult continuing education. As a result of my own recent dissertation research, I will chronicle the creation of a schema designed to facilitate exploration into what the field "does" via classifying appropriate dissertations and other selected documents of current research.

The chapter begins with an overview of how adult continuing education has been historically defined. An examination of pragmatism , as a more appropriate philosophy of inquiry, is presented. This is followed by an explication of my classification system, the data analyzed, the matrix used in analysis, and initial findings. The chapter concludes with recommendations and observations for practitioners in the field.

DEFINITION AND CLARIFICATION OF ADULT EDUCATION TERMS

Since the beginning of professional studies in adult continuing education (ACE) numerous definitions of the field have emerged. All have tended to be contextualized within an interpretive analysis dynamic centered on thematic paradigms. Thus, ACE can be interpreted as a "movement" devoted to the education of adults (Boyd, Apps, & Associates, 1980, pp. 10–11), as a "process" of "systematic and sustained learning" (Darkenwald & Merriam, 1982, p. 9), and "as a field of professional practice" (Merriam & Cunningham, 1989, p. 19).

Jarvis (1990) noted that "the term [ACE] is first used in Thomas Pole's *History and Origins and Progress of Adult Schools* (p. 6). He noted that some scholars "wish to restrict [ACE] to certain forms of planned process, such as those having a humanistic basis, but other scholars would want to restrict the process to certain types of learning[s]" (p. 6). Courtney (Merriam & Cunningham, 1989, p. 16.) noted that the "first systematic effort at defining adult [continuing] education in the modern era came with the founding of the American Association for Adult Education (AAAE) in 1926". Lindeman (1926) built on the thematic paradigms previously mentioned by expressing the notion that "adult [continuing] education is confined to adults because adulthood, maturity, defines its limits" (p. 5) He further noted that it is a "process" revolving around a set of circumstances. ACE begins where regular education leaves off. It is situationally dependent, experientially based, and "transformat[ive]" (p. 27).

Darkenwald and Merriam (1982) provided the following definition that "adult [continuing] education is a process whereby persons whose major social roles are characteristic of adult status undertake systematic and sustained learning activities for the purpose of bringing about changes in knowledge, attitudes, values, or skills" (p. 9). Knowles (1980), reflecting themes mentioned earlier, defined adult continuing education in terms surrounding three different topics: the "process" through which adults learn; the "organized activities" [i.e., institutional settings] surrounding adult learning; and the social practice that brings adults together "into a discrete social system" wherein adults engage in learning activities (p. 25). Stubblefield and Rachal (1992) wrote, after a comprehensive overview of the origins of the term "adult [continuing] education" based on tracing what the varied terms conveyed from 1815 to the present day, clarification of meanings of "adult [continuing] education" had to be based on the social or institutional contexts of learning. Their taxonomy contextualized the term within three paradigms: home education, popular education, and educational extension and concluded, without attempting to give a definitive definition, that the task of defining adult education is heavily dependent on the conceptual base that grounds one's inquiry. Courtney quoting Liveright and Haygood in the *Handbook of Adult and Continuing Education* (Merriam & Cunningham, 1989) observed that:

> Finally, it may be useful to invoke what is probably one of the most carefully crafted definitions in the literature, one which has enjoyed popularity, emerging as it did from one of the more neglected events in our history, the Exeter Conference of 1969: a process whereby persons who no longer attend school on a regular full-time basis . . . undertake sequential and organized activities with the conscious intention of bringing about changes in information, knowledge, understanding, or skill appreciation and attitudes; or for the purpose of identifying or solving personal or community problems (p. 17).

Lastly, Anderson (1993), completed possibly the most comprehensive investigation of definitions of ACPE and adult education resulted from her dissertation study at the University of North Texas. She discovered that there were over 283 different definitions of adult education.

I can therefore observe that defining ACE has been an arduous task involving many researchers. Suffice it to say, ACE seems to possess a chameleon like ability to define itself around the unique needs generated by the time and place it exists in. I cannot predict if there will ever be a clearly drafted definition of the field. What I do feel is that adult educators would be better served by adopting a philosophical approach that is systematically directed at discerning the actual practice of ACE as it exists in our every day "lifeworld" (Braaten, 1991). I believe that pragmatism augmented by phenomenology offers the most viable philosophic approach. Much of the credit for my coming to this belief rests with the philosophical observations of Dr. Sherman Stanage at Northern Illinois University.

OVERVIEW OF PRAGMATISM

The intellectual grounding of ACPE has, in my opinion, been traditionally based on understanding relationships individuals have with societies and organizations they work within. From its early "liberal-progressive" tradition, through social based critiques of class and power relationships of the modern era, to the rise of "personal growth" and human resource development, ACPE has attempted to form a philosophy without, in my opinion, much success. If philosophy is "the rational investigation of the *truth* and *principles of being, knowledge* or *conduct*"[my emphasis] (*Randon House Webster's College Dictionary,* p. 1014) then ACPE has historically presented methods of educational practice as philosophies. The end result is that the field seems to lack a comprehensive philosophical "meaning making system" with which to investigate the world it exists in (Stanage, 1987). I will argue that turning to pragmatism offers the adult continuing educator a solution to this dilemma.

Pragmatism is a "meaning making system" centered on understanding that any given object of study will have practical effects on some "thing" (Stanage, 1987). It presumes that an object's accumulated effects are the "whole of our conception" of the object being studied (Auspitz, 1983, p. 59). It is a philosophy that stresses, I believe, the relation of theory to praxis so that the realities of existence are revealed through reflection about experience gained as an outcome of directed action. Thus, knowledge tends to become instrumental—a tool for organizing experience satisfactorily. Truths are beliefs that are "successively [re]confirmed until they converge on a final determination" (Audi, 1995, p. 638) of meaning about the phenomenon under study. I believe that pragmatism, as exemplified by Peirce, stressed that knowledge is the product of its historical and social context. Peirce contended that fixed beliefs (habits) tend to solidify thinking about an object in ways that can limit inquiry (Houser & Kloesel, 1992) He further pointed out that knowledge is "cumulative" and continuously growing (Yu, 1994, p. 3). Thus, pragmatism grounds one within a context that emphasizes the interaction of a "community of inquirers" working towards a common goal eventually leading to a consensus over what "is" the reality of the "object" being studied. So, I believe, adult continuing education in the professions is best studied by a community of scholars willing to pragmatically access what it is "doing" freed from the incumbrance of trying to write a comprehensive definition. ACPE now becomes an *action oriented practice* best understood through scientific, systematic examination of its literature through the lens of a comprehensive "meaning making" system.

RESEARCH PROJECT

No study of ACPE can become "scientific" (i.e., severely examined) until it "provides itself with a suitable technical nomenclature" (MacKinnon, 1985, p. 161) or schema through which it can be studied. For the past two years I have been working in the Research and Evaluation In Adult Continuing Education (RE/ACE) Office of Northern Illinois University (NIU) creating and validating such a "meaning making system." I have *tested* this system by cataloging close to 8,000 adult education dissertations. I did this because, as Peters and Jarvis (1991) have noted, doctoral dissertations in the field of adult education "are examples of neglected literature" that are under-utilized and in need of further study. Brunner noted that "description, as accurate and precise as possible, is truly the first step in analysis" (p. 219).

IMPACT OF STUDY

Testing the classification schema by classifying dissertations has provided a unique new instrument for investigating the complex nature of ACPE. Thus, a coherent research schema, I believe, enhances the ability of present and future researchers to investigate the field. Application of this schema to a wide range of literature also expands ones ability to pragmatically comprehend the present state of research in ACPE.

METHODOLOGY

Two *Handbook[s] of Adult Education* written as part of a series of similar works (Smith et al., 1970; Merriam & Cunningham, 1989) gave much attention to research trends in adult continuing education and the number of graduate programs granting degrees. Smith

(1970) noted an early need to understand the "rapidly expanding programs" of the field of adult education (p. 138). He was concerned with identifying and critically evaluating the scholarly work of investigators in adult education in order to chronicle the growth of theory building in graduate education. I argue that this is also true for ACPE as a specific subset of the field.

These two *Handbooks* are laudatory of dissertation and practitioner research; they seem to indicate that some ordering was required, especially for theory building or definition. They suggest that research on research—meta-research—was needed in order to create "theoretical maps of the research territory [in order to] synthesize theory" (Deshler in Smith, p. 159) and delineate current practices. Such "mapping" can be accomplished via indexing this body of knowledge as a form of meta-research. The schema employed in this study now needs description.

INITIAL SCHEMA DESIGN PROCESS

Designing the schema was a staged process. The first phase consisted of *five distinct steps. Step One,* I conducted an extensive review of adult education literature with the objective of culling out as many relevant terms for use as coding descriptors as possible. I then targeted contemporary terms that I believed were being applied to adult education research in current practice and incorporated them into the schema. *Step Two,* I assigned those descriptors to headings I believed were appropriate. I added descriptors while still consciously retaining numeric space between each in order to ensure future expansion. *Step Three,* I circulated the initial schema for internal evaluation within the adult education office I am employed in. Once that evaluation was completed, I implemented appropriate revisions. Of critical concern at this stage was an over-arching need for terminology clarity and I made schema changes after periodic consultation with concerned adult educators in my office in order to validate my decision making process. These individuals acted as a constant "reality check" throughout this process. *Step Four,* the revised schema was printed and disseminated to the adult education faculty of Northern Illinois University (NIU). Nine professors of adult education were involved in this evaluation stage and critical additions reflecting contemporary issues in adult educational doctoral studies (specifically in research methodologies, adult learning characteristics, assessment procedures, instructional methods, and technologically related delivery systems) were made.

Once this external faculty evaluation was completed and appropriate schema alterations had been made, the first version of the revised schema seemed ready for *Step Five*—final external review. I requested that adult education doctoral students evaluate the schema for both content and appropriate terminology. After consulting the *Publication Manual of the American Psychological Association* for nonbiased terminology, appropriate changes were made (Knapp, 1994).

As presently constituted the *Roger DeCrow/William Rainey Harper Memorial International Classification System of Adult Education* classifies data as shown at the end of this chapter.

LITERATURE STUDIED FOR THIS CHAPTER

The literature being looked at reflects a limited view of ACPE. Two specific databases were analyzed. The first was the aforementioned RE/ACE Dissertation Database. The second were a wide range of document abstracts pulled from the ERIC (Educational Research Information Consortium) database on ACE for the years 1991 through 1995. They range from 248 journal articles, to 8 monographs, 34 symposia proceedings, 9 bibliographies, and 156 descriptive studies. All these were gathered by using the limited search term "adult continuing education."

DOCUMENT CODING

Precise coding required a concise, staged coding technique. The dissertation data had been coding prior to the research for this chapter. The ERIC documents were coded specifically for this project. All coding was done utilizing the abstracts supplied by dissertation researchers and ERIC abstractors. The instrument for coding these documents was myself. Each document, no matter its source, was read in order to determine

R = What is the research methodology? (0011–0035)
N = Is the dissertation done on a non-ACE subject? (0060)
S = Who are the subjects being studied? (0070–7150)
I = Who are the institutional sponsors? (8000–8900)
O = Is the problem being researched outside the United States? (9000–9950)

Once coded a method of analysis needed to be applied.

DESCRIPTION OF THE ANALYSIS MATRIX

ACPE tends to use similar if not "essentially the same kinds of facilities, techniques, and thought process[es]" (Houle, 1980, p.15). My purpose in writing this chapter it to describe an analysis of select current research literature (dissertations and ERIC manuscripts) with the purpose of delineating select portions of current research inquiry. The matrix for analysis combines data analysis which incorporated the DeCrow System with observations interpreted through three "viewpoints" of the relationship of CPE to society (Cervero in Merriam & Cunningham, 1989, pp. 518–519). These are as follows:

- The Functionalist Viewpoint = which posits that "the professions are service- or community-oriented occupations applying a systematic body of knowledge to problems that are highly relevant to the central values of society" (p. 518).
- The Conflict Viewpoint=which "asserts that professions are in conflict with other groups in society for power, status, and money" (p. 518). This relationship "lies in the oppressive system of which professionals are a part" (p. 519).
- The Critical Viewpoint=which assumes that professionals construct the problem from the situation and are critically aware of these choices and their implications (Schön, 1987). The end purpose of continuing education thus becomes centered on "understand[ing] the ethical and political, as well as the technical, dimensions of their work" (p. 519).

OBSERVATIONS AND RECOMMENDATIONS FOR THE FIELD OF ACPE

The most prolific professions doing continuing education as reflected in the literature studied for this chapter were medical doctors, nurses, and related health practitioners (50 dissertations and 96 articles); librarians and information technologists (53 articles and 4 dissertations); real estate brokers (29 articles and 10 dissertations); accountants (7 dissertations and 2 articles); and architectects (3 articles and 4 dissertations). The overarching purpose for research was to describe a phenomenon in ACPE (121 dissertations and 216 articles). The dominant research method was the survey (65 articles and 2 dissertations) with program evaluation (22 articles and 16 dissertations and experimental studies (7 articles and 20 dissertations) following behind. Case study methodology was sporadically employed (5 articles and 6 dissertations), whereas critical analysis techniques were applied very infrequently (9 articles and 1 dissertation). The main learning modalities studied in order of frequency were motivational factors for participation in learning (8 articles and 47 dissertations) and learning styles (27 articles and 16 dissertations). Finally, an emerging theme for study were applications of technology to learning (57 articles and 3 dissertations).

The data supports the contention that a "functionalist viewpoint" dominates ACPE practice. ACPE continuously surveys and assesses client needs for enhancement of current skills and practices. This is natural given that many writers are scholars whose function in their organization is to support and enhance preexisting structural / learning needs. ACPE seems to be ruled by the following research methods. First and foremost is the quantitative based assessment of educational need. Second, is the evaluation of existing programs. Third, is the description of applicable technological solutions to aforementioned educational needs. Future directions in professional development are studied but critical inquiry and non-mainstream, qualitative based data gathering techniques remain far down on the list of methods employed.

One can therefore conclude that the field is growing and prospering. But, given the prevalence of "instrumental" methods employed to support and evaluate on-going programing, there has been little critical analysis of ethical (only 4 articles) or foundational reasons for the existence of ACPE.

In conclusion, I have argued in this chapter that adult continuing educators need to consider adopting a philosophic stance that encourages analysis of the field's diversity of thought in ways that encourage greater understanding of what adult continuing education in the professions "is" through systematic clarification of what it "does." I am not arguing for a specific "kind" of ACPE practice. But I do believe that we need to more systematically critique the field's response to a the educational world it exists in. A changing society's needs demand no less.

As presently constituted the *Roger DeCrow/William Rainey Harper Memorial International Classification System of Adult Education* classifies data as follows:

0000   Information Sources
         0001   Periodicals
         0002   Books, Brochures, and Book Chapter
         0003   Technical and Research Reports

0004   Proceedings of Meetings and Symposia
0005   Unpublished Work and Publications of Limited
       Circulation
0006   Reviews
0007   Bibliographies
0010   Methodology
    0011   Experimental/Model
    0012   Descriptive/Survey
    0013   Historical
    0014   Philosophical
    0015   Ethnography/Field Research
    0016   Case Study
    0017   Grounded Theory
    0018   Interactive (Action Research)
    0019   Critical
    0020   Futures Research (Delphi)
    0021   Surveys
    0023   Collaborative Study
    0025   Quantitative Based
    0030   Qualitative Based
    0031   Heuristic/Phenomenological
    0035   Mixed Methods
    0060   Non-ACE Dissertations
    0070   ACE Dissertations
    0100   Philosophy
    0105   Policies
    0110   General Objectives
    0125   Evaluation
    0150   Legislation
    0175   Finance
    0250   Studies and Planning—Local Level
    0300   Studies and Planning—State and Regional
    0350   Studies and Planning—National Level
    0500   History
    0550   Biography
    0800   Continuing Higher Education
    0900   Adult Education as a Field of Study
    0950   Adult Education Research
    0990   Reviews, Bibliographies, Information Sources
1100   Adult Learning Characteristics
    1150   Mental-Perceptual Abilities
    1160   Psychological-Personality Factors

3500   Communications-Instructional Devices
      3510   Hardware Development
      3520   Software Development
3600   Learning Facilities/Environmental Issues Related to Learning
      3610   Classroom Design
      3620   Safety
      3630   Parking
      3640   Transportation
      3650   Telephone Access
      3660   Breaks
      3670   Location
3800   Personnel and Staffing
      3820   Personnel Selection Policies and Practices
      3825   Support Services/Consultants
3900   Staff Training and Development
4000   Teachers, Leaders, Change Agents
4100   Law Enforcement, Correctional Personnel
4200   Administrators
4400   Funding Methods and Issues
4600   Education of Special Groups
      4620   Age Groups
      4625   Young Adults
      4630   Middle-aged
      4635   Older Adults
      4650   Sex Differences
      4655   Education of Women
      4680   Education of Men
      4690   Veterans
4700   Aptitude Groups
      4710   Low Aptitude
      4750   Disadvantaged Groups
      4760   Economically Deprived
      4770   Homeless
      4780   Migrant
4800   Minority
      4810   African American (Black American)
      4815   Black Non-Citizen
      4820   Hispanic (Latino)
      4830   Mexican American/Chicana/Chicano
      4840   Native American
      4850   Inuit (Eskimo)
      4860   Asian American

4870   Immigrant/Refugee/Migrant Workers
4880   Jewish/Yiddish
4900   Other Minority
5000   Disabled
    5005   Gifted
    5010   Mentally Disabled (includes Developmental, Learning Impairments & Attention Deficit Disorders)
    5025   Physically Disabled (includes Visual & Hearing Impairments)
    5040   Behavior Disorder-Drugs & Alcohol
    5050   Correctional Ed.-Inmate
5200   Program Areas
    5230   Adult Basic Education-General
    5231   ABE-Curriculum, Instructional Materials
    5232   ABE-Teachers, Administrators-Training of
    5233   ABE-Participant Characteristics
    5240   Family Literacy
    5250   Work-place Literacy
    5280   Literacy Training-Foreign
    5285   Literacy Training-Domestic
    5290   English as a Second Language
5300   Adult Secondary Education-GED
    5350   Adult Elementary Education
5400   Adult Higher Education-Academic Programming
5500   Community Services
    5550   Community Development Programs
5650   Nontraditional Studies
5700   Continuing Education In the Professions
    5725   Career Change
    5750   Engineering, Architecture
    5775   Mathematics
5800   Life Sciences
    5825   Social Sciences
    5850   Medicine and Health (MD/RN)
5900   Education
    5920   AE Learning Theory
    5930   Libraries, Museums, Information Sciences
    5950   Law
    5960   Law Enforcement
6000   Other Educational Areas
    6010   Religion

        6015   Ethics
        6020   Writing, Acting
        6021   Art
        6022   Music
        6025   Recreation, Leisure activities
        6030   Outdoor Education
        6040   Environmental Education
        6050   Military Professions
        6060   Public Administration
        6125   Social Work
        6130   Volunteers
        6150   Technical Education
6200   Work Place Education
        6210   Management
        6220   Supervision
        6230   Learning Organizations
        6240   Downsizing-Rightsizing
        6250   Organizational Change
        6260   Human Resource Development
        6270   Total Quality Management
6300   Labor Education
6500   Occupational Education
        6510   Industrial Training
        6520   Vocational Rehabilitation
        6550   Unskilled, Low Aptitude, Disadvantaged
        6575   New Careers, Aides, Paraprofessionals
        6600   Clerical
        6610   Sale
        6650   Service Occupations
        6700   Agriculture-Extension Services
        6710   Home Economics
        6720   Processing
        6735   Machine Trades
        6750   Bench-work
        6800   Structural Work
        6850   Other Occupations
        6900   Liberal Education
        6950   Health, Mental Health, Patient Education
                (LPN etc.)
7000   Home Management, Consumer Education,
        Sensitivity Training
        7020   Family, Parent Education

7050   Arts, Crafts, Home Related Recreation
7150   Cross Cultural Training
8000   Institutional Sponsors/Subjects
8001   Colleges, Universities
8005   Cooperative, Rural Extension
8010   Junior Colleges, Community Colleges
8015   Public Schools
8020   Business and Industry
8025   Armed Forces
8030   Private Schools
8040   Community Based Organizations
8050   Unions, Cooperatives
8100   Religious
8200   Libraries, Museums
8250   Proprietary Schools
8300   State, Local Governments
8400   State, Local Non-Governmental Organizations
8500   Federal Government
8600   National Non-Governmental Organization
8700   Voluntary Organizations
8800   Consortia
8900   Charitable Organizations
9000   International Perspective
9020   International Comparative Studies
9040   Developing Nations
9350   Canada
9400   Latin America
9410   South America
9420   Central America
9430   Mexico
9450   Caribbean
9500   Europe
9510   Soviet Union/Russia
9515   Former Soviet Republics
9520   Great Britain-Scotland
9525   Ireland
9530   Nordic Countries
9540   Germany
9570   Eastern Europe
9650   Middle-Near East
9700   Africa
9710   South Africa
9800   Asia

9810   Japan
9815   China-Taiwan
9820   China-Mainland
9950   Australia, New Zealand, Oceanic

REFERENCES

Anderson, M. M. (1993). A comprehensive review of definitions of adult education. *Dissertation Abstracts International, 53* (08), 2642 A. (University Microfilms No. AAC9300584).

Audi, R. et al. (Eds.). (1995). *The Cambridge dictionary of philosophy.* Cambridge: Cambridge University Press

Auspitz, J. L. (1983). The greatest living american philosopher. *Commentary,* December, 51–64.

Blunt, A., & Lee, J. (1994). The contribution of graduate student research to adult education/Adult Education Quarterly, 1969–1988. *Adult Education Quarterly, 44* (3), 125–144.

Boyd, R. D., Apps, J.W., and Associates. (1980). *Redefining the disciplines of adult education.* San Francisco: Jossey-Bass.

Bratten, J. (1991). *Habermas's Critical Theory of Society.* Albany: State University of New York Press

Brunner, E. S. (1960). Adult Education and its research needs. *Adult Education, X* (4), 218–227.

Costello, R. B. et al. (Eds.). (1990). *Random House Webster's college dictionary.* New York: Random House.

Couglah, M. A., & Moss, G. M., (1969). Adult education as a field of study and its implications for the preparation of adult educators. *Adult Education Journal, XIX* (2), 127–134.

Darkenwald, G. G., & Merriam, S. B. (1982). *Adult education: Foundations of practice.* New York: HarperCollins.

D'Onofrio, A., Lawler, P., O'Malley, J. P., & Wilhite, S. C. (1993). Dissertation supervision: A new path, an old guide and reflections on William James. *Continuing Higher Education Review, 57* (3), 130–146.

Elias, J. L., & Merriam, S. B. (1984). *Philosophical foundations of adult education.* Malabar: Krieger.

Houle, C. O. (1980). *Continuing learning in the professions.* San Francisco: Jossey-Bass.

Houser, N., & Kloesel, C. (Eds.). (1992). *The essential peirce: Selected philosophical writings,* vol. 1 (1867–1893). Bloomington: Indiana University Press.

Jarvis, P. (Ed.). (1990). *An international dictionary of adult and continuing education.* London: Routledge.

Knapp, S. et. al. (Eds.).(1994). *Publication manual of the american psychological association* (4th ed.). Washington: American Psychological Association.

Knowles, M. S. (1980). *The modern practice of adult education: From pedagogy to andragogy.* Chicago: Follett.

Lindeman, E. (1926). *The meaning of adult education.* New York: New Republic.

MacKinnon, B. (Ed.). (1985). *American philosophy: A historical anthology.* Albany: State University of New York Press.

Merriam, S. B., & Cunningham, P. M. (1989). *Handbook of adult and continuing education.* San Francisco: Jossey-Bass.

Ness, F. W. (Ed.). (1957). *A guide to graduate study: Programs leading to the Ph.D. degree.* Washington, DC: Association of American Colleges.

Peters, J. M., & Jarvis, P. (1991). *Adult education: Evolution and achievements in a developing field of study.* San Francisco: Jossey-Bass.

Rose, A. (1996). Posing an ideal society: Adult education's role in defining a vision for America. *Adult Learning, 7* (3), 5 and 12.

Schön, D. A., (1987). *The Reflective Practitioner.,* New York: Basic Books.

Smith, R. M., Aker, G. F., & Kidd, J. R. (Eds.). (1970). *Handbook of adult education.* New York: Macmillian.

Stanage, S. M. (1987). *Adult education and phenomenological research: New directions for theory, practice, and research.* Malabar: Krieger.

Stubblefield, H. W., & Rachal, J. R. (1992). On the origins of the term and meanings of "adult education" in the united states. *Adult Education Quarterly, 42* (2), 106–176.

Yu, C. H. (1994). *Abduction? deduction? induction?: is there a logic of exploratory data analysis.* Paper presented at the annual meeting of the American Educational Research Association, New Orleans, LA.

2

Wellness for Professionals
Michele Hamil

To keep the body in good health is a duty. . . .
Otherwise we shall not be able to keep our mind strong and clear.

Buddha

The link between good health and a strong mind has been understood for centuries. Good health is the basis for life and learning; it allows people to think clearly and to act consciously.

Educators frequently separate mind and body, teaching only to the mind. By considering learners holistically, continuing educators can improve learning and help individuals and organizations meet their goals. This chapter provides a practical guide to enhancing individual and organizational quality of life by fostering a state of wellness.

THE CONCEPT OF WELLNESS

Wellness describes the status of a person's overall health. It is a philosophy of optimal well-being, an attitude toward life, a way of being, and a lifestyle that promotes health, vigor, and energy (Griggs, 1990).

A key tenet of wellness is the concept of self-care. Self-care involves accepting personal responsibility for one's own health (Griggs, 1990). Traditionally we have given responsibility for our health to others, for example, health care practitioners, employers, counselors, and family members. Taking a wellness perspective means taking responsibility for one's own health and using those caregivers as resources.

Proactivity is another key tenet of wellness. Being proactive about one's health means taking positive steps to avoid disease and injury (Griggs, 1990). This involves dealing with health issues before they become problems. For example, people can exercise and eat nutri-

21

tious foods in order to avoid a heart attack, rather than waiting until after a heart attack to care of themselves. Or people can choose occupations which are appropriate to their values, skills, and interests rather than experiencing the stress involved in working in an unsuitable position.

A person can be well without being completely healthy. Wellness means being the best you can be without accepting traditional limitations such as age, gender, or genetics (Powers, 1994). A person living with an illness such as diabetes can lead a well lifestyle despite having a chronic disease. An elderly person can enjoy the benefits of a well lifestyle even while coping with the aches and pains which accompany old age.

Wellness is a balance of physical, emotional, spiritual, intellectual, occupational, and social aspects (Powers, 1994). Each of these dimensions is intricately woven into our existence; therefore, it is important to understand and strive for continuous growth within each dimension, and to maintain an equal balance of all dimensions (Powers, 1994).

The physical dimension of health involves the functional operation of the body. Exercise, diet, drug use, smoking, sleep habits, medical checkups, and fitness are all physical dimensions of health (Powers, 1994).

The intellectual dimension of health involves the use of the mind. Such things as reading, critical thinking, applying information, keeping abreast of current events, and the ongoing pursuit of knowledge are included in the intellectual dimension of health (Powers, 1994).

The emotional dimension of health involves awareness, acceptance, and management of emotions; coping with life's ups and downs; adjusting to change; understanding personal strengths and limitations; and maintaining intimate relationships (Powers, 1994).

The social dimension of health includes interactions with other people. Appreciating differences, getting along, exhibiting fairness, and displaying concern for mankind and the environment are examples of the social dimension of health (Powers, 1994).

The spiritual dimension of health involves the development of the inner self and soul. It includes identifying the purpose and meaning of life, developing a sense of right and wrong, exhibiting ethical behavior, distinguishing innermost values and needs, and identifying a philosophy of life (Powers, 1994).

The occupational dimension of health deals with job/vocation. Important aspects of the occupational dimension of health include identifying internal and external rewards needed from a career, balancing career and personal life, and clarifying personal motivations and challenges regarding work (Powers, 1994).

WELLNESS AND LEARNING

Wellness and learning are inextricably linked: good health optimizes learning, and optimal learning capacities are a means to good health. If the goal of continuing educators is to help professionals learn, then wellness cannot be left out of continuing education.

Wellness can be approached using three strategies which work together to inform, encourage change, and support change. First, awareness strategies are educational in nature and help professionals recognize their need to make behavioral and attitudinal changes. Second, lifestyle change interventions help professionals change behaviors and attitudes. Third, supportive environment programs create a helpful environment for change. Each of these approaches is described in more detail below.

Awareness Strategies

Awareness strategies are defined as "a variety of communication dissemination and information transfer activities that are intended to enhance the knowledge levels of individuals, help catalyze and reinforce behavior change, while intentionally leading to improved individual health and productivity (Chapman, 1994, p. 163).

The role of awareness strategies and activities is generally threefold. First, awareness strategies communicate relevant information that helps to prepare individuals for health-behavior change. Second, awareness activities empower individuals to formulate a personal application of the newly acquired information. Third, awareness strategies enable individuals to gain access to applicable support services and technology that aid in the reinforcement of new health behaviors. In short, awareness provides information, empowers change, and connects individuals with services and resources to facilitate and maintain change (Chapman, 1994).

Awareness is the first stage of affecting change in health behaviors. Awareness strategies can take the form of informational classes and seminars, media campaigns, or screenings for various medical conditions. They are most beneficial when offered in conjunction with lifestyle change interventions and supportive environment programs. Creating awareness of health issues motivates professionals to change their unhealthy behaviors and adopt healthy lifestyle habits.

Lifestyle Change Interventions

Lifestyle change interventions go a step beyond awareness strategies by helping professionals to actually change their unhealthy behaviors. Changes might include quitting smoking, exercising on a regular basis, successfully managing stress, eating more nutritious foods, or combining exercise with nutritious eating to lose weight. The most successful lifestyle change interventions use a combination of health education, behavior modification, experiential practice, and feedback opportunities, and they allow sufficient time to elapse for behavior changes to occur.

Lifestyle change interventions are of value to professionals and the organizations in which they work for four important reasons. First, exhibiting healthy behaviors can result in improved health status, which in turn can lead to reduced medical problems and the costs associated with them. Second, lifestyle change interventions improve a professional's outlook and physical and emotional capacity to be more productive at work. Third, lifestyle change programs can provide a considerable morale boost and public relations angle. Finally, the social nature of lifestyle change interventions provides professionals additional opportunities to acquaint themselves with each other, which can help them work together more effectively.

A problem with lifestyle change interventions is their failure to sustain long-term behavior change. Without environmental support for their change, most smokers who quit smoking resume the habit, and most people who lose weight gain it back within one year. The best way to reduce these lapses is through supportive environment programs (O'Donnell, 1994).

Supportive Environment Programs

The goal of supportive environment programs is to create and maintain environments within the work setting which encourage healthy lifestyles. A supportive environment is critical to helping people maintain newly acquired healthy lifestyle habits. Work environments that support healthy lifestyles can be created by establishing healthy physical settings, policies, and organizational culture (O'Donnell, 1994).

In the context of physical settings, providing wellness initiatives located at the workplace is the most powerful opportunity for improving health behaviors. On-site wellness programming efforts have a significantly higher level of participation than off-site wellness programming efforts. Other common supportive aspects of the physical setting include providing healthful foods in the cafeteria and vending machines, furnishing lockers and showers convenient to exercisers, and removing cigarette machines and ashtrays from common areas.

Organizational policies which foster healthy lifestyles include making all professionals eligible for wellness programming, encouraging professionals to participate in programs through flexible work scheduling, instituting nonsmoking policies, establishing alcohol free organizational activities, funding medical care coverage programs so they reward good health practices instead of poor health, and restructuring absenteeism policies to reward remaining healthy rather than being sick. Some policies allow professionals' families to participate in wellness programs. Including families in the wellness process improves their well-being and encourages support for behavioral changes at home. Leading edge organizations have taken the idea of supportive environment programs even further to include the design of jobs and creation of a healthy organizational culture.

CONTINUING PROFESSIONAL EDUCATION AND WELLNESS

Providers of continuing professional education should embrace wellness not only as a means of helping learners, but also for its organizational benefits. Organizationally, wellness programs provide a strategic advantage for enhancing performance. Wellness programs positively influence worker productivity (Wolfe, Ulrich, & Parker, 1987), control health care and health-related costs, and minimize the potentially negative health effects of the organizational changes brought about by competitive realities (Chen, 1989a, 1989b).

To achieve the benefits of wellness, providers of continuing education should use the three wellness strategies (awareness strategies, lifestyle change intervention, and supportive environment programs) to offer professionals the opportunity to develop each of the six aspects of health (physical, emotional, spiritual, intellectual, occupational, and social). Continuing educators within higher education, human resource development, consulting functions, and associations can all focus on creating awareness of the importance of health issues. Lifestyle change interventions and supportive environment programs are most successfully approached by continuing educators in consulting and human resource development positions.

Table 2.1 visually represents the programming opportunities

Table 2.1 Wellness Program Development Opportunities

	Emotional	Spiritual	Intellectual	Occupa-tional	Social	Physical
Awareness Strategies						
Lifestyle Change Interventions						
Supportive Environment Programs						

available to continuing educators. To ensure that a holistic approach to wellness is taken, each aspect of wellness is addressed at each of the three levels of intervention. Programming should be offered in each segment of the grid based on the needs of participants.

A MODEL FOR THE CREATION OF WELLNESS PROGRAMS

Some continuing educators will see the benefit of institutionalizing a holistic wellness in their organizational setting. For those continuing educators, the following process was developed to guide the creation of wellness programs that will address all the wellness needs of professionals (Hamil, 1996). Table 2.2 provides an overview of the model, which is described in detail thereafter.

Phase One: Determine Appropriateness of a Wellness Intervention

The first phase of the process is an assessment to determine if developing a wellness program is the appropriate intervention to reach top management's desired outcomes. To this end, information is obtained regarding general reasons why top management may be interested in creating a wellness program. Understanding the expected gains from implementing a wellness program is imperative in successfully evaluating the usefulness of a wellness program to reach those goals.

If top management's goals are congruent with the types of outcomes a wellness program can provide, such as reduced health care costs, diminished stress, increased productivity, improved morale,

Table 2.2 Overview of Wellness Program Creation Process

Phase One	• Determine appropriateness of a wellness intervention
Phase Two	• Assess the organization's state of readiness 　• Evaluate management support 　• Ascertain professionals' support 　• Appraise organizational environment support 　　• Review organizational policies 　　• Examine physical setting 　　• Scrutinize organizational culture
Phase Three	• Design the program 　• Create a mission, vision, and goals 　　• Assess organizational needs 　　• Discover professionals' needs and interests' 　　• Determine internal and community links 　• Plan the wellness program 　　• Decide what programs will be offered 　　　• Prescribe level of impact 　　　• Set level of intensity 　　　• Determine program topics 　　• Establish where programs will take place 　　• Plan who will run the wellness program and individual program initiatives 　　• Establish the policies and procedures under which the wellness program will operate 　　　• Fix eligibility requirements 　　　• Constitute incentives to participation 　• Define how and when the program will be evaluated
Phase Four	• Obtain management approval and funding
Phase Five	• Implement plan 　• Hire and prepare staff
Phase Six	• Conduct programs
Phase Seven	• Evaluate, update, and revise the overall program

and lower health risks, then the planning process can move into phase two in order to determine the organization's state of readiness for a wellness program.

If top management's goals for the wellness program are not those which can be reached through health promotion activities, a wellness program should not be considered. In this case, other change-promoting interventions may be suggested.

Phase Two: Assess the Organization's State of Readiness

In the second phase of the model, the organization's state of readiness to support wellness initiatives is assessed. In this analysis, top management, professionals, and the organizational environment are studied to determine the level of support each will provide the organization's overall wellness effort. Wellness programs require the support of top management, professionals, and most importantly the culture of the organization itself in order to champion healthy people and a healthy environment. It is difficult to create a healthy organization if its members are unhealthy, just as it is difficult for people to maintain their health in an organization that behaves in unhealthy ways (Weinstein, 1989).

Evaluate Management Support

Upper management backing and interest for health promotion is imperative in order to secure adequate funding of the wellness program initially and over time. Upper management is charged with increasing an organization's profitability. Knowing that, the key to obtaining and maintaining upper management's support is showing the extent to which a wellness program can and does make a direct or indirect contribution to improving profitability.

Ascertain Professionals' Support

Supportive management aside, professionals themselves must be interested in participating in health promotion activities. The level of interest is determined by going directly to the professionals. This can be accomplished most effectively through an opinion survey or focus groups. (Surveys and focus groups determine the level of support for a wellness program, and can include more specific information on the types of programming in which professionals would participate if a wellness program is adopted. Including information on specific interests is more time-consuming up-front, but will save conducting another survey if the wellness program goes forward.) If professionals are uninterested, educational programs can be offered to increase awareness of the benefits of being well. Wellness programs should not be mandated, so professionals' interest is key to the success of a wellness program.

Appraise Organizational Environment Support

An accurate assessment of the organizational environment is crucial in evaluating whether or not an organization is ready to institute a wellness program. Preparing to create a healthy workplace requires assuming a systems approach: acknowledging that each worker is part of an open, dynamic system, affected by and acting upon internal and external environments (Weinstein, 1989). An organization's environment is influenced heavily by three factors: its policies, organizational culture, and physical setting. These three areas must support wellness activities in order to reap the benefits of health promotion efforts.

Review Organizational Policies.   An assessment is made of the health-enhancing policies the organization has or does not have. A no-smoking policy supports efforts made by a wellness program. A flex-time policy boosts wellness program participation. A policy that allows excessive alcohol usage at organization functions may send a signal that the organization's environment condones unhealthy behaviors.

An organization's absenteeism policy frequently reflects attitudes toward wellness. Most absenteeism policies benefit professionals who are unhealthy, but policies which offer well-days instead of sick-days reward remaining healthy. Such a health-promoting policy indicates that an organization has made a commitment to wellness and its wellness program is likely to prosper.

Examine Physical Setting.   Along with an organization's policies, its physical setting influences the work environment. Assessing how the physical setting supports a healthy workplace is an important part of determining how strongly health promotion activities will be supported by the organization. Positive indicators of a supportive physical setting include healthful foods sold in the cafeteria and vending machines; ergonomically engineered office desks and chairs; the absence of ashtrays and cigarette machines; clean, brightly-lit, and well-maintained work areas; and an effective safety program.

Scrutinize Organizational Culture.   Policies and physical environments help shape the nebulous concept of organizational culture. Organizational culture is comprised of the social systems and environments that exist within an organization, including at least five important concepts: (1) values—heartfelt beliefs about the appropriate way to approach living; (2) cultural norms—expected and accepted behaviors; (3) peer support; (4) organizational support—the systems and structures of an organization manifested through formal policies and informal activities; and (5) organizational climate—an organizational culture's capacity to bring about constructive change (Allen & Bellingham, 1994).

For the wellness philosophy to flourish, social systems and environments conducive to health-promoting behaviors are essential (Brehm, 1993). Among the most powerful of cultural influences affecting wellness are modeling, reward systems, orientation, training, rites and rituals, and patterns of relationship development (Allen, 1993). These elements should be considered closely.

In assessing the organizational culture, the job itself cannot be ignored. Weinstein (1989) believes that more attention should be paid to the nature and structure of the work experience itself as part of a holistic wellness package. An assessment of the work experience includes studying three key variables: (1) The way the organization is structured: Flat structures support wellness activities better than vertical, bureaucratic structures. (2) Job design: Professionals empowered to make decisions about their work are more inclined to healthy behaviors. (3) Expectations of good performance: Climates that reward people for consistent, excessive overtime, for example, are not supportive of healthy lifestyles.

Once an analysis of an organization's policies, physical setting, and organizational culture is complete, results are objectively scrutinized to determine the level of support the organizational environment will provide a wellness program. If support in one or more of these areas is lacking, efforts should be made to increase these necessary support mechanisms before continuing to plan the wellness program. If support in these areas is impossible to obtain, a wellness program should not be considered. When the organizational environment is supportive of wellness efforts, a wellness program can then be designed.

Phase Three: Design the Program
Create a Mission, Vision, and Goals

The first and most important element in planning a successful wellness program is determining a health promotion vision and mission in order to establish specific wellness program goals.

The vision statement describes the long-term success of the wellness program. With the creation of a vision statement, planning becomes outcome oriented. By beginning with the final desired outcome, the factors important to that outcome can be diagnosed before the intervention is designed, thus creating an intervention that is focused on problems rather than symptoms of problems. The mission statement outlines the importance of the wellness program, and reports what the program is to accomplish in the short term. A written set of goals can then be determined to provide specific direction for obtaining desired outcomes.

Many organizations want to improve the health, well-being, endurance and productivity of professionals, their dependents, and retirees. They also want to reduce costs associated with workers' compensation, disability claims, medical insurance, and absenteeism. Improved morale and image are also commonly desired outcomes. Mission and vision statements most often revolve around these issues.

In goal-setting, three types of objectives are usually established: (1) Performance goals deal with financial outcomes and changes in health behaviors. (2) Programmatic goals include workshop attendance, self-help material distribution levels, task-force participation, and other indicators of program success. (3) Cultural goals are created to make the organizational environment more conducive to wellness, and include development of specific health promotion values, norms, and peer support (Allen & Bellingham, 1994).

Goals typically involve promoting understanding of the benefits of a healthy lifestyle, providing professionals with a means of assessing their own lifestyles and current health status, offering professionals opportunities to improve their health by changing lifestyles and health habits, and contributing to a work environment that supports positive lifestyle practices (McAllister & Broeder, 1993). To facilitate evaluation, goals should be stated in behavioral terms.

Assess Organizational Needs. To create a mission, vision and goals for a wellness program, a primary source of information is management's overall expectations of the program determined in phase one. Based on those expectations, an assessment of specific organization needs is undertaken. This assessment includes an evaluation of external factors including competition, community, and national influences, as well as internal factors such as safety issues, turnover, absenteeism, morale, productivity, and insurance claims paid by the organization. Areas of high cost to the organization are targeted in order to achieve maximum savings early in the program's existence. Also necessary in establishing wellness program goals is an assessment of professionals' needs and interests, and information on available internal and community resources.

Discover Professionals' Needs and Interests.   Following an assessment of the organization, the professionals' needs and interests are determined. This assessment yields two important outcomes: First, it determines which health problems are most prevalent in the workforce and the behavioral and environmental factors which cause them, and second, it ascertains what personal wellness changes professionals would like to make and the behavioral and environmental factors which support them.

Along with their health needs, employees' personal wellness interests are determined. If professionals' specific personal wellness interests were not examined during phase two, such an inquiry is completed at this point.

In addition to their needs and interests in personal change, professionals should be asked what organizational changes would improve their wellness. This provides further information with which to identify and address quality of life issues on an organizational and individual level.

Determine Internal and Community Links.   The more a wellness program functions interdependently within the systems already created inside an organization, the fewer wellness program components will have to be created from the ground up, and the more ingrained wellness will become in the structure of the organization.

Structural links between the wellness program and other health-related organizational functions are critical. It is important that a wellness program's goals be developed such that they are congruent with those of other organizational health-related initiatives. Developing a wellness program without reference to other health programs can result in duplication and/or inconsistency of effort. Long-range plans that concurrently consider occupational health services and wellness programs should be developed (Seidler, 1993).

Links to the community can be especially important in maximizing a wellness program budget while still maintaining a commitment to high quality. Community resources such as Weight Watchers, hospitals, health clubs, and community colleges can provide quality wellness services at low or no cost. Organizational wellness program goals should include mutually beneficial interactions with the community.

Once management objectives, organizational needs, professionals' needs and interests, and internal and external links are clear, a vision, mission, and set of specific short-term goals for the wellness program are articulated. When creating program goals, the highest priority health problems should be pursued. To select the problems of highest priority, the following questions should be considered:

1. Which problems will potentially provide the greatest health care cost savings to the organization? Consider problems that highly correlate with the occurrence of death, disease, days lost from work, rehabilitation costs, and disability.
2. Which problems will potentially provide the greatest increase in productivity to the organization?
3. Are the problems of high-risk subpopulations addressed?
4. Which problems are most easily and quickly solved?
5. Which problems are professionals most interested in addressing? Which problems are professionals not interested in addressing?
6. Which problems are not being addressed by other agencies in the community? Can services to the community be provided?
7. Which problems can be addressed given the constraints of and opportunities available in the current organizational environment?
8. Which problems can be addressed given budgetary and staffing parameters?

In setting realistic goals, it is important to remember that relapses to poor health behaviors will occur; significantly deteriorated health conditions will not improve in less than five years; major improvements in health conditions require major effort; 100% participation in programs should not be expected; a large financial investment may be required to yield significant reductions in health care expenditures within a few years; absenteeism rates will not drop off immediately; and increased job output will not occur from all participants in the program.

When complete, wellness program goals will indicate who will receive the program, what health benefit they should receive, how much of that benefit should be achieved, and by when it should it be achieved.

Plan the Wellness Program

The vision, mission, and goals are the basis of a specific plan for creating the wellness program. A detailed and comprehensive plan includes the following actions: (1) Decide what particular programs will be offered to address the priorities established. (2) Determine where programs will take place. (3) Plan who will run the wellness program and individual program initiatives. (4) Establish the policies and procedures under which the wellness program will operate. (5) Define how and when the program will be evaluated. Each of these decision-points is addressed below.

Decide What Programs Will Be Offered. Once priorities are established, specific goals are determined for the educational, exercise, recreational, family, health-assessment, and social opportunities that will be offered on an ongoing basis. Three major programming decisions center on (1) the desired level of impact of the program, (2) the desired intensity of the program, and (3) the topics covered by the program (O'Donnell, 1994).

The level of impact should be determined by the organizational goals to be achieved as a result of the program. The most effective wellness programs offer professionals the chance to improve their health and well-being through a combination of awareness strategies, lifestyle change interventions, and supportive environment programs.

Strong impact can also be made by targeting programs to at-risk populations—the 10% of professionals who are responsible for 70% of medical care costs. Programming for this group has the potential to reduce medical care costs dramatically.

The level of intensity of the program is determined by the degree of success desired in program goals, the level of intensity needed to achieve success, and the health conditions and practices of participating professionals. Level of intensity is compounded by increasing the quantity of resources invested, upping staff levels provided, and lengthening time spent by participants in a program. Increased intensity of a wellness program generally translates into increased success in meeting objectives.

Program topics will follow the results of the goal setting process, and reflect a holistic attitude toward wellness. Topics are best presented in a combination of formats including self-management materials, classroom education, physical fitness training, and health screenings/assessments. Table 2.3 lists the goals that various programs can be expected to achieve.

Establish Where Programs Will Take Place. Physical facility needs become apparent when the wellness curriculum has been decided. Participation is greater when a wellness facility is located at the place of employment rather than at an off-site facility. However,

Table 2.3   Goals Achieved by Specific Programs

Program	Goals program achieves
Blood Pressure Screening	• Shrink medical care costs
Child Care	• Increase morale • Curtail stress
Elder Care	• Increase morale • Curtail stress
Employee Assistance Program	• Increase morale • Improve company image • Shrink medical care costs • Curtail stress
Fitness	• Increase morale • Cut workers' compensation • Ease physical exhaustion • Curtail stress • Mitigate cardiovascular disease • Diminish obesity • Decrease back problems • Lower hypertension • Alleviate smoking • Abate injuries
Nutrition/Weight Control	• Mitigate cardiovascular disease • Diminish obesity • Lower hypertension
Policy Evaluation and Change	• Increase morale • Shrink medical care costs • Curtail stress
Smoking Cessation/No Smoking Policy	• Improve company image • Alleviate smoking • Shrink medical care costs
Stress Management	• Increase morale • Ease physical exhaustion • Curtail stress • Alleviate smoking
Wellness Ambassador Program	• Increase morale • Improve company image
Ergonomic Audit	• Decrease back problems

the benefits of increased participation must be weighed against the costs of building, renting or remodeling space at the worksite and the costs of maintaining a facility over time. Organizations making a serious, long-term commitment to improve the health of their professionals should provide on-site facilities if financially feasible.

Physical facility needs can be dealt with creatively to increase participation and decrease expenses. Participation multiplies when wellness programming is brought directly to professionals' work areas. Wellness materials displayed on public bulletin boards, walking programs which allow professionals to participate within their building, and health screenings and educational workshops held in employee break rooms and cafeterias are ways to offer convenient programming which incurs no facility costs.

Plan Who Will Run the Wellness Program and Individual Program Initiatives.   Staffing decisions stem from the goals of the wellness program and the specific programs being offered. In general, health promotion professionals should run the wellness program.
Ideally, these individuals have expertise in all of the following areas: organization theory; group process; adult education principles; management; communication and marketing methods; instructional design process; and clinical aspects of health promotion including health assessment, fitness, nutrition, stress management, smoking cessation, medical self-care, and social health.

Another important consideration in staffing the wellness center is choosing people who embody a wellness lifestyle. One of the most powerful concepts in changing peoples' behavior involves modeling. If staff members consistently advocate positive health through their actions and words, good health becomes a natural part of the environment (Anspaugh, Ezel, & Godman, 1983; Schaller, 1981).

Establish the Policies and Procedures Under Which the Wellness Program Will Operate.   Procedures for operating the program are outlined during the planning process. Plans are devised to address procedures such as scheduling workshops, classes and events; promoting wellness and wellness activities; maintaining facilities; budgeting; registering and tracking participants; and managing equipment.

Policies guiding the operation of the program are also established at this time. Decisions are made regarding fees, hours of operation, participant code of conduct, confidentiality, and rules and regulations regarding use of facilities and equipment. Eligibility requirements and incentives to participation will also be decided. Eligibility and incentives are addressed below.

Fix Eligibility Requirements.   The size of the wellness program and the method for selecting professionals for the program is determined during the planning process. The program can be made available to all professionals or only to selected professionals. It can be offered to spouses, children, and significant others. Research shows that wellness program effectiveness compounds when all professionals, retirees, and their families are allowed to use the wellness program. Chenoweth (1995) states that programs must be directed to dependents, and retirees as well as professionals, considering that dependents and retirees often consume twice as many health care dollars as do professionals.

Inclusionary policies not only save money, they also enhance the effectiveness of the wellness program. Lifestyle change, one of the most important goals of all wellness programs, requires the support of work groups and families. Including all professionals and their families in wellness efforts helps them support each other through change. Maintaining positive lifestyle choices and fostering a wellness approach to living can only be achieved when there is support and encouragement by the surrounding environments (Weinstein, 1989; Powers, 1994).

Constitute Incentives to Participation.   When professionals are provided incentives to take part in a wellness program, participation usually increases and with it, positive results of the program. Offering professionals time during the workday to participate in wellness activities is an important incentive to participation. This can be accomplished by offering a flex-time policy which allows professionals control over their arrival, departure, and lunch times throughout the day to best accommodate wellness program participation. Another incentive to participation is to offer professionals the opportunity to take part in wellness activities on organization time. Frequently these programs allow professionals half an hour out of their regular workday to participate in wellness activities.

Another incentive to participation in wellness activities is offering professionals a rebate on insurance costs for good health. Such programs reduce an employee's cost for health insurance if agreed upon health goals are met and maintained. The benefits and costs of these incentives are weighed by the organization to determine whether they will be instituted.

Define How and When the Program Will Be Evaluated. The
basic evaluation plan is specified during the design phase. Decisions
are made regarding what aspects of the program to evaluate, when
to evaluate, how, by whom, and for what purpose. In making these
decisions it is important to take into consideration that meaningful
behavior changes can occur within six months of program initiation,
but changes in health status lag behind considerably. Health outcomes may not be measurable for at least one to two years after program initiation.

Evaluation is based on the wellness program goals determined in
phase one. Evaluations commonly include an appraisal of the program processes, the effect of the program on participants' behaviors,
and the impact of the program on health status, health-related costs,
and quality of life (Green & Kreuter, 1991).

Phase Four: Obtain Management
Approval and Funding

Phase four of the model involves approaching management for approval and funding of the project. Along with the design plan, a budget for development and maintenance of the program (including insurance costs), and a cost/benefit analysis are completed and
submitted to management sponsoring the program. (If the cost/ben-
efit analysis shows total benefits do not exceed total costs, the program as it is planned is not a worthwhile investment, and the program design needs to be revised before submission to management.)

In presenting the proposal to management, the health promotion
program should be marketed as a long-term investment that will
benefit the organization, not as an extravagant benefit that can be
cut when money is short. The ultimate goal of organizational health
promotion programs—to make the organization better able to
achieve its strategic goals—should be emphasized.

Phase Five: Implement the Plan

Once the design phase is complete and management has approved
the budget, the plan can be implemented. In the implementation
phase, all the plans developed in the design phase are carried out.
This includes building, remodeling or renting a physical facility; developing creative, innovative, and fun educational and exercise programs and events; and creating self-management and reference materials. Hiring and preparing the staff is among the first and most
important functions in implementing the plan.

Hire and Prepare the Staff

Hiring and organizing people who will evolve into a strong health promotion team provides the leadership necessary for successful programming. During the staffing function, recruit and hire qualified job candidates, provide orientations to new professionals, identify internal professionals and arrange for them to join the wellness staff on a full- or part-time basis, train the staff in skills needed to achieve program goals, tailor staff roles and responsibilities around program goals, and establish communication channels to enhance interpersonal and interdepartmental communication and teamwork (Chenoweth, 1995).

Phase Six: Conduct the Program

This phase marks the beginning of professionals' participation in wellness activities. At this time plans made in the design phase are carried out: Educational and exercise programs are conducted, policies and procedures are enacted, self-study materials are made available, and events are mounted.

Actions to carry out, monitor, and maintain these activities are undertaken. These include promoting wellness activities to achieve increased participation, managing efficient systems for program operation and administration, maintaining the facility and equipment, monitoring the budget, directing the wellness ambassador program, continuing to develop the wellness staff through training and multidimensional roles, planning and staging special events, evaluating and revising individual classes and workshops, guaranteeing a high level of program quality, and providing regular information reports on health status and practices of each department.

Phase Seven: Evaluate, Update, and Revise the Program

After the period of time specified during planning, the wellness program's effectiveness at meeting its stated goals is evaluated. Follow the decisions made during the planning process regarding the aspects of the program to be evaluated, how they are to be evaluated, by whom, and for what purpose.

Assess the results of the evaluation to determine strengths and weaknesses of the program. Establish the root causes of successes and failures of the various aspects of the program. Apply the program's success factors to improve weak areas of the program. Address ideas and initiate plans to revise or replace failing programs.

Every two years, the entire model will again be used to reexamine the wellness program to ensure that it keeps up with the changing needs of the organization and professionals.

SUMMARY

Whether instituted at an organizational level or practiced on an individual level, a state of wellness is necessary to maximize lifelong learning for successful professional practice. Continuing educators have the opportunity and responsibility to promote wellness through education, behavior change interventions, and the creation of supportive environments. Taking a wellness approach to continuing professional education involves the whole person in learning experiences which improves learning, productivity, and quality of life.

REFERENCES

Allen, J. (1993). Concepts in culture change. Wellness Connections, 3(1) 4–11.

Allen, J., & Bellingham, R. (1994). Building supportive cultural environments. In M. P. O'Donnell & J. S. Harris (Eds.), Health Promotion in the Workplace (pp. 204–216). Albany, NY: Delmar Publishing.

Anspaugh, D. J., Ezel, G., & Godman, K. N. (1983). Teaching today's health. Columbus, OH: Merrill.

Brehm, B. A. (1993). Essays on wellness. New York: HarperCollins.

Chapman, L. S. (1994). Awareness strategies. In M. P. O'Donnell & J. S. Harris (Eds.), Health Promotion in the Workplace (pp. 163-184). Albany, NY: Delmar.

Chen, M. S. (1989a). The most important influences in health promotion: Continuation of the panel discussion. [Interview with J. Michael McGinnis]. Health Education, 20(3), 34–35.

Chen, M. S. (1989b). The most important influences in health promotion: Continuation of the panel discussion. [Interview with Julie Davis-Colan]. Health Education, 20(4), 39.

Chenoweth, D. (1995). Getting the greatest bang for the buck. Occupational Health and Safety, 64, 25–26.

Green, L. W., & Kreuter, M. W. (1991). Health promotion planning: An educational and environmental approach. Mountain View, CA: Mayfield Publishing.

Griggs, R. (1990). Personal wellness: Your most profitable agenda. Los Altos, CA: Crisp Publications.

Hamil, M. A. (1996). Creating healthy workplaces: A model for developing corporate wellness programs. Unpublished doctoral dissertation, Northern Illinois University, DeKalb, IL.

McAllister, R., & Broeder, C. E. (1993). Wellness strategies help workers adopt health habits in lifestyles. Occupational Health and Safety, 62, 50–60.

O'Donnell, M. P. (1994). Employers' financial perspective on health promotion. In M. P. O'Donnell & J. S. Harris (Eds.), Health Promotion in the Workplace. Albany, NY: Delmar.

Powers, D. (1994). Understanding and working with an emphasis on wellness. Thresholds in Education, XX(1), 4–7.

Schaller, W. E. (1981). The school health program. Philadelphia, PA: Saunders College Press.

Seidler, S. M. (1993). The health project: Using model program data to design effective health promotion programs. Compensation and Benefits Review, 25, 30–37.

Weinstein, M. S. (1989). Lifestyle, stress and work: Strategies for health promotion. In A. Kaplun & E. Wenzel (Eds.), Health Promotion in the Working World (pp. 13–20). Heidelberg, Germany: Springer-Verlag.

Wolfe, R., Ulrich, D., & Parker, D. (1987). Employee health management programs: Review, critique, and research agenda. Journal of Management, 13, 603–615.

3

Continuing Education for the Professions: The Catalyst for Workplace Empowerment

Jane R. Flagello

As we move to the beginning of a new millennium, there is increased emphasis being placed on the changing nature of work, the breaking of the implied employer/employee contract, and the perception that there is an increased desire on the part of professionals to participate in meaningful activities within the work setting. Concomitant with this change in how adults perceive work is the increased recognition of the importance of continuing learning and preparation for a changing professional workforce so that it may compete effectively in a dynamic global economy. Bridges (1994) explores the reconceptualization of the job from a set grouping of tasks to a full range of interrelated activities that will require increasingly sophisticated levels of skill development. Others (Drucker, 1993; Kanter, 1989; Peters, 1992; Wheatley, 1992) who write and speak about the changing nature of the workplace have done the same thing.

The metagoal of all of the recent emphasis on changes within the workplace seems to be the desire to plant the seed that a new era has begun in America and the professional workforce had better wake up to it and take action. Change is the only constant and in order to change, each person will have to take more responsibility for keeping pace with technology and what that technology is doing within the workplace. Ongoing education, or more precisely continuous learning, both on a formal and an informal level, will be the requirement for all employees to remain competent about an ever-expanding body of knowledge and be key players on the playing field of life.

This chapter will explore continuing education within the professions as the catalyst to empowerment in the workplace. It is the potential that empowerment offers that presents professionals with a significant freedom, not often explored as a positive opportunity by many in today's society. As the old paternalistic corporate order declines and more companies are faced with the harsh realities of survival in a changing economic landscape, the entitlement mentality must give way to one of professional responsibility and self-efficacy. Unfortunately, this is often not represented by the media and others in power in a positive light. The phrasing above, "continuing education within the professions" has been used in order to look at the possibilities of ongoing learning and continuing education from a more inclusive framework. While not working in what might be categorized as a traditional profession (doctor, lawyer, teacher, clergy, architect), where certification, licensing and other means of controlling membership are employed, many more adults today consider themselves to be professionals (McGuire, 1993; Sullivan, 1995). As technology and knowledge expands, specialists are required for more and more activities and tasks. This concept of specialization made necessary by the increasing complexity of modern life can be seen as an extension of Adam Smith's original theory of the division of labor into specialties (Menand, 1995). Specialists, while highly skilled in their specific specialties, are often not as skilled in other aspects of business and professional life that will be requirements of our future workplaces. These include but are not limited to skills in team work, collaborative enterprise and partnership, conflict resolution within a win/win framework, communication within a multicultural community, leadership and entrepreneurship.

Knowing all of these new skill requirements, however, is not enough. The transformation necessary will require a full three-step process of knowing, accepting and then acting on that knowledge to initiate the transformative change. Understanding this transformative change process begins the discussion of empowerment with learning as the catalyst that makes a truly empowered professional work force an exciting possibility. An initial discussion of the term empowerment will be followed by a discussion of the economic realities that make learning/education a wise decision by all who offer service to an expanding market. The power debate is required in any discussion of empowerment, as it is the holding and yielding of power that constitutes the word's meaning. The chapter will conclude with an examination of the potential and opportunities that an empowered workforce brings to a changing workplace.

In this chapter the term professional will be acknowledged in its broadest possible sense, making it inclusive of many more people as opposed to adopting the more elitist view. Professional will not be considered as a label, title or rank, but rather an attitude about how one does one's chosen vocation. This view shatters the context of the professional as an elitist and moves the discussion into the realm of personal action and personal choice. All who seek to be seen as a professional need only develop the attitude and mind set of a professional. It becomes inclusive and invites participation in a myriad of learning projects that will enable and enhance the person's skills and competence. Being professional also carries with it a moral element of action beyond self-service and toward social good. This aspect of professionalism is too often overlooked by many who would claim use of the title. True empowerment acts as the foundation for professional action as it is a force which engenders not only an attitude and status, but also a mind set of trustworthy interaction between the professional and those served.

Empowerment is the contradiction of corporate America. Regardless of the articles and rhetoric extolling the virtues of an empowered workplace and an empowered professional, in reality, an empowered professional is the antithesis of what many of those currently in power in corporate America want. Ultimately, however, it is what must be achieved by all who work, especially by those who work in professional positions. If we are to reinvent the organization to enable it to meet the challenges of a new century, we must begin with the people who make up that organization. For in the most elementary analysis, an organization is nothing if not a group of people with common goals working together to achieve those goals. Extending this one step further, the professional has historically been looked upon as a leader within the workplace and the community. An empowered professional then becomes the true leader for a changing tomorrow.

Empowerment frees the professional to choose, collaborate, and commit. It is about ownership, responsibility, and outcomes that are congruent with personal choices. In a truly empowered professional person, beliefs and values combine with a higher order sense of responsibility toward the larger organization and the larger community. In many ways empowerment requires the professional person to abdicate an implied company security for one that is self-created, one with intention and purpose stemming from the professional endeavor and linked to it by virtue of the commitment the professional makes to his or her profession, not some perceived corporate caretaker. This cannot be forced or faked. According to Renesch, "a West-

ern tendency has been to adapt-to take on the form, the semblance
of change-without embracing the underlying principles. We have a
habit of taking on the appearance of doing it right without commit-
ting ourselves to the substance" (1994, p. 1). A truly empowered professional is not merely adaptive; he/she is generative and is reflective. These are higher order learning skills not taught within the
current context of professional education. They require an ongoing
educational commitment of a very different sort from rote learning
or skill training and development geared toward passing a certification and/or licensing examination. The door to continuing education,
lifelong learning, and empowerment opens.

THE ECONOMICS OF EMPOWERMENT

An empowered professional workforce is economically more viable as organizations recognize that the components of competitive
advantage have become less difficult to achieve. There are several
trends that have been identified that clearly require empowered
professionals. New competitors entering dynamically changing
markets, creating products and services that were once owned by
old line, established companies tops this list. Second is the acceptance of the fact that knowledge is growing exponentially. The
knowledge base doubles every 7 years and in some industries in
even shorter time periods (Davis and Botkin, 1994). People are being asked to do more, to be multiskilled, multitalented and to add
value at every step of an operation or process. Ideas of collaboration with adversaries working as partners requires learning the
skills associated with concepts of teamwork, partnership and cooperation from both sides of the corporate table, employer and employee. Referring to the Renesch quote, this collaborative process
cannot be done in an adaptive fashion, neither as a convenience,
nor as a manipulation. Working as a member of a team, collabora-
tively, as partners will require an inner transformation by many
people in power positions. Finally, the opportunities offered by empowerment are tremendous. Empowered people create their lives
and take responsibility for themselves. Empowered people change
the balance of economic power and alters the competitive playing
field considerably. Who better to provide the leadership on all of
these trend fronts than the professional?

The emerging workforce with professionals filling their leadership
roles must become one of shared aspirations, one that fosters creativity in all of its activities, and one that fully engages individuals

in meaningful work. Empowerment initiates the process of generative, creative learning, a style of learning that offers a fuller, richer, more meaningful life for all who understand how to incorporate its power into their everyday activities. Without this generative learning ability, it becomes economically unfeasible to produce the myriad of products and services that the 21st century organization will need to produce in order to compete effectively on a global scale. The complexity of the task is too enormous to control at the micromanagement level. The costs are too great in manpower, productivity, efficiency, resource utilization, and quality. There are too many customized operations to manage and control and too few able managers to be everywhere overseeing all aspects of the operation.

The realities of new economy require a higher degree of risk taking from organizations that can only exist in companies where all levels of employees feel a sense of ownership and responsibility. Increased risk taking must also become part of the repertoire of individuals in the work force. Professionals must begin to challenge themselves to live at a higher level than existence, to continuous growth and development, to learn how to make choices and decisions, and evaluate the extended time parameters of the decisions and choices they made, to own their outcomes and become responsible for themselves, their families, their workplaces, and their communities. These two factors, ownership and responsibility, are the essential elements of empowerment, but they are elements that must be learned and developed and they come with a price. "A good life for anyone now depends upon conduct that is collectively as well as individually responsible" (Sullivan, 1995, p. xiv).

THE EMPOWERING JOURNEY

The word *empowerment* seems to have taken on a life of its own over the course of the last few years as it has become yet another management buzz word. And just as every journey begins with a first step, empowerment is a journey too. It is a journey that requires a step inward. The current frustration with the dreaded "E" word exists and many companies are having problems trying to empower their workforce because they fail to recognize and respect the inner nature of the empowerment journey. A deeper understanding of the concept of empowerment becomes crucial because an empowered workforce is the reality of the future, and being empowered must become second nature to a larger percentage of the professional population. Empowerment lies outside of the context of the actual job duties being performed. A doctor, lawyer, or teacher may do the job it-self well, be highly regarded for his or her skill within the profession and still be powerless. The bottom line in this debate is simple. No one can empower anyone else. Empowerment is an inside job, per-haps the ultimate inside job.

The word itself combines the prefix *"em"* a variant of *"en"* which means "put into" or "into" with the root word *"power"* which means "the ability or capacity to act effectively." *Empower* then comes to mean "to invest with legal power, to authorize; to enable or permit." Finally, the addition of the suffix *"ment"* indicates product, means, action or state and is usually added to verbs. When that is added to *empower,* the noun *empowerment* is born with a meaning as "one be-ing invested, enabled and permitted with the legal authorization to initiate his/her ability or capacity to act effectively."

Empowerment is about the recognition that each person does have power and it is the effective use of this personal level of power that creates the dynamic energy that leads to creating the outcomes peo-ple want most. It is not about "getting," not about controlling others, not about benefits or raises, not about doing more with less. Block (1993) described empowerment as being about sovereignty and said that it is the

> act of standing on our own ground, discovering our own voice, making our own choices . . . It stems from a mindset that tells us that we have within ourselves the authority to act and to speak and to serve . . . we do not need permission to feel or to take what matters into our own hands. (p. 36)

As one can clearly see, this description changes the scope of em-powerment from something someone else gives or bestows upon a person to something that each of us takes for ourselves, creates for ourselves. Outcomes generated through empowerment become more than materialistic gratification, and they usually extend to society beyond the individual. Empowered people recognize this extension of outcomes to a community larger than themselves. This also pre-sents the inherent problem with the concept of empowerment: too many people are waiting for someone else to empower them!

For too long many people have felt powerless; victims of society, of bad bosses, bad teachers, bad parents, and bad environments. They have turned to the government, to entitlements, to demanding some-one else let them in and take care of their needs rather than looking within to determine the best path to personally fulfilling those needs. The cocoon of security offered by others robs people of their own abilities and energies. The promise of empowerment is in its ability to build personal efficacy into a force for change at an individual, familial, community and at a societal level.

Barner (1994) suggests that the process is twofold. First is the empowerment component, which constitutes a power shift from bureaucracy to individuals so that people can "get in touch with their own personal power" (p. 34). The second component addresses the general need for people to develop the competencies to manage this power and autonomy because empowerment establishes a different relationship with all of the factors that adults have in their lives. Professionals need to learn how to become empowered.

Empowerment can be truly experienced only when the real values, beliefs, meaning schemas, and goals are freed from confinement and socialized responses and are genuine to the person, drawn out and then reflected upon. "To empower me is to enable me" (Stanage, 1987, p. 168). All the guises of external control and manipulation cease to have relevance and the powering force centers upon the person to act on his or her own behalf. Until the professional persons learn the art of empowering themselves, it will never become their reality.

LEARNING AS CATALYST

Inherent here is an adult's ability to know his or her inner self with depth and clarity. It is this dimension of self-awareness or self-knowledge that provides the inner security that then frees the adult to proactively explore a myriad of external forces and opportunities without fear of losing, but rather with the empowered sense of enhancing the living experience. More and more professionals are recognizing the importance of learning as a key element in their process of becoming empowered. Learning helps remove the fear of something happening or not happening from a person's actions. Learning creates and builds confidence in one's total abilities, not just one's professional capabilities. An inner strength of character, integrity, and trust develops for and with others that enables the professional and acts as a foundation for actions within that professional's personal and professional spheres of operation. Empowered professionals legitimize themselves. It is this inner sense of value, of validation that leads to actions and intentions in harmony with others rather than in competition or conflict with others.

Learning becomes the catalyst to growing these abilities and capacities to perform. Strong and confident performance increases one's sense of value and self-worth, which then encourages more learning projects and continuous personal and professional growth. It is an iterative process. Learning offers opportunity to all who seek it out. It does not discriminate and is there for the taking in a variety of forms and contexts. This type of learning is not a discussion of segmented course work delivered on a variety of skill areas. The context being described here is more than schooling. According to Marsick (1987), ". . . learning is the way in which individuals or groups acquire, interpret, reorganize, change or assimilate a related cluster of information, skills and feelings. . . is also the primary way people construct meaning in their personal and shared organizational lives" (p. 4). Learning encompasses a complete range of projects that enables people to fully engage with all of the various facets of their lives. Learning is the bridge that links an empowered person with the myriad dimensions of life.

The paradox here is that many professionals are already overeducated for the jobs they hold; they are underemployed and their work becomes boring, rote, and meaningless (Harman & Hormann, 1990; Raines & Day-Lower, 1986). At the same time, they are undereducated about how to lead a fulfilling life, with their profession as only one component of that life. Learning must become more than training for a job or career; it must take on a new prominence in the activities in which adults engage. "Learning becomes the voyage of exploration, of questing and experimenting" (Handy, 1989, p. 10).

Continuing the learning process to enable empowerment will not be an easy task as it is at this point of conscious learning that professionals are faced for the first time with the need to challenge and often relinquish many of their beliefs and assumptions about status, ranking, and how life is to be lived, what life is all about. They begin to develop an inner awareness of what aspects of life provides them with meaning and value, what constitutes their fundamental motivations and what character traits are necessary to achieve the life they really want to be living. They also look into the mirror and see an image that supports these character traits or lives outside of them, attempting to make excuses as to why they don't matter in this or that situation. Empowerment begins as professionals proactively engage in and focus their attention, energies, behaviors, and choices on those relationships and experiences which fulfill that meaning and value schema (Covey, 1989; Heath, 1991; Kaufman & Raphael, 1991). These changed behaviors show up in every facet of their lives, especially in the workplace and the workplace begins to change as a result of professionals challenging the socialized status quo and wanting more for themselves and for others.

REINVENTING THE WORKPLACE
FOR THE 21ST CENTURY

Change is needed within the workplace to facilitate the new breed of professional that is now clearly vital to corporate America. The management/employee friction (us versus them, haves and have nots) currently felt in many workplaces (and in society in general) will be exacerbated unless and until more professionals learn how to act from a mode of empowered participation. This will require many professionals to learn how to operate in a different way.

Several organizations have been implementing education components into yearly performance management systems, hoping that forced learning will increase an employee's value to that organization. This forced learning component has also been forced on professionals, but is usually targeted at increasing skills within the professional skill set. Unfortunately, adding value is not about doing "seat-time" and although specific skill sets may be improved, many of the higher order benefits of education that these organizations seek (knowing-in-action, reflection-in-action) are lost as they require conformance to education programs and forced attendance. The rationale behind the learning component is valid, but learning cannot be forced. The good is lost in the policy.

The workplace can become the primary benefactor of the increased professional self-efficacy that comes from empowered action. As professionals develop their capacities to learn via empowered action, their capabilities will also be enhanced to initiate, utilize, incorporate, and reflect upon new information and processes. Clearly, those professionals' ability to add value to the company's operation increases. The creative energy generated here is both immense and contagious. The operative word above, however, is "can," for the workplace "can" also stifle and suppress. People try to dominate what they fear or feel threatened by, and professionals are not immune to this type of behavior. According to Senge (1990), adults have learned many self-protective and defensive routines, and these are deeply imbedded into daily operating styles, so deep they are often difficult to detect. Empowered adults intimidate those who fear for their own security, and in a time when people view the world from a scarcity mentality (Covey, 1989), a survivalist approach is all too common. It is the environment created within the organization, by the leadership of that organization, which holds the key to successful incorporation of the empowerment initiative at the professional level or its total repression.

On the surface an environment conducive to an empowered work force seems easy to create and maintain. It is, however, this appearance of simplicity that both belies the power of empowerment and the difficulty in achieving this type of environment. Creating an empowered professional work force will require a paradigm shift about how professionals perceive their work. The movement to a knowledge age (Drucker, 1993; Handy, 1989; Harman & Hormann, 1990) will fundamentally transform work and subsequently leisure and life. The promise of technology will finally be actualized. What will take place in this transformation will be the realization that technology will free more people from the job cycle and allow them to engage in work from a different perspective. "Work will cease to be a means of survival and become a means of joining with others in extending creation because it will now be experienced as connected to all of creation in a meaningful way" (Mollner, 1992, p. 103). We are now in the initial and often painful stages of this transformation.

Greenleaf (1977), Block (1993), DePree (1989), Kostenbaum (1991), Senge, (1990), Wheatley (1992) and many others have described a workplace where an individual's potential is developed in concert with an organization's potential, where systems and structures are fluid, and where a sense of community and partnership has replaced the power and control mechanisms which diminish so many. Witness the humanness shown by Aaron Feuerstein after his textile mill burned just before Christmas 1995. He pledged to rebuild and promised to continue to pay salaries and benefits during the rebuilding process. "I haven't really done anything. I don't deserve credit. Corporate America has made it so that when you behave the way I did, it{s abnormal" was his reaction to the reaction of others about his actions (Wulf, 1996). An environment that thinks this behavior abnormal is not an environment conducive to empowerment.

The language of the workplace is also in the process of changing as words enter the vocabulary of work that had previously been reserved for home, church, and community. Words like partner and collaborate and cooperate join with ideas like creating relationships with vendors, suppliers, customers, and employees to signal a workplace trying to free itself from controlling mechanisms and shifting to embody new constructions of collaborative and unified enterprise.In addition, more occupations are taking the label of professional to give themselves a perceived sense of elitism and importance, hoping that this will elevate them to positions where they cannot be downsized. While many in corporate America quickly dismiss these concepts as idealistic, utopian or naive it is perhaps because they see their own actions as being less than what the Judeo-Christian ethic presents as foundational tenets to being human.

It is the relationship of people to people and then people to organizations that must be more honestly and sincerely addressed. The tie that binds one person to another, and people to each other through organizations has indeed frayed beyond any simplistic external workshop, management technique or repair strategy. One of the goals of this transformation to an empowered workforce must be to restore the human element in the workplace and honor in the act of work itself. Perhaps, we must learn how to be human. Who better to lead the way than the professionals who offer us so much leadership in the concrete fields of science, technology, and education.

EMPOWERED WORKPLACES

The one reality that permeates all of our organizations is quite simply that organizations are made up of people, by people, and for people. At the end of any chain of command, any decision to do anything, there will be some perceived benefit to some group of people. The need is to expand this circle of beneficiaries, to move beyond personal greed and selfishness, to view the workplace and professionals within the workplace as integral to our success overall. Wheatley (1992) quotes from Robert Haas, CEO of The Levi Strauss Company, ". . . we are at the center of a seamless web of mutual responsibility and collaboration . . . a seamless partnership, with interrelationships and mutual commitments" (p. 140). The instruments needed to accomplish this expansion are not to be found in change programs, but in changed people.

What is required is a new social contract based on different, more current assumptions and philosophies about how to live, how to love, and how to conduct business, and one that presents these concepts as interrelated elements of a complete being. Work must become more fully integrated into each adult's life, not as a means to other ends, but as a meaningful endeavor in and of itself. People must see themselves as working together for common interests not "for the man." It is this synergy of purposes that will enable employees who want to do the very best job they can, who want to learn how to better serve the organization, and therefore, better serve themselves and their families.

This synergy is "a shift of mind—from seeing ourselves as separate from the world to connected to the world, from seeing problems as caused by someone or 'something' out there to seeing how our own actions create the problems we experience" (Senge, 1990, p. 12–13). In order to bring about this type of change, professional need to continue to learn about themselves and about others because learning creates change. Herein lies the opportunity for the continuing education community to create alliances with workplaces to incorporate the learning act into the daily routine. As organizations look for autonomous action from the professional ranks, those professionals must learn how to act in an autonomous fashion, how to reflect on their actions and how to enhance and improve the various processes within their venue. And they must learn how to do this together.

> No educational institution . . . tries to equip students with the elementary skills of effectiveness as members of an organization: ability to present ideas orally and in writing; ability to work with people; ability to shape and direct one's own work, contributions, career; and generally skills in making organization a tool for one's own aspirations and achievements and for the realization of values. (Drucker, 1989, p. 247)

Several management consultants have labeled this as organizational learning. The concept of a learning organization (Argyris & Schön, 1978; Senge, 1990) has been defined as one where ". . . people continually expand their capacity to create the results they truly desire, where new and expansive patterns of thinking are nurtured, where collective aspiration is set free, and where people are continually learning how to learn together" (Senge, 1990, p. 3). In the final analysis, "A learning organization is a place where people are continually discovering how they create their reality. And how they can change it" (Senge, 1990, p. 13).

Empowerment is about bringing all of these elements together. It is about creation and growth for everyone, on an individual and organizational level. DePree (1989) talks about business as "a place of fulfilled potential . . . a gift to be what I can be . . . the opportunity to serve . . . the gift of challenge . . . the gift of meaning" (p. 59–60). An empowered work force can accomplish this.

While it is true that the external environment of business will continue to be unpredictable and will require organizations to be agile, there are several principles that can be incorporated into the internal environment of an organization to facilitate the empowerment process. First and foremost, organizations must become forums for open dialogue and free expression. All employees must be able to work without the fear of retribution or punishment. Questioning organizational actions, sharing in decision-making, and sharing in reward and compensation programs as equals must become routinely accepted. Experimentation and inquiry must become the norm. Constraints of a machine age mentality must give way to flexible operating procedures in order to accommodate the changing needs of a diverse work force. The concept of blame must be eliminated and replaced by a shared mind set of goals and outcomes to which all are committed. All employees must be encouraged to learn and grow beyond current job assignments.

CONTINUING PROFESSIONAL EDUCATION OPENS THE DOOR

All of these elements require learning; learning as a process of continual renewal becomes the catalyst that decreases the fear of obsolescence and empowers employees to reach new goals and strive for their fullest potential. Facilitating the process of continual renewal is the opportunity that the workplace holds for continuing professional educators: to make this non-skill-based education more easily available to a wider audience. It also must be made nonthreatening. Professionals do not like to open themselves up any more than many members of the general workforce.

Continuing professional educators must recognize the specific needs of the professional outside of skill development. Empowerment learning is a softer curriculum, one that is full of naysayers. Outcomes take longer to realize. Many of the skills that professionals need to learn to become truly empowered require them to give up some of their positional power.

Continuing professional educators can lead the way. Learning how to become empowered is different from many other types of learning that CPE offers. It is a different animal and must be offered in a format that enhances the learning and reduces the risk. CPE can and should establish delivery systems that bring empowerment education to the professional at times and in a forum that offers all of the benefits and eliminates the fear of exposure. Many professionals may shy away from the very type of learning required to learn how to become empowered. It may be seen as too threatening to the professional who is suppose to know it all.

However, the possibilities made available through technology become the pot of gold at the end of the rainbow for just this type of learning. CPE must explore new mediums of delivery including the virtual classroom now possible on the World Wide Web. Access to the latest technology is a trait of many professionals and CPE must use this characteristic to its advantage.

CPE must become more aggressive in seeking funding and creating partnerships with organizations that already have this technology. Together, programs can be developed that professionals can tap into from the safety of their own homes, at times conducive to their effective participation. Some of this is probably being done informally now; groups setting up chat rooms to explore the external universe. CPE needs only to focus the conversation on the inner universe to make empowerment learning a reality. CPE professionals must guide the journey of adults into their inner worlds; to take the leadership role and ask the tough questions. CPE professionals must also be there to companion the reflective process. Perhaps, therefore, it is also the CPE professional who must first take his or her own journey.

Continuing professional educators often wait in the wings bemoaning low participation and wondering why so few take advantage of courses offered. They make lists about program length, costs, access, etc. But year after year, many CPE programs repeat the same mistakes. Learning how to become empowered is a need of most professionals now engaged in active work. The market is there. CPE needs only step up to the plate and empower themselves to deliver the service, without regard for exactly which CPE group is getting the cash. As the world changes there will be enough to go around and together, we can achieve an empowered professional workforce and share in an abundance of opportunities that will lie ahead.

REFERENCES

Argyris C., & Schön, D. A. (1978). *Organizational learning: A theory of action perspective*. Reading, MA: Addison-Welsey.

Barner, R. (1994). Enablement: The key to empowerment. *Training and Development Journal, 48* (6), 33–36

Block, P. (1993) *Stewardship: Choosing service over self-interest*. San Francisco: Berrett-Koehler.

Bridges, W. (1994). *JobShift: How to prosper in a workplace without jobs*. Reading, MA: Addison-Wesley.

Covey, S. R. (1989). *The seven habits of highly effective people*. New York: Simon & Schuster.

Davis, S. M., & Botkin, J. W. (1994). *The monster under the bed: How business is mastering the opportunity of knowledge for profit*. New York: Simon & Schuster.

DePree, M. (1989). *Leadership is an art*. New York: Doubleday.

Drucker, P. F. (1993). *Post-captialist society*. New York: HarperCollins.

Drucker, P. F. (1989). *The new realities*. New York: Harper Row.

Greenleaf, R. K. (1977). *Servant leaderhsip: A journey into the nature of legitimate power and greatness*. New York: Paulist Press.

Handy, C. (1989). *The age of unreason*. Cambridge, MA: Harvard University Press.

Harman, W., & Hormann, J. (1990). *Creative work: The constructive role of business in a transforming society*. Indianapolis, IN: Knowledge Systems.

Heath, D. H. (1991) *Fulfilling lives: Paths to maturity and success*. San Francisco: Jossey-Bass.

Heider, J. (1986). *The tao of leadership: Lao Tzu's tao te ching adapted for a new age*. New York: Bantam Books.

Kanter, R. M. (1989). *When giants learn to dance: Mastering the challenges of strategy, arrangement, and careers in the 1990s*. New York: Simon & Schuster.

Kaufman, G., & Raphael, L. (1991). *The dynamics of power*. Rochester, VT: Schenkman Books.

Koestenbaum, P. (1991). *Leadership: The inner side of greatness*. San Francisco: Jossey-Bass.

Marsick, V. J. (1987). New paradigms for learning in the workplace. In V. Marsick (Ed.) *Learning in the workplace*. New York: Croom Helm.

McGuire, C. H. (1993). Sociocultural changes affecting professions and professionals. In L. Curry, J. F. Wergin, and Associates (Eds.), *Educating professionals: Responding to new expectations for competence and accountability*. San Francisco: Jossey-Bass. pp. 3–16.

Menand, L. (1995, March 3). The trashing of professionalism. *New York Times Magazine*, pp. 41–43.

Mollner, T. (1992). "The 21st-century corporation: The tribe of the relationship age." In J. Renesch (Ed.), *New traditions in business: Spirit and leadership in the 21st century* (pp. 95–106). San Francisco: Berrett-Koehler.

Peters, T. (1992). *Liberation Management*. New York: Knopf.

Raines, J. C., & Day-Lower, D. C. (1986). *Modern work and human meaning*. Philadelphia: Westminster Press.

Renesch, J (1994). A commitment to a change context. In J. Renesch (ed.), *Leadership in a new era: Visionary approaches to the biggest crisis of our time* (pp.1–6). San Francisco: Sterling & Stone.

Senge, P. M. (1990). *The fifth discipline*. New York: Doubleday.

Stanage, S. (1987). *Adult education and phenomenological research: New directions for theory and practice*. Malabar, FL: Krieger.

Sullivan M. (1995). *Work and integrity: The crisis and promise of professionalism in america*. New York: HarperCollins.

Wheatley, M. J. (1992). *Leadership and the new science: Learning about organizations from an orderly universe*. San Francisco: Berrett-Koehler.

Wulf, S. (1996, January 8). The glow from the fire. *Time*, p. 49.

4

The Infusion/Utilization of Critical Thinking Skills in Professional Practice

Arnold Bickham

Professions do not teach or expose individuals to critical thinking for the most part as they go through the process of becoming a professional. Every profession may want to examine itself, and highlight those areas where critical thinking and continuing professional education are flourishing. Professionals need to know that critical thinking today may be one of the more important skills and mindsets that they have.

OVERVIEW OF PROFESSIONAL PRACTICE

Definitions: Critical Thinking

Critical thinking should be considered as part of an entire process of learning that continues throughout the life span. One purpose of the knowledge base in the field of adult education is to serve as a tool to stimulate and promote critical thinking about what we do as educators of adults. The two central activities of critical thinking are identifying and challenging assumptions and exploring alternative ways of thinking and acting (Brookfield, 1987). Basic to critical thinking is categorizing and asking questions about information and incidents appearing in life and in print. For instance, Apps (1985) suggests that besides reading, participating in the arts, thinking, writing, discussing, and taking action is a valuable strategy for analyzing practice. Professional activity should consist of instrumental problem solving guided by scientific theory and technique(Schön, 1983). Essential to any definition of a profession is the notion of established competence through standardized, rigorous training, principled standards of practice, and unselfish service to society. Licensing provisions and laws defining scope of practice assume an explicated, specialized body of knowledge. We may regard critical thinking initially as the determination of the meaning, and the acceptability of a statement. To engage in critical thinking is to engage in judgment-making, but judgment-making of a specific kind. The critical thinking judgments that we make characterize and involve five kinds of things: laws, principles, or hypotheses; statements; arguments; terms; and problems (Drake, 1976, p. 30).

Knowledge

The key assumption underlying the acquisition of knowledge is that learning is cumulative in nature. Professionals think about specific cases. They decide practice and judge individuals based on comparisons with previous, similar experiences. No meaning or learning occurs in isolation from experience. Schön (1983) calls the dominant understanding of professional knowledge "technical rationality." In this view, they conceive of knowledge as basic and applied research that has four essential properties: "It is specialized, firmly bounded, scientific, and standardized" (p. 23). The experienced professional selects the appropriate knowledge to apply to situations of practice. The model assumes that knowing is in the actions of professionals. Spontaneous actions that professionals take do not stem from a rule or plan that was in the mind before the action, although they may stem from internal categories or checklists. Experienced professionals constantly make decisions for which they cannot state the bases or theories on which they formed their judgments. Schön (1983) calls this knowing-in-action. Knowing-in-action has three properties: (1) actions and judgments that professionals know how to carry out without thinking about them before or during performance; (2) there is no awareness of having learned to do these things; and (3) an inability to describe the knowing that the action reveals (p.54). It is not at all clear that knowing-in-action represents critical thinking.

Profession, Professional

Educators need to define more precisely what they mean by profession and professional. What constitutes them has been an issue of intense debate for decades, and any consensus on definition is difficult to establish. The most common way to decide which occupations

we accept as professions in the United States has been to use the categories of the federal government's Bureau of the Census (Cervero,
1989). According to Curry and Wergin (1993), a profession is an occupation that regulates itself through systematic, required training
and collegial discipline; that has a base in technological, specialized
knowledge; and that has a service, rather than a profit, orientation
enshrined in its code of conduct. Specialized knowledge remains essential for professional practice. He says there are only those occupations that we commonly regard as professions and those that are
not. Some amount of higher education must be prerequisite to classification of a profession. Most managers, airline pilots, and legal as-
sistants fail to meet this criterion. In contrast, the least restrictive
definition includes all of the occupations included in the Census Bureau's category of professional workers, such as business executives,
teachers, nurses, and lawyers.

Drake (1976) has summarized some of what we know of the term
professional (p. 71):

1. Its root notion is a title, which refers to certain specialized
   kinds of occupations.
2. We apply it mostly to highly-specialized occupations, such as
   doctors or lawyers, but can also apply it to artists, nurses,
   teachers, and the like.
3. It is involved with deriving a livelihood from a particular sort
   of endeavor, but not always or not necessarily.
4. In certain situations it is used to signify a sort of "level of excellence."

Skills

The professions encompass occupational groups, that share specialized skills requiring extensive systematic and scholarly training.
They restrict access with rigorous entrance and exit requirements,
and because of their importance to society, claim high social prestige
(Curry & Wergin, 1993). They list the *helping* professions, such as
nursing, social work, teaching, and the ministry; the *entrepreneurial*
professions, such as journalism, business, and law; and the *technical*
professions, such as architecture, engineering, and the military (p.
xiii). Something they do labels people as professionals, not their
earnings. Their annual or lifetime incomes are not what *makes* them
professionals, but the result of it. We have thought of continuing pro-

fessional education historically as imparting skills that better human life. In addition, people need certain basic, physical skills to survive in a profession.

Skill denotes certain processes, which may be quite complicated. Skills are activities or abilities that do not extend universally through the population. Educators recognize they exist because not everyone has them. This explains why welding is called a skill, but breathing is not. Breathing, sitting, and walking seem to be natural abilities or activities; yet, skills are acquired. The term "skill" is associated with the sorts of abilities and processes, which metalsmiths, welders, cabinetmakers, and stonemasons engage in. Skills are not associated generally with what doctors, lawyers, representatives, inventors, and musicians do. "Skill" is not usually associated with the performing arts or with the so-called fine arts. The term talent generally signifies the creative processes or activities that overall characterize the arts of Caruso, Picasso, or Toscanini. Such labels as a skilled cardiovascular surgeon and a skilled lawyer are misapplications of the term "skill," in that the respective professions presuppose a host of skills merely to become licensed members in them. To speak of someone as a skilled educational philosopher, a skilled representative, or a skilled inventor seems redundant. The term may be used with many morally and/or socially desirable activities. In addition, the term skill may be associated with certain frowned-upon or undesirable actions, like illegally forging a person's name on a bank document to obtain money.

Purpose: Goals, Mission

The goals of critical thinking and of continuing professional education, should concern the entire profession. Every professional needs to understand the central mission of the profession. The mission is concerned with developments in its basic disciplines. Those developments improve competence by using theories and techniques of innovative practice. They require applications of ethical principles in a constantly changing work and social environment. They strengthen and sustain a responsibly coherent profession in all the ways, to preserve an appropriate perspective on worklife. Self-conceptions and ways of work are also continuously evolving. Worklife does not engulf them, because they collaborate with members of other professions. He or she represents the profession responsibly in all relationships with the persons served.

Classifications

Professionals are classified in many different ways. Stark, Lowther and Haggerty (1986) identify twelve professional fields: architecture, business administration, dentistry, education, engineering, journalism, law, library science, medicine, nursing, pharmacy, and social work. The key in his classification is training, which professionals are much more likely to have than nonprofessionals. Continuing education programs exist today, which embody management, architecture, engineering, law, medicine, pharmacy, veterinary medicine, social work, nursing home administration, the military, nursing, public school education, and many other professions (Cervero, 1989). Houle (1980) called the following groups professionals: accountants, architects, clergy, dentists, engineers, foresters, health care administrators, lawyers, librarians, military officers, nurses, pharmacists, physicians and surgeons, school administrators, school teachers, social workers, and veterinarians.

CURRENT ISSUES FACING PROFESSIONS

The professions are central to the functioning of society. As in adult education, professionals must assume responsibility for their own learning (Brookfield, 1984; Knox, 1986). Most professionals now espouse the importance of lifelong professional education. They feel that being up to date in knowledge and skill ensures competence. The teaching role is most important in helping professionals become critical thinkers (Brookfield, 1987). This emphasis highlights the importance of teaching as a tool for distributing knowledge. Reading is only one way of stimulating critical thinking. Publications, in and of themselves, do not lead to critical thinking. Graduate courses, workshops, informal networks, and continuing education can aid in the development of critical thinking. A comprehensive strategy for continuing professional education requires clarification of the roles and goals of professionals as learners. Practitioners engage in critical thinking throughout their working lives, through reading, discussions with colleagues, formal and informal educational programs, and the problem solving activities of their everyday practice. From this perspective, professionals are neither entirely independent nor entirely dependent in the learning situation (Brookfield, 1986). Instead, they must use appropriate external expertise and assistance, while the individual simultaneously maintains ultimate control over the critical thinking process.

Reflection

The process of reflection and analyzing priorities and practices in adult education offers several benefits to professionals and the professions (Apps, 1985). These benefits may involve helping them reflect and expand their awareness of ways to practice, which helps their profession critically develop and analyze its role in society (Brockett, 1991). In this process of reflection, professionals' use of their body of knowledge enables them to think critically about what they do and why they do it. Their experiences may even serve as tools for encouraging and supporting critical thinking.

Competency

Across the professions, we have championed education to promote competency and as a necessity for distributing new knowledge (Cervero & Scanlan, 1985). Professionals fill the adult education literature with multiple perspectives on institutions, programs, practices, issues, and research within the field. Critical thinking can provide a convenient and often accessible way to use the ideas, gleaned from the literature. Continuing education rarely addresses attitudes and strengths, such as interpersonal skills and motivation, or the events and personal weaknesses that impair competence. The intellectual autonomy and highly specialized knowledge they possess often confine professionals to practice within specific boundaries. This specialized knowledge often requires long and intensive preparation, and high standards of achievement and conduct, which positively influence the conduct and commitment of professionals. State regulatory agencies and private certifying agencies have experimented with a variety of methods to promote continued competency and accountability of professionals. Self-assessment inventories, periodic reexaminations, chart audits, peer reviews, practice audits, and computerized simulations are examples. Whether these ensure critical thinking is not clear. Although the movement from voluntary to mandatory continuing education is gaining popularity, no widely accepted method to assure continued competency within professional groups exists.

Wholeness

Development of critical thinking by professionals is itself a social act. In discharging their common social responsibilities, it makes a person publicly accountable and responsive for his or her judgments and decisions. Critical thinking should encourage a genuine concern for societal problems and the ethical consequences of professional action (Cervero, Azzaretto, & Associates, 1990). Schön (1983) describes it as a learning strategy that demands an integrative and a "reflection-in-action" orientation. Kolb (1988) broadens this learning strategy to that of wholeness. Mid-career and older professionals face new tasks requiring new skills—especially integrative skills necessary to seek balance between career, family, personal well-being, and a desire to contribute to society. Kolb identifies this as the need to develop mind power versus muscle power. This mind power focuses on knowledge creation, capture, transfer, and use.

Knowledge

All educational activities for professionals are based on beliefs about how professionals know and incorporate knowledge into practice. More knowledge increases the effectiveness of professionals and the value of their services to society. On the other hand, many fields are advancing so rapidly that mastering and maintaining a professional knowledge base is becoming very difficult for practitioners. The long-term result of such a trend is creation of experts who know a great deal about very little and almost nothing about anything else. Whimbey and Lochhead, (1991) have written extensively about the conditions under which professionals learn best, and what role experience plays in learning. The assumption that professions are service-oriented occupations, currently dominates the provision of continuing education for professions. These occupations apply a systematic body of knowledge to problems that are about the central values of society. The viewpoint highlights the functional value of professional activity for the maintenance of society.

Regarding the source of professional knowledge and critical thinking, Schön (1987) argues that the professional has built up a repertoire of practical knowledge. We generally understand practical knowledge as a list or supply of examples, understandings, actions, images, practical principles, scenarios, or rules of thumb that we have developed primarily through experience. Experienced professionals, in trying to make sense of a situation, see it as something already present in the repertoire. They do not apply this accumulated knowledge from the repertoire in a real-life fashion, but let it function as a metaphor or exemplar for helping to define the new situation. Most professionals are not fully aware of the knowledge in their repertoire. It is as important to help them make this knowledge explicit as to help them to develop new knowledge. Critical thinking is a way for professionals to foster use of their repertoire of practical knowledge to construct an understanding of current situations of practice.

Expertise

Studies of expertise in a variety of professions, such as medicine, nursing, and teaching, support the importance of practical knowledge, implicit knowledge, and understanding. They learn the knowledge through experience in professional practice. A major difference between experts and novices is the extent of practical knowledge possessed by the experts. The knowledge is based on their repertoire of experience solving complex problems of practice. An extensive body of research in medical problem solving shows that experienced physicians do not, in fact, address the problems confronted in practice in the way suggested by the model of applied science (Curry, Wergin, & Associates, 1993). They quickly formulate and confirm hypotheses based on their repertoire of experience with similar medical problems, a process consistent with the knowledge of reflective practice. This research also proves that the superiority of experts over novices stems not so much from their superior general clinical reasoning skills; it comes from their breadth and depth of experience in clinical reasoning with similar medical problems, in all their complexity. These complex situations include, among others, multiple interacting problems and conflicting values embedded in multiple practice situations.

Learning: Schema Theory

Psychologists have always been interested in how people learn. The dominant orientation in critical thinking has changed from behavioristic to cognitive learning, the study of the mind and how it functions. Glaser (1984) uses schema theory to explain acquired knowledge. Schema theory describes how we organize knowledge in our minds, and how cognitive structures facilitate its use in particular situations. In this theory, schemata represent knowledge that we experience, interrelationships between situations and events that normally occur. Schemata are prototypes in memory of frequently experienced situations that people use to construct interpretations of related situations. We can think of schemata as internal checklists that professionals use as they face new situations; also, they may be internal models used by professionals to evaluate new situations critically. As one compares the schemata with the situation, if it fails to account for certain aspects, "it can either be accepted temporarily, rejected, modified, or replaced" (Glaser, 1984, p. 100). Professionals arrange educational contexts to test, evaluate, and modify their existing schemata. In this way, they can achieve some resolution between old knowledge structures and propose new ones.

Reflection-in-Action

We have called this process of thinking in action, reflection-in-action (Schön, 1987), intuition, or problem finding (cognitive psychologists). A study of practitioners in the fields of engineering, architecture, management, psychotherapy and town planning, for example, found that a kind of "reflection-in-action" characterized outstanding professional practice (Schön, 1983). Although the idea of a reflective practicum (continuing professional education) is general, it takes very different forms in different professions (Schön, 1987). People learn together by doing and by dealing with complex problems of practice. They learn in a virtual world, which represents but is not identical to the world of practice. Participants can try again and control the pace of their learning. In a reflective practicum novices learn from experts through reciprocal reflection-in-action related to demonstrations and exemplars of practice; in it, experienced professionals may also learn with each other through reflection-about-action.

Knowing-in-Action

Knowing-in-action, tacit knowledge, knowing more than one can say, and reflection-in-action are the fundamental elements of reflective practice. Articulation of practice, whether in writing or another form (such as demonstrations, written exemplars, or mutual reflection-in-action), is generally considered essential for guidance in development of skilled practice. In responding to the questions about the knowledge and competencies needed for reflective practice and how are they found, Schön (1987) argues for the central role of knowing-in-action, learned through experience, reflection-in-action, and reflection-about-action. These three competencies account for the skill that practitioners bring to situations of complexity, uniqueness, and value conflict. Besides knowing-in-action, Schön views reflection-in-action and reflection-about-action as central to the "art" by which practitioners deal well with situations of uncertainty, instability, uniqueness, and value conflict. Unlike practical knowledge, which is unique to an individual professional's practice, the process by which knowledge is used is a universal, humanly cognitive act. Professionals use similar skills to construct an understanding of situations both within and outside their practice.

Continuing Professional Education: A Continuum

Continuing professional education is no longer a luxury but a necessity. Cervero and Young (1987) claimed that professional leaders of the past assumed participation in learning throughout life. Professionals now realize the young graduate is not prepared to participate for the next half century without the benefit of critical thinking skills. The volume and rate of knowledge have increased in the past two decades. Leaders in those professions perhaps most affected (e.g., medicine, accounting) recently began to recognize the urgency for practitioners to continue their formal learning. Continuing professional education is a distinctive answer, which has evolved from traditional continuing education. It builds on previous formal education, but also takes into account the informal learning that accompanies professional practice and the need to integrate new knowledge via critical thinking. Most significantly, continuing professional education must be effective in helping practitioners enhance their performance as the embodiment of critical thinking.

Using critical thinking, continuing professional education is becoming increasingly differentiated from the educational practices of preprofessional education. Many professionals think of themselves as continuing educators, though they may not have had any experience in the preprofessional education of the groups with whom they work. In building their continuing education systems, most professionals rely on knowledge and structures in their own professions for guidance and models. The leaders of most professions believe that their own members must direct the continuing education function. This frame of reference assumes that the continuing education systems of various professions have little in common.

Many writers have noted the similarities in the continuing education efforts of individual professions about goals, processes, and issues (Brookfield, 1986; Cervero, 1988; Cervero & Scanlan, 1985; Houle, 1980; LeBreton et al., 1979; Nowlen, 1988; Stern, 1983; Whimbey & Lochhead, 1991). To talk intelligently about continuing professional education explicitly, we have to examine the differences between professions and other occupations. The problem of defining professions has a long history. One approach considers all occupations to exist on a continuum of professionalization. Regarding terms like professional, use in a continuum fashion is best, with the clear uses and the misuses being considered components within the continuum. Without apparently misusing the term, we often speak of professional athletes, writers, nurses, artists, and the like. Neither are indisputable clear uses nor outright misuses of the term *professional,* these might be borderline instances of usage and seem to lie somewhere near the middle of the continuum. We have modified a diagram offered by Drake (1976, p. 67).

CONTINUUM FOR THE TERM "PROFESSIONAL"		
CLEAR USES	BORDERLINE USES	MISUSES
Doctors Musicians	*Athletes Nurses Artists*	*Street-cleaners*

We predicate the term *professional* to certain activities, occupations, or endeavors in which the "ordinary" person could not engage satisfactorily. Many people do not consider precision toolmakers, and even veterinarians, on a par with medical doctors, as professionals. Either training or talent may be the crucial factor in any analysis of the term. There are complicated tasks, which require a specific sort of training to succeed at them. Certainly nursing, singing, painting, and the like do require a particular degree of training or talent. An explanation for this seems to lie in what Drake (1976) might call the "social value" of each occupation, that is, the extent to which the society as a whole values each.

Drake (1976) sees professionals as "the elite part of the American working force comprising doctors and lawyers" (p. 27). This is one use of the term. Viewed objectively, nevertheless, there is more open-ended use of the term professional. It is any working individual who has a particular skill or service, who derives the bulk of his or her income from rendering it. One might note that the term professional seems to have two undisputed referents, namely, lawyers and medical doctors. Then, continuing with the process, one would go on to cite an example of what might be a definite misapplication or misuse of the term—as in predicating the term professional to a group of street cleaners.

Active Practitioners: A Continuum

Houle (1980, pp. 156–161) identifies a continuum of active practitioners in continuing professional education. He calls them innovators, pacesetters, middle majority, laggards, and facilitators. People called innovators are at the upper end of his continuum. They continuously seek to improve their performance, at times in highly unconventional ways. Untested ideas and practices attract them. Innovators are likely to participate extensively in educational activities and to favor sophisticated learning pursuits. They have clear-cut plans of independent learning. They undertake investigations, seek and cherish part-time teaching positions, belong to groups that have restricted membership. Innovators take pride in being more advanced in their practice than their colleagues. They read highly specialized journals, attend invitational seminars, and leave their work occasionally to engage in full-time study. Innovators are intolerant of those who show fewer arduous, meretricious efforts to learn. They often ignore or are contemptuous of formal programs of continuing education. Most innovators take delight in broadening their education beyond their basic professions to become expert in another field of study.

Pacesetters feel the need to be progressive in their practice, but are not eager to be the first to try a new idea. They wait until ideas have been well tested. This judgmentally correct quality of their characters wins respect and makes them legitimizers and gatekeepers of innovation for their professions. Pacesetters position themselves between innovators and the majority adopters. They value exposure to new ideas and techniques, but maintain an attitude of conservatism toward avant-gardism. The pacesetters are concerned about the profession itself and feel a definite need to organize, conduct, or take part in its structures and functions. Pacesetters strongly support group learning endeavors. They are leaders of such activities as meetings of professional societies, conventions, exhibits, short courses, lecture series, conferences, and efforts to learn within institutional settings such as schools, welfare agencies, hospitals, and libraries.

The *middle majority* make up the great body of professionals (Houle, 1980). They gradually adopt innovations. At the upper levels, they often win support for a change because pacesetters approve it. At the lower levels, are those who are often not in direct touch with the "leaders" of the profession. They eventually adopt new practices because they have become so generally accepted that colleagues and clients would raise questions if they continued older techniques. As the level of educational participation by professionals declines, the number of reasons for resistance to learning increases, as does the general distaste for or apathy toward continuing professional education.

The lowest group of active professionals is the *laggards* (Houle, 1980). Laggards learn only what they must know to stay in practice. Their performance is so poor that they are a source of embarrassment to their colleagues and a menace to their clients. When young, they may have had their eyes fixed on dedicated service to society; now they have fallen into routine. They offer many excuses for this sad state: scarcity of competition, disillusionment with their profession, envy, apathy, unhappy personal life, alcoholism or other addictions, a fixation upon some single method, adequate private income, the tyranny of unbreakable habits of work, failure to perceive that the practice of their vocation has changed, low achievement motivation, failure to understand the need to keep on learning, belief that they can no longer learn, and many others. Laggards cause extreme concern to their colleagues and to the policy makers of society. A profession has selected them, trained them, admitted them to practice, and must now fight to protect their perquisites. Since society licenses them, it has a formal stake in their ability. Laggards do not respond properly to their privileged position—their ideas have hardened. Their old skills deteriorate and they adopt the few new ones, by osmosis or because of pressure to change. Their chief source of new information is sales agents of supplies, equipment, and services, who usually cloak their approach to professionals with the aura of education. They have a high need to resist continuing professional education. They believe that it costs too much time and money, not realizing that ignorance is even more expensive.

Facilitators make up that the final group (Houle, 1980). Their titles may reflect the profession they serve, but they share only part time or not at all in its central activity. The work of facilitators lies outside the mainstream of practice, though designed to uphold and strengthen it. They teach, give training or continuing professional education seminars, do research, study, organize, administer, regulate, coordinate, and engage in other activities that advance the profession. Facilitators work in universities, associations, government offices, foundations, and other places. Some professionals feel that facilitators who have not spent years in professional work cannot simply understand the profession or work effectively to help and reinforce it. The dangers of being facilitators are great. Even for well-trained, experienced persons, they are certain to lose eventually the sense of uniqueness of the specific cases with which they must always deal (Houle, 1980). The facilitator must develop special skills, such as research, teaching, editing, organizing, or administering. Facilitators must bear the chief administrative burden of continuing professional education for the professions. Their livelihoods often depend on it, since they often work directly with learners—teaching, giving lectures, writing papers, or editing. More frequently, they arrange for other people, chiefly innovators and pacesetters, to carry out major instructional responsibilities.

Expanded Definition: Critical Thinking, Professionals, Continuing Education

Cervero (1989) distills the various viewpoints about the relationship between the professions and society into three different categories. The *functionalist* approach stresses the value of professional activity for the maintenance of an orderly society. The key idea in the functionalist viewpoint is expertise. Although the model of professional knowledge based on the functionalist viewpoint accurately represents some forms of learning, a critical viewpoint is emerging, which accounts more effectively for how professionals learn. Where functionalism sees well-defined problems, the critical viewpoint assumes that professionals ask questions and construct the problem from the situation. As professionals make choices about what problems to solve and how to solve them, this approach stresses the need to be critically aware of these choices and their implications. In this view point, there is agreement about what is good professional practice. The *conflict* approach says that professions differ from other groups in society as to power, status, and money. The key notion here is power. The *critical* viewpoint assumes that professionals construct the problem from the situation. Professionals are always making choices about which problems to solve and how to solve them. This approach stresses the need for professionals to be critically aware of their choices and the implications (Schön, 1987).

There has to be a call for reform, if the professions are to survive in the 21st century (Curry & Wergin, 1993). We need to develop a different way of thinking about professional training and continuing education. The authors identify a gap between theory and practice as they develop their theme, which is responding to the requirements for "stronger bonds between our systems of education and our systems of practice" (p. xvi). The important message they convey is that continuing professional education must be more integrated with practice if it is to be effective. In addition, we must break down the epistemological and pedagogical barriers separating knowledge construction and theory from actual professional practice.

Current criticism of continuing professional education's performance in preparing graduates for professional practice environments is wide-ranging. The criticism is long-standing as well. The poor relationship between a course of study and occupational success is well known. As well, no relationship is found between academic grades and subsequent professional performance for business, education, and medicine graduates.

There is a need for postgraduate continuing professional education. This "future study" allows professionals to learn new techniques and develop awareness of new knowledge in their fields. Critical thinking's primary emphasis should be upon the actions of individuals and groups who seek to fulfill their own potentialities (Houle, 1980). They learn advanced and subtle bodies of knowledge by study, apprenticeship, and practice. They can evidently achieve adequate knowledge and competence only by maintaining and increasing the use of continuing professional education.

Professions have their own knowledge bases and codes of practice; their own lore, terminology, and points of view; their own mysteries and secret places. Certain dominant ideas guide all professions. As they turn to the task of educating their members, they use essentially the same kinds of facilities, techniques, and thought processes. Those who seek goals for a profession use one or more of three major modes of learning: inquiry, instruction, and performance (Houle, 1980, pp. 31–33). *Inquiry* is the process of creating some new idea, technique, policy, or strategy of action. Sometimes they employ this mode in a structured fashion through discussion and encounter groups. Professionals learn new ideas or new ways of thinking through seminars, clinics, and guided experiences. *Instruction* is the process of disseminating established skills, knowledge, or sensitiveness. The mode of *performance* is the process of internalizing an idea or using critical thinking habitually. In that way, it becomes a fundamental part of the way in which a learner thinks about and undertakes his or her work.

Nonparticipation

There are many reasons for nonparticipation in critical thinking and continuing professional education—Dao's research suggests nine clusters (1975). In order of frequency they are as follows:

1. Not enough time to participate in educational activities.
2. Unawareness of educational activities available.
3. They do not value results of educational activities. (They doubt that the learning will prove worthwhile and hold the conviction that experience, not education, is the best teacher)
4. Individual and personal problems make it too difficult to participate. (Poor transportation, costs, ill health, problems of safety, and other factors)
5. Too difficult to succeed in educational activities. (They fear that the instruction itself may be too demanding, that there will be insufficient time to devote to study, that aging has caused abilities to decline, that a new group or new way of life will be too challenging, or that public failure will be harmful.)
6. Negative feelings toward that the institution offering instruction.
7. Negative experiences in educational activities.
8. Indifference to educational activities.
9. Against the social norms to participate in educational activities. (Social disapproval and the fear of being ridiculed by peers, colleagues, or family)

Core Competencies

Each profession has a set of core competencies. Core knowledge or theory is the foundational bedrock for the attainment of all competencies. Theory guides practice, which mastery of relevant concepts must precede. At least three factors create and exacerbate problems for all professionals: (1) the rapid growth of specialized knowledge, (2) the application of new technologies to practice, and (3) the expansion of professional obligations to include new clients or recipients of service. Stark, Lowther, and Hagerty (1986) write about *conceptual, technical,* and *integrative* competencies (pp. 22–40). Conceptual competencies may not reside specifically in knowledge or theory but we characterize them as integral to the professional. Mastery of theory must be present for successful attainment of other competencies and for successful practice. Conceptual competencies include such attributes as values, attitudes, and cognitive capability; which include problem-solving skills, creative capabilities, and critical thinking. Technical competence refers to an individual's ability to perform fundamental skills required of any member of the profession. In various professions, they closely relate technical competence to conceptual competence. The "craft" aspect of professional preparation is clearly unique to each field. Skills needed are distinguishable by profession; therefore, there is less commonality across continuing professional education programs with respect to technical competence. Further, it is more difficult for individuals we do not train in a profession to understand the technical literature written about competence. This contributes to the view that continuing professional education is narrow (Stark, Lowther, & Hagerty, 1986). Integrative competence is the ability to meld information and examinations to make informed judgments about appropriate professional strategies that we employ in practice. We have also defined integrative competence as "professional judgment or critical thinking." Among professional educators, the use of the word "integration" relates more closely to the process by which we get this competence. Exhibiting integrative competence infers that a critical thinking process has occurred, employing skills such as reasoning, decision making, and problem solving gotten through prior knowledge and experience. Work experience is an important element in the perfection of integrative competence. Factors such as judgment and problem-solving skill are difficult to nurture within the time constraints of a continuing professional education program. After a career has begun, integrative competence may be a crucial factor in distinguishing the merely competent professional from the acknowledged expert.

Houle (1980, p. 305) states it best:

> The primary responsibility for critical thinking in continuing professional education should rest on the individual. Critical thinking seeks to learn from each new situation, no matter how familiar, by viewing it creatively. The ideal for every profession is that individuals should feel a deep and continuing concern for carrying out their own education out at a high level throughout a lifetime of practice. Professionals must feel it with special urgency, for once they achieve their formal status, we usually protect them in it for life. Professionals must collaborate to maintain the life and vitality of their thought and practice. They must participate in groups and associations that provide new ways to scrutinize and improve practice. Critical thinking requires re-

moval from time to time for intensive periods of study. Professionals do not merely get new knowledge but also gain a broader perspective so that, upon returning to service, they view matters in a new light. They must, in short, use every means of continuing education available so that their work retains the dedication, lucidity, and freshness of its early years. Only in this way can critical thinking achieve its essential continuity, gradually blending new ideas and techniques.

Higher Order Thinking Skills

At least three elements seem to make a difference in professional gains in thinking skills: (1) discussion, (2) explicit emphasis on problem-solving procedures and methods using varied examples, and (3) verbalization of methods and strategies to encourage development of metacognition (Stroup & Allen, 1992). Heiman and Slomianko (1985) discuss certain approaches and strategies, which can help create an environment that fosters the development of critical thinking and other higher order thinking skills. They review courses and programs that make thinking the subject of instruction. Professionals focus on the key aspects of higher order thinking, and scientific experimentation and methodology, which play key roles in developing critical thinking skills. They suggest giving professionals opportunities for continual, explicit practice. The old adage, "practice makes perfect," has some merit in developing critical-thinking skills. Professionals will not develop these skills if instructors tell them what to do, when to do it, and how to do it. Questioning and developing an investigative nature are also key strategies. Testing must reinforce the development of higher order thinking skills and not just subject matter acquisition. One of the most common complaints is that higher order thinking skills are very difficult to test. Essay questions are usually the easiest way to evaluate critical thinking, but evaluation becomes cumbersome and time consuming. Perhaps the best known program for improving thinking skills is by Whimbey and Lochhead (1991). The authors emphasize work on verbal reasoning, analogies, and solving mathematical word problems. They maintain that skills with these general processes will transfer to more specific reasoning tasks.

VISIONS FOR THE FUTURE

Goals

Critical thinking may involve the desire to reach a personal goal, a social goal, a desire to know, and to comply with formal requirements (Houle, 1980). Professionals may have a desire to gain knowledge for the sake of knowing. They may derive pleasure from learning, enjoy mental exercises, and want to remain in command of learning skills. They may want to achieve a personal goal, which the knowledge gained will make possible. Professionals may have to learn certain knowledge to do the necessary functions better. Critical thinking may reflect a desire to earn credit required by an employer. Its use may meet certain conditions required for membership by certain groups, or meet requirements of some authority (Houle, 1980; Spear & Mocker, 1989; Whimbey & Lochhead, 1991; Stroup & Allen, 1992).

The adult education goals of coverage and breadth are of value here because they provide a context for thought. We experience a larger context for our critical thinking the more we read, ask questions, and see and hear, which furnishes more and greater the opportunity for fresh and imaginative thought. Another goal of continuing professional education, is to establish the kind of context in which thinking is most valuable. Thought is not thought without standards against which to measure and evaluate new ideas and experiences. So a companion goal of continuing education is to develop values in students that are appropriate to educated people. Value formation is one of the more controversial features of education. Whose values and what values get fostered? What standards are used to judge them? Most would agree that higher education values the quest for truth, freedom of expression, service to others, and a desire for excellence.

Teaching Critical-Thinking Skills

We can teach critical-thinking skills. The teaching of critical thinking in continuing professional education begins with educators who are themselves critical thinkers. Adult education must be concerned with the training of such teachers for programs that model critical thinking rather than programs designed to deposit information into the heads of learners. "Teach them how to think and they will teach themselves the facts" (Spear & Mocker, 1989, p. 648). As we give professionals continual opportunities to think critically, they improve their critical thinking. We must also give them the opportunity to discuss their thought processes and train them in the art of questioning (Whimbey & Lochhead, 1991).

The foremost goal of continuing professional education is to teach professionals to develop and hone critical-thinking skills. A critical viewpoint is emerging based on the premise that individuals trained in the field of continuing education have the most appropriate background for this function. The quest for truth begins here. Higher level thinking involves at least the ability to reason without being overpowered by personal biases and experiences. It includes the ability to marshal evidence from outside sources, and the ability to evaluate the opinions of others and appreciate the best of them. We must have a variety of experiences to which we can react and address our thoughts, in order for thinking to be most effective.

Competency

Future regulators will be concerned with the maintenance of professional competency in the face of rapid growth in technology and knowledge. Measurement and maintenance of professional competency are difficult yet crucial. Educators and professionals are becoming aware that they must plan preprofessional education with continuing education in mind. Critical thinking then takes on a new meaning in continuing professional education. It becomes a self-sustaining process of experiencing, reflecting, forming new ideas, and testing one's judgment and abilities in action.

Defining the Core

The dominant objectives of critical thinking include learning and mastery of theoretical and practical knowledge. Also, the habitual use of this knowledge and skill about a profession to solve the problems that arise in practice is important (Houle, 1980). As many members of a profession as possible should be concerned with clarifying its defining functions. Professionals should use critical thinking to accomplish mastery of at least the foundations of the information and theory that comprise the knowledge base of the profession. They should use theoretical knowledge to solve specific problems that arise in the practical affairs of society. Critical thinking should allow professionals to use practical knowledge and techniques that have grown out of the profession's core disciplines. It will allow professionals to seek self-enhancement throughout their years of continuing professional education and work. New personal dimensions of knowledge, skill, and sensitiveness will develop through the arduous study of topics not directly related to their occupation. They use formal training to establish critical thinking in continuing professional education. Professional education transmits the essential body of knowledge and technique to all recognized professionals. Formal credentialing should use critical thinking to test the capacity of individual professionals to do their duties at an acceptable level and, sometimes, to license those it qualifies.

Phenomenology

However, a new and emerging view goes well beyond any of these positions and must therefore be termed "radical." It holds that we must reconceptualize critical thinking as an activity that normally occurs throughout all of life. To improve and infuse critical thinking into continuing professional education, professionals should consciously raise questions: What do we know? How do we know? Why do we accept or believe? What is the evidence for? when studying some body of material or approaching a problem (Stroup & Allen, 1992; Stanage, 1987). They should clearly and explicitly be aware of gaps in available information. This includes recognizing when they reach a conclusion or decide without complete information, and being able to tolerate the ambiguity and uncertainty. They should recognize that words are symbols for ideas and not the ideas themselves. Professionals practice probing for assumptions (especially the implicit, unarticulated assumptions) behind a line of reasoning. They draw inferences from data, observation, or other evidence, and recognize when firm inferences cannot be drawn. Professionals employ critical thinking to discriminate between inductive and deductive reasoning, that is, being aware when they are making an argument from the particular to the general or from the general to the particular. Testing lines of reasoning and conclusions develops self reliance for internal consistency. Through these processes, professionals develop a self confidence concerning their own thinking and reasoning processes.

CONCLUSION

In the future, adult education will take a leading role in fostering critical thinking as a major component of continuing professional education. We know, however, that the critical thinking ability is unevenly distributed among those in the field of adult education. For all its protestations to the contrary, education traditionally has fixed its attention on information transfer with a blind belief that critical thinking is a natural and inevitable by-product. The two are, of course, unrelated, since critical thinking predates education by thousands of years and is present in the general population without regard to formal learning.

REFERENCES

Apps, J. W. (1985). *Improving practice in continuing education: Modern approaches for understanding the field and determining priorities.* San Francisco: Jossey-Bass.

Brockett, R. G. (1991a). Disseminating and using adult education knowledge. In J. M. Peters, P. Jarvis, & Associates (Eds.) *Adult Education.* San Francisco: Jossey-Bass.

Brockett, R. G. (1991b). *Professional development for educators of adults.* San Francisco: Jossey-Bass.

Brookfield, S. D. (1984). *Adult learners, adult education, and the community.* New York: Teachers College Press.

Brookfield, S. D. (1986). *Understanding and facilitating adult learning.* San Francisco: Jossey-Bass.

Brookfield, S. D. (1987). *Developing critical thinkers: Challenging adults to explore alternative ways of thinking and acting.* San Francisco: Jossey-Bass.

Cervero, R. M. (1989). Continuing education for the professions. In S. B. Merriam & P. M. Cunningham (Eds.) *Handbook of Adult and Continuing Education.* San Francisco: Jossey-Bass.

Cervero, R. M. (1988). *Effective practice in continuing professional education.* San Francisco: Jossey-Bass.

Cervero, R. M., Azzaretto, J. F., & Associates. (1990). Visions for the future of continuing professional education. Athens, GA.: University of Georgia Center for Continuing Education.

Cervero, R. M., & Scanlan, C. L. (Eds.). (1985). Problems and prospects in continuing professional education. *New Directions for Continuing Education,* no. 27. San Francisco: Jossey-Bass.

Cervero, R. M., & Young, W. H. (1987). The organization and provision of continuing professional education: A critical review and synthesis. In J. C. Smart (Ed.) *Higher education: Handbook of theory and research,* Vol. 3, pp. 402–431). New York: Agathon.

Curry, L., Wergin, J. F., & Associates. (1993). *Educating professionals: Responding to new expectations for competence and accountability.* San Francisco: Jossey-Bass.

Drake, J. A. (1976). *Teaching critical thinking.* Danville, IL: Interstate Publishers.

Dao, M. N. (1975). The orientations toward nonparticipation in adult education. Doctoral Dissertation. Chicago: University of Chicago Press.

Glaser, R. (1984). Education and thinking: The role of knowledge. *American Psychologist, 39,* 93–104.

Heiman, M., & Slomianko. (1985). *Critical thinking skills.* Washington, DC: National Education Association.

Houle, C. O. (1980). *Continuing learning in the professions.* San Francisco: Jossey-Bass.

Knox, A. B. (1986). Helping adults learn. San Francisco: Jossey-Bass.

Kolb, D. A. (1988). Integrity, advanced professional development, and learning. In Srivastva & Associates, (Eds.), *Executive integrity: The search for high human values in organizational life.* San Francisco: Jossey-Bass.

LeBreton, P. P., & others (Eds.) (1979). *The evaluation of continuing education for professionals: A systems view.* Seattle: University Of Washington Press.

McKnight, J. (1977). The professional service business. *Social Policy, 8,* 110–116.

Nowlen, P. M. (1988). *A new approach to continuing education for business and the professions: The performance model.* New York: Macmillan.

Schön, D. A. (1983). *The reflective practitioner: How professionals think in action.* New York: Basic Books.

Schön, D. A. (1987). *Educating the reflective practitioner: Toward a new design for teaching and learning in the professions.* San Francisco: Jossey-Bass.

Spear, G. E., & D. W. Mocker. (1989). The future of adult education. In S. B. Merriam & P. M. Cunningham (Eds.) *Handbook of adult and continuing education.* San Francisco: Jossey-Bass.

Stanage, S. M. (1987). *Adult education and phenomenological research: New directions for theory, practice, and research.* Malabar, FL: Krieger.

Stark, J. S., Lowther, M. A., & Hagerty, B.M.K. (1986). Responsive professional education: Balancing outcomes and opportunities. *ASHE-ERIC Higher Education Report No. 3.* Washington, DC: Association for the Study of Higher Education.

Stern, M. S. (Ed.). (1983). *Power and conflict in continuing professional education.* Belmont, CA: Wadsworth.

Stroup, D. J., & R. D. Allen. (1992). *Critical thinking: A collection of readings.* Dubuque, IA: Brown.

Whimbey, A., & Lochhead, J. (1991). *Problem solving and comprehension.* Hillsdale, NJ: Erlbaum.

5

On Their Own:
Professionals Need
Entrepreneurship Education
Zira J. Smith

Lemuel is an attorney in private practice. When asked if his legal education included any courses to help him learn how to establish and operate a law office as a business, he responded that it had not. After Lemuel finished law school, he worked for Legal Aid for a number of years and then, like many lawyers, he decided to go into business for himself. He revealed that he never developed a business before he opened his law office and that he learned how to operate the business side of his practice through trial and error. He says there should be more education on self-employment for attorneys, because there is a great need for it.

Henderson is an accountant who operates a one-person office. Like Lemuel, his professional accounting education did not include entrepreneurship concepts to help him know how to turn his accounting skills into a self-supporting business. He worked at a bank for several years before making the decision to start his own business. He says he is still learning what he needs to do daily, through the experience of action and corrective action. He strongly believes more entrepreneurship information should be included in the education for accountants because most of them are certain to be involved in self-employment activity during some portion of their careers.

Peter is a doctor of naprapathy. He shares an office with two other colleagues. His four-year degree from the Chicago National College of Naprapathy prepared him for this work. It did not prepare him to operate a business, which is inevitable for many professionals. Naprapaths open their own offices or practice from their homes. Few gain experience working for other individuals or organizations. All the naprapaths in Peter's office learned to market their businesses, advertise, manage office staff, and develop customer/client relations by the seat of their pants—through practical experience. Peter says there is a great need to learn the skills of self-employment. He thinks the economy would expand overnight if the concepts of entrepreneurship were included as components of a professional's education.

Shirley is a teacher in private practice, a choice that is increasingly popular among educators. Her business is educational computing training and consulting for teachers. Shirley was a teacher in the public school system before she started her business. After 17 years in the classroom, she said she was experiencing "burnout," which is unavoidable for most teachers in urban public schools. Shirley loves to teach, but needed more control over the conditions, so she developed her business to serve teachers like herself in a way that is compatible with her need for "job satisfaction." She developed basic knowledge of how to use the computer to make teachers' work easier, but she developed knowledge of how to turn that knowledge into a business on her own through trial and error.

Cervero (1988) documents the history of problems in trying to define what constitutes a professional, and concludes that public acceptance of credentials as necessary to provide a specific service is one of the methods employed by the public at large. However, no matter which dictionary you choose, the definition for entrepreneurs is about the same: people who have created a commercial endeavor that requires considerable initiative and risk. And, no matter how you look at it, these professional practitioners in business for themselves, doing the kind of work that they want to do, are entrepreneurs. All have had to learn on their own how to be in business after completing the basic requirements for entry into their profession. They learned the skills of their profession in university classrooms. Yet, while going into business was almost inevitable, they were not prepared for their destiny by their professional education programs. These are not isolated exceptional cases, they are the norm for professionals. A majority of professional school graduates engage in some self-employment activity during their work lives. What these professionals are doing today will be commonplace for most of the population in the United States in the future. As many as half of all individuals will be self-employed. Jeremy Rifkin (1995) cites a study that forecasts that within 30 years, as little as 2 percent of the world's current labor force will be needed to produce all the goods necessary for total demand. Rifkin projects that for the year 2045, less than 20% of the adult population will work full-time. Today a new business begins every 24 seconds; an estimated 1,600 new home-based businesses start every day. In 1991, 16 million people were making it on their own from home and 10% of all work being done in the United States was being done at home. These numbers are growing at an impressive rate of over 20% a year. According to the Small Business Administration, as more businesses develop, the rate of small business failure is going down, citing a 25% decrease since the mid 1980s, or a 70% success rate according to a study of the National Federation of Independent Business which surveyed 3,000 new businesses.

Once professionals leave their universities qualified to practice their profession, they find that they must seek information outside those universities about how to actually implement their skills in a business. Even if they go to work for others they usually become more proficient as professionals rather than skilled as business operators. The sometimes painful, costly, stumbling process that our professionals described is the way most of them learn to operate a business. Unfortunately, it is also the way that almost all business owners learn. This learn-everything-as-you-go method can cost a business owner a lot of money and it takes a psychological toll on confidence and trust in oneself. It may also be a factor in making the decision to stay open or to close a business's doors. Readily available access to self-employment information specifically geared to the kinds of businesses started by professionals is important to help them establish and maintain a healthy business.

PROFESSIONALS NEED FOR ENTREPRENEURSHIP EDUCATION

In their book, *Making It on Your Own,* Paul and Sarah Edwards (1991) distinguish between traditional entrepreneurial aspirations and what they describe as a new breed of entrepreneur, a *propreneur,* a *pro*-fessional who is an entre-*preneur.* This new entrepreneur is quite different from the classic one who loves the business of business. For the traditional entrepreneur, business is like a game and money is the scorecard. The classic entrepreneur may move eagerly from venture to venture, loving the business of doing business.

These goals are not those of propreneurs who usually set out on their own in order to have greater control over their lives, to work on their own terms in their own way, as Shirley revealed. Propreneurs want to create a livelihood for themselves that enables them to do more meaningful work, enjoying life more while doing what they know how to do best. They're more interested in doing the work of their business than in running it. Yet, they are highly motivated to be their own bosses. They have good ideas, valuable skills, and talents. They are willing to work hard but they're not prepared to operate a business, nor do they desire to do so. Today's new entrepreneurs are professionals, artists, and service providers and that's what they want to do. They're more interested in working *in* the business than *on* it.

They may find some aspects of doing business uncomfortable and intimidating; such as selling, negotiating a deal, projecting profits and losses, managing cash flow, financial planning and marketing. But without these functions there is no work. So this experienced professional is now faced with learning as much about running a business as possible. Unfortunately, however, much of the available information about becoming one's own boss is geared to classical entrepreneurs and advocates getting even more involved in the business side of operations. The books and courses they turn to for help usually focus on how to become sophisticated at marketing, negotiating, and other strategies in order to grow make a company larger and more profitable. For propreneurs these activities just mean taking more time away from doing the work they actually want to do. What they need are practical ways to streamline the business side of self-employment so they can profitably pursue their work.

WHAT IS ENTREPRENEURSHIP EDUCATION?

Entrepreneurship education, according to Dr. Thomas Murray, Executive Director of the Illinois Institute for Entrepreneurship Education, consists primarily of three multifaceted components. They are (1) mindset change, (2) assessment of strengths, and (3) skills of small business creation. Dr. Murray describes mindset change as essentially "moving from a mindset of entitlement and dependence on a job, to acceptance of the notion of responsibility for creating and maintaining work to provide for yourself."

Mindset Change

Working for one's self is the second most popular desire for Americans, after owning one's own home, particularly in times of stress either on the job or during periods of unemployment. In the past these stress situations were identified as more likely to predict business startup than any other factor. Cooper (1983) describes them as dislocations or pushes, forces which cause a person to move out of a comfortable rut. Today, corporate downsizing, relocations, and opportunities for self-employment through competing for work now being outsourced are responsible for the boom in small business creation. However, working for oneself means leaving behind the paycheck mentality and the classical approach to doing business. It means operating with a new approach. Professionals have developed the paycheck mentality because that is what is normally taught in homes and in schools. Children were told by parents that if they were good and did what they were told, they'd be rewarded. In school the same structure applied; follow the rules, work hard, know the right answers and do what the teacher said and to achieve good grades and all the perks of child society. All this was preparation for the roles adults would fill in the workplace where they would be rewarded with a paycheck, for following the rules and directions of the supervisor.

Good employees learned to operate effectively within a system of rules. Classic entrepreneurs are noted for identifying themselves as having rebelled against rules, even as children, taking delight in standing out from the crowd. They may have made poor grades in school, gotten lots of traffic tickets, or had a history of business failures. The new breed of entrepreneurs don't match that nonconformist profile. They usually did their best in school and have been good employees, sometimes they were the cream of the crop. They are highly achievement oriented and strive for excellence in their work. This group is actually well prepared to excel in serving their clients and customers. But their mental challenge will be in learning to break out of the limitations of paycheck thinking so they can survive in the creative, free-form world of self-employment.

The entrepreneur's world does not have fixed rules, and very little comes to those who wait as employers may have advised good employees. Quality and performance are a given, and not a determiner of success. Once participants become familiar with how it really works, it is a world of unlimited possibilities, with no plateaus, dead ends, or glass ceilings, a world that can be shaped by the professional.

Assessment of Strengths

How do individuals evaluate their potential to work for themselves? Should aspiring entrepreneurs take self-scoring quizzes found in popular books and magazines that gage entrepreneurial skills? Like the books and courses touted as help for business owners, these quizzes are based on characteristics that have been identified in studies of classic entrepreneurs. Nonetheless, millions of propreneurs are earning a living in their own businesses. In research conducted with self-employed adults with low education skills, Smith (1994) confirmed that individuals don't have to be entrepreneurs in the classical sense to survive and thrive on their own. Likewise, Steven Balkin's (1989) study documented the long history of entrepreneurship among low-income people. Dr. Murray indicates that assessment of strengths means taking inventory of a person's talents, knowledge, skills, and lifestyle to determine compatibility for an entrepreneurial life. When recognized and valued the innate or learned talents possessed can be used to plan for a better life. It is like the difference between starting a road trip in a strange car or one put through a thorough analysis. Understanding what the car is capable of doing helps the driver determine on which roads and under what conditions the automobile will perform best, as well as the worst. Once understood what is actually known people can plan how to handle the things not known or things individuals are not prepared to handle. All the skills developed in life are the foundation upon which to build a career or a business. Individuals need to know, understand, and accept them all in order to move forward with life goals. Unfortunately, our schools teach us proficiency after proficiency with little regard for teaching us how to learn about ourselves including our own strengths and weaknesses.

Skills of Small Business

The third component of entrepreneurship education that Dr. Murray identifies is development of the skills needed to start and operate a small business. Although professionals may have developed some technical knowledge and skills at which they may have excelled when they applied them in somebody else's business, professionals have not learned what it takes to make a business work so that they can sell their skills for themselves. Potential propreneurs need to prepare a business plan that will compel them to think through and have some basic understanding of those business-oriented skills identified earlier that can be intimidating. The business plan should include the identification of and learning activities involved in gaining competence or at least awareness in the components viewed as significant for successful business operations including: the compatibility between business opportunities and a propreneur's skills; the possible types of business ownership; business management including marketing and financial management; business location options; human and technological resource management; legal issues involved in the various types of ownerships and operations; and the help available to the new business owner from various sources including local and national government agencies (Ashmore & Pritz (1983).

In addition to the skills pertinent to running a business, personal traits and skills also help to determine whether someone is suited to self-employment. In the Smith study (1994), self-employed adult student participants identified numerous personal characteristics that were important to customer satisfaction and retention. Among the desired traits were being honesty, service-orientation, positive attitude, good communication skills, respectfulness, and the ability to make people feel important.

CURRENT ENTREPRENEURSHIP EDUCATION AVAILABLE TO PROFESSIONALS

Professionals are full of contradictory ambitions. On one hand they want the anticipated rewards of the new and novel, but on the other hand they still cling to the old and familiar. The desire for freedom and to be in charge is accomplished when professionals actually go out on their own. Many would call this state of affairs as very desirable. Then fear enters the decision-making process. Can professionals really be in control or will they make a mess and lose all that they have? These are the fears that surface for most people when they leave the security of a paycheck. Can professionals assume full responsibility for their own destiny? Under these unfamiliar circumstances, professionals may try to cope by pulling on old ways of thinking and it is only natural to want to operate from the paycheck mentality that has been so familiar for so long. People may try hard to run their self-employed lives in much the same way they worked as employees. But it doesn't work. The shift from working in a professional position of influence where one wielded power and authority, to being a sole practitioner can be a jolt. The feelings of power and control turn to feelings of powerlessness and loss of control. The logical dependable world gives way to the unknown. Schools have prepared people to get a job and become consumers of other peoples' jobs. So when the familiar and society-sanctioned status is left, professionals are confronted with having to make an adjustment in the approach to earning a living. People are still most likely to be viewing the world from a paycheck mentality and expect life to work the way it had when they were employed. Thinking that if you follow directions carefully, you will succeed, sooner or later can be a confusing, frightening, and a pressure-filled experience for the new self-employed individual.

Professionals need help (1) To acquire information for understanding about creating and operating a one-person business, (2) To explore the option of self-employment through developing a plan for a business, and (3) To start and manage a small business. Adults enter any learning activity at different levels of understanding, experience, and need. It is so for professionals interested in entrepreneurship education. They fall all along the continuum of "never thought of it before and have no idea what it would mean" to "They have been in business before but they need help to do it differently this time."

Lemuel, the attorney, indicated that recently more information of this type is available to attorneys through monthly newsletters published by Bar Associations, and through joining self-help sections of these associations. He also reported that off-shoot businesses have been created by private contractors specifically to help attorneys set up their own practice. He said that the Illinois Institute for Continuing Legal Education publishes a manual to help lawyers with small business management, but feels there is a great need for more of this kind of information for attorneys. Peter says that he has not seen self-employment information available through any of the naprapathic associations aimed at his profession. His profession just became licensed 3 years ago and they are working with research and development issues. But like Lemuel, he has noticed an increasing number of private training contractors targeting naprapaths to help them set up and operate a business. He says there is a great need for naprapaths to have this kind of training.

I met Shirley when she served as a speaker in one my entrepreneurship education for educators classes. Once she found out what the class actually taught, she indicated an interest in joining the class so that she could become more familiar with the skills needed for a small business. She said she had taken business planning courses at a couple of agencies in the city, and has learned the things she knows from picking up information wherever she could. She is a real inspiration for teachers who say they can't do "anything other than teach," depreciating the value of the vast marketable skills they have acquired through teaching. Shirley's success convinced them that there is active exciting life beyond the classroom. Henderson recounts his continuing struggle to have more control over the outcomes of his business by learning how to handle the business duties of his accounting practice more effectively. He and I frequently discuss his need to develop different marketing strategies and to create more efficient recordkeeping systems. He regularly updates his accounting skills through yearly participation in classes, but he has never taken classes to acquaint himself with the business side of his office.

Though statistics readily available to everyone indicate that self-employment activity is on the rise, initiatives to prepare professionals to take advantage of opportunities to work through self-employment have not been incorporated into professional education. School career offices maintain listings of the decreasing number of wage jobs soliciting workers at less than desirable pay, but do not champion the notion of creating work that may better sustain their graduates. To explore and encourage such an option is outside the scope of what many professional schools consider their mission. They are primarily in the business of preparing workers for employers. They fail to equip their students with realistic present and future employment data and projections. One fact is that currently a full 30% of college graduates march directly from commencement into the ranks of the unemployed or underemployed. But schools think they have discharged their obligations to students by teaching professional knowledge and skills. If their graduates cannot find jobs, then they must learn how to earn a living on their own.

Today, the field of entrepreneurship education for professionals is wide open for development. What is typically available to professionals to help them start a business, is geared to the goals of a traditional entrepreneur, mastering complex business skills to steadily grow a larger company. The reason most professionals give for starting their own business is to be in control of the work that they love to do, not to develop a bigger and better widget. Effective entrepreneurship educators of professionals will have to design programs that specifically take these workers' goals into consideration. Professionals require distinctively streamlined methods to manage one-person operations, not merely scaled down versions of what is known about managing larger companies (Whitmyer, et al., 1989). Professionals will have questions from abstract and general, to narrowly precise. Program designers will need to have a broad range of expertise as well as a vast referral resource system to meet extensive interests. Regardless of the effort that will be required of professional schools and associations, the need for entrepreneurship preparation for professionals must be addressed in their organizations. To continue to turn a blind eye to professional workers' struggles to earn a living and take care of themselves is negligent behavior with which educators do not need to associate or perpetuate.

REFERENCES

Ashmore, M. C., & Pritz, S. G. (1983). *PACE (revised) instructor guides, levels 1, 2, and 3.* The National Center for Research in Vocational Education. Columbus, OH: Ohio State University.

Balkin, S. (1989). *Self-employment for low income people.* New York: Praeger.

Cervero, R. M. (1988). *Effective continuing education for professionals.* San Francisco: Jossey-Bass.

Cooper, A. C. (1983). *Entrepreneurship: Starting a new business.* Institute for Enterprise Advancement, Purdue University.

Edwards, P., & Edwards S. (1991). *Making it on your own.* New York: G. P. Putnam's Sons.

Rifkin, J. (1995 May/June). After work: A blueprint for social harmony in a world without jobs. *Utne Reader,* 52–63.

Smith, Z. J. (1994). *Self-employment skills training for adults with low skills; educational survival strategy: A model for oral instruction.* Unpublished doctoral dissertation. Northern Illinois University, DeKalb, IL

Whitmyer, C., Rasberry, S., & Phillips, M. (1989). *Running a one-person business.* Berkeley, CA: Ten Speed Press.

6

Implications and Impact of Emerging Communications Technologies

Brenda G. Young

Well-informed people know it is impossible to transmit the voice over wires and that were it possible to do so, the thing would be of no practical value.

—*Editorial in the* Boston Post *commenting on the arrest for fraud of Joshua Coopersmith who had been attempting to raise funds for work on a telephone 1865. (Cerf & Navasky, 1984 p. 205)*

A CONTEXT FOR NEW AND EMERGING TECHNOLOGIES

To understand what is happening with new communications technology it is important to know the context in which it has developed. For example, if I tell a person "100,000," the reaction is likely to be "100,000 what?" Without a context the number has no meaning. If I tell someone that the budget for paper has gone up $100,000 over last year's budget and is now 25% of all office expenses compared to 13% last year, the number 100,000 now has meaning. This meaning has occurred because there is a context which provides a useful framework for evaluation.

So much is happening with technology that it is difficult for most people to find an appropriate context for evaluation. Even though the costs for advancing technology are dropping almost exponentially, the costs associated with keeping up with changing technology can be significant and incorrect decisions can be costly. As computers and communications equipment have moved out of the back offices and become central to the way people do business, they have inherited all the problems that have always been around in the traditional functional areas of the business. For professionals who have not kept up with technology, this can create a management headache of epic proportions.

One thing that has not changed radically in the last few years is the very human way in which people respond to technology. This human response fits in with what I call the "law of critters," which holds that a critter of any kind will be true to itself. A dog is not a cat, is not a goat, is not a bear, and a human is not a computer. A dog will eventually act like a dog and a human will act like a human. People know this law of critters, but when it comes to technology, they keep forgetting, and become frustrated when humans revert to their form and start acting, inevitably, like humans. Thus, it is very beneficial to have more information about how humans react to new technologies, and what issues should be considered when adopting emerging technologies. To gain additional understanding about our current situation with new communication technologies, it would be helpful to look at how humans have reacted in the past to other new tools, technologies, or ideas. These reactions can give us some valuable insights into the issues to consider when adopting and adapting to emerging technologies.

Humans have a brain that has two ways of understanding and processing information, the left brain, for cognitive, linear thinking, and the right brain for affective, multilevel thinking. The right brain thinks in pictures, or imagery, and can be considered the "silent observer." It sees, hears, and feels, but for the most part, it cannot speak. The left brain, however, is the repository of language. When people speak of their "gut" telling them something, what they mean is that years of experience collected by their right brain tells them something. Whether or not individuals are fully aware of right brain processes, they are still there. Left brains are reality- and data-oriented, while right brains are process- and planning-oriented (Herrmann, 1990).

Also located in the brain is something called the reticular formation, which is the incoming information "traffic cop." It allows us to live and function in a chaotic world without being overloaded with sensory information. This ability can be both good and bad. It is good because it allows us to function, but it can be bad if we are filtering out information we really need to have brought to our conscious attention. For example, this filtering mechanism would explain why users usually ask only for incremental improvements to current applications and technology. Until the reticular formation allows information into our brain to see all the possibilities of a new technology through using it, people may not fully comprehend how a new technology will work for them. By understanding how people adapt to new technology, we can avoid some of the pitfalls of the "eighteen-month effect" when users become comfortable with the new technology and broaden their use of it well beyond their initial inclinations (Herrmann, 1990).

A REVIEW OF OTHER ADAPTATIONS TO TECHNOLOGY

Looking at the way other technologies or ideas have been integrated into general usage will provide further insight. After Christopher Columbus and other explorers proved the world was not flat, it did not take long for people to adapt to this new knowledge. The change from the handwritten word to the printing press, the use of beasts of burden for agricultural activities, the discovery of gunpowder, created significant changes in society when they were introduced. In his prescient book *Information Payoff*, Paul Strassman states:

> Understanding the patterns of the past is essential for interpreting where we are at present and where we will go in the future . . . We can view each major stage of historical development in terms of the methods it used to manage its principal source of wealth. Mankind has always used tools to aid in its managerial endeavors; information technology is simply the most recent of them. If we are to understand its far-reaching consequences, we must take a broad view of our progress. (1985 p. 203)

Strassman outlines four general stages of societal development relative to the main economic activity of the time. The first stage is a hunting society, and is organized around a tribal locus. Its primary resource is nature and its products. It must be concerned with extracting food, clothing, and shelter from the natural environment. At the hunting society stage labor is unceasing to maintain the hunting society.

The next stage is an agricultural society. The agricultural form is feudal with its primary resource centered in whatever land it owns and it must extract wealth from that land. Again unceasing labor is necessary to sustain society.

An industrial society is nationalistic. Its primary resource is capital, and it focuses on extracting wealth from its capital assets. Unceasing labor is necessary to create a growing surplus.

An information/service society requires global cooperation. Its primary resource is knowledge and it is concerned with extraction of wealth from the capabilities of its people. A service society requires an incessant investigation into creating new and superior services.

Michael Porter in his book *The Competitive Advantage of Nations,* states that companies that achieve competitive advantage do so through acts of innovation. Innovation can be in new technology, new ways of doing things or both, and much of this innovation is incremental. It depends more on an accumulation of small insights and advances than on a single, major technological breakthrough. For international markets, innovation must anticipate both domestic and foreign needs. Innovations which respond only to the domestic market will actually impede success on the international market. Companies, and individuals, ignore innovation and its consequences at their own peril, because competitors will eventually, and inevitably, overtake any company that stops improving and innovating (Porter, 1990).

During the Industrial Revolution huge efficiencies in production were realized over manual production processes. For example, if one man could produce an X amount of chain in one hour, a chain-making machine could make upwards of *80 times* that amount in one hour. This enormous jump in productivity fueled the Industrial Revolution. With such a gain in productivity it no longer made economic sense to continue to use human labor at certain tasks. Furthermore machines changed the way work was done. Thus, if one man could dig a posthole in one hour (i.e., 60 minutes), it did not necessarily follow that sixty men could dig a posthole in one minute.

Looking at the transportation and related industries more recently, there are similarities to today's economic environment. The 20th century began with a lot of activity and innovation in the transportation industries. People left their horses behind and traded them in for cars, trucks, and trains. Then people took to the air, broke the sound barrier, created modern jet aircraft, and even hopped a rocket to the moon to collect a few rocks. Along the way, many of the issues which are being debated in the computer and communications industries were parallelled in the transportation industry. Take standards, for example. A great deal of money, effort, and perhaps even some guile was expended in determining the exact width of train tracks. A similar situation occurred in countries all over the world. For example, there was much maneuvering and even some intrigue in England over which size track to use as a standard for the British

Empire. Between Europe and Russia, track widths were incompatible and a lengthy stopover was required to adapt a train to the different sized track.

> Rail travel at high speed is not possible because passengers, unable to breathe, would die of asphyxia.
> —Dr. Dionysus Lardner (1793–1859) (Professor of Natural Philosophy and Astronomy at University College, London). (Cerf & Navasky, 1984, p. 232)

In the automobile industry, there were public and private debates over the type of energy systems to be used. (e.g., internal combustion/gasoline powered motors vs. electric motors) Social and development factors had to be in place, as well. Public assent and policy had to be developed for roads and other publicly supported infrastructure.

> The horse is here to stay, but the automobile is only a novelty—a fad!
> —President of the Michigan Savings Bank, advising Horace Rackham (Henry Ford's lawyer) not to invest in the Ford Motor Company, 1903.

> • Throwing caution to the winds, Rackham disregarded his banker's advice and bought $5,000 worth of stock. When he sold his shares several years later, they were worth $12.5 million. (Cerf & Navasky, 1984, p. 228)

SIGNIFICANT FACTORS IN THE ADVANCEMENT OF NEW TECHNOLOGIES

The modern computer and communications industries had their beginnings at the start of this century, as well, but really did not take center stage until recently. The major factors driving the changes in the computer and telecommunications industries include the following:

- the changing nature of the global business community;
- profound increases in computer chip processing speeds and storage capacities;
- the increasing importance of the service sector in the marketplace; and
- the evolving nature of information as a commodity.

The last factor whereby information is now a commodity is of particular interest here. Information is unlike other economic consumables used throughout human history. It cannot be consumed the way a tree, or a ton of raw metal ore, or other commodities have been consumed. Indeed, when using information, the most likely outcome is that more information is produced (Strassman, 1985). However, as with other inventions or discoveries which have transformed society, it is difficult to know the full impact of a new technology before it is fully integrated into general usage.

> I watched his [Samuel Morse's] countenance closely, to see if he was not deranged . . . and I was assured by other Senators after we left the room that they had no confidence in it.
>
> —Oliver Hampton Smith (U.S. Senator from Indiana), after a demonstration by Samuel Morse of his telegraph to members of Congress, 1842. (Cerf & Navasky, 1984, p. 204)

For those trying to keep up with technology, gaining a comfortable perspective in order to make better decisions is very important. The major reason to keep up with technology is centered around the *gradual way it makes you change* the way you do your business (Strassman, 1985).

> Worthless.
>
> —Sir George Bidell Airy, K.I.C.B., M.A., LL.D., D.C.L., F.R.S., F.R.A.S. (Astronomer Royal of Great Britain), estimating for the Chancellor of the Exchequer the potential value of the "analytical engine" inventor Charles Babbage, September 15, 1842. (Cerf & Navasky, 1984, p. 208)

With each new generation of technology, there is a great deal of uneasiness concerning which direction to take. Instead of isolated transactions which can be automated, organizations now need to be concerned with the entire process which would be migrating to new platforms. Newer technology allows companies to enlarge types of functions which can be handled by computers. As communications technologies converge with computer technologies, there is very little guidance in helping professionals make decisions. As the work of organizations has migrated down from mainframes to minicomputers, to PCs and LANs, people in organizations have not necessarily kept up with the changes. With hindsight, it can be asked why people did not recognize what was happening, but it is not always easy to recognize a juggernaut.

> I have travelled the length and breadth of this country, and have talked with the best people in business administration. I can assure you on the highest authority that data processing is a fad and won't last out the year.
>
> —Editor in charge of business books at Prentice-Hall publishers, responding to Karl V. Karlstrom (a junior editor who had recommended a manuscript on the new science of data processing), c. 1957. (Cerf & Navasky, 1984, p. 209)

> I think there is a world market for about five computers.
>
> —Remark attributed to Thomas J. Watson (Chairman of the Board of International Business Machines), 1943. (Cerf & Navasky, 1984, p. 208)

THE EMERGING IMPORTANCE OF CULTURE IN AN INFORMATION/SERVICE SOCIETY

In an information/service society we need to redefine organizations as fundamentally providers of services. It, thus, is easier to understand and make decisions about the processes that supply those services. For example, an automobile manufacturer would consider itself as primarily a provider of the service of transportation, and secondarily as a manufacturer of automobiles. It is important to understand that it is the *culture* of an organization *which actually delivers the service.* With this understanding it is easier to make necessary changes to processes as migration to new technology occurs, and to provide documentation and training.

> For God's sake go down to reception and get rid of a lunatic who's down there. He says he's got a machine for seeing by wireless! Watch him—he may have a razor on him.
>
> —Editor of the Daily Express, London refusing to see John Logic Baird (the invention of television), 1925. Cerf and Navasky p. 207

The top three priorities to changing work in the automated office are training, training, and training. Office automation is primarily a social and only secondarily a technological phenomenon. If we consider organizations as providing services, and the culture of the organization delivers the service, then effective training is critical to changing the culture (Strassman, 1990). To train effectively, an organization must be aware of its culture and modify the training message to fit the culture. Organizations need to understand and redefine training as an acculturation process, as well as its traditional definition and role of providing instructions. It is also important to enlarge the context of training and link the tactical with the strategic (i.e., the "what to learn" as well as the "why of learning" it). A better understanding of the larger culture in general, and the corporate culture in particular, will allow the providers of emerging technology to identify better methods of introducing new products and services.

As Alvin Toffler (1970) noted the information revolution is closely connected with a change from a mass culture economy to a multiple-choice economy as well as a rising level of social diversity. As society and the economy become more differentiated, it becomes increasingly important to exchange information among subgroups in order to maintain integration of the system. Toffler also calls for changes in our education systems to help people manage and cope with a changing environment (p. 365).

As organizations are forced to operate in increasingly complex environments, an organization needs to be aware of possible changes in the external environment in order to adapt to new opportunities or constraints. For example, new technologies might obsolesce current or planned production processes, or changing social conditions may change the use or acceptance of a product (e.g., the social trend to healthier lifestyles and the decreasing use of cigarettes). Organizations need the best information possible to help them understand what is happening now and what is likely to happen in the future. The monumental changes in the world's political, financial, social, and economic landscape can work to the benefit of a company which is keeping up with the convergence of computer and telecommunications technologies because these changes are intimately linked to these technologies and the services (Toffler, 1970, p.365). A company which is alert to these changes will have more lead time than its competitors to react and make the necessary changes.

> How can he [Thomas Alva Edison] call it a wonderful success when everyone acquainted with the subject will recognize it as a conspicuous failure?
>
> —Henry Morton (Professor of Physics and President of the Stevens Institute of Technology) commenting on Edison's electric light bulb, December 28, 1879. (Cerf and Navasky, 1984, p. 203)

Looking at how electricity as a new technology was actually adopted for commercial and residential usage provides other useful insights to help us understand our current situation. In his book *Electrifying America: Social Meanings of a New Technology,* author David Nye cautions the reader to avoid thinking of "the home," or "the factory," or "the city" as static, passive things that somehow transformed themselves in a process called "electrification." Rather, we should think of every institution as a "social space that incorporates electricity at a certain historical juncture as part of its ongoing environment." The process of electrification took place through a series of choices and was based only *partly* on technical considerations. To appreciate this process better, a clearer understanding of the many contexts in which Americans decided to use electricity is necessary.

> They chose, for example, not to live in cities with collectivized electrical services, but rather in suburban homes with individual appliances. They preferred the automobile to the electric trolley, home washing machines to commercial laundries. Americans adopted electrical technologies in a wide range of social, political, economic, and aesthetic contexts, weaving them into the fabric of experience. The light bulb itself was not merely a substitute for gas lighting, but facilitated social transformations. (Nye, 1990, p. x)

There are times in human history when events, or discoveries, or technologies become the starting point for great changes in society, in history, and even in the way humans come to think of themselves. The discovery of oxygen was a singular event in the development of modern science and the scientific method. Eventually, this discovery and the concurrent use of the scientific method, had a profound influence on philosophy and the rationalist movement. For example, Freud was greatly influenced by the scientific method in his development of psychiatry and his work and studies of the subconscious mind. In turn, Freud's work ultimately had a strong influence on literature and the arts, as exhibited for example, in the works of the surrealist artists. The effects of Freud and the surrealists can still be seen in the work of some of today's advertisers.

When events are moving very quickly around us, it makes it difficult to understand and know what the implications might be. The great 20th century bioethicist, René DuBos cautioned people to beware of a tendency to project into the future the effects of today's events into tomorrow's likely outcome. He called this the *rational* future versus the *willed* future. Humans have the ability to adapt and to change and to "will" a different course of events for their future.

Again, putting events into context can be very helpful. Context provides a structure for evaluation and a starting point for action.

IMPORTANT ASPECTS OF CULTURE

Another part of the context in which humans operate is their culture. Large portions of human behavior are culturally influenced. Culture controls human behavior in a nonrational but nevertheless persistent fashion. It frequently affects people on an unconscious level. Culture resides so deep within people that they often cannot recognize their own cultural attributes until they face those in another culture. Cultural patterns provide the routine, largely unexamined options followed by most people most of the time. Cultural attributes go beyond mere habit, and are *the automatic option* when there are no particular reasons for choosing another pattern of behavior (Hofstede, 1980).

The former Soviet Union can be viewed primarily as a failed social experiment because the leaders of the Bolshevik revolution did not understand culture's influences. The dramatic changes going on in Soviet society at the end of the 20th century had their roots in the events which occurred at the beginning of this century. The Bolsheviks did not just want to obtain power in Russia, they wanted to restructure society, the culture of the country, and, indeed, the world. Their failure to change society to their vision has been profound and irrefutable. The Bolsheviks did not know the strength and resiliency of culture as an influencing and moderating factor in making changes. The only changes that have truly taken effect are those which were compatible with the culture in the first place, in spite of ruthless leaders, such as Stalin who were resolute in using any means possible to force their vision on an unwilling populace. The Bolsheviks were even less successful in effecting changes in countries which had no common basis in culture with the Russian culture, or with each other (Gitelman, 1988).

One definition of culture is the way human beings understand the world, representing a shared way of being, evaluating, and doing that is passed from one generation to the next. Thus, culture is used as a tool for humans to interpret behavior, but the trouble lies in that an individual's cultural perspective may be too narrow to allow for a full, objective understanding of other people and other cultures. To understand the role of culture, companies must also distinguish beliefs from values, although they are often considered identical. People may view values as a particular kind of belief. Therefore, a person's attitude toward any object is a function of his or her beliefs about that object (Gitelman, 1988).

A person's values are relatively resistant to change, while a belief may change when the individual receives new information. In many cases, values can be thought of as intervening between beliefs and attitudes. For example, a belief that New York is the cultural capital of the world may lead to a favorable attitude toward New York by someone who values culture. However, whereas a value is a single belief, an attitude refers to an organization of several beliefs that are all focused on a given object or situation. People tend to regard their own values as superior to those of others. This unconscious identity with one's own cultural values has been considered the root problem of most international business problems. Fortunately, these value differences can be overcome if professionals are willing to show a tolerance for diversity (Ronen, 1986).

Many aspects of culture can be important. Language is a significant element of culture, and it should be considered for obvious differences as well as the subtle influence it has on thinking and on cultural identities. Communication is central to most human relationships and is a very important aspect of culture. Not just speech, but also writing and nonverbal behaviors such as gestures and facial expressions should be considered. Religion can be considered another aspect of culture, and it establishes taboos, moral standards, and reflects the principal values of a people. Other cultural institutions include the family, the educational system, peers, and peer groups. Additional attributes include the problems of and attitudes toward time, communications, work, relationships, space, and power. Individuals can be seen as one of the chief ways in which cultural goods and meanings assume their cultural significance. (Ronen, 1986).

Culture is quite often placed on the periphery of the usual consumer behavior diagram in most textbooks. This type of model supposes that a person is always a "maximizing" creature who makes all choices devoted to the cultivation of advantage. This model also places a person outside of any cultural context, with one exception for the attachment of meaning to goods, and ignores the question of whether other meanings might be attached to something. However, if something can be seen as a vehicle of cultural meanings, then individuals can be seen as one of the chief ways in which cultural goods and meanings assume their cultural significance. Following this logic, people would be considered meaning centered rather than information centered (Ronen, 1986).

THE IMPORTANCE OF MEANING

It would be wise to treat culture as meaning and then assume that this meaning is in constant circulation among people. There is a conventional process for the movement of cultural meaning in consumer societies. Meaning begins in the general culture and then moves to consumer goods through advertising and the "fashion" system. The process is completed when consumers transfer the meaning of the elements into the product through a sudden act of "recognition." This process occurs because consumers need meaning to build the self and their world (McCracken, 1990).

Humans have a strong need for meaning which is also reflected culturally in religion. As mentioned above, a person's cultural value system can be subconscious and internalized as a "belief system" by which the person evaluates the world. This belief system has been more formally studied and described by James W. Fowler, a theologian at Emory University in Atlanta. Based on the work of Lawrence Kohlberg, the famous developmental psychologist, Fowler asserts that before people come to think of themselves as Catholics, Protestants, Jews, Muslims, or whatever, people are already engaged in issues of faith. A person's level of faith development will have a direct relationship to his or her perception of the world and an interpretation of the world and all of life's events. Fowler notes that whether people are nonbelievers, agnostics or atheists, people are concerned with how to put their lives together and with what will make life worth living. Moreover, people look for something to love that loves them, something to value that gives value in return, something to honor and respect that has the power to sustain their being, that is, something which provides meaning to them (Fowler, 1981).

It will also follow that people will reject or resist those things which do not give them value. Through an understanding of what Fowler is saying it is possible to understand why people may be very resistant to new technologies, because of the fear of a loss of meaning. Here, I would caution the reader to not underestimate the importance of the human need for meaning. In a time of corporate downsizing and rapid changes, the need for meaning will weave itself into many of the issues which are both created and affected by new technologies. The downside to this issue is that people may feel overwhelmed by the pressures of time, bewildered by the quantity of information and the changes required of them, and feel dehumanized by impersonal technologies. If people also feel they are dealing with an indifferent management or a hostile work environment, the consequences will be real and inevitable.

Theologians speak of religions as cumulative traditions, and people see a cumulative tradition as the various expressions of the faith of people in the past. These expressions may take many forms including narratives, myths, prophecies, texts of scripture or law, oral traditions, music, dance, rites, liturgies, and so on (Fowler, 1981). If we substitute "corporate culture" for religion in the previous sentences, it is not too much of a stretch to say that the culture of a company has its own set of myths, oral traditions, prophecies, and rites.

Looking at mythology as yet another aspect of culture, we can also find evidence of modern-day urban mythology around us. Examples of urban myth reflect the types of subconscious worries people have about living in modern society. An example of modern mythology is seen in the popular culture's fascination with UFOs. Whether you believe in unidentified flying objects or not, their popularity in contemporary culture reflects a symbolic form of the free-floating anxiety which modern peoples feel toward their culture and technologies.

A FAILURE TO RECOGNIZE THE SIGNIFICANCE OF A NEW TECHNOLOGY

This chapter has covered how humans have adapted to other innovations or new technologies, briefly reviewed the social and economic contexts of a global/service society, examined the increasing need to monitor and understand various aspects of culture, and covered the need for meaning in human activities. Looking at new communications technologies such as videoconferencing, enterprise networks, unified messaging (i.e., bringing voice mail, fax mail, and e-mail to either a PC or telephone interface), and the Internet, the unexamined assumption has been that if providers give people enough information, or a new technology, they will automatically know what it means and know what to do with it. Scholars would caution that the assumption has been that people will somehow reason their way to the best use of something (Shank, 1996). However, when looking at the historical introduction to new tools, technology, or ideas, people seldom immediately recognize the significance of a transforming technology or idea, and may indeed reject it as a fad, foolhardy, or worse (Strassman, 1985).

It is difficult to understand when an innovation has far-reaching consequences. Many people need overwhelming evidence of its significance before they can acknowledge that something about the situation is different. How far down the road with a new technology, a changed environment, or an innovative idea do people have to get before they realize that something is different? Consider the big three automakers in their initial assessment of Japanese automakers, or IBM in its assessment of minicomputers, personal computers, and LANs (Local Area Networks). Here I am not talking about an unsuccessful new product launch such as New Coke, rather I am talking about a failure to recognize a fundamental change in the work and social environment.

THE IMPACT OF NEW COMMUNICATION TECHNOLOGIES

Looking only at the current educational structure (and ignoring other institutional structures, such as political or social structures), the changes in information technology are putting educational providers at a crossroads. One path is a continuation of Industrial Age models of education and continuing education. The other path is a change to Information Age models of education and continuing education. The accumulation of changes in information technologies have become great enough to create the true point of departure from the Industrial Age into the Information Age. For those institutions which do not recognize the transformation, there may be a "Wait for me! I'm your leader!" situation. I keep thinking it is similar to the famous story of the University of Bologna, Italy, around the 15th century when students and administrators could not agree and the students decided to abandon the administration and move the university down the road. When considering the impact of new communication technologies, the most significant changes will center around timing, volume of information, decentralization, and what I call "the democratization of technology."

In the Industrial Age, companies and institutions focused on training and education in a very linear fashion. Particularly, in our educational institutions, people have been forced to cover the same amount of material in the same measures of time (isochronous learning). The new technologies will now allow people to learn in a "discontinuous" time (asynchronous learning). An argument could be made for correspondence courses as a form of asynchronous learning which has been in place, but correspondence courses are to asynchronous learning as a quill pen and paper are to the Internet. Students and lifelong learners will be able to pace their subject matter training according to their ability. For certain applications, such as a help desk, it is already possible to determine the skill set of a person and adjust the information a person would see on his or her computer screen to his or her skill set.

Videoconferencing is about to become as ubiquitous as faxing, but videoconferencing is not just a phone call with pictures, as TV was not simply radio with pictures, or another form of moving picture. Adjustments in using this new technology will need to be made. Videoconferencing is not quite the same thing as having a person in the same room. However, it is a significant improvement over simple teleconferencing, particularly where seeing the presentation material, or a physical object which is being discussed, or sharing a document in real time on a PC is important to the discussion, or where the participants do not share the same primary language. Videoconferencing is already changing the learning landscape, and will continue to do so.

Timing is another area where the new communications technologies will have profound effects in changing the way we work and in training and education. As timing is affected, we will need to change the way we look at the following: our definition of what constitutes a "course," and when a course is completed; how to deal with certification; quality control issues; and socialization and acculturation issues. There also will be a need to deal with issues relating to loyalty or team building. Managers will need to be coaches/trainers who help people manage themselves better. The new technologies will require people to be much more self-disciplined. If I might be somewhat prescriptive here, companies and individuals will need to partner in continuing professional education. It is not good for either companies or individuals to have an organization full of people with outdated skills. Individuals will need to take more responsibility for keeping themselves current with new technology, and organizations will need to be better facilitators of this continuous learning process.

The new communication and processing technologies are unlike anything we have ever faced in human history in one very significant aspect. These new technologies do not consume, or use up, a commodity in the way that a ton of iron ore, or a tree, or a farm product is consumed. When we use information, it is possible for the original information to remain and to be generally increased. For so much of our human history, the ability to communicate with others and acquire information has been a very difficult task. Voice mail messages, faxes, e-mail, cellular and other mobile communications, and now videoconferencing are all available. With the Internet, an astounding amount of information is available to anyone with a computer and a modem. Consider that an average person who lived in the Middle Ages might live an entire lifetime and not ever come in contact with the amount of information available in one major Sunday newspaper.

Because of the ever-increasing volume of information available to people now and the exponentially increasing amount of information available in the future, keeping up with the volume of information without being overwhelmed will be a major issue for professionals. As ever, new communication technologies are evolving to help professionals manage the volume, but it will require people to change the way they do their work. Professionals will also have to learn to differentiate the quality of the information available to them. Management will also have to focus on the impact of the volume of information and be ever-vigilant on the quality issue. For example, requiring people to provide outdated, and essentially meaningless reports just because it is possible to do so, does nothing to add value to the organization. Management will want to focus on how to help professionals do what professionals do best, that is, to make informed, meaningful decisions and to make those high value decisions more often.

New and emerging communication technologies are allowing organizations and professionals to decentralize from the Industrial Age model of a centralized workplace. With unified messaging, for example, an employee can receive voice, fax, and e-mail using either a PC or a telephone at any location with a good connection to modern communications technologies. The Internet and World Wide Web are expanding these capabilities, and the availability of videoconferencing means that employees can even participate in meetings without actually being there.

Some of the effects of decentralization are beginning to emerge. Again managers will need to redefine their roles by becoming better facilitators to accomplish the job. To perform their new role they will need to be more pragmatic about how the work of an organization is done. Work may take on more of a project orientation rather than a daily transaction orientation. Managers, professionals and other employees will need to focus more on situational leadership than rigid hierarchical structures. The goal is to complete the work and to be less focused on how to do it. However, organizations still have a political component to them. Professionals will need to deal with the issue of "face time" to career building.

The "democratization of technology" has also been an important component of new communication technologies. Large, proprietary mainframes have given way to minicomputers, PCs and eventually to LANs and are continuing to evolve to client server technologies. In the process, technology has been "democratized," where initially only a relative few people had access to technology and information, now the majority of people within an organization have access to technology and information. New skill sets are in the process of being developed by people in the organization to use these new technologies. With the increasing use of enterprise networks, involving local and wide-area networks, e-mail has become the natural network application. e-mail is more than an addition to voice mail systems. "e-mail can redirect your entire focus, from managing transactions to managing human relationships" (Baker, 1994).

SUMMARY

This chapter has described some of the ways humans have adapted to previous innovations or new technologies, the contexts of a global/service society, the need to understand various aspects of culture, and the need for meaning in human activities. It is difficult to understand when an innovation has far-reaching consequences. The unexamined assumption has been that if you give people enough information, or a new technology, they will know what it means and know what to do with it. However, when looking at the historical introduction to new tools, technology, or ideas, people seldom immediately recognize the significance of a transforming technology or idea, and may indeed reject it as a fad, foolhardy, or worse. As new technologies become more prevalent, the most significant changes will center around timing, volume of information, decentralization, and what I call "the democratization of technology." Many changes will be needed to adapt successfully to these technologies, and perhaps the best approach is to assume the answers are out there somewhere, we just have to work together to find them.

Everything that can be invented has been invented.

—Charles H. Duell (Commissioner of U.S. Office of Patents), urging President William McKinley to abolish his office, 1899. (Cerf and Navasky, 1984, p. 203)

REFERENCES

Baker, R. H. (1994).*Networking the enterprise*. New York: McGraw-Hill.
Cerf, C., & Navasky, V. (1984). *The experts speak: The definitive compendium of authoritative misinformation*. New York: Pantheon Books.
Fowler, J. W. (1981). *Stages of faith*. San Francisco: Harper & Row.
Gitelman, Z. (1988). *Politics and culture in the Soviet Union*, Ann Arbor, MI: University of Michigan, 6.

Herrmann, N. (1990). *The creative brain.* Lake Lure, NC: Brain Books.

Hofstede, G. H. (1980). *Culture's consequences.* Beverly Hills, CA: Sage.

McCracken, G. (1990, January). Culture and consumer behavior: An anthropological perspective, *Journal of the Market Research Society,* 3–11.

Nye, D. (1990). *Electrifying America: Social meanings of a new technology.* Cambridge, MA: MIT Press.

Porter, M. (1990). *The competitive advantage of nations.* Harvard Business Review, 73–93.

Ronen, S. (1986). *Comparative and multinational management.* New York: Wiley, 19.

Shank, G. (1996, February). Professor, Educational Psychology, Northern Illinois University, interview.

Strassman, P. (1985). *Information payoff: The transformation of work in the electronic age.* New York: Free Press.

Toffler, A. (1970). *Future Shock,* New York: Random House. p. 365.

7

The Role of Continuing Professional Education in a Virtual Organization

Deborah Lavin Colky and Michael Colky

INTRODUCTION

Our world moves at an accelerated pace. Many things for which people were willing to wait in the past are now available instantaneously. Groceries, clothing, and household goods can be ordered merely by dialing the twenty-four hour number, faxing, or accessing the company's file on the Internet. Banking can be done at any time of day. Vacations can be arranged and people can book their own reservations. Through technology, our boundaries are limitless. Instant access to thousands of venues by phone, fax, or computer exist. In the global marketplace, business is conducted at any time of day all over the world. This business climate has created an almost unbelievable customer expectation: customers now expect to receive services and products on demand. In order to meet this expectation, businesses must be able to provide services and products around the clock, and they must be totally accessible to the customer. Along with this customer expectation, employees are requiring more personal time, more quality family time, and more balance in their lives. One attempt to address all of these needs is to establish a virtual organization.

WHAT IS A VIRTUAL ORGANIZATION?

A virtual organization is a way of organizing a business. This organization model is a natural evolution, resulting from three trends: the globalization of the marketplace, increasing competition, and growing technology. Sometimes called telecommuting, definitions

111

range from simply working at home to the more complicated combination of flexiplace, flexitime, and electronic communications (Piskurich, 1996). The most common example of a virtual organization is a situation where workers are linked to the corporate office electronically, but work from their homes. From home, these workers are able to do the work that they normally would in an office, including receiving telephone calls from customers. The fact that these employees are working from home is not known by the customer.

What the virtual organization is becoming, however, is a network of professionals with notebook computers, with modem and fax, and mobile telephones, connecting with each other and the home office from anywhere in the world. To accommodate the growing population of virtual organization workers, many companies have converted traditional office space to a series of "hotel" cubicles: cubicles that are used by telecommuters on a day-to-day or even on an hourly basis. The office, then, is a concept, not a place.

It is important to note that a virtual organization is not just a string of workers, working on independent projects. A characteristic of the virtual organization is that it links together those workers who are part of a *team*. Virtual organization workers are *not* independent contractors, although independent contractors may be part of the team on specific projects. Virtual organization professionals are employees who just happen to perform their jobs outside of the traditional workplace, outside of the traditional worktime, and via electronic linkages. They are part of the team on a particular project or in a specific department, even if they are not physically present.

As our world becomes smaller, modern business is motivated to do things faster, and to be ever-closer to the customer. The emerging virtual workplace provides unlimited opportunities for working around the clock, providing products and services at an almost nonstop pace. Since virtual organization workers are not bound by traditional offices, they are able to be in the field, always accessible to the customer. Work is performed in virtual space—out of sight, if not out of touch. The virtual organization professional is measured by the work that is done, not where that work was performed.

WHAT ARE THE NEEDS OF VIRTUAL ORGANIZATION PROFESSIONALS?

There are many reasons why a professional chooses to be part of a virtual organization. Among the top reasons listed are (1) the need for independence; (2) the need for a work-family balance; (3) the need for a better work environment—a "quiet" place to work in order to be more productive (Gordon, 1996); and (4) the need for more flexibility, both in the way time is spent in the day, and in work style. Work-at-home employees often view telecommuting as a way to reduce stress because they are working in a familiar, comfortable environment, and they did not have to fight any rush hour traffic to be there. Working from home has the added stress-relieving benefits of reducing "work clothing" costs and commuting costs. All virtual organization professionals are able to save tremendous amounts of time by eliminating the need to commute to a particular place and by being electronically linked so that information is always and immediately available.

Companies have their own reasons for establishing virtual organizations, and these reasons are only sometimes compatible with the needs of the workers. The company needs include (1) getting closer to the customer; (2) saving costs on things such as office and parking space; (3) meeting Environmental Protection Agency and Americans with Disabilities Act regulations; and (4) increasing employee retention by providing a flexible scheduling advantage to them (Piskurich, 1996). This desirable benefit also helps in recruiting the best and the brightest. No matter what the underlying need is, telecommuting is not going to be successful unless two matters are in place: the worker and the company both have to be *prepared* for the virtual office situation.

The company must have a clear reason for telecommuting, and ultimately that reason is based on the bottom line, in terms of quicker customer response and lowered costs. It is to the company's advantage to ensure that managers and nontelecommuters understand what the virtual organization means, how it works, and how virtual organization colleagues are to be treated. The company also has a responsibility to select the best candidates for telecommuting. The first step in that selection process is developing policies and procedures for telecommuters—like a "rule book" for the virtual organization.

Since many workers actually become less productive when telecommuting because they are not prepared for the change in work style and lifestyle, certain competencies should be achieved before an employee is considered as a candidate for the virtual office. Telecommuting works best when people are self-motivated, entrepreneurial, moderately social, flexible, responsible, trustworthy, committed, task oriented, good time managers, and already successful in their jobs (Gordon, 1996). There are some physical space requirements, as well. Work-at-home professionals, for example, need to have a quiet, dedicated space in which to establish an office, with a desk, files, electronic equipment and telephone lines.

Virtual organization workers' needs tend to be distinctly different *before* telecommuting than *during* telecommuting. Although telecommuting appears to be a solution to the workers' personal concerns listed earlier in this section, once the virtual office becomes a reality, the needs of the worker change, becoming much more job-focused and much less personal-focused. The work/family balance sought by at-home workers, in particular, may turn out to be more of a dream than reality. If a worker is a workaholic, he or she will have a difficult time leaving an office that is always there. Virtual organization workers often suffer a sense of loneliness or isolation. They feel out of the loop on decisions and even something as seemingly trivial as general office repartee. Their colleagues may not return their telephone calls or e-mails. Once workers are out of the office and not part of the regular culture, they are quickly forgotten. Being away from the office can affect a virtual organization professional's career. In an era when companies are downsizing, not being physically present in the office could lead some to believe that the worker is not productive and, therefore, not needed. Nontelecommuters as well as supervisors of virtual office workers often do not know how to include telecommuters in their regular meetings and other office communication.

HOW CAN CONTINUING PROFESSIONAL EDUCATION MEET VIRTUAL ORGANIZATION NEEDS?

To succeed, the virtual organization needs to build trust. Paradoxically, the more virtual an organization becomes, the more its people need to meet in person (Handy, 1995). To paraphrase John Naisbett, high tech needs high touch. By definition, a virtual organization is an entity that has people, many of whom may not have met and do not live in the same part of the country, working together on a team. A common situation would be one where a team member working in the corporate office in one state has to trust that another team member in another location will act appropriately when making decisions on a project. This situation demands a great deal of trust between two strangers.

Another aspect of trust needed in a virtual organization is the trust between a telecommuter and his or her supervisor. Supervisors are accustomed to seeing their employees working. Visibility means productivity. A virtual organization is based on an entirely different premise: results, not volume. It is difficult for some supervisors to supervise when they cannot see their employees. Questions arise about the virtual organization employee's use of time.

Continuing professional education can play a key role in fostering trust among team members in a virtual organization and between supervisors and virtual organization workers. Training interventions on topics such as team building (for team members) and coaching (for supervisors) can reinforce common goals, common vision, and shared commitment. The training must be reinforced and constantly updated to ensure continuous learning and growth.

According to those who have been part of a virtual organization, the single most important reason that these organizations fail is that the people who are directly involved in making the concept work have been ill-prepared. People who are going to begin telecommuting have to be prepared for the many changes that will occur in their work lives and home lives, and companies are responsible for training their people on the competencies needed to succeed in this networked environment. The needs are logical and obvious. Continuing professional education on topics such as company policies and procedures, computer skills, decision making, time management, organization skills, and communication skills are essential. A worker who no longer has a desk or files at hand will need to have organization skills. One who no longer has a structured work week will need time management skills. Communicating electronically calls for better computer skills. A worker who does not have a supervisor in the next office needs to be confident about his or her decision-making skills. The training provided should be as realistic as possible so that it is meaningful.

Supervisors and nontelecommuters need to understand how to include telecommuters in their regular meetings, emergency meetings and other communications. The concept of inclusion is one that has not been addressed well in current virtual organizations. It requires a great deal of planning and changes in attitude, thinking and behavior. Continuing professional education should be an essential part of this change process.

WHAT IS THE FUTURE OF CONTINUING PROFESSIONAL EDUCATION IN THE VIRTUAL ORGANIZATION?

As the demand to be closer to the customer and to produce in a 24-hour cycle grows, so will virtual organizations. Link Resources Corporation, a New York-based research firm, recently released figures from its 1994 annual work-at-home survey. The number of telecommuters has been on an upward trend. In 1994, more than 8.8 million corporate employees spent part of every work week at home and that number is ever-increasing. Telecommuting is by far the fastest-growing segment of at-home workers. Although the future of the virtual organization is tied, to some extent, to the future of global wireless communication, the effectiveness of virtual organizations will be dependent on the attitude and behavior shifts of employees and employers.

Technology and multimedia will play a larger role in the delivery of continuing professional education, but the classroom will be even more necessary than it is now. As the distance between workers increases, so will the need for more interpersonal time and training. People will have to come together to build trust and teams; to combat the feeling of isolation the virtual organization professional will experience; and to question the decisions of upper management. Managers will continue to need training as the web of the virtual workplace multiplies. At this point continuing professional education's role will grow. Continuing professional education will knit virtual organization professionals together. Companies will support continuing professional education efforts because they will see the bottom-line benefit of having a well-prepared, well-integrated network of professionals. The future opportunities for continuing professional education, like cyberspace, is boundless.

REFERENCES

Gil Gordon interview. (1996, March). *Gil Gordon Associates,* Monmouth Junction, NJ.

Handy, Charles. (1995, May–June). Trust and the virtual organization. *Harvard Business Review,* 40–50.

Piskurich, George M. (1996, February). Making telecommuting work. *Training,* 20–27.

Sharoff, Robert. (1995, September). Take stock of telecommutes. *Crain's Small Business,* 17.

8

The Problems and the Promise of Diversity in the Professions: Implications for Continuing Professional Education

LaVerne Gyant

In a society facing profound and rapid change universities [businesses and government] must work diligently to provide quality education to a greater number of students, in a wider variety of formats and settings . . . (Council of Graduate Schools, 1989, p. 4).

What is diversity and why should it be included in every phase of our society—education, politics, economics, and socialization? Is it so important that we included everyone? Must we be sensitive and has an understanding of the various racial/ethnic, gender, and economic status of those we come in contact with? Why "can't we all just" be one? Why can't we see each other without seeing color or gender? These questions will not be answered within this chapter. However, these questions should be of concern to those who are administrating, planning, and facilitating continuing professional education.

In searching for the answers to the above questions, this chapter will briefly discuss the history of blacks and their participation in formal and informal continuing professional education. By discussing the history of blacks, I hope to provide some insight as to why and if continuing professional education has neglected diverse populations, and if so, how can we improve and increase diverse populations' participation in continuing professional education.

In the sixties, continuing professional educators recognized that racial/ethnic groups and women were not being served. So they sought to address this void. However, they have been successful in

117

improving programs for women, but not for racial/ethnic groups. This situation is evident by the increased number of continuing professional programs designed for women and the number of women who are attending them. According to Kramer (1989) continuing professional education has been on the periphery in its efforts to expand access and opportunity to racial/ethnic groups. Yet, with its capabilities, resources, innovation, and adaptability, continuing professional education could be in the forefront for creating and developing a cultural diverse environment in education, business, politics, and government. Continuing educators have the opportunity to develop programs which will enhance the personal interest, professional development, basic skills and knowledge of racial/ethnic groups. Continuing professional education also has the opportunity to assist culturally diverse populations in gaining control of their lives, relationships, and careers—"to be all they can be."

Historically racial/ethnic groups have recognized the "opportunity to learn" and participate in continuing professional education as a key to equal opportunities (Baratz-Snowden, 1993). They recognize that via education, higher and continuing professional education, they will be able to obtain success—personal, professional, economical. Thus, they tend to participate in programs which provide them the opportunity to increase their technical and vocational skills, improve their community, learn about the political system, how to start their own business, and learn about their own cultural and historical experiences.

Education is our passport to the future, for tomorrow belongs to the people who prepare for it today,

(Malcolm X 1986, p. 43).

The history of blacks participating in formal and informal continuing professional education programs is a long and rich one. Adult and continuing professional education was necessary in the Africans' struggle to survive, for self-determination, advancement, and freedom (Franklin, 1984). Due to laws and restriction regarding the education of Africans, "they demanded education, for themselves and for their children, and they created the means to appropriate the knowledge they need for social and productive relations" (Butchart, 1990, p. 46).

Blacks utilized adult and continuing professional education, especially informal education, in the various social movements—slavery, abolition, Civil War, Reconstruction, migration, Harlem Renaissance, and the civil rights movement. Continuing professional education programs were sponsored by organizations and clubs, churches, conventions, and the press, as well as black colleges/universities. These programs provided blacks with educational activities to pursue economic development, career training, political debate, and basic educational needs.

An early example of continuing professional education was offered by the Free African Society. The purpose of the Free African Society was to uplift the black community by teaching thrift, improving the morals of its members and society, assist the needy, and to provide security for members in case of unemployment, illness, or death (Ihle, 1990). Via the Free African Society its members assisted in the establishment of several black churches and schools and sponsored several conventions, where they could discuss issues relating to the welfare of enslaved and freed Africans, how to develop their own businesses, and how to work with whites who were interested in providing them and their children with an education. The Minerva Literary Society provided black women with the opportunity to read and discuss their original compositions, to hear talks on the moral improvement and influence of women on family life. (Ihle, 1990). Voluntary organizations and clubs such as the Free African Society, the Minerva Literary Society, the Banneker Institute, and the National Association of Colored Women have always been in the forefront in providing opportunities for both individual and community improvements (Ross-Gordon, 1991; Porter, 1936).

The black press has been recognized as an important form for continuing professional education. The black press—magazines and newspapers—offered "useful knowledge of every kind, and every thing" (Barrow, 1977–78, p. 119). It was through this median that blacks were able to "plead their own cause" (Freedom Journal, 1827). The black press served as a forum for protest and self-definition, and allowed readers to become aware of and articulate their opinions, learn about local, national, and international issues and achievements of blacks, employment and career opportunities, and some how to's. The *Freedom Journal, Amsterdam News, Defender, Voice of the Negro, Horizon, Journal of Negro Education* are only a few examples of black press. The content of these programs and activities were well beyond basic adult education of its day.

National conventions for blacks began around the 1830s in Philadelphia. These conventions, which were sponsored by white and black organizations, focused on enfranchisement, equal rights, abolition, economic development, and education. The early efforts of national conventions, organizations and clubs, churches, and the black press are still continuing today via Opportunities Industrial Center (OIC), the Urban League, Nation of Islam, the Association for the Study of African American Life and History, *Jet, Essences, Journal of Black Studies, Dollars and Sense,* and Black Entertainment Television.

Early supporters of continuing professional education include but are not limited to Booker T. Washington, Alain L. Locke, Marcus Garvey, Ambrose Caliver, Anna J. Cooper, Nannie Helen Burroughs, and Septima Clark. These individuals viewed education as an avenue to "change the conditions among the masses of Negro people" (McGee, 1984, p. 16). It was this belief which led them to sponsor and support various avenues of continuing professional education. Little attention has been given to the various programs Booker T. Washington sponsored via Tuskegee Normal and Industrial School. These programs include the Moveable School Project where students from the Tuskegee programs went to the fields to teach adults and children how to read and understand the value of education . . . how to pickle, can, and preserve; how to prepare and season food; how to make starch and bluing for laundry out of the potato . . . how to cure and keep meat in hot weather; how to rotate crops; and how to manage an efficient and profitable farm (Gyant, 1988; McGee, 1984). Tuskegee also sponsored several conferences which were attended by farmers, mechanics, schoolteachers, and ministers who viewed the conferences as their "one day of schoolin' a year" (Thrasher, 1969). The purpose of the conferences was to inform participants how to secure their own property, improve their life style and way of living, and how to attain an education (Washington, 1904). An outgrowth of these conferences was the formation of local farmers' clubs and the National Business League.

Along these same lines, Alain L. Locke, Ira Reid, and E. F. Frazier in conjunction with the American Association of Adult Education (AAAE), Carnegie Corporation, and Julius Rosenwald Foundation organized several library programs in Atlanta, Georgia, and Harlem, New York. These library programs offered participants the opportunity to gain skills which would not only improved their employment and educational possibilities, but their leadership skills as well. The programs were comprehensive and were classified as creative and recreative—music, art, theater, literature; informative—forums, panel discussions, lecture series, radio talk shows; practical—child care, parent education, counseling for special needs; library services—book clubs, story hours, readers' advisory service (Rose, 1936; Hayden & DuBois, 1977).

Today similar programs can be found in many racial/ethnic communities. Yet, these programs are generally sponsored by one of many racial/ethnic organizations/clubs or churches. Within the black community one can find several male mentoring programs, rites of passages programs for both children and adults, and economic development programs. For example, after the Million Man March (October 16, 1995), Black Entertainment Television has highlighted some of the programs various organizations and churches have started prior to and after the march.

Locke (1935–36) once stated "that the key to an intellectual interest is a strong emotional drive and in Negro adult education we should boldly capitalize the motivation of racial interest" (352). Heeding these words, early and contemporary black organizations/clubs, churches, institutions, and media have provided the black community with various forms of continuing professional education programs. They have made it possible not only for the "elite" but for the masses to attempt to reach beyond their racial interests and pursue the same goals of mainstream society (Locke).

In reviewing some of the continuing professional education programs found within the black community, we learn how education, formal and informal, provided blacks the opportunity to deal critically and creatively with reality and how to participate in the transformation of their world (Freire, 1970).

Education heals, giving new information, new knowledge of who they are and what they are.

(Na'im Akbar, 1993).

Within the literature on continuing professional education, there is minimal information on diversity. Ross-Gordon (1991) notes that adult education research has not taken an interest in understanding the needs or racial/ethnic adults—First Nation Groups (Native Americans), African Americans, Asian Americans, Latinos. She notes research on these groups have been inadvertently excluded from major publications in both adult and continuing professional education. For example, there has been little research done on the 1945 special issue of the *Journal of Negro Education* which was dedicated to various aspects of adult and continuing professional education within the black community. Some of the topics in this issue included "Adult education programs of Negro parent-teacher associations," "Adult education for Negroes in the Armed Forces," "Adult education in public libraries and museums," "Wider use of audio visuals in adult education for Negroes," and "Neglected areas in adult education."

In a literature review several articles focusing on continuing professional education and marginal groups were found in various issues of the *Journal of Negro Education, Western Journal of Black Studies, Journal of Black Studies, Black Issues of Higher Education, Hispanic Engineering, and Journal of American Indian Education*. These articles covered such issues as "Opportunity to learn: Implications for professional development" (Baratz-Snowden, 1993) and "A plan for the special preparation of attorneys in effective writing skills" (Stone, 1983). Information on continuing professional education programs could also be found in secular magazines such as *Essences, Dollars and Sense, Pittsburgh Courier*. In a similar review of adult and continuing professional journals, minimal information was found. Thus, we can understand why Ross-Gordon states that research on racial/ethnic groups has been excluded from major publications.

Why is this? Is the need for continuing professional education within diverse groups seen as unnecessary? Are research and programs offered by diverse groups not seen as valid? Are continuing professional education administrators, planners, and facilitators hesitant because they are not familiar with these groups? their history and resources? are they not ready to discuss the fact that racism and sexism persist in every phase of our every day?

> *I feel on much better ground with people who say "I'm working on overcoming my racism." We've got to approach this problem with as much humility and generosity as we possibly can.*
>
>   (Andrew Young, 1993)

Amstutz (1994) addresses the issue of race and gender in adult education by noting that racism and sexism persist in adult and continuing education for several reasons—differences in interpretation of events and issues, omission of facts and/or theories, assumptions that all theories are applicable to all groups, discriminatory institutional policies, and lack of experiences with and sensitivity to other cultures. Administrators, planners, and facilitators in continuing professional education should examine these reasons and acknowledge that racism and sexism exist and affect whites as well as marginal groups. By making this recognition, we see changes in both personal and professional interaction. "Personal change refers to changing one's beliefs and actions as an educator as well as in other areas of life. Professional change refers to educating others about racism and sexism, creating more equitable institutional practices, and confronting biases in and through professional associations" (Hayes, 1994, pp. 77–78). If administrators, planners, and facilitators heed these words, they will begin to provide programs and activities which will meet the needs of all people.

Racial/ethnic populations participation in continuing professional education is invisible. Santos and Richardson(1988) note by failing to address racial/ethnic inclusion, we are undermining the foundation of society, delaying efforts in building a competitive work force, questioning the educational systems capacity to provide equal education for all, and the systems efforts to meet the rapid demographic changes. Kramer (1989) continues by stating "the presence of Black [and other racial/ethnic] adult students would likely contribute significantly to the needs and interest of all Black [and racial/ethnic] students" (p. 3). If educational institutions, businesses, agencies, and government continue to exclude these groups, society will eventually lose what minimal gains it has achieved. With the recall of affirmative action, set asides, and race based scholarship, we are already losing "qualified" and "talented" men and women from the African American, Latino, Asian, and First Nation community. The loss of these talented and skilled men and women reduce society's competitive edge, places a strain on domestic resources, and continues to cause conflict between these groups and mainstream society.

In some ways the invisibility of racial/ethnic groups in continuing professional education can be considered a barometer for this loss. Yet, there are some examples where individuals from these groups have succeed without participating in any type of continuing professional education programs. Les Brown, a noted motivational speaker, disc jockey, and former state representative, has only a high school diploma and is one of the most recognized speakers in this country. In his book *Live Your Dreams* (1992), he notes that reading, contacting people who inspired him, attending programs and seminars within his budget, were fundamental in his goal to become a motivational speaker. Members of racial/ethnic groups tend to learn via the television, radio, and newspaper. In her study on disadvantaged older adults, Heisel (1986) found that "older persons were actively involved in purposeful learning activities . . . the interest and activities . . . were informal, nontraditional learning" (p. 19). She also notes that their efforts for self-directed learning were a sign of learning motivation and activity. Would these self-directed avenues be considered continuing professional education? Some would say no because it did not occur in a formalized, structured environment. Others would say yes, because learning is an ongoing process. Regardless of whom you side with, self-directed learning has been the continuing professional education avenue many racial/ethnic, elderly, women, and others have used to become productive, competitive, knowledgeable, and empowering individuals.

If there is exclusion and lack of participation by racial/ethnic groups, what are some of the reasons for this invisibility? One reason is centered around the fact many of these programs are sponsored by white institutions. Many of "these institutions have to come to grips with some historical factors" (as quoted in O'Brien, 1990, p. 6) which have prevented their participation in various activities. These factors include such things as unfriendly and uncomfortable environments, feelings of alienation, and lack of leadership by members of their own groups. Another reason is some find the programs "a waste of time" or "they were unaware of the existences of such programs" (Bass, 1972). Other reasons for non-participation are centered around location and cost of the programs. The final reason may be due to conflicting family responsibilities. On the other hand, there are some racial/ethnic individuals who have found continuing professional education "as a second chance," and an avenue to help them personally and professional. With this in mind, members of racial/ethnic groups view continuing professional education with some skepticism and a positive attitude. Bass (1972) suggests that these views may serve as a key to persuade demonstrate how these programs can improve their lifestyle and living conditions, employment opportunities, and community.

In meeting this challenge administrators, planners, and facilitators must acknowledge the fact that many of the programs they create have not been compatible with or excluded the needs and values of the racial/ethnic groups. Programs don't have to focus on racial/ethnic issues. Rather it is important administrators, planners, and facilitators have some awareness of their audiences, their various learning styles, their educational characteristics and needs, and recognize and respect the experiences of their audiences. Locke (1934) wrote

> Let us be aware of adult education, not merely for the good of the Negro but mainly in the interest of effective adult education in general. Where the physical separation of one racial group from another in the pursuit of their education seems dictated by circumstances, let us guard the values, standards, and objectives most zealously and keep them constant and universal. (p. 419).

Educators must also recognize that needs assessments and evaluations may have to be designed in a way to provide the information necessary to plan programs or activities which will increase the participation and meet needs and values of the racial/ethnic groups. Jackson (1980) and Heisel (1986) agree administrators, planners, and facilitators should be aware of racial/ethnic groups "formal and informal learning activities and attitudes toward learning" (p. 15) in their development of strategies to increase programs and participation by racial/ethnic groups.

The task for adult educationists . . . lies in discovering and using ways to generate serious and sustained interests.

(Locke, 1935–36, p. 352).

With increases in racial/ethnic groups, elderly, and early retirees, the number of individuals needing and seeking continuing professional education will increase. They will be seeking assistance in vocational/technical training, workplace technology, early retirement, economic development, and parenting. Likewise with the changes in welfare reform, health care, and the information highway continuing professional education should be planning programs for and developing strategies to encourage the participation of racial/ethnic groups, elderly, homeless, displaced workers, and welfare recipients. By examining some of the issues previously discussed in this chapter and by (a) enhancing and creating alternative assessment and evaluation; (b) enhancing the visibility of and including members of the various groups in the planning, implementation, and teaching of programs; (c) developing inclusive curriculums and programs; (d) providing flexible cost for participants; (e) disseminating information in local and community media, churches, organizations, and stores; and (f) creating a supportive and welcome environment there is an opportunity to increase participation (Gordon, 1992; Brsicoe & Ross-Gordon, 1989; Bass, 1972).

Managing, teaching, and planning diversity programs in continuing professional education is not just a social responsibility, it is an economic and human responsibility. Managing, teaching, and planning diversity programs help to create a cooperative, appreciative, open learning experience for everyone. Managing, teaching, and planning diversity programs help us to look at people as individuals, and to see their strengths and weaknesses. Managing, teaching, and planning diversity programs are about helping people to work together productively, build a better world, while learning to respect and value each other differences and similarities.

The real value of race, the positive value . . . [is] the great contribution it could make to the diversity as well as the unity the human race.

(Holmes, 1965, p. 83).

REFERENCES

Akbar, N. (1993). Education. In D. Winbush Riley (Ed.), *My soul looks back 'less I forget: A collection of quotations by people of color,* 115.

Amstutz, D. (1994). Staff development: Addressing issues of race and gender. In E. Hayes & S. A. J. Colin III, *Confronting racisim and sexism,* 39–51. San Francisco: Jossey Bass.

Baratz-Snowden, J. C. (1993). Opportunity to learn: Impact for professional development, *Journal of Negro Education, 62* (3), 311–321.

Barrow, L. C. (1977–1978). Our own cause: Freedom's journal and the beginnings of the black press. *Journalism History, 4,* 119, 121.

Bass, F. L. (1972). Impact of the Black experience on attitudes toward continuing education. *Adult Education,* 22:3, 207–277.

Briscoe, D. B., and Ross-Gordon, J. M. (1989). Racial and ethnic minorities and adult education. In S. B. Merriam & P. M. Cunningham (Eds.), *Handbook of adult and continuing education,* 583–598.

Brown, L. (1992). *Live Your Dreams.* New York: Morrow.

Butchart, R. E. (1990). Schooling for a freed people: The education of adult freedman, 1861–1871. In H. G. Neufeldt & L. McGee (Eds.), *Education of the African American adult,* 45–58.

Council of Graduate Schools, (1989). *Off campus graduate education.* Washington, DC

Franklin, V. P. (1984). *Black self-determination: A cultural history of the faith of the fathers.* Westport, CT: Lawerence Hill.

Freire, P. (1970). *Pedagogy of the oppressed.* New York: Herder and Herder.

Freedom's Journal (1827) as quoted in H. G. Neufeldt & L. McGee (Eds.), *Education of the African American adult,* 78.

Gordon, J. (1992). Rethinking diversity. *Training, 29*:1, 23–30.

Gyant, L. (1988). Contributors to adult education: Booker T. Washington, George Washington Carver, Alain L. Locke, & Ambrose Caliver. *Journal of Black Studies, 19*:1. 9–110.

Hayden, R. C., & DuBois, E. E. (1977). Drum major for black adult education: Alain L. Locke *Western Journal of Black Studies, 1,* 293–296.

Hayes, E. (1994). Developing a personal and professional agenda for change. In E. Hayes & S. A. J. Colin III, *Confronting racism and sexism,* 77–89.

Heisel, M. A. (1986). Learning activities of disadvantaged older adults. *Community Education Research Digest,* 1:1, 14–21.

Holmes, E. C. (1965). Alain L. Locke and the adult education movement. *Journal of Negro Education,* 34:1, 5–10.

Ihle, E. L. (1990). Education of the free blacks before the civil war. In H. G. Neufeldt & L. McGee, *Education of the African American adult,* pp. 11–23.

Jackson, J. J. (1980). *Minorities and Aging.* Belmont, CA: Wadsworth.

Kramer, J. L. (1989). Continuing education in a multicultural society: Challenges of access and environment. *Continuing Higher Education,* 37:1, 2–4.

Locke, A. L. (1935–36). The intellectual interest of Negroes. *Journal of Adult Education,* 8:3, 352.

Locke, A. L. (1934). Reciprocity instead of regimentation. *Journal of Adult Education, 6,* 418–420.

Malcolm X (1986). Self-reliance. In J. Cheatham Bell (Ed.), *Famous black quotations and some not so famous,* 43.

McGee, L. (1984). Booker T. Washington and George Washington Carver: A tandem of and adult education at Tuskegee Institue. *Lifelong Learning, 8*:12, 12–18.

O'Brien, E. (March 1, 1990). Continuing education programs not reaching minority populations. *Black Issues in Higher Education, 6*:24, 6–8.

Porter, D. B. (1936). The organizational education activities of Negro literary society, 1828–1846. *Journal of Negro Education, 5,* 555–576.

Rose, E. (1936) The Harlem experiment. *Journal of Adult Education, 7,* 55.

Ross-Gordon, J. M. (1991). Needed: A multicultural perspective for adult education research. *Adult Education Quarterly, 42*:1, 1–16.

Ross-Gordon, J. M. (1990). Informal adult education and learning in African American women's voluntary organizations. Paper presented at the American Education Research Association, Boston.

de los Stantos, Jr. A., & Richardson, R. C. (1988). 12 principles for good institutional practices in removing race/ethnicity as a factor in college completion. *Education Record, 69*:3, 43–47.

Stone, E. (1983). A plan for special preparation of attorneys in effective writing skills. *Journal of Negro Education, 52*:3, 374–331.

Thrasher, M.B. (1969). *Tuskegee: Its struggle: Its story and its work.* New York: Negro University Press.

Washington, B.T. (1904). *Working with the Hands.* Garden City, NY: Doubleday.

Young, A. (1993). Racism, in D. Winbush Riley (Ed.), My soul looks back less I forget: A collection of quotations by people of color, 337.

9

Systematic Efforts in Continuing Professional Education Focusing on Mandatory Continuing Professional Education

William H. Young

THE DINOSAUR IS STILL ALIVE AND WELL—WHY IT IS SO?

Introduction

The history and philosophy of mandatory continuing professional education and current points of view concerning it have been explored in the literature, debated at national, regional, and state educational forums, and discussed within the walls of institutions and other "workplaces" where affected professionals gather. If one formulated an opinion from a synthesis of information gleaned from these sources, it would be difficult to favor mandatory continuing professional education, since there is growing concern and condemnation of the mandated principle as it is applied to professional education. A great deal of criticism has been launched by individuals who apparently have not conceptualized the rationale that gave birth to mandatory continuing professional education and who have not recognized the benefits derived. I hope this chapter will point out the place of mandatory continuing professional education within the mandated principle, show the major benefits derived, and direct critics to more meaningful scientific inquiry (Young, 1980, p. 12).

This preamble launched my first article about mandatory continuing professional education over 15 years ago when the people in charge of editing the *Illinois Adult Continuing Educators Association Journal* called me to find out if I would be interested in writing an article that provided a positive viewpoint about mandatory continuing professional education. I was honored to been selected and I proceeded to write and submit my article. When I received a copy of the publication, I discovered that I was the only author who dedicated time and effort describing the positive aspects about mandatory continuing professional education. The article was later published in the *Yearbook of Adult and Continuing Education* (Young, 1980). Although no one would ever verify my suspicions, I firmly believe that I was chosen to write the article and later the book chapter not because of my literary talents but because I was the only one available who would say anything positive about mandatory continuing professional education.

Quest for New Information

Instead of looking at all of the reasons we should not be involved in mandatory continuing professional education (CPE), I decided to describe the issues based upon the fact that mandatory CPE is increasing among the professions, and there must be compelling reasons for this apparent support for mandated activity. It is difficult to create a refreshing approach in discussing the issues surrounding mandatory CPE. I pondered this thought for about two months before I realized that I had the opportunity right in front of me one Wednesday evening while I was providing some thoughts on mandatory CPE to my 1996 spring semester continuing education for professional groups graduate education class. Many of the 30 students in this class were involved in the administration of continuing professional education in higher education, the associations, employer based human resource development, or in private pratice. Others had a research interest in the field and still others were interested in pursuing a CPE career.

I decided that I would create a modified nominal group process technique to attempt to uncover new thoughts about the reasons different domains have embraced mandatory CPE. Over the years, the literature has identified higher education, professional associations, employing agencies, and governmental agencies as the four major types of organizations that provide mandatory CPE. The individual practitioner and society in general are major stakeholders also. I divided the class into six groups of five professionals/students each. Those students sitting in the front right side of the room were to provide no more than three reasons why higher education institutions were involved in mandatory continuing professional education. Those students in the middle section of the right side of the room were to provide no more than three reasons why the associations were involved in mandatory CPE. The students in the back right side dealt with the government. The students in the left rear section worked with the reasons the employers were involved in mandatory CPE. The students in the middle left side section were initially concerned with society in general and the students in the left side front were to come up with no more than three reasons the professional practitioner was involved in mandatory CPE. Within 5 to 7 minutes the six groups accomplished their initial tasks and passed their paperwork to the group next to them going clockwise. Each time the group was to arrive at no more than three reasons for involvement in mandatory CPE. After each group had dealt with all six domains, phase two of the process began. Each group had in its possession the paperwork for one of the domains. A spokesperson for each group identified all of the reasons for involvement by the six different groups. At this time, clarification and emphasis were provided by any members of the class including the instructor. The reasons were redefined and placed into larger inclusive categories, if necessary. No attempt to prioritize the reasons was made because the purpose of the exercise was to unearth any new or different reasons that have not been found in the literature.

The reasons why higher education institutions were involved in mandatory continuing professional education were

1. Within its mission;
2. Receive financial rewards;
3. Create another method of job security for faculty;
4. Recruit new students to degree programs;
5. Determines needs for change within the profession;
6. Creates exclusivity and elitist status for the professions involved;
7. Raises intellectual standards within the profession;
8. Protects professionals from litigation
9. Improves the quality of professional practice; and
10. Response to governmental mandates for higher education involvement.

The reasons for professional association involvement gleaned from this activity were

1. Increase the quality, quantity, and diversity of the membership;
2. Improve professional services;

3. Increase revenues;
4. Promote political activity among the membership.
5. Keep members current with changes;
6. Control the population of professionals engaged in practice;
7. Increase leadership and control of the profession;
8. Improve and increase prestige in the profession;
9. Respond to the legal requirements for mandatory CPE;
10. Create networking among members; and
11. Increase training and education in the profession.

According to the results of the group process, employers were involved in mandatory CPE for the following reasons:

1. Increase quality of services;
2. Promotes rapid change in corporate cultures.
3. Increase bottom line and market share;
4. Used as another recruiting tool;
5. Means of employee control;
6. Increases knowledge and skills across the organization;
7. Alternative to financial benefits;
8. Keeps individual employee skills up to date;
9. Tool to decrease insurance costs;
10. Keeps employees motivated and feeling vested in the organization;
11. Means of Employee evaluation and promotion;
12. Protects employees and the employer from litigation; and
13. Reduces "settler" mentality in favor of "pioneering" attitudes.

The reasons government agencies are involved included

1. Protection against litigation;
2. Control;
3. Gain society's acceptance of professional competence;
4. Appearance of concern and involvement;
5. Reflection of society's concerns;
6. Revenue source;
7. Quality of life for citizens in the delivery of professional services;
8. Comply with the law;
9. Creates standards across a given profession;

10. Insures proper training, licensure and certification;
11. A mechanism to help maintain an adequate supply of professionals;
12. Mandates uniformity across state or other geographical and jurisdictional boundaries.

The reasons society is involved in mandatory CPE include

1. Protection from litigation;
2. Desire for professional to be current;
3. Enhances quality of life for everyone;
4. Creates standards of professional practice and better professional performance;
5. Increases prestige in world market;
6. Increases status of the professions; and
7. Increases technological advancement within the professions.

The reasons individual practitioners support mandatory CPE are as follows:

1. Protection against litigation;
2. Maintain employability;
3. Self-improvement;
4. Prestige;
5. Economic advancement;
6. Narrowing the field of competition;
7. Helps define professional self-worth;
8. Response to legal requirements or employer/association mandates;
9. Bridging and broadening the career path;
10. Credentialing;
11. Networking; and
12. Defend the profession.

If agreement between and among the six domains increases the importance of the factors, it should be noted that avoiding litigation, increasing revenues, and maintaining uniform standards of practice within the profession were considered reasons for involvement by higher education, associations, employing agencies, governmental bodies, society at large and the individual professional practitioner. There were several reasons that were unique to each domain and have not received much, if any, attention in the literature. For example, employers used mandatory CPE as an alternative to financial fringe benefits. The employers, associations, and higher education were involved in mandatory CPE in order to recruit students/members or employees to the organizations.

A Synthesis

Cy Houle fueled the debate on mandatory CPE as early as 1980 when he stated that he believed that requirements for participation in educational activities were seldom, if ever justifiable. Several adult educators led the charge against organizations such as the American Medical Association when they said that preplanned, institutionally sponsored knowledge dissemination programs were not the types of educational activities most worthy of professional participation. Recently Candy, (1995) set forth the notion that self-directed learning projects (called self-guided study 15 years ago) were very important, and he inferred that it was preferential to institutionally, preplanned lecture based 1-hour presentations. George Miller (1967, 320–326) believed that there must be a link between education and professional performance in order for continuing medical education to be viable. In a 1985 dissertation Pajor suggested that the positive side of MCPE (mandatory CPE) is founded on the belief that it will protect the public from professionals who are too lazy, uninterested, or egotistical to participate in mandatory CPE. He believed that mandatory CPE would remove from the roll those who no longer were practicing or interested in keeping current professionally and would result in better informed practitioners (Pajor, 3). Several scholars have stated that it is easier to legislate seat time, clock hours, classroom time that it is to create measures for competency and professional performance.

Over the years Louis Phillips has championed the positive outlook. In 1987, Phillips noted that professionals themselves approve of requirements for mandatory CPE. He further stated that professional laggards are finding renewed interest in the profession via mandated continuing education activities. Phillips also believed that leading edge professionals examine new ways of improving their own practice based on upon improvements suggested through systematic continuing education efforts.

Cervero (1988) noted that more and more professionals are required to participate in some form of continuing education. Failure to participate could result in losing the right to practice, loss of membership, forfeiting compensation and/or not gaining reregistation, re-licensure or recertification. Cervero contends that the most common use of mandatory CPE is as a basis for relicensure and recertification and that all 50 states use participation in continuing education as a basis for the relicensure of at least one profession. Dr. Cervero also reminded us that little evidence has shown any positive correlation between participation in continuing education and changes in professional practice.

Barbara LeGrand who has been both a practitioner and a scholar in the field of continuing professional education for over 20 years has been critical of mandatory continuing professional education, but in a later publication Dr. LeGrand pointed to the improvement of continuing professional education based upon it being made systematic via the mandated principle (1992).

Requirements for professionals to participate in systematic non-credit, postdegree educational activity began in the early 1970's. From the beginning through today, social and political forces, not academic rationales, are responsible for the increase in mandatory continuing professional education. Among these forces are (1) widespread public concern about professional competence and performance; (2) failures of the professions and their employers to police their incompetent and impaired; (3) public perceptions of inflated costs for services rendered; and (4) unequal access to quality care and services.

Governmental bodies, professional associations and employers of professionals have used mandatory continuing professional education as a method to quell public concern about professional incompetence. The newspapers are constantly filled with stories about airplane pilot error, ministerial misconduct, amputation of the wrong arm or leg, bank fraud by insiders, and most recently computer viruses initiated by information systems professionals. Many clients/patients/parishioners have firsthand information about impairment when they see surgeons and airplane pilots drinking too much alcohol, see a nutritionist eating junk food, or find out that their religious leader committed an unthinkable crime against their children. These stories and the personal experiences will not go away. It is much easier to legislate classroom activities than it is to restrict or rescind licenses to practice. It appears next to impossible for professions to create standards of practice that go beyond minimal levels of competence. MCPE will go on being used as a method to promote positive public image by informing the public that all members of a profession are engaged in educational activity that helps maintain, expand, and extend competence and performance.

The professions have failed miserably in disciplining their members. My experience working with professional groups tells me that up to 30% of any given profession is either incompetent, impaired, or otherwise unable to perform at expected standards/levels of practice. Drug and alcohol abuse, lack of physical, mental and emotional wellness, debilitating disease, and unethical/immoral behavior contribute to poor practice. The professions and their employers have not limited the practice of those within their ranks who do more harm than good. Mandatory continuing professional education has been used as the cure when remedial education coupled with lifestyle changes should be prescribed.

The costs of professional intervention have risen to a point that people are beginning to buy or create do-it-yourself kits to save money. Citizens are becoming their own financial planners, travel agents, tax accountants, lawyers, architects, and health care professionals in order to maintain financial solvency. The costs of a 24-hour hospital stay, 3 hours of a lawyer's time, and an architect's house plan are simply outrageous. The professions believe that mandatory continuing professional education will be seen by the public as one reason fees for service must be high.

Very few people get the best services performed by the best professionals. There are very few "dream teams" available to the ordinary citizen. To combat public perception of unequal access to quality care and services, education for everybody is mandated. The public should assume that if all are educated, all will be competent in an equal way.

It sounds as if mandatory continuing professional education has been used and abused as a means to protect the professions against public scrutiny and criticism. *The economic, political, and administrative compelling agendas have increased the use of mandatory continuing professional education beyond the criticism leveled against this form of education for the purposes sought.* Government, employers, associations, and higher education have been co-partners in using the classroom as a convenient vehicle to defend the professions against attacks of incompetent and impaired practice.

At continuing education meetings, educators have debated mandatory versus voluntary continuing professional education issue for at least 25 years. I remember well the arguments set forth by the proponents talking about legitimacy, quality, accountability, uniformity, and sponsor control versus the naysayers who fostered freedom of choice, self-directedness, and education directly related to performance outcomes, and professional responsibility. The minute one involves educators in the CPE equation, the programs must sooner or later fit into the educators' paradigm. Historically, a great idea is developed into a noncredit activity sponsored by an individual or group surviving or thriving at the margins of the profession. When the idea has received enough praise and credibility, it is offered in yet another type of noncredit activity sponsored by a mainstream organization. Faculty members in higher education, association executives, and human resource development officers begin the painstaking process of recognizing the importance of the discovery or idea. Upon acceptance, educators are not happy leaving well enough alone. They have to find ways to legitimize the activity from their own paradigm using quality, accountability, and uniformity measures within their educational paradigm to continue the curriculum process. In higher education, the new program is integrated within a graduate education course, later when it has aged sufficiently, it is developed into its own graduate education course, and finally, it is introduced into the undergraduate education program as a new idea or discovery in the field. By this time, the profession's innovators and pacesetters have moved forward and the new program has been labeled a historical archive. In the associations, the educators reluctantly take the new idea and the initial successes experienced at the margins and place the new idea into their own programs which will lead eventually to inclusion in a mandatory CPE activity as it ages into professional acceptance on a large scale. The mandatory activity is said to have "credit" via some kind of continuing education unit designation but can never be transferred into higher education "credit." The new program is offered again and again until the market dries up. Human resource development managers afraid of being outsourced, displaced, or simply ignored are the last group of educators to deal with the new idea. It has to be legitimated by the associations or pioneering higher education institutions before employer based education accepts it. Acceptance places the new idea into some kind of employer based training program. The educators' paradigm is to build a concrete wall around the idea and make it a requirement in higher education, a mandatory program sponsored by the association, or a condition of employment by employer based educators. Anyway you look at it, the idea is doomed to fit into some kind of mandatory activity.

One of the most disturbing facts about mandatory CPE deals with the role of faculty in higher education. Many of the critics of mandatory CPE, sit around the association, employer and government tables as high paid consultants and craft mandatory CPE programs for professional groups. Once these faculty members cash their consultant checks, they begin to write articles criticizing the monster they helped create.

In summary, the dinosaur, the multimillion dollar mandatory continuing professional education enterprise, is alive and well and increasing in importance, sophistication and power.

THE ALTERNATIVE

Episodic live lectures, workshops, and seminars held in exotic vacation areas offered at exorbitant fees have been the trademark of the continuing professional education programs sponsored by professional organizations, higher education institutions, private for profit CPE organizations, and to some extent, employer agencies. In recent years, these "learning" activities have been accredited by respected organizations and have been produced as part of mandatory CPE requirements for recertification, relicensure, or reregistration. To a lesser extent the 1 hour every Tuesday morning lecture will give way to alternative methods of mandatory CPE in the very near future also. What does this alternative look like?

CPE professionals have been exposed to every conceivable curricular trend, teaching method, and learning style inventory available. For years, we have been bombarded with concepts such as teacher-focused, learning-centered, self-directed, group-oriented, problem-based, performance audit, customer/client-focused, and distance education. Newer concepts such as technology delivery, the virtual curriculum, and just-in-time education are making the rounds. We have tried every conceivable method and we continue to look for the method that will provide the best results. The problem is not curricular or methods centered. The problem is in the area of financial management.

CPE professionals have not invested in the presentation components in their programs. More money is spent on luncheons and dinners or housing and tours in a CPE program than on preparing presentations for professionals. More money is spent on promotion and faculty honoraria than on the presentation of subject matter. Room rental and speaker travel costs exceed costs associated with program material preparation. And lastly more money is treated as "profit" than is provided for the presentation of appropriate content. CPE professionals have to reconsider the reallocation of funds within program budgets to present materials in a way that directs the use of knowledge and skills into professional practice. A new financial management paradigm must be created that takes CPE personnel from the budget page to the content presentation page. As most of you know, CPE professionals start planning meetings with their organizational budget form. This budget form is now a lock step CPE professional's paradigm that creates episodic lecture/slide-based presentations. If we could divert 10% of the promotion, room rental, faculty fees and travel, meal expenses, travel and room costs into the development of appropriate learning activities, we would begin to have an impact on practice-based educational interventions. Given the reallocation of funding, this new alternative would begin to take shape.

Immediate changes in curriculum would occur. The shift from the European model of teacher as the extensive source of knowledge would dramatically shift to eclectic sources of knowledge placed within a learner-centered environment. If this shift is done, there would be no need for a big room at a fancy hotel, no need for faculty to present in a live format, and no need for housing and food service. Systematic CPE will take on new meaning. The alternative will still be systematic but will be systematic from the learners' point of view and not from the sponsors' point of view.

People could subscribe to a two-way interactive pay per view basis and lock into information and activities that are important to the learner or the learning organization. Every CPE professional knows about the curricular models and instructional/learner methods that need to be used to create this alternative model; however, very few have conceptualized the problem as one of reallocating funds within the program budgets to begin the process of moving the dinosaur to the modern age. An eclectic model utilizing just-in-time, learner-centered, practice-based, technology-driven environments is the plan for the future. This eclectic model will not replace the dinosaur but it will change the focus of CPE from episodic live lectures held in vacationland to programming more responsive to the needs of the practitioner, the employer and the society at large. Put it together, your professional customers will love it.

REFERENCES

Candy, P. C. (1995). Physician teach thyself: The place of self-directed learning in continuing medical education. *The Journal of Continuing Education in the Health Professions, 15,* 80-90.

Cervero, Ronald M. (1988). *Effective continuing education for professionals,* San Francisco: Jossey-Bass.

Houle, C. O., (1980). *Continuing learning in the professions.* San Francisco: Jossey-Bass.

LeGrand, Barbara F. (1992, summer). A change of heart: Continuing professional education should be mandatory. *New Directions for Adult and Continuing Education. 54.* San Francisco: Jossey-Bass.

Miller, George E. (1967). Continuing education for what? *Journal of Medical Education, 42* (7), 320-326.

Pajor, Michael (1985). Comparative analysis of licensee attitudes toward continuing education in real estate. (Doctoral Dissertation, Northern Illinois University) Department of Learning, Development, and Special Education. LD2411.6.P1511985.

Phillips, L. E. (1987). Is mandatory continuing professional education working? *Mobius. 7* (1), 57-64.

Young, W. H. (1980, winter). Mandatory continuing professional education: The bright side of the picture. *The Journal of the Illinois Adult and Continuing Educators Association, Inc. Setting the Pace,* 1:1.

Young, W. H., (1980-1981). Mandatory continuing professional education: The bright side of the picture. *Yearbook of Adult and Continuing Education,* (6th ed.). Marquis Media, 526-530.

Part II
The Role of Continuing Professional Education in Resolving Critical Issues Facing Selected Professions

10

Continuing Medical Education in Transition: The Evolution of a New Paradigm

Katherine Pijanowski

A DEFINITION OF CONTINUING MEDICAL EDUCATION

Individuals seeking medical attention in this country are likely to interact with an entire team of health care professionals. While continuing education for all health care professionals is critical, this chapter will focus upon continuing medical education which is specifically designed for the physician. The American Medical Association (AMA) has defined continuing medical education (CME) as those

> Educational activities which serve to maintain, develop, or increase the knowledge, skills, professional performance and relationships that a physician uses to provide services for patients, the public, or the profession. The content of CME is that body of knowledge and skills generally recognized and accepted by the profession as within the basic medical sciences, the discipline of clinical medicine, and the provision of health care to the public.—(AMA, 1993)

Not all learning activities in which physicians engage are considered to be CME by the AMA; educational pursuits which are not directly linked with the medical profession are not considered continuing medical education.

A number of mechanisms by which a physician may continue his or her professional education exists. Journal reading, collaboration with colleagues, interactions with pharmaceutical or equipment representatives, utilization of audiotapes, videotapes, or computer software, research for lecturing or writing and attendance of formal educational activities all constitute continuing professional education for physicians. The term CME, however, typically connotes the attendance of a formal educational activity which has been coordinated by a traditional CME provider (Davis & Mazmanian, 1994). According to Richards and Cohen (1980), a formal CME activity consists of a series of programs, lasting for up to five days, frequently requiring travel. The evolving CME paradigm presented in this chapter suggests that activities beyond those which occur in a formal setting should be incorporated into an expanded conception of CME.

THE CME ENTERPRISE

There are approximately 2,500 CME providers in the United States (Wentz & Harrison, 1994); provision of CME may or may not be the provider's primary organizational function. Medical schools, specialty medical societies, voluntary health organizations, state medical associations, hospitals, not-for-profit foundations and for-profit corporations are among those organizations which provide CME for physicians.

Providers of CME may or may not be accredited. A study conducted by Slotnick, Lichtenauer, and Raszkowski (1995) indicated that physicians prefer to attend CME activities which are offered by accredited providers.

ACCREDITATION OF CME SPONSORS

In the United States, organizations which sponsor CME activities can voluntarily apply for accreditation from the Accreditation Council for Continuing Medical Education (ACCME). Established in 1981, the ACCME comprises representatives from the following seven organizations:

1. The American Board of Medical Specialties
2. The American Hospital Association
3. The American Medical Association
4. The Association of American Medical Colleges
5. The Association for Hospital Medical Education
6. The Council of Medical Specialty Societies
7. The Federation of State Medical Boards

The secretary of the Department of Health and Human Services appoints a federal representative to serve on the council each year. Additionally, a public representative is elected by the council to participate for a one year period (Maitland, 1992).

The Accreditation Review Committee, which consists of two representatives selected by each of the seven member organizations, evaluates applications for accreditation and makes recommendations for accreditation periods to the council. The accreditation process was established to promote quality within educational programs and integrity within those institutions providing the CME programs (Maitland, 1992). The standards for quality and integrity used by the ACCME and state medical associations to determine eligibility for and status of accreditation are outlined in the *Essentials and Guidelines for Accreditation of Sponsors of Continuing Medical Education* (ACCME, 1984). In order to initially receive or to maintain accreditation, institutional providers of CME must comply with each of the following *Essentials:*

Essential 1:   The sponsor shall have a written statement of its continuing medical education mission, formally approved by its governing body.

Essential 2:   The sponsor shall have established procedures for identifying and analyzing the continuing medical educational needs and interests of prospective participants.

Essential 3:   The sponsor shall have explicit objectives for each CME activity.

Essential 4:   The sponsor shall design and implement educational activities consistent in content and method with the stated objectives.

Essential 5:   The sponsor shall evaluate the effectiveness of its overall continuing medical education program and of its component activities and use this information in its CME planning.

Essential 6:   The sponsor shall provide evidence that management procedures and other necessary resources are available and effectively used to fulfill its continuing medical education missions.

Essential 7:   The sponsor shall accept responsibility that the *Essentials* are met by educational activities which it jointly sponsors with nonaccredited entities.

Applicants for accreditation at the national level initially receive a 2-year provisional status; the provisional status may be extended for a maximum of 2 additional years. Institutions unable to achieve full accreditation status after a four year provisional period will return to a nonaccredited status. Periods of accreditation vary in length according to the extent to which compliance with the *Essentials* has been achieved. The maximum period of accreditation is 6 years; typically, institutions which are in good standing are awarded a four-year accreditation period. Institutions achieving less than substantial compliance with the *Essentials* are accredited for fewer than four years. In those instances where compliance with the *Essentials* is insufficient, a probationary accreditation status is granted.

The ACCME awards institutional providers of continuing medical education an accreditation status allowing them to offer programs for CME credit which is recognized by the American Medical Association (AMA). Physicians intending to earn the Physician's Recognition Award (PRA), awarded by the AMA, are likely to seek out CME experiences which will yield credit applicable to award requirements. Other professional groups, including the American Academy of Family Physicians, the American College of Preventive Medicine, and the Emergency Physician Group, have also established similar criteria for the award of CME credit. A study conducted by Slotnick et al. (1995) indicated that most significant factor in a physician's decision to participate in a CME activity was the availability of CME credit.

THE PHYSICIAN AS LEARNER

Physician characteristics such as age, speciality, stage of career, and practice setting influence the extent to which one engages in CME activities (Slotnick et al., 1995; Lockyer et al., 1994; Moore, Bennett, et al., 1994). Similar indicators of participation in continuing education are reported in the adult education literature; Merriam and Caffarella (1991) noted that adult participation in continuing education activities could be correlated with select characteristics including prior education, age, and professional employment status.

Physicians choose to engage in CME for a number of reasons. Research conducted by Grotelueschen (1985) identified five main reasons for physician participation in continuing education:

1. To maintain current abilities;
2. To provide better health care services to patients;
3. To be challenged by colleagues in the field;

4. To maintain an identity within the medical profession; and

5. To enhance professional security.

Moore, Bennett, et al. (1994) contrasted *reasons* for participation with *purposes* for participation; several studies they cited indicated that the primary *purpose* for physician participation in CME is to remain current with advances in medicine. Other educational purposes reported include validation of previous learning and practices, board preparation, and remediation. Socializing and increasing potential earning power were noted as less important purposes for physician participation in CME, although the study reported by Slotnick et al. (1995) did identify fulfillment of the psychological needs of security, affiliation, and self-esteem as factors motivating physician participation in CME.

Slotnick et al. (1995) described criteria used by physicians to select CME activities. Physicians reportedly prefer to attend educational programs which award CME credit; CME credit is often required to renew licensure, to maintain association memberships, to attain fellowship status in specialty societies, and to establish and maintain hospital privileges. Additionally, CME credit enables physicians to claim expenses associated with their educational pursuits as a tax deduction.

According to Knowles (1990), adults engage in learning activities to the extent in which they perceive their job performance and/or problem-solving ability will be favorably enhanced by the experience. Slotnick et al. (1995) demonstrated that adult learning theory is representative of physicians as learners; physicians prefer to engage in learning activities which enable them to learn about new problem-solving techniques, new standards of practice, and innovative techniques in diagnosis and treatment.

The research conducted by Slotnick et al. (1995), which has been referred to repeatedly in this chapter, resulted in a reconceptualization of CME which characterizes endeavors in continuing education as activities which compete for resources within a physician's professional and personal life. Participation in CME activities is costly to a physician in terms of lost patient revenue as well as the expense associated with program attendance. Physician reliability is taxed by CME participation; the physician is not available to patients and must rely upon colleagues to provide patient care coverage. Finally, attendance of CME activities which require travel puts additional strain upon physician family and personal commitments.

OPERATIONAL DISSONANCE: A CALL FOR TRANSITION

Although CME has been the subject of a significant amount of research activity within the last decade (Wentz & Harrison, 1994), the literature indicates that CME practice has not changed in response to research findings (Moore, Green, et al., 1994). In spite of numerous studies suggesting ways in which the provision of CME could be improved, current CME practices bear an uncomfortable resemblance to the "traditional" practice of CME.

The current system of CME depends upon the number of credit hours earned as the primary outcome measurement of a learning experience. Requirements for the Physician's Recognition Award, established by the AMA, for example, include a prescribed number of credit hours; neither a personal needs assessment, nor an individual learning agenda are required as a means for determining which learning activities might be most appropriate. Many agencies, such as hospitals, state medical licensing boards, medical specialty boards, and specialty societies, have adopted the PRA standards for their own purposes (Maitland, 1992); consequently, a system which rewards "seat-time" rather than learning or improved patient care is perpetuated (Moore, Green, et al., 1994).

Continuing medical education programs tend to be dominated by lecture formats which are episodic in nature rather than reinforcing. Arguably, lecturing continues to be one of the most efficient and effective means of disseminating information (Apps, 1991). A study conducted by Silverberg, Taylor-Vaisey, Szalai, and Tipping (1995) indicated that formal lectures continue to be an appropriate CME format to facilitate knowledge retention. It is important to note, however, that the acquisition of information is not synonymous with learning. Premi (1994) reported that identification and consideration of individual learning needs are rarely components of traditional CME; furthermore, the traditional lecture format emphasizes information transfer rather that the integration of new knowledge into physician practice.

The overdependence upon a lecture format in traditional CME places those physicians who optimally learn through other techniques at a constant disadvantage. Smith (1982) defined learning style as those "preferences, dispositions, and tendencies that influence one's learning" (p. 60). CME activities must be designed to accommodate the diversity in learning style preferences of the physician population served. The traditional approach to CME prompts physicians to base their educational pursuits upon learning opportunities which are available and convenient rather than those which are consistent with personal learning needs, styles, and agendas. Consequently, participation in CME activities tends to be sporadic rather than purposefully planned and cumulative.

While many CME providers directly involve the constituencies they serve in the needs assessment process, this effort provides only a limited opportunity for collaboration between the physician and the CME provider. The adult education literature suggests that more significant learner involvement in the planning process is critical to the provision of a meaningful learning experience. According to Smith (1982), the first condition for the provision of an optimal adult learning experience is inviting and incorporating learner input into the purpose, content, format, and evaluation of the educational program. More than 30 years ago, Miller (1963) recognized the importance of interaction between CME providers and their audience in order to ensure program relevance to practice and to facilitate improvement in physician practices. According to Bennett and Casebeer (1995), "When learners collaborate in defining the clinical question or problem, the desired outcome, and the methods, rate, and sequence of educational experiences, learner satisfaction and the adoption of new knowledge, skills, and attitudes increase" (p. 75).

The provision of educational activities, for many CME providers, is not a primary institutional goal. Operating on a cost-recovery basis or being held accountable for attaining a prescribed profit margin has resulted in an emphasis upon quantity of programs coordinated rather than upon the quality of practice-altering learning experiences. Success is measured in terms of number of courses offered, number of participants registered, number of CME credits awarded, and number of tuition dollars generated (Bennett & Casebeer, 1995). Brookfield's (1986) recount of an "enrollment economy" is strikingly similar to the traditional CME planning model described by Bennett and Casebeer (1995):

> It is an adaptive, reactive enterprise, condemned by its desperate search for students to follow curricular fads and popular fancies irrespective of their educational merit. This search sometimes results in courses and programs of real educational merit in which felt learner needs are met. Often, though, it results in a superficially attractive program that has no lasting educational value. (p. 229)

Interestingly, Moore, Bennett, et al. (1994) characterized "traditional CME" as having a "focus on course production driven by an enrollment economy" (p. 5).

The planning cycle for formal CME activities, particularly those which take the form of an annual conference, prohibits CME providers from addressing the educational needs of their audience in a timely fashion. Evaluation forms from one conference often provide needs assessment data for the planning of a CME event which will not occur for another twelve months. The traditional notion of CME must expand to include those activities which are better able to respond to emerging learner needs more immediately; CME providers must dedicate some of their resources to the development of programs which assist physicians with the identification of personal learning needs which arise in response to the dynamic changes in medicine and technology and support individual learning agendas which allow them to maintain currentness in the practice of medicine.

Bennett and Casebeer (1995) identified lack of impact upon physician performance as the most critical deficiency in the traditional CME model. According to Dixon's (1978) discussion of evaluation criteria for continuing education in the health professions, a CME activity has the potential to influence four increasingly complex and significant outcome levels:

1. Participant satisfaction
2. Increased physician competence
3. Changes in physician practice
4. Enhanced patient care

The literature indicates that traditional CME offerings typically achieve participant satisfaction and occasionally facilitate increases in physician competence. Research conducted by Bertram and Brooks-Bertram (1977), Lloyd and Abrahamson (1979), Haynes and associates (1984), Beaudry (1989), Stein (1990), McLaughlin and Donaldson (1991), and Davis et al. (1992), concluded that participation in traditional CME activities rarely translates into changed physician practice. Unfortunately, there is little evidence linking physician participation in CME with improved health care outcomes (Premi, 1994). It is believed by some that the development of working alliances between quality management and CME systems will provide the mechanism whereby CME will be able to facilitate change in physician behavior (Moore, 1995).

The current system of CME is organized to serve the administrative convenience of providers, regulators, and participants; its utilitarian nature narrowly focuses upon the development of vocational skills and completely neglects the needs of the physician as a lifelong learner (Mazmanian & Duff, 1994). In an address entitled *The Importance of Post-Graduate Study,* Sir William Osler, on July 4, 1900, acknowledged the importance of lifelong learning to the medical profession (McGovern & Roland, 1969). However, the American Medical Association's definition of CME specifically excludes those educational activities which are not professionally oriented; "Continuing educational activities which respond to a physician's nonprofessional educational needs or interests, such as personal financial planning, and appreciation of literature or music, are not CME" (AMA, 1993).

The ever-accelerating pace at which knowledge is created in the medical field suggests that the traditional conception of CME should be expanded to include activities which address a broader range of learner needs. According to Mawby (1986), the unsubstantiated, yet underlying assumption that those individuals who have been certified in the medical profession are prepared to engage in self-directed continuing education, is not entirely accurate. Premi (1994) pointed out that undergraduate medical education and residency training do not provide any instruction in learning how to learn; he further suggested that it therefore seems "presumptuous" to expect physicians to be capable of managing the lifelong learning required by their profession (p. 205).

Smith (1982) described learning how to learn as a phenomenon which involves "processing, or acquiring, the knowledge and skill to learn effectively in whatever learning situations one encounters" (p. 19). According to Jennett and Swanson (1994), physicians who are capable of identifying their own personal practice strengths and weaknesses, locating resources to satisfy their learning needs, and evaluating the quality of care they provide, are "more able to maintain their professional competence" (p. 75). In order to facilitate change in physician practices and to ultimately impact patient care outcomes, the orientation of traditional CME must be modified; the importance of and need for training in learning how to learn must be acknowledged. The introduction of learning how to learn could potentially empower individuals to utilize the CME system to satisfy their own personal lifelong learning needs. Training in learning how to learn will enable physicians to realize more meaning from the formal learning activities in which they engage as well as to learn from their day to day professional experiences.

SELECTED ISSUES CHALLENGING "BUSINESS AS USUAL" CME

Emerging Health Care Issues in the United States

Public concern about the access to health care and the quality and cost of health care services has moved the issue of health care reform to a priority position on the current administration's agenda (Jay & Anderson, 1993). As the United States health care system continues to shift toward a managed-care environment, the practice of medicine and the related system of CME will have to change. A focus on primary care rather than tertiary care, health promotion and disease prevention, cost-effective clinical decision making, and health-care outcomes that improve health status will characterize the transformed health care system (Leist, 1995). The establishment of a nationwide managed care environment will have many implications for CME; educational activities will become learner centered and will respond to individual learning needs. Quality management principles will link CME with measurable outcomes of patient care.

The changing demographics of the individuals practicing medicine *and* the individuals receiving health care services significantly impact the health care system. The female population of physicians in this country has increased at a rate four times faster than that of male physicians (Wentz & Harrison, 1994). The number of physicians participating in group practice increased by 54% between the years 1980 and 1988; the number of physicians engaging in solo practice has dramatically decreased. The average age of physicians is declining; in 1992, 50% of licensed physicians were 44 years old or younger. Demographic information has been linked to participation rates in the literature (Bennett, 1994); Lockyer et al. (1988) determined that CME courses are more frequently attended by younger physicians.

The United States population is expanding continuously because of increased births, improved longevity, and immigration (Pories, Smout, Morris, & Lewkow, 1994). A correlation can be drawn between the aging of the population and increases in health care spending; individuals aged 65 years and older spend three times the national average on health care (Wentz & Harrison, 1994). Individuals who are 85 years and older reportedly spend 7.5 times the national average on health care. The distribution of the population is also changing. According to Pories et al. (1994), the migration of individuals to suburban areas has resulted in the consolidation of health care providers into larger and more comprehensive health care institutions.

The variety of patient health conditions encountered by physicians continues to broaden. Injuries related to trauma and complications associated with acquired immunodeficiency syndrome (AIDS) introduce new challenges to the practice of medicine in urban treatment centers (Pories et al., 1994).

Social conditions introduce unique complexities to the provision of health care in America. Illiteracy, drug use, malnutrition, domestic violence, teenage and childhood pregnancy, and welfare dependency (Pories et al., 1994) are challenges faced by the some of the individuals seeking health care in this country; physicians must be prepared to deal with the contextual issues associated with presenting health issues.

The ethnic composition of the United States is changing. English is not the primary language in all communities. Physician awareness of cultural diversity must be heightened. More important, physicians must be trained to recognize diseases which have an ethnic or cultural component (Pories et al., 1994).

Hospitals and health care organizations are beginning to adopt continuous quality improvement (CQI) techniques to analyze the processes and outcomes of the health care services they provide (Moore, Green, et al., 1994). The primary means by which CQI techniques are being incorporated into the health care system is through the development of practice guidelines. Practice guidelines have been defined as systematically constructed statements which inform physician decision making about appropriate health care for specific clinical circumstances (Kelly & Swartout, 1990).

Development of pharmaceutical products, protocols, procedures, medical technology, and information technology continually advance the heath care profession. At the same time, the rate at which these innovations are introduced challenge the CME provider's ability to provide state-of-the-art education and the physician's ability to remain current in the field. According to Sequeira et al. (1994), CME providers must attend to five issues when instituting new technology:

1. Data must be analyzed to verify the validity and reliability of the technology before broadly introducing it;
2. The utilization of any potentially lethal technology must be taught on a one-on-one basis;
3. Initially, new technology must be introduced to a small num-

ber of physicians; once the original trainees develop competency and confidence, they may share their expertise with colleagues;

4. Credentialing in the use of new technology should be awarded based upon the ability to perform the acquired skill and judgment to perform the skill appropriately; and

5. The Quality Assurance Department must maintain a record of all case histories; documentation of any complications must be included (p. 823).

The extent to which patient care has been effective can be measured by the health status of the patient. Outcomes measure is a tool which can be used to measure and analyze the health status of patients. Data concerning the health status of clients is collected both from patients and from providers. The data is compiled, analyzed, and disbursed to providers for comparison purposes. Outcomes measurement can be undertaken to determine the effectiveness of routine care, prescribed treatment, or alternative interventions (Moore, Green, et al., 1994). The establishment of a profiling system which monitors and reports instances of physician clinical performance and patient medical histories has significant ramifications. Although profiling would enable CME providers to design timely educational interventions and to respond to individual learner needs, the implementation of a regulatory system which makes information regarding physician competence and medical histories public compromises physician and patient confidentiality. Furthermore, the implications for physician and organizational liability have not been thoroughly explored in the literature.

Emerging Issues for the Practicing Physician

The changing environment of health care generates a number of issues for practicing physicians. The managed care approach to health care provides an impetus for those physicians who have been trained and practice in specialized areas of medicine to seek primary care training.

Recertification has become increasingly popular as a means of verifying physician competency. According to Wentz and Harrison (1994), 21 of the 21 boards of the American Board of Medical Specialties have endorsed recertification. Credentialing requirements for clinical privileges, association membership, and employment with managed care organizations continue to escalate.

Continuous quality improvement efforts are characterized by more closely monitored resource appropriation, more conservative management of risk, and heightened physician accountability (Wentz & Harrison, 1994). The increasing demand for physicians to demonstrate their competence in a changing world of medicine suggests that CME providers must continuously adjust to meet the evolving needs of the physician learner.

The Emerging Need for an Integrated Health Care System

Although CME has not yet been addressed by the health care debate (Wentz & Harrison, 1994), education must be considered as a central component of any newly devised or modified system. An integrated health care system which includes CME would ensure that the needs of physicians learners are met. Profiling is a technique which compares the clinical practice patterns of physicians and resulting patient outcomes; an integrated health care system could implement physician profiling not only as a means for assessment of quality improvement, provider performance, and resource appropriation (Jay & Anderson, 1993), but also as a mechanism for conducting an educational needs assessment.

Until recently, due to the diversity and lack of cohesion among CME providers (Jay & Anderson, 1993), CME has not actively contributed to the development of health care policy. To ensure that health care policy is adopted and disseminated by CME providers, that policies which support physician lifelong learning are initiated, and that research will be conducted in the areas of health care policy and CME, it is imperative that CME providers actively contribute to the development of policy as members of an integrated health care system.

The creation of an integrated health care system would enable CME providers to link patient health status to CME intervention. The integration of CME into the health care system would allow CME administrators access to information regarding health care outcomes which might contribute to a more accurate determination of the effectiveness of CME programs.

Emerging Issues in Accreditation

In a session entitled *1995 in Review: Update on New ACCME Policies, Procedures and Interpretations* at the 1996 Alliance for CME

Conference, the Associate Executive Director (Capizzi) of the Accreditation Council for Continuing Medical Education (ACCME) and the Executive Director and Secretary (Kopelow) of the ACCME discussed accreditation issues which surfaced in 1995 and the role the ACCME intends to assume within the evolving CME paradigm. As part of a strategic planning process, ACCME reportedly intends to develop a new accreditation system; this session was the first public presentation of the framework for the proposed system.

A managed care environment would be appropriately served by the proposed system; accreditation will become oriented toward health care outcomes. Accordingly, CME will become a "self-directed enterprise" wherein providers will have the capacity to respond to the needs of their own physician learner populations. Learner needs will be met with a variety of educational formats including distance learning and personalized educational plans; a more holistic approach toward the physician as learner will be undertaken.

CME providers operating within the revised accreditation system will consistently engage in the following activities:

- Identification of learning needs of the target audience;
- Promotion of interaction between learners and educators;
- Provision of feedback to the learners;
- Measurement of quality of educational products in terms of changes in practice;
- Appropriation of organizational resources calibrated to the scope of the educational program; and
- Evaluation of all activities related to the development and delivery of educational programs.

Kopelow indicated that the ACCME will be establishing a mechanism whereby input from all stakeholders may be considered for incorporation into the revised accreditation system. The current accreditation system will remain functional while pilot projects are being undertaken; a means for transitioning from the current system to a revised system will be developed. The ACCME intends to begin implementing the new accreditation system sometime in 1996.

According to Capizzi and Kopelow (1996), the new accreditation system will focus on CME outcomes rather than on the process of CME. The goal to modify the current accreditation system is to facilitate the development of CME programs which encourage change in physician practice and which positively impact the health status of patients served.

BEYOND TRADITION: CREATING A CME PARADIGM FOR THE 21ST CENTURY

The changing environment in which health care is delivered clearly requires that the system which facilitates the continuing education of physicians must also change. A commitment to focus upon changed physician practices and improvement in the health care status of patients served rather than upon the dissemination of scientific data and the accumulation of CME credit will characterize the CME paradigm shift. When the emphasis of CME becomes patient wellness and the ability of the physicians to effect improved states of health, CME will be recognized as a valuable component of the health care system. In order for CME to achieve its intended impact upon physician knowledge and practice and to ultimately contribute to the well-being of patients served, the manner in which CME activities are conducted must undergo a dramatic transformation.

A Learner-centered Orientation to CME

Continuing medical education activities must assume a learner-centered orientation; the current emphasis upon the process of planning educational activities does little more than perpetuate the myth that "seat time" automatically translates into competence.

The identification of learning needs, learning style preferences, and the subsequent evaluation of learning experiences has not been present in traditional undergraduate, graduate, or CME. The assumption that physicians are capable of directing their own lifelong learning has been perpetuated by the traditional notion of CME. The new CME paradigm must account for and address the need for physicians to learn how to learn. Smith (1982) described "learning-how-to-learn" training as a process which prepares individuals to be integrally involved in the planning , management, and evaluation of their own lifelong educational pursuits. Similarly, Premi (1994) defined individualized CME as "the educational practice that assists and enhances the learning process by which a physician conceives, plans, implements, completes, and evaluates CME activities designed to maintain and enhance his or her medical practice competency" (p. 203).

Fox, Davis, and Wentz (1994) proposed that the design and function of CME should emerge from what is understood about how physicians change and learn. These authors indicated that in order to elicit changes in physician behavior, CME planners must attend to the issues of frequency, intensity, and timing of an educational intervention. Additionally, Fox et al.(1994) reported that those interventions which are linked to feedback derived from actual practice have more potential for effecting changes in performance. Finally, the degree to which the proposed change is consistent with personal goals greatly impacts the likelihood of the change occurring (Mann, 1994).

Continuing medical education must be driven by the learning needs of its constituents; physicians must be actively involved in the identification of personal learning needs. In the future, the cost and availability of speakers will no longer determine educational agendas. As members of an integrated health care system, data generated through chart review and chart stimulated recall (Jennett et al., 1995), among other techniques, will be available to CME providers; data about clinical performance, patient outcomes, and resource utilization will facilitate the coordination of education which is individually (as well as) organizationally, and professionally relevant.

The diversity among learners will be acknowledged. CME will no longer adhere to a "one-size-fits-all" model. Blake et al. (1995) echoed the significance of recognizing differences in learning styles; the identification and accommodation of individual learning style preferences establishes a climate which is conducive to learning. A variety of educational experiences will be made available to physicians; innovations in educational formats will allow individuals to engage in educational pursuits which accommodate personal learning styles.

The current dichotomy which exists between formal and informal CME activities will disappear. Self-directed learning activities such as journal reading, collaboration with colleagues, interaction with pharmaceutical representatives, conducting research and writing, utilization of self-assessment instruments, and the employment of medical informatics must be universally valued as legitimate CME activities. Mann and Ribble (1994) reported that a survey commissioned by the (ACCME) indicated that the primary criterion for choosing to attend a CME activity was the granting of CME credit. Therefore, legitimatizing self-directed learning projects will likely accelerate the designation of CME credits for nonformal, CME activities (Candy, 1995).

Research indicated that multiple sources of corroborating information are required before a physician will employ a change in clinical practice (Lockyer, Mazmanian, Moore, Harrison, & Knox, 1994). Educators will assist physicians with the development of individual educational plans utilizing multiple resources as a means for purposefully directing personal lifelong learning agendas. Equally as important, CME providers must appropriate increasing percentages of their resources to the development and support of self-directed, informal, learning activities.

Learning from Experience

Learning from experience, in the case of physicians, involves learning which is realized from the practice of medicine rather than from a instructor-directed activity. According to Mast and Davis (1994), learning from experience is critical to a physician's ability to accommodate changes in clinical practice. The CME of the future will acknowledge medical practice as a legitimate context for learning; physician on-the-job experience will be incorporated into the CME paradigm. Schön's (1987) model of "reflective practice" can be used as a mechanism for assisting physicians to learn from their experience in a clinical setting (Fox & Craig, 1994).

The first stage of Schön's model, "knowing-in-action, "refers to that knowledge which is embedded and which can be accessed with very little effort. The second step is characterized by the presentation of an unusual case resulting in "surprise." When a physician encounters a unique situation which cannot be readily explained by knowing-in-action, he or she progresses to the third level of Schön's model, "reflection-in-action."

Reflection-in-action is characterized by a reconstruction of the condition or event with the intent of resolving the problem. Based upon the conclusions drawn from reflection-in-action, the physician will determine a plan of action such as prescribing a medication, conducting a procedure or recommending a treatment in order to resolve the clinical dilemma; Schön termed the fourth stage of the model the "experiment."

The final stage of Schön's model allows that which has been learned from a unique clinical experience to be evaluated and to become assimilated into one's store of knowledge. Accordingly, the physician reflects upon how the dilemma was analyzed and the steps taken to resolve it; the physician engages in "reflection-on-action." Reflection-on-action allows the physician to establish a new frame of reference which can be utilized in future patient encounters; the learning which has occurred as a result of the encounter with the unique patient condition will enable the physician to draw upon a broader knowledge base the next time that he or she engages in knowing-in-action.

Reflection upon practice as a mechanism for learning is a skill that can be developed (Fox & Craig, 1994). A study undertaken by Campbell et al. (1995) invited physicians to use a journal to maintain a record of their CME activities. Physicians were asked to identify issues addressed by CME activities, CME formats utilized, and the outcomes of engaging in each CME activity. The authors concluded that keeping a journal assists physicians to reflect upon their patient care activities. Hoftvedt and Mjell (1993) suggested the formation of peer review groups as a means for collectively engaging in reflection on practice. Physicians were able to heighten their self-awareness of clinical strengths and weaknesses as a result of asking colleagues the question, "What could I have done differently?" (p. 237). Formal training in becoming a "reflective practioner" must be incorporated into the CME of the future so that physicians may more effectively learn in the informal but valuable educational context of the clinical practice setting.

The CME Educator as a Facilitator of Change

Continuing medical education activities no longer will consist of a unidirectional dissemination of information which is never integrated into the provision of heath care services; the role of CME educators will be to guide the transfer of newly acquired knowledge and skills into practice. Educators will assume the role of facilitator; a variety of techniques will be implemented to foster physician learning.

Although it is likely that didactic sessions will continue to be utilized in a number of instances; context rather than convenience must determine the choice of instructional methodology. Examples of methodological alternatives include the use of journals, academic detailing, computer-aided instruction, including interactive modalities, educational influentials, simulations, role plays, electronic reminders, and standardized patients.

Research undertaken by Scott (1994) suggested that the immediate feedback yielded by computer-aided instruction supports its use as a CME delivery method. Parker and Mazmanian (1992) encouraged CME providers to consider the use of learning contracts as a way of maximizing the learning realized from traditional seminars. According to Jennett and Pearson (1992), learning contracts typically involve a one- to three-year commitment to participate in a variety of learning activities under the supervision of a mentor. Nicol (1995) similarly recommended the use of portfolio learning, also under the guidance of a mentor, as a way to ensure that CME is relevant and meaningful.

A study conducted by Silverberg et al. (1995) determined that lectures may be appropriately used as an instructional methodology when the educational objective is knowledge retention. However, lectures which incorporate the utilization of audience response systems and touch pad technology can render even the largest CME didactic sessions interactive (Blandford & Lockyer, 1995).

Traditional CME has been characteristically limited in terms of access, convenience, and relevance. According to a study conducted by Lott (1995), physicians in rural areas tend to be at a disadvantage in securing state-of-the-art information about medical innovations in techniques, treatment, and therapy. Distance learning formats of the future will ensure the accessibility and relevance of CME. As a result of a study developed and produced by the Virginia Hospital Television Network of the Office of Medical Education at the Medical College of Virginia/Virginia Commonwealth University, Hampton, Mazmanian, and Smith (1994) concluded that videoconferencing may be a valuable format for CME for physicians located in geographically isolated areas. Telemedicine (consultation and diagnosis using telecommunications), teleradiology, (analysis of transmitted medical images), and desktop medical conferencing will enable physicians located in even the most remote areas to access late-breaking information.

New Skills Required by CME Professionals

The evolution of a new CME paradigm is accompanied by the need for CME professionals to develop a more sophisticated skill set. A survey conducted by Casebeer et al. (1995) identified three areas in which CME professionals of the future will need to develop skills and knowledge: educational technology, self-directed learning, and quality improvement. Given the implications of the predicted institution of a national managed health care system, the identification of these concepts as targeted areas in which CME professionals should develop expertise is not surprising.

Changes in the Environment
Generate New Educational Needs

The impending managed care environment will generate unique physician learning needs. CME activities which address wellness and patient education will be offered in response to an emphasis on preventive medicine. Physician-specialists may need retraining in the provision of primary care services (Wentz & Harrison, 1994), although research indicates that this proposition may be resisted (Bing-You et al., 1995). Education concerned with managed care and integrated delivery systems will help physicians to cope with the changing environment of health care. The expectation that the new health care system will comprise multiple health care professionals functioning as a team will be met with the coordination of educational offerings devoted to teambuilding in the health care environment.

The Incorporation of Continuous Quality Improvement

The application of a continuous quality improvement model to the provision of health care will be reflected in CME. Defined as "a structured approach for creating organization-wide participation in planning and implementing an organization's operations to guarantee that high quality products and services are provided" (Moore, 1995), quality management will seek to reduce variations which occur in the processes associated with the practice of medicine.

According to Moore, Green, et al. (1994), quality improvement teams will be formed for the purpose of examining processes which resulted in patient outcomes assessed as being less than satisfactory. Consequently, practice guidelines will be revised or newly developed and evaluated using statistical process control techniques. Acceptable practice guidelines will be disseminated throughout the medical community utilizing a variety of instructional methodologies, including journals, newsletters, conferences, and distance learning techniques. According to Lockyer (1994), if clinical practice guidelines are going to result in changed practices, physicians must be introduced to the guidelines; further, the physician must be reminded to utilize the guidelines and the implementation of appropriate guidelines must be reinforced.

Alternative Models for the Provision of CME

Increased physician learner needs and shrinking CME provider resources will likely result in the strategic formation of alliances. Mazmanian and Duff (1994) described a successful Area Health Education Center (AHEC) as a newly established organization in which the education of health care professionals is regionalized; the effective AHEC regularly interacts with the educational and health service delivery institutions within the community to ensure a timely response to emerging educational needs (American College of Physicians, 1995). Gorton et al., (1995) suggested that AHECs be utilized as repositories for practice guidelines; this practice would ensure that clinical guidelines are accessible to all health care professionals.

Mazmanian and Duff (1994) proposed innovative independent learning centers that resemble AHECs but would be characterized by a more centralized financial and performance-based system devoted to studying the following issues: (1) measurable outcomes of CME, (2) accessibility of research to community members, (3) the physician as learner, (4) the value of accreditation, and (5) the accessibility and quality of health care. These investigators believed that such independent learning centers will provide channels for governmental policy monitoring, contribute to the establishment of professional standards of quality, yield valuable research to facilitate decision making by individuals and communities, and assure physicians that their educational needs are being appropriately met.

Lockyer et al. (1994) recommended that alliances should be formed between CME providers and other health care providers to optimally diffuse information regarding medical innovations. These authors further observed that the continuing education of physician, nurses, other health care professionals, patients, and the community be synchronized so that innovations can be uniformly and universally implemented. Indications of a team-oriented approach to health care delivery of the future seem to support this recommendation.

Mann and Ribble (1994) posited that the incorporation of self-directed learning activities into the legitimate CME enterprise will require the establishment of collaborative relationships between CME providers and other resources. Distance learning projects will require the manipulation of information-management systems; physicians will need instruction in how to access and utilize these systems. It is probable the CME providers will need to establish liaisons with librarians and informatics specialists in order to provide their learner constituencies with the services and resources needed.

ETHICAL CONSIDERATIONS FOR THE PROVISION OF CME

The changing health care environment complicates an already complex process of CME planning. Ethical practice is a central issue to planning CME; the CME administrator must constantly decide whose interests will be represented and how those interests will be served.

Medical liability is a central issue to the provision of health care. Liability claims are on the rise and the percentage of total U.S. health expenditures associated with liability costs is escalating (Wentz & Harrison, 1994). The proposed focus of CME upon changes in physician practice and improved patient health status implies a new accountability for CME providers. To date, malpractice suits have not been extensively associated with CME in the literature. The legal implications of a physician-centered CME model committed to improvement of patient care and health status remain to be seen.

Information regarding physician practice patterns, resource appropriation, and patient outcomes would be readily accessible to CME providers in an integrated health care system. If CME providers are dually committed to serve the interests of physicians and those of patients, information regarding physician performance and the need for remediation will likely result in conflict. If the CME provider is to acquire the capability of responding to physician learner needs, access to information regarding performance will be essential. On the other hand, if the CME provider has access to information intimating that physician performance is less than satisfactory, will it become incumbent upon that organization to report deficiencies in physician performance? Issues of confidentiality and informed consumerism are likely to surface.

All adult education program planners must negotiate between competing interests within a context of limited resources and asymmetrical relationships (Cervero & Wilson, 1994). Those stakeholders whose interests must be considered in planning CME include physician learners, CME educators, CME administrators, CME provider leadership, and the public. According to Cervero and Wilson(1995), in order to ethically engage in program planning, one must rigorously preserve democratic process, otherwise, CME programs would always be developed primarily to serve the interests of those in power. Democratizing planning ensures that all people affected by a proposed CME program would have the opportunity to contribute to it. Cervero and Wilson (1995) further argued that the politicking undertaken by CME program planners is ultimately as important as the educational program itself due to the reconstruction of social and political relationships which occurs as a result of negotiation. CME planning is not a neutral process; the power inherent in the activity of planning CME for physicians cannot be ignored. CME administrators must apply their knowledge and relationships in order to address the needs of their learner population and the health care issues of those patients served by their constituency.

THE EVOLUTION OF A NEW CME PARADIGM

It is clear that the primary focus of the new CME paradigm will be to improve patient health care through the facilitation of change in physician practice. In order to facilitate improved patient care, CME providers must place the physician as learner at the center of CME planning. The learner will actively assume responsibility for the identification of learning needs and the management of a personal lifelong learning agenda. The new CME paradigm will promote and provide the opportunity for the acquisition of skills needed to engage in self-determined, self-regulated CME.

In contrast to operating as a neutral coordinator of irrelevant learning activities, the CME provider will act as an agent for change by promptly responding to the educational needs of the learner population. Accreditation will no longer serve as a mechanism for monitoring the administration of CME; it will provide a framework for CME operations which are committed to knowledge integration, changed practice, and improved patient care outcomes.

CONCLUSION

As CME providers become recognized as components of an integrated health care system, information regarding *changes* in clinical performance, patient outcomes, and resource utilization will become accessible. The difficulty will lie in trying to attribute these changes to any specific CME activity. The pivotal issue driving the described paradigm shift in CME is the commitment by CME providers to place the patient, as well as the physician learner, at the center of the educative process. The enterprise will no longer exist as an isolated, ineffectual, albeit revenue-generating, activity. Continuing medical education will become a dynamic force within an integrated health care system; transformational, action oriented, lifelong learning will characterize the CME paradigm of the future.

REFERENCES

American College of Physicians. (1995). Rural primary care. *Annals of internal medicine, 122* (5), 380–390.

American Medical Association. (1993). *The Physician's Recognition Award: 1993 Information Booklet*. Chicago: American Medical Association.

Apps, J. W. *Mastering the teaching of adults*. (1991). Malabar, FL: Krieger.

Beaudry, J. S. (1989). The effectivenss of continuing medical education: A qualitative Syntheses. *Journal of Continuing Education in the Health Professions, 9,* 285–307.

Bennett, N. (1994). Developmental perspectives in learning. In D. A. Davis & R. D. Fox (Eds.), *The physician as learner: Linking research to practice.* Chicago: American Medical Association.

Bennett, N. L., & Casebeer, L. L. (1995). Evolution of planning in CME. *The Journal of Continuing Education in the Health Professions,* 15, 70–79.

Bertram, D. A., & Brooks-Bertram, P. A. (1977). The evaluation of continuing medical education: A literature review. *Health Education Monograph,* 5, 330–362.

Bing-You, R. G., Wennberg, D. E., & Crichton, J. E. (1995). Retraining specialists for primary care: Exploring issues at one academic medical center. *The Journal of Continuing Education in the Health Professions,* 15, 23–30.

Blake, G., Montgomery, D., Walley, E., Beebe, D., & Replogle, W. (1995). Residents' formal knowledge acquisition and preferred learning styles. *Family Medicine,* 27, 35–38.

Blanford, L., & Lockyer, J. (1995). Audience response systems and touch pad technology: Their role in CME. *The Journal of Continuing Education in the Health Professions,* 15, 52–57.

Brookfield, S. D. (1986). *Understanding and facilitating adult learning.* San Francisco: Jossey-Bass.

Campbell, C., Parboosingh, J. T., Fox, R. D., & Gondocz, S. T. (1995). Diary use for physicians to record self-directed continuing medical education. *The Journal of Continuing Education in the Health Professions,* 15, 209–216.

Candy, P. C. (1995). Physician teach thyself: The place of self-directed learning in continuing medical education. *The Journal of Continuing Education in the Health Professions,* 15, 80–90.

Capizzi, S. A., & Kopelow, M. (1996, January). "1995 In review: Update on new ACCME policies, procedures and interpretations. Orlando, FL: Presentation at the 1996 Alliance for Continuing Medical Education Annual Conference.

Casebeer, L., Jay, S., Leist, J., Brink, T., & Miller, V. (1995). Skills and knowledge needed by the CME professional in the twenty-first century. *The Journal of Continuing Education in the Health Professions,* 15, 227–230.

Cervero, R. M., & Wilson, A. K. (1995). Responsible planning for continuing education in the health professions. *The Journal of Continuing Education in the Health Professions,* 15, 196–202.

Cervero, R. M., & Wilson, A. L. (1994). *Planning Responsibly for Adult Education.* San Francisco: Jossey-Bass.

Davis, D. A., Thomson, M. A., Oxman, A. D., & Haynes, R. B., (1992). Evidence for the effectivenss of CME: A review of 50 randomized controlled trials. *JAMA, 268,* 1111–1117.

Davis, D., Lindsay, E., & Mazmanian, P. (1994). The effectiveness of CME interventions. In D. A. Davis & R. D. Fox (Eds.), *The physician as learner: Linking research to practice.* Chicago: American Medical Association.

Dixon, J. (1978). Evaluation criteria in studies of continuing education in the health professions: A critical review and a suggested strategy. *Evaluation of the Health Professions, 1,* 47–65.

Essentials and guidelines for accreditation of sponsors of continuing medical education for physicians. (1984). Lake Bluff, IL: Accreditation Council for Continuing Medical Education.

Fox, R., & Craig, J. (1994). Future directions in research on physicians as learners." In D. A. Davis & R. D. Fox (Eds.), *The Physician as learner: Linking research to practice.* Chicago, IL: American Medical Association.

Fox, R., Davis, D., & Wentz, D. (1994) The case for research on continuing medical education. In D. A. Davis & R. D. Fox (Eds.), *The physician as learner: Linking research to practice.* Chicago: American Medical Association.

Gorton, T. A., Cranford, C. O., Golden, W. E., Walls, R. C., & Pawelak, J. E. (1995). Primary care physicians' response to the dissemination of practice guidelines. *Archives of Family Medicine, 4* (2), 135–142.

Groteleuschen, A. D. (1985). Assessing professionals' reasons for participating in continuing education." In R. M. Cervero & C. L. Scanlan (Eds.), *Problems and prospects in continuing professional education.* New Directions for Continuing Education, *27.* San Francisco: Jossey-Bass.

Hampton, C. L., Mazmanian, P. E., & Smith, T. J. (1994). The interactive videoconference: An effective CME delivery system. *The Journal of Continuing Education in the Health Professions, 14,* 83–89.

Haynes, R. B., Davis, D. A., McKibbon, A., & Tugwell, P. (1984). A critical appraisal of the efficacy of continuing medical education. *JAMA, 251,* 61–64.

Hoftvedt, B. O. & Mjell, J. (1993). Referrals: Peer review as continuing medical education. *Teaching and Learning in Medicine, 5* (4), 234–287.

Jay, S. J., & Anderson, J.G. (1993). Continuing medical education and public policy in an era of health reform. *The Journal of Continuing Education in the Health Professions, 13,* 195–209.

Jennett, P. A.,& Pearson, T. G. (1992). Educational responses to practice-based learning: Recent innovations in medicine. *New Directions for Adult and Continuing Education,* no. 53. San Francisco: Jossey Bass.

Jennett, P. A., Scott, S.M., Atkinson, M.A., Crutcher, R.A., Hogan, D B., Elford, R. W., Maccannell, K. L., & Baumber, J. S. (1995). Patient charts and physician office management decisions: Chart audit and chart stimulated recall. *The Journal of Continuing Education in the Health Professions, 15,* 31–39.

Jennett, P. A., & Swanson, R. W. (1994). Traditional and new approaches to CME: Perceptions of a variety of CME activities. *The Journal of Continuing Education in the Health Professions, 14,* 75–82.

Kelly, J. T., & Swartout , J. E. (1990). Development of practice parameters by physician organizations. *QRB, 15,* 54–57.

Knowles, M. (1990). *The Adult Learner: A Neglected Species.* Houston, TX: Gulf Publishing Company.

Leist, J. C. (1995). The alliance and continuing medical education face transition. *Almanac,* 1995,*17* (12),1.

Lloyd J. S., & Abrahamson, S. (1979). Effectiveness of continuing medical education: A review of the evidence. *Evaluation of Health Professions, 2,* 251–280.

Lockyer, J. (1994). Clinical Practice guidelines and the CME office. *The Journal of Continuing Education in the Health Professions, 14* 46–55.

Lockyer, J., Mazmanian, P., Moore, D., Harrison, A., & Knox, A. (1994). The adoption of innovation. In D. A. Davis and R. D. Fox (Eds.), *The physician as learner: Linking research to practice.* Chicago: American Medical Association.

Lott, D. R. (1995). Obstacles to self-paced learning for rural physicians. *The Journal of Continuing Education in the Health Professions, 15,* 203–208.

Maitland, F. (1992). Accreditation of sponsors and certification of Credit. In A. B. Rosof & W. C. Felch, (Eds.), *Continuing medical education: A primer.* New York: Praeger.

Mann, K. V. (1994). Educating medical students: Lessons from research in continuing education. *Academic Medicine, 69,* (1), 41–47.

Mann, K., & Ribble, J. (1994). The role of motivation in self-directed learning. In D. A. Davis & R. D. Fox (Eds.), *The physician as learner: Linking research to practice.* Chicago: American Medical Association.

Mast, T., & Davis, D. (1994). Concepts of competence. In D. A. Davis & R. D. Fox (Eds.), *The physician as learner: Linking research to practice.* Chicago: American Medical Association.

Mawby, R. G. (1986). Lifelong learning and the professional, *Mobius, 6,* 35–39.

Mazmanian, P., & Duff, W. (1994). Beyond accreditation and the enterprise of CME: An alternative model linking independent learning centers and health services research. In D. A. Davis & R. D. Fox (Eds.), *The physician as learner: Linking research to practice.* Chicago: American Medical Association.

McGovern, J. P., & Roland, C. G. (1969). *William Osler: The continuing education.* Springfield, IL: Thomas.

McLaughlin, P. J., & Donaldson, J. F. (1991). Education of continuing medical education programs: Selected literature, 1984–1988. *Journal of Continuing Education in the Health Professions, 11,* 65–84.

Merriam, S. B., & Caffarella, R. S. (1991). *Learning in adulthood.* San Francisco: Jossey-Bass.

Miller, G E. (1963). Medical care: Its social and organizational aspects: The continuing education of physicians. *New England Journal of Medicine, 269.6,* 295–299.

Moore, D., Bennet, N., Knox, A., & Kristofco, R. (1994). Participation in formal CME: Factors affecting decision-making. In D. A. Davis & R. D. Fox (Eds.), *The physician as learner: Linking research to practice.* Chicago: American Medical Association.

Moore, D. E., Green, J. S., Jay, S. J., Leist, J C., & Maitland, F. M. (1994). "Creating a new paradigm for CME: Seizing opportunities within the health care revolution." *The Journal of Continuing Education in the Health Professions, 14,* 4–31.

Moore, D. E. (1995). "Moving CME closer to the clinical encounter: The promise of quality management and CME." *The Journal of Continuing Education in the Health Professions, 15,* 135–145.

Nicol, F. (1995). Making reaccreditation meaningful. *The British Journal of General Practice: The Journal of the Royal College of General Practioners, 45* (395), 321–324.

Parker, F. W., & Mazmanian, P. E. (1992). Commitments, learning contracts, and seminars in hospital-based CME: Change in knowledge and behavior. *The Journal of Continuing Education in the Health Professions, 12,* 49–63.

Pories, W. J., Smout, J. C., Morris, A., & Lewkow, V. E. (1994). U.S. health care reform: Will it change postgraduate surgical education? *World Journal of Surgery, 18 (5),* 745–752.

Premi, J. (1994). Individualized continuing medical education. In D. A. Davis & R. D. Fox (Eds.), *The physician as learner: Linking research to practice.* Chicago: American Medical Association.

Richards, R. K., & Cohen, R. M. Why physicians attend traditional CME programs. *Journal of Medical Education,* 1980, *55,* 479–485.

Schon, D. A. (1987). *Educating the reflective practioner: Toward a new design for teaching and learning in the professions.* San Francisco: Jossey-Bass.

Scott, C. J. (1994). Applied adult learning theory: Broadening traditional CME programs with self-guided, computer-assisted learning. *The Journal of Continuing Education in the Health Professions, 14,* 91–99.

Sequeira, R., Weinbaum, F., Satterfield, J., Chassin, J., & Mock, L. (1994). Credentialing physicians for new technology: The physician's learning curve must not harm the patient. *The American Surgeon, 60* (11), 821–823.

Silverberg, J., Taylor-Vaisey, A., Szalai, J. O., & Tipping, J. (1995). Lectures, interactive learning, and knowledge retention in continuing medical education. *The Journal of Continuing Education in the Health Professions I, 15,* 231–234.

Slotnick, H. B., Lichtenauer, David F., & Raszkowski, R. R. (1995). "Rethinking continuing medical education." *The Journal of Continuing Education in the Health Professions, 15,* 8–22.

Smith, R. M. (1982). *Learning how to learn: Applied theory for adults.* Englewood Cliffs, NJ: Cambridge Adult Education.

Stein, L. S. (1990). The effectiveness of continuing medical education: Eight research reports. *Journal of Medical Education, 56,* 103–110

Wentz, D., & Harrison, A. (1994). Forces for change in the CME environment. In D. A. Davis & R. D. Fox (Eds.), *The physician as learner: Linking research to practice.* Chicago: American Medical Association.

11

The Lamp Burns Brightly: Trends in Continuing Education for Nursing

Anne M. Devney

INTRODUCTION

As professionals dedicated to human caring, nurses endeavor to fulfill their responsibilities in a manner that demonstrates commitment to quality health care. They recognize their obligation and responsibility to keep abreast of rapid advances in the technology of delivering care. Continuing education (CE) is seen by nurses as an essential means of acquiring new skills and knowledge, as well as updating skills previously learned to improve health care delivery. As a way of meeting this goal, a variety of strategies have been developed over the years including mandatory continuing education in some areas. In addition, some states require evidence of attendance at continuing education programs for relicensure. Today, nurses are now challenged more than ever to seek, analyze, refine, and critically evaluate the application of new knowledge generated by new technology and research in the clinical arena. Continuing education can serve as a survival strategy for those nurses who need to cross-train to improve their chances of job retention. There are ever-increasing ways to choose to deliver and receive continuing education, some of which are designed for nurses who are not located in densely populated geographic or technically rich areas. This chapter is designed to explore the current and potential means by which professional nurses seek, implement, and expand their practicing knowledge and skills.

BACKGROUND

Throughout its history, practitioners have spent much time and effort trying to identify nursing as a separate and unique profession.

As Diers (1991) pointed out, "Nursing does not suffer from lack of attempted definition" (p. 5). She noted the influence of the political and legislative arenas in the world of social change. Simple words and phrases do little to describe or embrace the scope of current professional practice. Continuing to expand on a research and experiential base to describe and explain the art, science, and management of direct health care delivery, nurses have gone from general care of the sick toward ever-increasing medical and nursing specialty roles and expanding responsibilities in administration, education, and research. With the expansion of practice, nurses continue to define, test, and improve upon the established knowledge base.

Despite the fact that the overwhelming majority of nurses continue to be prepared for entry into professional practice at three different levels (hospital diploma programs, associate degree programs, and baccalaureate degree programs), the expansion of the general and technical knowledge base demands that all members of the profession continue educational pursuits in order to maintain and improve their competency in the delivery of patient care. Rath et al. declared, "Nurses have a responsibility to patients, a professional responsibility to organizations, and an individual responsibility to maintain a high level of current and relevant knowledge and skill" (1996, p. 12). If continuing education is designed to improve and maintain competency in practice and the quality of health care (Oliver, 1984; Waddell, 1991), how do nurses continue to seek and test new knowledge? What motivates these professionals? What are the trends? What is in the future to expand one's knowledge base and professional skills?

DeSilets (1995) recently surveyed 866 nurses at a national nursing conference to find out reasons for their participation in continuing education. Five conceptual factors were identified: (1) professional improvement and development; (2) professional service; (3) collegial learning and interaction; (4) personal benefits and job security; and (5) professional commitment and reflection. There was a statistically significant difference between the nurses' responses in relation to their basic nursing education, years in professional service, and length of time in their present position. Baccalaureate prepared nurses rated professional improvement and development, collegial learning and interaction the most influential. Associate degree prepared nurses placed professional service at the top and diploma prepared nurses rated professional service, professional commitment and reflection incentives highest in importance. The shorter the length of time nurses had in their present position, the greater the importance they placed on "continuing education for reasons related to collegial learning and interaction while those in their present positions for the longest periods of time were more concerned with professional commitment and reflection reasons" (p. 207). Knowledge of the various reasons for individual participation in continuing education can be used effectively by program planners and instructional designers to target their audiences.

CURRENT ISSUES

The development of a scientific knowledge base upon which to build nursing care is sought by nurses in administrative, research, education, and practice arenas. Research is undertaken to improve prior knowledge and integrate recent technological developments into the clinical setting. It is difficult to ensure that the results of research by nursing colleagues are received and utilized by administrators, educators, and clinicians. However, continuing education offers a means to translate new information into practical application. Historically, Florence Nightingale conducted research attempting to blend knowledge, practice, and patient care together, but her pioneering efforts of investigation were not continued. Instead, over the years nurses used other, less scientific means to learn, develop skills, and seek new knowledge. Now, as Weiler, Buckwalter, and Titler (1994) observed, "the profession has once again embraced Nightingale's ideals as evidenced by the establishment and increasing stature of the National Institute of Nursing Research" (p. 61) and numerous other vehicles to encourage, nurture and continue research.

How is the knowledge acquired through research introduced into practice? What are the main issues preventing easy assimilation of knowledge into practice by clinicians? This topic was reviewed by Funk, Tornquist, and Champagne (1995) through an extensive meta analysis. They noted barriers to dissemination of research findings into practice to include "lack of awareness of the research . . . insufficient authority to change patient care procedures . . . insufficient time on the job to implement new ideas . . . [and use of] statistical analyses [which] are not understandable" (p. 397). Nurses consistently identified the need for increased support by administrators and colleagues for more time to "review and implement research findings" (p. 399) in an environment which encourages the use, continuation, and evaluation of research.

Continuing education was one of the key factors seen as a means of improving nurses' research utilization by enhancing communication between nurse-colleagues and accessibility to research findings and reports, conferences, and in-service training. With the decreasing availability of health care dollars, providers at all levels are urged to foster research and continuing education in creative ways, including collaborative relationships. Funk et al. (1995) also noted the importance of including research-to-practice concepts early in basic nursing programs so that nurses entering the field have an understanding of how to incorporate research into their practice. They proposed a model to cope with current research-to-practice issues and recommend that dissemination of research findings occur with regularity and using a variety of avenues to increase accessibility, that is, through publication in specialty journals and on-line databases, personal dialogue, during conference-based opportunities, and through institutions of learning. Their recommendations clearly emphasize continuing education as a means to conceptualize and conduct research and to implement research findings into practice.

Cronenwett (1995) described the importance of research utilization and emphasized continuing education and accessibility to research as means of integrating new knowledge into practice. As she noted, "Perusing the journals once a month is not sufficient. Access [to information] involves both the ability to search for and the ability to understand the contents of what is read" (p. 431). She described two models of research dissemination: decision driven and conceptual. The decision-driven models are in place when nurses are able to access and interpret the literature, use integrative research reviews to consult with experts to resolve practice problems, and attend conferences where colleagues can exchange research findings and practice techniques. Conceptual models of research dissemination occur in environments supportive of research utilization. Cronenwett noted that nurses who engage in discussion about research and its applicability to their own practice are more likely to integrate and evaluate new knowledge into their care. Journal clubs, journal accessibility, formation of research committees to assess the relevancy of findings are additional means of incorporating continuing educational strategies into current practice (Cronenwett, 1995). But there are now several modes of delivering continuing professional education. The "information superhighway" is increasingly accessible and nurses are cruising that highway, engaging in dialogue that was once only imagined.

WHAT'S NEW?

As has been noted, continuing education is a long-standing tradition and expectation within the nursing profession. Nevertheless, continuing education in nursing cannot be limited to hospital staff development workshops and sessions. Because nurses practice in a multitude of settings, a variety of approaches and opportunities exist to provide needed educational opportunities. New technologies now permeate traditional delivery of instruction. No longer are nurses limited to passive delivery of information using lectures, correspondence courses, videotapes, audiotapes, or reading texts and journals, interspersed with seminar participation or occasional chats over coffee. Now, multimedia are preferred. In other words, the lessons/programs are designed to take advantage of more than one of the five senses to deliver the content whenever possible. For example, two-way satellite transmission can now enhance conferences, connecting participants in disparate geographical locations, giving them a chance to engage in interactive real-time dialogue. Newer personal computers add sound and motion to instruction. Laser disks can also be added to computer programs bringing exceptionally clear visual enhancement to the subject matter content. Learners can respond to embedded questions using touch screens or a mouse and the program will change according to their answers. Interactive video/laser discs and compact discs—read only memory (CD-ROM) bring exceptional quality, detail, and longevity to individual and group instruction. Programs are available which detail anatomy, physiology, clinical procedures, and communication skills. The capabilities of such technology offer learners opportunities to deal with acute or chronic clinical simulations in a safe, nonthreatening environment. They are given the chance to examine various problem-solving approaches and receive feedback on their choices. Some programs include sensorized manikins as a way to test cognitive and psychomotor skills, such as basic or advanced cardiac life-support.

Individuals can log onto the Internet and the information superhighway, gaining access to thousands of colleagues and other resources such as the National Institute of Health, the Library of Congress, and numerous other databases. Electronic mail or e-mail provides a forum for problem solving and information sharing with colleagues around the world. Questions cover any number of topics including dress codes for college health professionals, cases for discussion, hepatitis B immunization programs, issues of risky student behaviors, tuberculosis screening programs, the pros and cons of melatonin, and new illegal substances being abused.

Designers of education via "virtual reality" strive to put learners into scenarios as real as possible in the hope that simulated practice will translate into actual safe, competent delivery of care. Nurses can take a "trip" on the information superhighway, into cyberspace, and go to the "Virtual Nursing College" (VNC). Offering several areas of discussion and information, the "VNC is a virtual learning and teaching environment that uses concept-resource mapping, multimedia and full access to Internet and virtual reality" (One can get there by using the following Internet address code: FTP.langara.bc.ca/pub/nursing/vnc.htm).

To illustrate this expanding resource, take a look at some areas undergoing development within the VNC: "Project Cybernurse," "Interactive Seminar," "Virtual Clinic—NurseMOO." The "Nursing Practice Seminar II" is being revised "to meet the changing needs of nursing students in the Nursing Seminar of Term IV of the collaborative curriculum. Entering the search term "Nursing" lists accessible related topics such as "The Family—Family related resources from birth onwards," the "Maternal & Child Health Network," "Guide to Clinical Preventive Services," "Virtual Hospital," and "Psychiatry and Psychology." "Nursing Research" including the "Virtual Nursing Research Collaboratory" and a "Qualitative Research Page" is under development and is intended to "make it a link to a database of nursing research, searchable by topic, researcher, etc." (FTP.langara.bc.ca/pub/nursing/vnc.htm, p. 3). What an exciting time to be seeking ways to learn and integrate new information—to witness and be a part of the cutting edge!

In addition to the latest in the electronic world, many educators present several new cognitive possibilities for nurses to deal with the inherent challenge of translating research-based knowledge to safe and effective clinical nursing practice. For example, concept maps are offered as a means of teaching and learning nursing subject content matter in a way that will be meaningful for both the care provider and the receiver. The maps are designed so that participants in basic nursing curricula as well as continuing education/staff development workshops will be "able to link concepts from different domains of knowledge, to what is actually seen and observed in a client care situation" (Daley, 1996, p. 17). It is felt that concept maps serve as an effective "methodology to assess students' thinking" (p. 24) as they go about the nursing process in providing care in the clinical settings. In addition, concept maps are seen as a tool students could use to further demonstrate the blending of theory and practice as they move through the curriculum. Instructors can likewise use the instrument to individualize assignments and "promote conceptual thinking" (p. 25) as students progress from one course to another.

Rath and her colleagues proposed the use of a "four-phase approach to an individualized enhancement program that incorporates job expectations and competencies" (1996, p. 12). Following adult learning principles, the phases consist of assessing learners' needs, developing learning objectives, reviewing learning resources, and evaluation of the experience. This type of approach could result in competency-based outcomes which can be used as a guide congruent with accepted standards of practice and a means of quality assurance.

Another strategy, storytelling, is presented as a method to develop staff members in a long-term care (LTC) facility (Mayers, 1995). Narratives written about aspects of LTC serve as a catalyst to generate meaningful discussion by staff members. Many themes can be illustrated in anecdotes occurring within the LTC facility. Such stories can describe the frustrations and care dilemmas that can occur with situations dealing with memory loss, loneliness, and surviving one's spouse and other family members. Staff members are encouraged to pick up the story materials or take them home and reflect on the scenarios. As Mayers noted, "presenting a story about a problem situation can reduce the problem to manageable components" (p. 281), giving staff members the opportunity to discuss possible answers and alternative ways of managing the situation. Such a technique can be an adjunct to inservice programs that send care givers to classrooms, removing them from the clinical area.

THE IMPACT OF TECHNOLOGY ON KNOWLEDGE ACCESS AND AVAILABILITY

Traditional strategies of continuing education—are they alive and well? Yes, the seminars, conferences, workshops, conversations with colleagues still exist and good things continue to happen in this venue. In each of these areas, participants share information with one another and get immediate feedback on their level of understanding and yet, many still seek greater levels of interactivity. One e-mail respondent reflects the attitude of many colleagues when she wrote, "I am probably not unlike others . . . I read journals, go to professional conferences, continued my higher ed and just finished a master's degree

. . . " (M. Powell, personal communication, February 7, 1996). Such a statement implies the extent to which many professionals go to maintain and/or improve their skills and understanding.

There are many technologies available to deliver instruction to individuals, groups, locally or at a distant site. Educational technology is changing day-by-day and instructional designers strive to use the latest and greatest bells and whistles to present instruction. Bernard Gifford, Ph.D., the Chair and Chief Instructional Officer of Academic Systems Corporation, described a learner-centered courseware at a recent presentation to the National League for Nursing's Council of Baccalaureate and Higher Degree Programs in the fall of 1995. He declared that the success of this model can be attributed to the interactivity offered by technology. Gifford further stated, "I believe that we have to change more than the tools and techniques traditionally used to teach and learn . . . [We] as faculty have to manage more than 'symbol transfer' from a teacher to the student in a 'lockstep' transmission mode" (Garon, 1996, p. 1). Translating abstract concepts into meaningful knowledge and practical skills must be done within the appropriate situational and cultural context. As teachers, learners, instructional designers, and administrators, it is imperative that we look to the creative possibilities offered by the current state-of-the-art technologies. How can practitioners assimilate new information and integrate it into practice? Did the new information make a difference? Is there a change in participants' practice? Can any change be attributed solely to continuing education?

Correspondence courses are a familiar form of distance learning that still offer nurses a way to earn continuing education units. The learner and instructor are at different sites and communication of course content, feedback, and tests to measure achievement of objectives are done by mail. However, even correspondence courses can now take on new meaning. In the past, learners would sign up for a course, receive material in the mail, complete the lessons at their leisure or in a specified time frame, mail them back to the instructor, and then wait for feedback. Unfortunately, the feedback can be a long time in coming and seldom is there any real dialogue with the instructor/expert. It is often difficult to ascertain if the course material is translated from theory into clinical practice. But now, advances in the world of instructional technology provides both learners and instructors many new opportunities.

Nancy Di Mauro, R.N.C., Director of Continuing Education with the American Journal of Nursing Company (AJN), is investigating ways to improve the delivery and interactivity of instruction within the distance educational setting (personal communication, February

22, 1996). The number of individual nurses taking part in continuing education programs for staff development with the AJN has been increasing monthly. Responding to concerns of limited learner and expert interaction, Ms. Di Mauro is working with instructional designers to provide an interactive learning environment using the computer and other technologies. For example, the AJN moved its electronic bulletin board information to the World Wide Web (WWW) and can be accessed using the address "http://www.ajn.org" on the Internet. AJNs educators are now offering different types of continuing education classes using the www as the vehicle. Some of the programs put learners in touch with librarians who give instruction and assignments via e-mail. Learners can download current information from the electronic bulletin board to complete their course work.

"Nursing Rounds" is a home study program that includes actual clinical problems within the hospital setting. A clinical nurse specialist (CNS) "goes on the rounds" with the participants. Learners complete a pretest regarding the problem, go to the "bedside" with the CNS, complete the posttest, and receive feedback to their answers including a bibliography from the CNS. Feedback is tailored to their experience—from novice to expert levels. As of this writing educators and the American Nurse Credentialing Center are seeking objective data to document changes in behavior as a result of the Nursing Rounds and other learning experiences (Di Mauro, personal communication, February 22, 1996).

But the new technologies and the electronic media: how are they being used and by whom? Actually, nurses have been leading the way in technology for several years through collaborative consortia, university-sponsored programs, private foundations, and individual consultants. Computer-assisted instruction (CAI), CD-ROM, and interactive videodisk (IVD) programs are being added to nursing curricula and are used in many ways. Instructors include CAI in conjunction with classroom presentations and as a resource for further learning assignments. Learners use these programs individually and in small groups. In some institutions, learning centers are open daily around the clock. "They sit before a networked computer learning station and are instructed in a variety of formats and languages, including text, graphics, animation, simulation, visualization, etc." (Garon, 1996, p. 3). The number of subjects addressed with this medium grows with the technology and the creativity of program planners and instructional designers. A current listing of available programs can be found in a directory complied by Christine Bolwell, R.N., M.S.N. which is updated annually.

Nurses have been breaking into cyberspace and surfing the net in great numbers. In addition to the AJNs World Wide Web page, nurses log onto "NurseNet—A Global Forum for Nursing Issues." The nurses (and physicians) in college health can enter the College Health Server and pose all kinds of questions, raise issues of concern, and chat with their colleagues. One respondent to the question of continuing education posed on the electronic network stated her wish for a special interest group of occupational health nurses to form on the network (L. Gemmill, personal communication, February 18, 1996). Another stated her hope, "I am very interested in offering the Health Education Electronic Forum [HEEF] as a source for continuing education for nurses. Are there any nurses out there willing to offer CEUs on the HEEF?" (M. Pejsach, personal communication, February 8, 1996). And still another person noted she uses her access to the Internet to "log into MEDLINE to do searches for medical articles. The newest thing that I plan to investigate is obtaining college credits and taking courses over the internet" (M. Powell, personal communication, February 7, 1996).

LEADERSHIP—ITS IMPACT DURING TIMES OF REORGANIZATION AND DWINDLING RESOURCES

Since "competence is used as an outcome for effective education, coping, and development" (Nagelsmith, 1995), continuing education must be strongly encouraged and facilitated by leaders of the profession. Unfortunately, "no definitive model guides nurses in their approach to CE" (Rath et al., 1996). Data suggest that the benefits of CE is more personal than professional with respect to increased competence in delivery of care (del Bueno, 1977; Ferrell, 1988; Oliver, 1984). However, evidence of competence is valued and sought for individual and institutional accreditation. Practitioners who are at risk in terms of skill and knowledge acquisition or maintenance of safe practice of care must be identified. This, as Nagelsmith noted, is the "paramount responsibility of the profession as a whole, and is of particular concern to those in staff development and basic education roles" (p. 248).

Roles continue to evolve, expand, and present new opportunities and challenges to clinicians, educators, and administrators. Nursing leaders must be willing to step out of and expand "comfort zones" and seek new horizons. Some leaders are more assistive than others. For many, continued education within the work environment is encouraged, but not facilitated and yet, the need is present both on an individual and institutional level. For example, concerning the implementation of new physical assessment skills gained by community health nurses, Oliver noted, "There must be a concerted effort by nursing administrators to encourage the integration of physical assessment with the nurses' assessment of client's needs" (1984, p. 134).

Individuals should take part in the assessment, planning, and evaluation of their learning objectives and programs. Comparison of current personal performance to accepted standards of practice can serve as a starting point. Rath et al. note the "Nurse Educational Assessment Program at McMaster University in Hamilton, Ontario" (p. 14) as an "innovative way" to do such an assessment. Using this one-day assessment program, evaluation by nurse peers "using standardized patients, short clinical exams, and multiple choice questions" (p. 14) provide participants with data for improvement and enhancement of practice. Learning objectives are translated into personalized competency-based outcomes. This permits the learner to be in touch with his or her knowledge and skill deficits. Learning resources such as expert consultants, preceptors, mediated instruction, and literature need to be available and readily accessible. As with all effective programs, individuals who take an active part in learning activities will gain the most.

CONCLUSION

Administrators, educators, and clinicians face some challenges to maintain standards of practice, the provision of high quality care, and keeping up with an ever-increasing body of professional and technical knowledge. Adequate time, money, staffing, and resources continue to be major problems. Newer technologies bring the added promise of rapid acquisition of information and yet, practitioners need that precious of resources—time to pursue continuing education, including how to use the new technologies of learning. Access to resources including the Internet and the World Wide Web can facilitate those pursuits. Individuals seek opportunities to prepare themselves for the unexpected in terms of change and dwindling resources. Professional nurses must remain steadfast in the pursuit of continuing education using both established and nontraditional means in order to enhance the quality of patient care. As Oliver put it, "Continuing education is not merely a matter of getting the latest information in the fastest way possible. Ultimately the goal . . . is the improvement of health care through change in the behavior or practice of nurses" (1984, p. 130).

The challenge is before us and nurses are seeking continuing education whether or not it is a requirement. Many nurses are leading the way. A brief "tour" in cyberspace will reveal the dialogue that continues even as you read this chapter: colleagues posing questions, exploring the issues, answering some questions, seeking reassurance, giving feedback, and giving pats on the back. And yet, note the irony of the following observation: of the respondents to the question posed on the Internet (How do you go about continuing education?), less than half replied that they were using the Internet! Enjoy your trips into the world of cyberspace, lifelong learning and continuing education!

EPILOGUE

As a note of interest, I posed the question of continuing education to college health nurses via the electronic mail system (e-mail). Although the question was delivered to 846 organizational sites, only five people replied. The question was also placed on NurseNet and one person replied. The respondents concurred with the usual means of knowledge acquisition: regional and national conferences, correspondence courses, inservice classes with colleagues, and journal articles (J. Barton, personal communication, February 7, 1996; P. Bradley, personal communication, February 8, 1996; M. Pejsach, personal communication, February 8, 1996; & M. Powell, personal communication, February 7, 1996). One respondent was a physician whose staff hold periodic "Interdisciplinary Case Conferences" which are planned because of the importance of the type of diagnostic condition and to "develop closer communication and collaboration between" nurses, physicians, and psychologists (H. Faigel, personal communication, February 8, 1996). Another respondent stated continuing education was mandatory in order to maintain certification in her particular specialty (L. Gemmill, personal communication, February 18, 1996).

REFERENCES

Bolwell, C. (1995). *Directory of nursing software*. (5th ed.). Athens, OH: Fuld Institute of Nursing Education.

Cronenwett, L. (1995). Effective methods for disseminating research findings to nurses in practice. *Nursing Clinics in North America, 30* (3), 429–38.

Daley, B. (1996). Concept maps: Linking nursing theory to clinical nursing practice. *Journal of Continuing Education in Nursing, 27* (1), 17–26.

del Bueno, D. (1977). Evaluation of continuing education workshops for in-service educators. *Journal of Continuing Education in Nursing, 8* (2), 13–16.

DeSilets, L. D. (1995). Assessing registered nurses' reasons for participation in continuing education. *Journal of Continuing Education in Nursing, 26* (5), 202–208.

Diers, D. (1994). What is nursing? *Current issues in nursing* (4th ed.). In J. McCloskey & H. Grace (Eds.), St. Louis: Mosby, 5.

Ferrel, M. J. (1988). The relationship of continuing education offerings to self-reported change in behavior. *Journal of Continuing Education in Nursing, 19* (1), 21–24.

Funk, S., Tornquist, E., & Champagne, M. (1995). Barriers and facilitators of research utilization. *Nursing Clinics of North America, 30*(3), 395–408.

Garon, L. (1996, Winter). Technology is the key to learning. *Open mind, 3* (1), 1, 3.

Mayers, K. (1995). Storytelling: A method to increase discussion, facilitate rapport with residents and share knowledge, among long-term care staff. *Journal of Continuing Education in Nursing, 26* (6), 280–282.

Nagelsmith, L. (1995). Competence: An evolving concept. *Journal of Continuing Education in Nursing, 26* (6), 245–248.

Oliver, S. (1984). The effects of continuing education on the clinical behavior of nurses. *Journal of Continuing Education in Nursing, 15* (4), 132–134.

Rath, D., Boblin-Cummings, S., Bauman, A., Parrott, E., & Parsons, M. (1996). Individualized enhancement programs for nurses that promote compctency. *Journal of Continuing Education in Nursing, 27* (1), 12–16.

Waddell, D. (1991). The effects of continuing education on nursing practice: A meta-analysis. *Journal of Continuing Education in Nursing, 22,* 113–118.

Weiler, K., Buckwalter, K., & Titler, M. (1994). Is nursing research used in practice? In J. McCloskey & H. Grace (Eds.) *Current issues in nursing.* 61–75.

12

Emerging Issues in Social Work: Implications for Continuing Professional Education

Sandra J. Mills

Social work is a profession so interwoven with society that "... what social workers do very much depends on the context of the times ... " (Gibelman, 1995, p. 64). Social work, a profession known by its advocacy for society's poor and disenfranchised groups, has been under assault and greatly challenged, as a result of sweeping changes in policy and attempts to balance the budget.

Social work's dedication to marginalized populations, its involvement in public sector programs and in services such as home visiting, are out of step with government cutbacks. Changes in social, economic, and political conditions, brought about by the 1994 elections, which propelled conservative lawmakers into power, have not been matched since the early inception of social work as a profession. Gibelman asserts that, "The conservative bent of the mid 1990s suggest that the areas of social work practice that were perceived as deeply entrenched and perhaps sacrosanct are indeed vulnerable" (Gibelman, 1995, p. 8).

DEFINITION AND PRACTICE CONTEXT

The most generally accepted definition of social work was adopted in 1970 by the Board of Directors of the National Association of Social Workers (NASW): "Social work is the professional activity of helping individuals, groups, or communities enhance or restore their capacity for social functioning and creating societal conditions favorable to this goal: (NASW, 1973, p. 4).

Social workers serve people of all ages and walks of life, in a variety of practice settings from children's residential facilities to nursing homes. They work in alcohol and drug abuse treatment centers, businesses, correctional facilities, family service agencies, hospitals, mental health clinics, private practice psychotherapy settings, public agencies, schools, and in a vast array of private community-based organizations. Social workers counsel, manage, organize, consult, teach, write, and do research.

> Four aspects of social work distinguish it from other professions: (1) its focus on the environment as a critical factor in creating and solving individual and social problems: (2) its acknowledgement of the importance of history in shaping the lives of people and communities; (3) its respect for people, their strengths, customs, traditions, and problem-solving capacities; and (4) its belief in both the inevitability and the desirability of change. (Reisch, 1995, p. 6)

"A number of factors are converging to change the environment in which social workers practice and the nature of practice itself." Say Strom and Gingerich, "Such influences include the growth of private social work practice, the passage of licensure and vendorship legislation, and the expansion of managed care and other forms of third-party provided services" (1993, p. 78).

Technological changes, including but not limited to the rapid transfer of information, changes in work environments, and the loss of many jobs to these changes are a challenge to social workers and the clients they serve. These challenges, along with those resulting from the major upheavals in the political direction of the country (changes in which the social work profession, through its stewardship of the poor, has a keen interest), represent the most critical outside forces currently facing the profession. The profession's struggle to define itself is the most critical internal issue which continues to challenge social work.

HISTORY

Social work is and has always been a profession with an identity crises. Originally rooted in psychoanalytic psychiatry, social workers turned their skills to the disadvantaged in the 1930s in the wake of the Great Depression. The profession is perhaps best known by the works of its most famous practitioner, Nobel Peace Prize winner, Jane Addams, the first woman ever to receive this distinction. Addams, founder of Hull House in Chicago, popularized the settlement house movement in the United States. This movement provided the framework for social work practice throughout the '30s and '40s.

Many social workers were involved in the conception and implementation of New Deal programs under Roosevelt. Harry Hopkins, known as the chief architect of the New Deal programs, and advisor to Roosevelt, was a social worker; as was Frances Perkins, Secretary of Labor and the first woman to direct a major governmental agency.

> The radicalism of the 1930s gave way in the subsequent decade to a patriotic fervor supporting total mobilization of resources to fight World War II. During the McCarthy era of the 1950s the profession reacted in much the same way as other parts of society: generally, social work became more conservative. This was manifested in a preoccupation with professionalization, the refinement of clinical techniques, and the use of more sophisticated analytic methods. (Specht & Courtney, 1994, p. ix)

Social work again lurched toward radicalism during the anti-war and civil rights movements of the 1960s and 1970s. Psychiatric social work took a back seat to community organization and advocacy during this period, but regained dominance as the clinical social work movement surfaced in the late 1970s.

Sometimes accused of being agents of social control, as a result of their association with public programs; many social workers prefer the prestige of an affiliation with the practice of therapy. In recent years social workers have increasingly turned their attention back to the mental health field. Many entered individual and group private practices, often referring to themselves as psychotherapists rather than social workers. Specht bemoans these events in the preface to his book on the subject:

> Today, a significant proportion of social workers are practicing psychotherapy, and doing so privately, with a primarily middle-class, professional, Caucasian clientele in the 20- to 40-year age group. The poor have not gone away; there are more of them than at any time in recent memory. Community life has deteriorated, and our social problems have gotten more difficult and complex. Certainly many professional social workers are still committed to the public social services, to helping poor people, and dealing with social problems like homelessness and child neglect, but a large part of the profession is adrift in the psychotherapeutic seas. (Specht, 1994, p. x)

The ambivalence of the profession to define itself is examined at length by Specht and Courtney in their book, *Unfaithful Angels* (1994). A book, the importance of which is described in the opening words of Marsh's rather critical evaluation:

This book will quite likely shape the debate and direction of social work education and practice in the early 21st century. It is fundamentally a treatise objecting to psychotherapy as the "major model" of social work practice and advocating a "community based system of social care." It is a book that makes a significant contribution by alerting us to important trends in social work practice and education. In identifying and discussing trends, however, it is a book that is long on moral indignation and short on fact and analysis. (1995, p. 125)

Despite Marsh's disagreement with the authors' data and interpretations, she concludes that

. . . it is fair to ask whether the voice of social workers on behalf of the poor has been loud enough . . . And, as we debate the direction of social work, we should ask ourselves whether we are providing the right services to the right people in the right places and whether we are developing the knowledge base required to intervene most effectively. (1995, p. 130)

These words seem to lay a course for continuing social work education.

PARALLELS IN ADULT EDUCATION

It is interesting to note that the struggle to define the direction of the social work profession parallels the struggles in the field of adult education. Pittman states that

A fair number of the more distinguished academics in the field seem to fear that the actual practice of adult education is drifting-or stampeding-to their political right. Phyllis Cunningham, for example, suggested that adult education needs to be diverted from the study of institutions toward '. . . popular social movements, grass roots education, voluntary associations, and communities producing and disseminating knowledge as a human activity . . . ' The fear that adult education has abandoned its social reformist roots inspired the American Association of Adult and Continuing Education (AAACE) to stage a "trial" of the field. (1993, p. 58)

Professor Jack Mezirow indicated

All evidence points to abandonment of significant social goals, the default of leadership, the failure of our historic promise to serve as a means of realizing democracy's full potential and the decline of a once idealistic movement to a collective market mentality with a vested interest in serving only those who can afford to pay and in maintaining the status quo. (1990)

These comments could easily have been made about social work.

The social work profession is based on a belief in human dignity and social justice and a mission dedicated to creating a social environment and promoting the social exchange of people in it in a manner that acknowledges and reinforces that dignity (Steiner Briggs, & Gross, 1984). Gross believes that it is not enough for a profession to have a mission. That mission must be translated into objectives that implement the mission and against which a record of competence can be developed over time. Adding this dimension requires that the social work profession demonstrate a record of competence in creating social environments and developing forms of exchange between people and environments which support human dignity and social justice (Gross, 1992, p. 111). The mission and objectives of social work, like so many professions, are learned, passed on, and enhanced through continuing professional education.

ACADEMIC PREPARATION OF SOCIAL WORKERS

The majority of practicing professional social workers have either an undergraduate or a master's degree. A small number of workers have obtained doctorate degrees. Though an exact count of professional social workers is not available, the National Association of Social Workers (NASW), the largest professional organization representing social workers, boasts a membership of over 150,000. Gibelman and Schervish report that the Bureau of Labor Statistics (BLS) estimated that the total social work labor force was 603,000 in 1991 (1993, p. 4).

The Council on Social Work Accreditation (CSWE) is a non profit association of social work education programs and educators that serve as the accrediting body for baccalaureate and master's degree social work programs. According to the Fall 1995 CSWE membership publication, "The Reporter," the Council conducts accreditation functions for 400 accredited baccalaureate programs and 117 accredited master's programs. Another 38 baccalaureate and 12 master's programs were in candidacy awaiting accreditation.

Part-time and distance learning educational options are increasingly available through institutions of higher education to meet the demand of the growing number of nontraditional student applicants to Master of Social Work (MSW) programs. These students are often married and employed adults seeking graduate education close to home, in the evenings and on weekends.

Baccalaureate level social workers are educated from a generalist perspective. They are taught a range and diversity of practice behaviors and basic eclectic skills to be used with individuals, families, groups, and communities. Their competence, once trained, is not limited to a single specialty area. The generalist is capable of assuming complete and ultimate responsibility for his or her own working behavior. The generalist framework presents a holistic perspective (Baskind, 1984, pp. 13–15).

Master's level curriculums allow for specialization in direct (micro) and indirect (macro) practice. Macro practice has traditionally meant policy, planning and community organization, and administration. Political social work is considered macro level as well, though this is beginning to change, with CSWE's call for a more integrated practice design, as discussed later in this article.

Doctoral level education is predominately intended for students interested in research and teaching in higher education. Only 229 doctoral degrees were granted during 1992–93, while MSWs reached 12,583 (Lennon, 1994). A shortage of doctoral graduates entering teaching has created a vacuum in higher education in some areas of the country.

CONTINUING PROFESSIONAL EDUCATION

Continuing professional education for social workers, who have completed their formal education, is primarily geared to those engaged in direct practice. Very little information is available in the literature on social work continuing professional education. A review of 5 years of social work education journals revealed only one article dealing specifically with continuing education. That article, by Dattalo, is entitled "Perceived Continuing Education Needs of Licensed Clinical Social Workers." It sampled 507 licensed clinical social workers in Virginia. It also addresses the identity debate mentioned earlier, as 86% of the respondents describe their services as psychotherapy rather than social work. Dattalo concluded that because respondents expressed much interest in nonsocial work theories and little in topics historically associated with the profession, some schools could be unwilling or unable to offer the desired training (1994, pp. 217–227).

Private practice, due to insurance reimbursements and the popularity of individual, marriage, and family therapy with the upper and middle classes, has become far more lucrative than either public or not-for-profit agency practice. The clinical entrepreneurs, who engage in private practice, have driven the policies and practices of the major social work organizations for several years. Their desire for vendorship has been behind the social work profession's movement toward licensure in most states.

Continuing professional education for social workers is a rapidly growing field due to the proliferation of licensed social workers and licensed clinical social workers, and because of mandatory continuing social work education in most states.

In 1985, 18 states had mandatory continuing education requirements attached to their social work licensure laws. Presently, the profession of social work is regulated, in some form, in all 50 states, the Virgin Islands, Puerto Rico, and the District of Columbia. All but 17 of these locales require continuing education for licensure or certification renewal. Most require documentation, usually in the form of a certificate of attendance. Some states allow credit to be accumulated through self-directed learning. For example, Illinois allows a portion of the credits required for licensure renewal to be accumulated by listening to taped lectures, and others to be earned by teaching. Kansas requires the largest number of continuing education hours, 60 hours every 2 years, while California requires the fewest, 7 hours every 2 years. Most areas base the contact hours on clock hours of instruction (American Association of State Social Work Boards, 1995).

Graduate level courses approved by an institution of higher education fully accredited by a regional accrediting body are valid in most states, as long as the classes are provided by an academic department in the specialty in which the license is held or by a department in a closely related field. Seminars, workshops, or mini-courses oriented to the enhancement of social work practice, values, skills, and knowledge are the most popular methods used by professionals to obtain their continuing education units (CEUs). Providers must be approved by the state in most cases.

NASW set standards for continuing professional education in 1982. These standards are used in many of the states where continuing professional education is required. Broadly, the standards suggest that social workers (1) assume personal responsibility for their continuing education, (2) complete 90 hrs of instruction every 3 years, and (3) contribute to the development and improvement of continuing professional education. There are also standards for assessing providers and for administrators (NASW, 1982).

NASW has been a major provider and advertiser of continuing social work education throughout the country. A review of the Association's national newsletter, "NASW News," and NASW state chapter's newsletters, indicated that most of the continuing education being offered is psychotherapeutic in nature and much of it is offered by nonsocial workers.

As indicated previously, social work is currently having a resurgence. Debates in social work education journals and at professional conferences clearly indicate the need for the social work profession to speak out against the far reaching changes embodied in the Republican's "Contract with America." The "Contract" and the conservatives attempts to implement the "Personal Responsibility Act" have alerted social workers to the impending threat to the programs and clients traditionally served by the profession.

This statement from Michael Reisch, Director of the School of Social Work at San Francisco State University, taken from his keynote address, "It's Time to Step Up to the Plate: Political Action and the Right-Wing Agenda," at the NASW-California Legislative Days Conference in February 1995, perhaps best sums up the crises currently facing the social work profession.

> We are now asked to make fundamental political decisions about our society, choices that are literally matters of life and death, health and illness, opportunity and oppression, hope and despair, for millions of people. These choices concern issues at the core of the social work profession. They have a major impact on the lives of our clients and the day-to-day work we do in our agencies and communities. They require us to make political action a central, ongoing component of our work; to abandon the false image of professionalism which separate professional responsibilities from the harsh realities of poverty, power, and politics; to recognize, in the words of Maryland social worker-turned-Senator Barbara Mikulski, that politics is simply "social work with power."

Reisch goes on to caution the profession by stating

> We cannot practice social work in hermetically sealed, sanitized agencies. We cannot apply effectively what we have learned through our education and experience when we have fewer resources to assist more clients and when those clients come to us with greater and more complex needs. And we cannot change this stark reality by wringing our

hands in despair, retreating behind a veil of indifference, or taking yet another advanced seminar in stress management or psycho therapeu tic techniques. As long as individuals and communities are placed at a resource disadvantage by decisions of our elected and appointed officials, politics will pervade all aspects of our personal and professional lives. We must discard the notions that partisanship and conflict are incompatible with professionalism. Whether we like it or not, whether we relish combat or shy away from it, we are now engaged in an ideological and political war with individuals and groups who see us and our clients as the enemy. We have to give ourselves permission to vilify our opponents as they vilify us—not by engaging in name-calling or character assassination, but through targeting our use of facts and by appealing to the best instincts in people. We need to become responsible extremists in the cause of social justice to move the center of the political debate back toward the progressive end of the political spectrum.

Must the social worker profession once again face the dilemma of whether to turn its resources and efforts back to the public services and the needs of the poor and disenfranchised, or to continue to exert efforts to increase the wealth and prestige of private practitioners? It is assumed by most that the profession will not turn its back on the traditional recipients of social work, the poor. Rather, the debate includes the following: How shall future social workers be prepared for the dual roles of direct practice and political social work? Must we debate the merits of micro versus macro practice? Can we combine the strenghths of both areas of specialization? Is the profession prepared to do battle with the extreme right?

Fisher reminds us that Fabricant and Burghardt (1992) called upon the profession to use a generative practice model that includes integrated practice, multiple arenas, and the contextualizing and politicizing of social welfare problems, issues, and strategies (1995, p. 202). Fischer also mentions Rees's (1991) discussion of a more "integrated model" of education, in which all social work practice, from micro through macro interventions and in all settings, is treated as part of political social work. Rees defines this simply as good social work such as being political, focusing on power, learning skills from the micro through the macro levels, and linking policy to practice. Feminists, he says, have integrated methods in an empowerment-oriented practice model. Structuralists also posit an integrated methods approach to political social work as the best means of getting at the entrenched structural inequalities that cause both personal and social problems (Fisher, p. 196).

CSWE, which under its new standards emphasizes an integrated curriculum, has also taken an interest in political social work. In his first presidential statement, CSWE's Moses Newsome Jr. states

> One of the first areas to which I will turn my attention is improving the political clout of social work education and practice. For too long we have been absent from the bargaining table where research and training priorities are identified and social policies are developed. For social work education to be effective in the political arena, we must continue to work collaboratively with NASW, BPD (Baccalaurete Program Directors), NADD (National Association of Doctoral Educators), and GADE (Group for the Advancement of Doctoral Education) in the area of legislative advocacy. I am encouraged by the work already begun in this area under the leadership of NASW, which has helped the above organizations work collaboratively to disseminate policy-relevant information and develop political strategies.

Another area addressed by Newsome in the same statement involves leadership:

> Leadership development is a second issue that we in social work education and practice must address. It may be reassuring to assume that professional leaders will simply emerge from our ranks when the time is right. But the truth is that without our serious attention to leadership preparation, that we educate for service delivery are likely to be "managed" by other professionals. Individuals educated in business, public administration, law, psychology, or medicine—although certainly competent in their own right—do not possess the knowledge, values, and skills necessary for the promotion of the social work profession. We must, in my view, re-evaluate the curriculum content in community organization, administration and planning to determine how best to sensitize and prepare our students for taking a greater role in professional leadership. I have no illusion about converting all of our clinical students, but I do think we can do more to ensure that all students identify with professional values and are knowledgeable about the social welfare policies that impact our clients. (Newsome, 1995, p. 1)

Newsome closes with

> I hope that our profession will carry out the type of mentoring and socialization necessary to ensure the development of effective leaders in social work education and practice. For without vision manifested in leadership, our profession will cease to be as we know it-a champion for the underserved. (p. 2)

How does the social work profession intend to respond to the critical issue of an extremist political agenda, that threatens to eradicate its very existence; and a membership that increasingly cannot identify with its mission? CSWE has called on the deans and directors of schools of social work to involve their students in political social work. NASW has gone "on-line" with its legislative alerts so that schools can pick up on current information and act quickly to fend off attacks on the profession and the clients served, and they have started a member-to-member legislative network in an attempt to influence legislation affecting social work practice.

The Commission on Educational Policy has outlined its "Millennium Project" work plan entitled "Challenges and Prospects for Advancement for the 21st Century." Reviewed by the Commission on Conferences and Faculty Development, and the Publications and Media Commission, and approved by the Board of Directors of the Council on Social Work Education, the Millennium Project will continue through the year 2000.

Millennium Project goals are as follows:

1. Encourage dialogue on the content and structure of social work education needed to meet future challenges.
2. Promote scholarly exchange on social work education and practice.
3. Stimulate innovative conceptualizations of social work education and practice.
4. Foster the creation and evaluation of new program designs in social work education based on the above conceptualization.

Areas to be examined by social work scholars, under the Millennium Project include the following:

1. External environment of social work education and practice
   - Changes in the political, economic, and ideological environments and their effects on social policies;
   - Globalization and its impact;
   - Technological changes;
   - Demographic changes and their impact on clients, communities, students, and faculty;
   - The impact of multiculturalism on clients, students, and faculty;

- Market forces such as licensing, vendorship, occupational requirements, continuing education, and professional organizations such as NASW;
- Consumer demands and client and community needs;
- Changing service environments;
- Changes in funding services and patterns;
- Partnerships within the social work profession and with other professions and disciplines;
- Means for social work to provide leadership in addressing major social issues.

2. Mission and Purpose of Social Work Education and Practice
- Demographic changes;
- New and continuing social and economic problems;
- Developments in other professions, disciplines, and fields;
- The "boundaries" of social work practice and education in the 21st century.

3. Knowledge and Theory
- Evolving definitions of social work practice;
- Theoretical constructs and models;
- Areas and types of knowledge;
- Ways of knowing and the role of scholarship;
- Integration of different world views and perspectives;
- Use of theory and knowledge from other disciplines, interdisciplinary studies, and professions;
- Intellectual history of social work;
- The development of intellectual leadership;
- Dissemination of theory and knowledge.

4. Teaching and Pedagogy
- Discriminating among applications of information technology;
- Integrating research and practice;
- Research on how different student populations learn;
- Variety of instructional approaches;
- Practice-education collaborations;
- Evaluating teaching and pedagogy;
- Promoting and rewarding effective and innovative teaching.

5. Institutional Structure
- Alternative organizational structures for social work programs;

- Relationship between social work education and academic settings;
- Alternative venues for professional life-long learning;
- Reciprocal educational responsibilities of the practice and educational communities;
- Means for incorporating alternative world views and knowledge bases through the creation of linkages with other disciplines, consumer groups, practice community representatives, etc.;
- Alternative conceptualizations of levels of practice and education. (*Social Work Education Reporter,* Winter, 1995).

Schools of social work have struggled to engage students, many of whom are private practice oriented, in the political struggles of the day, by teaching a required number of macro level courses at both the baccalaureate and the master's levels. CSWE's recently revised standards now encourage an integrated approach to practice and discourage the division between micro, direct practice, and macro, indirect practice, courses. This new direction in accreditation standards may be just what is needed to make political and administrative level issues seem important to direct practice oriented students. By combining both micro and macro level subject matter, students may more easily see the interrelationships. They must be taught in a way that helps them to understand the direct impact that political policies have on practice.

CSWEs Millennium Project offers hope of reinfusing the profession with its root mission of advocating for and empowering marginalized populations.

It seems fitting to end this discussion with a quote from the Millennium Project Work Plan:

> In their brief histories, the social work profession and social work education have responded to a host of contemporary phenomena, societal needs, economic trends, political climates, demographic shifts, and emerging technologies. To fulfill our professional mission as we move into the 21st century, social work educators and practitioners must develop new conceptualizations of and approaches to social work education and practice.
>
> This need arises from unprecedented social, economic, demographic, and cultural changes that have transformed the U.S. and the world at large, and thus the nature of the environment in which social workers and social work educators will practice in the decades ahead. For social work to help resolve complex problems and issues emerging within this environment, it must explore the relationships among its current struc-

ture, functions, and conceptual frameworks; create innovative forms of social work practice, theory, and research; and develop and disseminate new knowledge to inform practice and education. It is the goal of the Millennium Project to serve as a catalyst for the emergence of these interactive processes (*Social Work Education Reporter,* Winter 1995).

SUMMARY

Given the certainty of change, outlined by Macarov (1991), social workers will need constant retraining and continuing education throughout their careers. The changing composition of families, an ever-enlarging aging population, work shortages and work place changes, including rapid advances in technology, a move from public sector to privatized services, and finally the relentless attack on the profession and the marginalized populations served; all of these areas are the challenges facing social workers now and well into the future.

Continuing education for social workers will need to focus on how to do more with less, in a shorter period of time, and in a hostile climate. Social workers should not assume that they will be automatically respected for what they do. They must learn to speak up loudly and to advocate for their work and the populations that they serve. An integrated approach to education that spans the breadth of the profession's interests and skills and incorporates new technologies and methods, in both micro and macro practice, is the most likely approach to succeed and to keep the profession from splintering even further.

In conclusion, social workers are licensed professionals with mandatory continuing education requirements in most states. Providers should, however, keep in mind that social workers are poorly paid, relative to their professional training. They therefore tend to prefer educational offerings which, along with being license approved, are also low cost, half day or full day events, conducted in settings close to where they work and reside. *Providers of continuing professional education for social workers would also do well to familiarize themselves with the critical issues facing the profession and with the council on social work education's "Millennium Project."*

REFERENCES

American Association of State Social Work Boards (AASSWB). (1995). *Continuing education manual.* Culpepper, VA: Author.

Baskind, F. R. (1994). *Defining generalist social work practice,* Lanham, MD: University Press of America.

Dattalo, P. (1994). Perceived continuing education needs of licensed clinical social workers. *Journal of Social Work Education, 30* (2), 217–227.

Fabricant, M., & Burghardt, S. (1992). *The welfare crisis and the transformation of social service work,* New York: Sharpe.

Fisher, R. (1995). Political social work. *Journal of Social Work Education, 31* (2). 194–202.

Frumkin, M. L. (1994). The millennium project: promoting the creative spirit in social work education. *Social Work Education Reporter, 42* (2). 1 & 8.

Gibelman, M. (1995). *What social workers do.* Washington, DC: NASW Press.

Gibelman, M., & Schervish, Phillip H. (1993). *Who we are.* Washington, DC: NASW Press.

Gross, G. M. (1992). A defining moment: The social work continuum revisited. *Journal of Social Work Education, 28,* 1.

Lennon, T. M. (1994). Statistics on social work education in the United States: 1993. Alexandria, VA: Council on Social Work Education.

Macarov, D. (1991). *Certain change: Social work practice in the future,* Silver Spring, MD: National Association of Social Workers.

Marsh J. (1995). Review essay on Harry Specht and Mark Courtney, Unfaithful angels, New York: Free Press, 1994, In *Journal of Sociology and Social Welfare,* 125–130.

Mezirow, J. (1990). Indictment, trial of adult/continuing education, Annual Conference, American Association for Adult Continuing Education, Salt Lake City, UT.

National Association of Social Workers. (1973). *Standards for social service manpower.* Washington, DC: NASW Press.

National Association of Social Workers. (1982). *Standards for continuing professional education.* Washington, DC: NASW Press.

Newsome, M. Jr. (1995). Vision manifested in leadership. *Social Work Education Reporter, 43* (3). 1–2.

Norlin, J. M (1995). Accreditation update. *Social Work Education Reporter, 43* (2). 4.

Pittman, V. (1993). Those who teach and those who do: contemporary rivalries. In R. C. Mason & W. H. Young (Eds.). *Challenge and change: Creating a new era of collaboration in adult continuing education,* DeKalb, IL. LEPS Press, 55–59.

Rees, S. (1991) *Archieving power: Practice and policy in social welfare.* North Sydney, Australia: Allen and Unwin.

Reisch, M. (1995, Spring/Summer). Its time to step up to the plate: political action and the right-wing agenda. *Social Work Education Reporter, 43* (2). 6–9.

Social Work Education Reporter (1994). 42 (1).

Social Work Education Reporter (1995). 43 (1).

Specht, H. & Courtney, M. E. (1994). *Unfaithful Angels.* New York: Free Press.

Steiner, J., Briggs, T., & Gross, G.(1984). Emerging social work traditions, profession and curriculum policy statements. *Journal of Education for Social Work, 20,* 23–31.

Strom, K., Strom, G., & Wallace J. (1993). Educating students for the new market realities. *Journal of Social Work Education, 29* (l), 78–87.

13

Continuing Education in Dietetics: Present Paradoxes and Changing Paradigms

Janet Regan-Klich

"The future will see a significant reorientation of the dietetics profession that will require continuous learning, rapid adaptation to innovation and change, and a flexible mindset." according to Sara Parks 1994, p. 843) a recent past president of the American Dietetics Association. Factors such as technological and medical advances, health care reform, changing legislation regulations, increased consumer expectations, new environments for the delivery of health care, changing demographic and social patterns, and accelerated change in day-to-day life, challenge the health care professional in ways that were unimaginable 25 years ago. In addition, the public has come to expect a higher quality care from its professionals. Professionals in today's society practice in an increasingly uncertain environment. Finn encourages dietitians to "probe the outer limits of our envelope" as dietitians become increasingly involved in new areas of practice. She exhorts dietitians to "broaden their skills to include marketing, management, creativity, and finance and . . . to take advantage of career opportunities in fields we previously hesitated to enter." She notes "We need the courage to perceive ourselves succeeding in new roles" (Finn & Rinke, 1989, 1441).

There is no doubt that the dietetics practitioner is challenged to maintain competence and grow professionally in the face of many uncertainties, competing demands and diminished resources. On the other hand, the opportunities have never appeared to be as opportune, diverse, and potentially rewarding for those who can adapt, be creative, and be engaged in a personalized plan for professional growth and development. Obviously, continuing education will play a significant role in the transition, though most likely in challenging ways.

The purpose of this chapter is threefold: (1) to show the evolution of continuing education within a professional dietetics organization and how the organization's approach and philosophy impacts its members; (2) to examine some paradoxes inherent in continuing education; and (3) to discuss ways in which the paradigm should and is changing for dietitians. Some curious discrepancies and "silences" within the dietetics continuing education literature will be explored and selected research findings and model programs will be discussed.

THE EVOLUTION OF CONTINUING EDUCATION WITHIN THE PROFESSION

The American Dietetics Association (ADA) has a membership of approximately 58,000 registered dietitians and 4,700 dietetic technicians. As a professional organization, it has taken its mandate seriously to protect the public by attesting to the professional competence of dietetics practitioners and it has worked diligently to position the dietitian as the "recognized nutrition specialist." The ADA has been in the vanguard with regards to registration and credentialing of its members, requiring continuing education according to established guidelines, tracking continuing education for its members and adapting policies and practices to changing realities.

In 1969, the membership voted in favor of a constitutional amendment that would establish the ADA registration program. Members meeting designated criteria of academic preparation, supervised practice, and successful completion of a qualifying examination would be able to use the status "registered dietitian", a legally protectable designation. This title carries with it a responsibility on the part of the practitioner to meet the requirements to complete 75 hours of approved continuing education every 5 years in order to maintain registration status. In taking this position, the ADA demonstrates its commitment to "protect the nutritional health, safety and welfare of the public by encouraging high standards of performance (Commission on Dietetic Registration, 1995).

At the same time, the association created the Commission on Dietetic Registration. (CDR). Whereas this office was once under the jurisdiction of ADA, it is now a separate and distinct entity responsible for all registration, licensure, credentialling and educational activities in support of these processes. The office develops, reviews, evaluates programs for quality, content and format. It also validates and administers the CDR entry-level registration examination.

For the registered dietitian, the CDR develops the guidelines for and approves continuing education activities. The CDR defines continuing education as education beyond that required for entry into the profession (Commission on Dietetic Registration, 1991). Educational activities that qualify for continuing education approval must meet certain guidelines: they must (1) update or enhance knowledge and skills required for competent performance beyond entry-level; (2) assess knowledge and skills; (3) provide opportunities for interdisciplinary learning; and (4) provide opportunities for professional growth and development. In the past, approval for continuing education activities was obtained prior to the event. A mechanism also exists for subsequent approval. More recent developments include a movement to self-directed learning plans. Members would determine, after a period of self-assessment and reflection, learning goals to enhance professional growth and development and in a series of activities to support such goals. Upon completion of the continuing education learning plan, the member would submit documentation for approval.

There is a wide range of continuing education activities which are considered appropriate. They include: self-assessment modules, self-study programs, videotapes of prior approved programs, viewing trade and educational exhibits (up to 3 hours per year), poster sessions (limit on hours), presentations, demonstrations, academic coursework, publications, research articles, technical articles, abstracts, books, book reviews, study groups and journal clubs. The *Journal of the American Dietetic Association* carries at least one article in each issue which is approved for continuing education credit. After reading the article, members complete the self-administered questionnaire and return it with a processing fee to receive one continuing education unit (CEU). The first article of this kind appeared in 1982 and became a regular feature by 1984. The level of sophistication of program content is rated to help the practitioners determine the most appropriate educational activities. Level I indicates a basic or general nature of the program. Level II indicates an intermediate area of knowledge and the program is beyond basic level. The Level III indicates an advanced practice topic. This level of program assumes a thorough knowledge of the literature and experience in the designated topic area and tends to be geared to recent advances and future directions.

Other accomplishments of the CDR office bear mention. The registration exam has been significantly revised since its inception. Whereas it was once based on knowledge content, it was revised in the early 1980s to reflect the results of role delineation studies of actual entry-level practices. CDR did a Predictive Validity Study to measure the relationship between the candidate's performance on the exam and performance on the job, a Content Analysis Project, and more recently has made a commitment to computer adaptive testing (CAT) which will be implemented in 1999 (Ruiz, Foltz, Lewis Reidy, 1995). In 1996, CDR completed a Practice Audit Survey which included feedback from employers as well as members.

To address the needs of the registered dietitian, CDR has worked with the American Dietetic Association to establish standards of practice for the profession. In 1986, a continuing education planning process was initiated and has been maintained since its inception. In addition to the Practice Audit Survey, CDR is also investigating issues of competency-based practice and is reexamining recertification procedures. Alternative methods of continuing education are also under discussion. Some of these considerations will be highlighted in other sections.

A particularly interesting project undertaken by CDR is its advanced practice specialty credential. CDR has taken a major step among professional groups in providing objective and legally defensible certification processes to recognize advanced level practitioners through its Fellows of the American Dietetic Association program. Specialty categories exsist for three areas of advanced practice: pediatrics, renal and metabolic support (Bogle, Belogon, Cassell, Catakis, Holler, & Flynn, 1993). There is discussion of doing the same for additional groups such as gerontology and food service management.

Challenges that the CDR faces include recertification issues and continuing education requirements. Confusion over professional designations due to state licensure activities is also a problem. For example, a person may be a "Licensed Dietitian" (L.D.) by virtue of passing the state licensure exam, but not a "Registered Dietitian",(R.D.) whereas another person may be both a R.D. and a L.D. The former could have less academic preparation with little or no supervised practice and conceivably compete for employment positions with others who meet the Association's and CDR's criteria for registration. Also, methods for the documentation of continuing education activities may differ from those required of the state licensure boards and those of CDR.

The CDR recognizes two factors which have contributed to the generally limited impact which continuing education has had across the professions. First, continuing education has generally ignored the need for learner reinforcement and skills development. Second, it has been assumed that professionals have the necessary skills to be effective lifelong learners who can be self-directed in their continuing professional education (Commission on Dietetic Registration, 1989).

In looking for ways to evaluate and redesign a recertification program for the membership, a competency assurance panel working with the Commission on Dietetic Registration has examined the present continuing professional education certification system. Strengths of this system, as identified by the group, indicates that it encourages lifelong learning, is accepted by practitioners, is easily accessible, affordable, and flexible, and is administratively manageable and attainable. The group also identified weaknesses of the present system that are worth noting. They felt that the current professional education certification system is not linked to competent performance. Without self-assessment, it is often not planned. Most practitioners select CPE activities based on interest, convenience or perceived needs, rather than on actual needs. This selection process, based on variables that may not be linked to actual needs. This selection process, based on variables that may not be linked to actual needs, makes CEUs too easily attainable. Several panel members indicated that ADA has not shown a commitment to the value of continuing professional education. Professional education by itself lacks efficacy and does not ensure continuing competency. Some system needs to be devised that includes periodic assessment that can assure the public, employers, and regulatory agencies of continuing practitioner competence.

At a time when the continuing education credit system is coming under fire for its inability to guarantee competence and the highest standards of practice among members, the CDR will need to work with members to help them adjust to the idea of the evolving reality of recertification. Practitioners will need to gain newer knowledge, skills and confidence to keep up with and adjust to technological and practice advancements. It will also have to address, along with the Association, some of the paradoxes that exist in the profession.

PARADOXES WITHIN THE DIETETICS PROFESSION
Membership Base

As one reviews the results of role delineation surveys and research surveys, one is struck by an interesting fact: the majority of the participants are generally under 40 years old, with varying years of practice and generally with a relatively equal distribution of undergraduate and graduate degrees. (Some exceptions do exist). What has happened to the mature, experienced practitioners? Are they invisible or are they leaving the profession?

Dissatisfaction with salary and a perception of the absence of a career ladder may lead some professionals to seek employment outside the profession. A number of journal articles have addressed the salary inequity issues. For their experience and academic training, dietitians are at the lowest end of the salary scale for all health care professionals. One former ADA president has acknowledged this phenomenon and noted the absence of experienced role models and peer mentors for new practitioners. If the profession's emphasis is on competency, it will need professionally trained and experienced practitioners who themselves, as lifelong learners, are well prepared and available to address the nutrition issues and public needs. The profession needs to stem the exodus of older members or provide opportunities for them to expand their job responsibilites while maintaining their affiliation with the association. Other possible reasons for the decline in active involvement or exodus may be seen in the next paradox.

Focus of Educational Activities

The profession's Code of Ethics (1988, p. 1592) reads "The dietetic practitioner assumes responsibility and accountability for personal competence in practice" presumably through ongoing continuing education and lifelong learning. Standard 4 of the ADA's Standards of Practice states that the dietetics practitioner continually engages in lifelong self-development to improve knowledge and skills. Despite this emphasis on the practitioner, almost all of the journal literature related to education, enhanced training, and an expanded knowledge base is geared to the undergraduate and graduate programs. It is as if the glaring spotlight and hopes for the profession have been focused on the entry-level practitioners. In fact there are probably few aspects of this population that have not been investigated and reported in the literature. By comparison, far fewer articles target the more experienced professional. It is as if they are consigned to the shadows.

A case in point is an article by Insull (1992) "Dietitians as Intervention Specialists: A continuing challenge for the 1990s." The article highlights the central role of the intervention specialist in the patient's care and advocates the dietitian's responsibilities and qualifications in this area. He also notes that the profession has not achieved its full potential in this area. Curiously though in proposing a schema of action for career development to address this gap, he situates the training needed to develop the knowledge and skills of an intervention specialist in the undergraduate dietetics curriculum. Perhaps, myopically, he fails to place the emphasis where it clearly belongs—on targeted continuing education programs geared to the practitioner who needs to make the next step. Dietitians who are going to succeed in becoming intervention specialists are those that have already achieved a level of proficiency in practice and need the extra support, assistance and guidance in developing the skills, knowledge base and self-confidence. They are less likely to return to the classroom setting unless there is a major incentive. They are more likely, however, to participate in continuing education activities, particularly those that address perceived or actual needs related to practice. Insull's proposal that such training occur in undergraduate, graduate and postgraduate programs overlooks the fact that students in those programs may lack sufficient intervention skills at a basic level and are thus poor candidates for preparation as specialists. Another example may be seen in Kaufman's (1989) question as to whether or not dietitians are prepared to work with handicapped infants. The question is certainly valid and the opportunities exist. However, in raising the question and proposing some guidelines to prepare for such a career move, the author focuses on the prepractitioner programs rather than on those practitioners who already have practical experience with a pediatric population. An article by Sneed, Burwell, and Anderson (1992) acknowledges that financial management is an increasingly important career choice for dietitians and that one-quarter of ADA members practice in management. Their article focused on undergraduate and graduate curriculums and did not address continuing education needs. Although more than 80% of respondents to their survey supported the establishment of a specialization certification in food service management, no mention was made of continuing education other than graduate preparation.

Heiss and Lopez (1991) conducted a survey of job time spent on education-related activities by registered dietitians and concluded that dietitians spent a significant amount of professional time engaged in such activities. The survey included six educational activities common to the different dietetic practice areas but omitted self-education or continuing education. It is ironic but understandable that professionals would concentrate on their service to others and neglect their own educational needs or count them as significant on-the-job activities. Yet they are significant. Slaughter, Kleypas, and Teague (1991) found that continuing education was one of the top five activities contributing most towards job satisfaction. It was not, however, among the list of the top five activities utilizing the majority of the dietitians' time. The researchers also found that 26% of their work day was involved in activities that ranked low in contributing to job satisfaction. The researchers concluded that if portions of those activities could be delegated to support personnel and nonprofessional staff, "the dietitian could devote more time to continuing education and medical rounds which provide higher job satisfaction" (Slaughter, Kleypas & Teague, 1991, p. 28).

Continuing education is significant and is likely to influence practice, thus it should not be overlooked. Yet it often is. Dwyer (1991) discusses the vision, objectives and strategies for the profession for the 21st century, but she neglects to implore members to be lifelong learners and avid consumers of continuing education. Perhaps members would benefit from more nudging in this direction.

Regardless of the area of practice, the literature cites examples of additional training needed "to probe the outer limits of our envelope" (Finn & Binke, 1989, 1441) yet continuing education is not mentioned—a glaring oversight! Invariably, journal authors suggest that the undergraduate or graduate curriculum be modified to include training in the topic under discussion. As a faculty member in an undergraduate program, I contend that there is hardly sufficient time to address basic needs and core knowledge. It is time that the profession realizes that the undergraduate and graduate preparatory programs have curriculums that are tightly constructed in accordance with the mandates from their own academic institutions as well as the association's mandated requirements, and that the focus of such programs is to teach basic skills and the knowledge foundations necessary for practice. I hope there is time in the already crowded curriculum to help the students develop positive attitudes towards lifelong learning and critical thinking skills. The tendency is to overwhelm the student and provide no time for critical reflection.

Professional development and career growth and enhancement is best left to continuing education. Few realize the extensive knowledge and skill base required by a current dietetics practitioner. Whereas a person might change careers six or seven times, a dietetics practitioner may in the course of her/his career work in five or six diverse practice settings yet remain within the same profession. The changing health care field and work setting offer fertile ground for professional continuing education efforts. But not necessarily continuing education efforts as they have traditionally been offered. This raises another paradox.

Praxis and Women's Ways of Knowing

In a profession that is predominately female, it is valid to raise the question about womens' ways of knowing and its application to continuing professional education. Gilligan (1992) in her seminal work

In a Different Voice offers evidence that women perceive and construe social reality differently from men and that women's sense of integrity appears to be entwined with an ethic of care. Belenky, Clinchy, Goldberger and Tarule (1996) proposed a model for womens' knowledge based on a relationship between the knower and the known, ranging from the Silent Knower to the Constructed Knower. They also include in their work a list of 11 educational dialectics (Appendix B) that could be incorporated into continuing education efforts—especially those that help the practitioner connect their learning with their practice and their approach to professional issues. Loughlin and Mott (1992) cite these works in their studies which suggests ways in which these findings might be used in continuing education. It is necessary before discussing this model to emphasize that they did not intend to create a "divisive polarity" but rather to present information that transcends polarity to enrich our perspective in considering alternative models of knowing and learning.

Given the demographic composition of the dietetics profession, the implications for Loughlin and Mott's work is clearly exciting, particularly with reference to the finding by Schiller, Foltz, and Campbell in their work on dietitians' self-perceptions and implications for leadership. In their research, they used a self-administered Life Styles Inventory and found that the two dominant styles on the circumflex scoring instrument were the Self Actualize Style and the Dependant Style. The group as a whole characterized as "seasoned professionals with substantive, though not extensive managerial experience" (Schiller, Foltz, & Campbell, 1993, p. 871). All members of the group had distinguished themselves in some way as to be invited to attend a regional leadership workshop where the Inventory was administered as part of the program. Interestingly, the Dependant group was also less likely to participate in continuing education activities.

Keeping these two groups in mind, Loughlin and Mott (1992) provided an interesting perspective with concrete implications for continuing education. In their studies they sought to investigate the learning experiences of women that in a sense empowered these women "to make commitments, to take risks, and to act creatively for change within society" (p. 83). The authors point out that the subjects' learning

is not confined to a particular context. Rather, the learning (was) achieved through self-refection on their daily concrete life experiences (which in turn) influenced both their personal and professional development. The nature of that learning was grounded in critical reflection on the underlying assumptions of their personal and professional knowledge. The insights that they then learned informed and motivated their action, sometimes within their personal lives and other times within their professional lives. (p. 81)

For the women in their study, the knowing and learning had to be rooted in their authentic selves. To arrive at this knowledge they had to critically reflect on their own assumptions of their personal and professional knowledge and to integrate this knowledge into their personal and professional identities. When they successfully achieved this, they became more self-directed in their choices, more tolerant in their ability to accept ambiguity. What distinguishes this process as having a female orientation is the degree to which women integrate reason and intuition in their knowing; the women achieved a "relatedness" and a "connectedness" in the process of this integration. The women who were able to make commitments, to take risks and to act creatively to change within society had a sense of self, their own personal uniqueness which informed and influenced their learning contributing to their own sense of authenticity.

Using the two groups of dietitians in Schiller, Foltz, and Campbell's study, one might raise the question as to whether or not the dietitians in the Self-Actualize group were more skilled in critical reflection or could articulate a description of themselves that reflected a sense of "connectedness." Conversely, one might question the extent to which this behavior occurred in dietitians in the Dependant style group. It would be interesting to compare the Self Actualize dietitians with the Dependant style dietitians in terms of their opportunities for and skills in critical reflection, encouragement for such expression, and the extent to which the work settings encouraged and supported efforts in self-assessment and self-expression. Loughlin and Mott (1992) cite an example from one of their studies in which a woman experienced a disorienting dilemma-acceptance into graduate school while her children were still young. Self-examination of her feelings lead to feelings of guilt. In assessing her underlying assumptions and talking with other female graduate students one woman began to realize she was not alone. The rest of the process led to a perspective transformation. Dietitians characterized by a Dependant style of leadership may not yet have experienced a disorienting dilemma and thus had not had to critically reflect on their underlying assumptions in a way that would lead them to a more authentic understanding of themselves. They may have chosen positions of safety and security which didn't challenge them. It is interesting to note that these dietitians were less likely to participate in continuing education events as noted above which also may have challenged them to reflect and act.

Interestingly enough for several of the women in Loughlin's and Mott's studies, their formal educational experiences did not facilitate this type of authentic learning process. A question for dietetics educators of future practitioners would be the extent to which educators foster this sense of authenticity or extinguish it by promoting conformity to competency standards.

The implications are also clear for continuing educators. Each program offering should engage the participant in some way that causes him or her to critically reflect on the expectations, assumptions and experiences they bring to the event. Dependant learning style dietitians may need additional assistance learning to identify their own voices and situated selves. Specifically the authors suggest that professional educators need to "(1) facilitate a process of centering learners' knowledge within their authentic self, (2) to facilitate the development of a connected and experientially focused language within the learning process, and (3) to create a context of relatedness among learners." The authors go on to describe a model in which this might be accomplished. Loughlin and Mott describe this process as one of "deriving our beliefs from our own experience." Only in this way can dietetic practitioners experience a sense of authorship of the knowledge that they constructed.

Although Schiller, Foltz, and Campbell's (1993) study on transformative leadership did not specifically address the critical reflection and action habits of the participants, it would be interesting to learn the extent to which those that were identified as Self-Actualized were in fact acting from a sense of their authentic selves. Or, if following the workshop, some moved from a Dependant style mode to a more Self-Actualize style. Since all who attended the leadership workshops had distinguished themselves in some way as to be invited, it is not likely that those in the Dependant style mode would be described as silent or Received Knowers according to Belenkey, Clinchy, Goldberger, and Tarule's (1986) categories. It would be interesting however to see the extent to which they would be identified as Subjective Knowers, Procedural Knowers, or Constructed Knowers.

Clearly the message to the academicians, mentors and continuing educators is to attend to the content to be learned while also providing opportunities for learners' to reflect, intuit, and integrate their learning into their personal and professional knowledge. This approach is likely to increase the learners' ability to act in an empowered way. This is what the profession claims it needs to face the multitude and complex challenges that exist. The profession of dietetics is sufficiently diverse and the needs to promote nutrition in an effective and efficient manner are sufficiently great that we should be less concerned about training competent practitioners in a traditional, theoretical/didactic and episodic mode and more about providing continuing education in an interactive, related manner that helps practitioners relate their thoughts to experience and challenges them to critically examine underlying assumptions that shape their practice. Which leads us to the next paradox.

Academicians' Involvement in Continuing Education

Continuing education is practice-based education, or it should be. The Commission on Dietetic Registration identifies is as "education beyond that required for entry into the profession" (Commission on Dietetic Registration, 1991). Traditionally, and perhaps appropriately, continuing education events involve either academic institutions and/or academicians who presumably have more experience in educational/learning designs, methodologies and delivery services. No data exists as to the practitioner/academician ratio of continuing education programs for dietitians but it is assumed to be great.

A paradox exists in the fact that what academicians consider important may or may not be relevant to practitioners. For example, Olmstead-Schafer, Story, and Haughton conducted a national Delphi survey of 85 public health nutrition leaders, practitioners, WIC directors and graduate public health faculty members to determine the future training needs in public health nutrition. It was interesting to note that of the most important public health issues and their nutritional implications, rankings differed somewhat between faculty and practitioners. For example,

> practitioners ranked the increasing populations of color and need for cultural skills as number 3, whereas faculty ranked it as number 11."
> Faculty ranked needs assessment, program planning and evaluation skills as number 3 whereas practitioners ranked it as number 9. Faculty ranked scientific foundations for dietary recommendations as number 6 whereas practitioners ranked it as number 16. (Olmstead-Schafer, Story, & Haughton, 1996, p. 283)

The top concerns of the public health practitioners include coalition and partnership building, increased participation in politics and the development of policy, greater cultural sensitivity and the development of culturally relevant programs and focus on cost-benefits of nutrition service. Implicit in this list is the realization that it is no longer sufficient to plan programs that are cognitively and content oriented. What the list of needs suggest is that there may be an emerging trend to incorporate more affective, psychosocial and interactive domains of learning for practitioners. Whereas the above survey did not specifically address training needs in terms of continuing education programs, it is interesting to note that Olmstead-Shafer, Story, and Haughton (1996) found that "ongoing communication and collaboration between universities and public health agencies is essential when reviewing and redesigning curriculums . . . and providers of continuing education can use the results to plan future educational activities" (p. 283). These needs challenge the continuing educator to develop programs that address practical and communication areas.

Even though the above refers to only one study of a limited size, other literature and experiences would suggest that clearly there is a gap between what academics perceive to be important and what practitioners find relevant to their positions. Programs that have practitioners as speakers are more likely to engage the learner, especially if they are conducted in an interactive manner and provide for practical applications of the subject matter. Academics may be thoroughly skilled in traditional didactic models but insufficiently grounded in adult education methodologies, adult learning theories and continuing education expertise to be effective in a nonacademic setting. They may tend to ignore nonformal and informal approaches to learning, practical competence and professional artistry. Their classroom style and orientation to rational, logical and orderly sequence of activities does not necessarily translate to the workshop setting for practitioners who have to function in a world that is characterized by "uncertainty, disorder and indeterminacy" (Schön, 1983, p. 16). Or, if it does, it does so in a limited manner.

Eraut (1994) claims that school administrators have six different kinds of knowledge: knowledge of people, situational knowledge, knowledge of practice, conceptual knowledge, process knowledge and control knowledge. Dietitians as professionals also possess different types of knowledge yet these remain undocumented. It would be curious to analyze and document the types of knowledge that continuing education programs address.

Mixed Messages

There is a very interesting dilemma unfolding over the issue of practitioner competence, recertification and continuing education and membership acceptance/resistance of the changing philosophies of these issues.

From the beginning, the ADA has supported the need for practitioners to be lifelong learners and has placed the responsibility for continuing education in the realm of the individual dietitian. To the practitioner this generally translates as the mandatory number of hours needed to maintain registration. Dietitians are less likely to see themselves as lifelong learners who periodically self assess practitioner skills and develop a personalized, written plan for self-development. This is not a model to which they have been socialized or trained. This fact is supported by research studies which have indicated that practitioners state their learning needs in terms of new and unfamiliar knowledge and skills; they are less likely to claim deficiencies related to skills used in daily practice or to actually develop written plans. Several practices besides the lack of training in this area seem to contribute to this deficiency.

Many continuing education activities have been planned haphazardly with the program content determined primarily by identification of new developments in the art and science of nutrition, the availability of someone knowledgeable and accessible, and the financial resources to sponsor a desired program rather than on the correlation with actual learner needs. Attendance of these events is sufficient to earn CEUs. Participants are not asked to demonstrate application of subject matter to practice or to demonstrate comprehension of subject or significant learnings.

Apart from the journal articles approved for continuing education credits, the dietetics literature is strangely silent on the subject of continuing education. There are few research studies documenting the effectiveness of a continuing education program or suggesting models to follow when planning such activities, methods and/or strategies to employ or the application of quality assurance techniques as part of a program evaluation. In the absence of such information, program planners are left to their own devices and resort to traditional methods of delivery.

Authors of articles published in the *Journal of the American Dietetic Association* seldom mention continuing education other than to state that their findings might be a subject for future continuing education. In general, articles conclude with a one or two sentence statement recommending continuing education as a route to knowledge or skills enhancement.

Nor does the current journal literature address the application needs of the practitioner. For example, after reading a journal article, the practitioner is likely to ask himself or herself "How would I apply this information to my own practice setting?" "What future learning must I complete to internalize this information and transform it for practice." "What implications does this information have for my own area of practice?" The same may be true for continuing education events. Journal authors should be encouraged to include in the discussion of their results a section "Implications of the research for Continuing Education" The Association and other professional societies could construct more explicit criteria for authors as to how information in the article can be operationalized through continuing education and/or self-directed avenues (strategies). Authors could help the reader to identify strategies for the acquisition of skills, and suggest a possible framework and/or timetable and process guidelines to help get the practitioner thinking about how such goals could be reasonably and relevantly achieved. Such actions reinforce the message that lifelong learning is a desirable and necessary skill. It also has the potential to engage the practitioner as well as the student in a way that has been previously ignored. The *Journal of the American Dietetic Association* could actually solicit articles demonstrating effective continuing education programs and practices that make a difference with a message to members about the need to be lifelong learners and effectively plan for their professional development.

When leaders within the profession write about their visions for the future, they paint a dynamic, well-informed, picture of where professionals need to be to position themselves competitively. Yet in almost all cases, they fail to mention the need for members to utilize continuing education as a vehicle to become more effective practitioners and lifelong learners capable of self-assessing, revisiting their underlying assumptions, improving their knowledge and skills in their current area of practice, or retooling their skills to be more competitive and competent in the marketplace. Although it is clearly implicit in any article of significance, it is probably time to make the message explicit. Continuing educators could take advantage of these knowledge-to-practice gaps to facilitate the application while simultaneously conditioning the practitioner to this way of practice.

There is a very significant effort on the part of the professional association, the Commission on Dietetic Registration and a number of committed members to examine the issues of competence, recertification, continuing education, assessment and training. They are actively working to move the profession into the 21st century and to deal with the complicated issues that such a challenge entails. As articulated at a Future Search Conference, they are looking at developing models for seamless education systems that include entry/reentry points at various levels tied to job opportunities. They are looking to develop simulated practice models and use technology to develop self-paced, interactive learning opportunities.

On the other hand an even larger group of the membership-at-large is unaware of the machinery in place and the depth and breadth of the effort that it is taking to move forward. To them the word "recertification" and an implied test generates anxiety, hostility, frustration, and resistance. They are more likely to view their professional association as an adversary rather than an advocate. As their job descriptions, roles and responsibilities change, often in an unpredictable and nontraditional manner, they are ill-prepared to see how the changes will benefit them. Neither the literature, the continuing education offerings nor their informal network has prepared them for what lies ahead. It is as if two separate worlds on this subject exist and have only begun to intersect with the 1995 publication of an ADA report on ADA leadership in regulatory reform to reengineer credentialing competency standards. It is ground fertile for a massive continuing education campaign to reorient practitioners and help them gain acceptance of the inevitable or empower them to contribute to the discussions.

Dietitians as Participants in Continuing Education

Dietitians take seriously the mandate of continuing education. Perhaps since a significant proportion of the membership entered the profession after the establishment of the mandate, they have not questioned the need for such activities.

Holli (1982), in her study of 194 dietitians documented that respondents spent a mean of 117.6 hours over a six-month period or 19.6 hours per month engaged in professional learning. An interesting finding that was also documented by Reddout (1991) was that dietitians devoted more time to learning activities that were not eligible for CDR continuing education credit. These non-CDR activities may have been self-directed, self initiated projects or job-related inservice programs that were ineligible for CDR credit. Eighty-eight percent of the dietitians reported self-initiated learning projects and dietitians spent a mean of 70.7 hours over a six month period engaged in such activities.

Several surveys of dietitians' needs in Illinois (Cross, Van Horn, Olson & Kamath, 1984) and Michigan (Mutch, Wenberg, 1986), as well as among several professional groups such as diabetes educators (Anderson, Arnold, Donnelly, Funnell, & Johnson, 1992) and public health nutritionists (Haughton & Shaw, 1992) indicate that of the CDR approved activities, clearly workshops, local, state and national meetings and symposia are the preferred mode of continuing education. Dietitians were less likely to use journal articles and videotapes, books, booklets and programmed instruction for continuing education. (Vickery & Cotunga, 1992). Greater use of these forms of continuing education may be seen in areas with limited access to CE events or where schedules or circumstances do not permit opportunities to participate in CE events. In two studies, RD respondents were least likely to use audiocassettes as a means of continuing education. The survey of Michigan dietitians (Mutch & Wenberg, 1986) indicated that respondents considered self-assessment, skill training, peer review and individual planning with a CE consultant as helpful even though they had not been previously utilized indicating a positive predisposition to these modes of learning.

The greatest barriers to participation appear to be time and lack of financial support. Most professionals report feeling overwhelmed with the day-to-day tasks of routine practice that they find it difficult to make time for continuing professional education. Such time constraints also impede the reflection and action parts of the process.

Lack of financial support for continuing education activities may be a significant factor when one considers the dietitians' low position on the allied health pay scale. When expenses for such activities are out-of-pocket, selectivity increases. My own personal experience with this fact occurred when planning an interdisciplinary workshop for allied health professionals and discussing registration fees. What was considered an acceptable registration fee by members of two other professions because of their higher salaries precluded the participation of all but a select group of dietitians. Geographic location and lack of high quality programs were also named as barriers to participation in one study but not to the same extent as time and financial considerations.

In Holli's (1992) survey, dietitians were in strong agreement with the statements "Learning activities I initiated have increased by competence to practice" (p. 55). They also had strong agreement that their self-initiated learning efforts met their continuing education needs, that the Association should provide CE programs, that employers should sponsor more programs and that Association programs had increased their competence to practice.

If such is the case, why the present dilemma? Where do the voices of discontent originate and based on what discussions? There is probably little empirical evidence but ample anecdotal evidence to support the new conversations on continuing education and recertification. But the tests of applicability, validity and ultimately membership acceptance have yet to be made. On one hand, given the dietitians' track record with continuing education activities, it is likely that they will support the changes suggested by the Association and CDR. On the other hand, the effort may be sufficiently threatening and perceived to be elitist as to cause rejection by the membership or an erosion of the membership base. An argument could be made that the extent to which the profession invests in continuing education efforts directed toward this end will determine the success of the transition. Only time will tell.

What is clear though is that the profession is changing along with modes of practice. Such changes necessitate paradigm shifts in light of new developments. Several of these changing paradigms are highlighted below.

CHANGING PARADIGMS

Impact of Technology

The introduction of the computer has had a profound impact on education and society. Increasingly, computers are used to perform a number of necessary functions from managing personal tasks to profoundly altering the way service is delivered and documented. Computers also raise interesting questions for continuing education. Gregoire and Nettles (1994) noted that decision-making is an important aspect of a job for a dietitian employed in food and nutrition services. Yet, despite the existence of availability of computer technology to assist in the decision making process, few food service managers use any form of quantitative or computerized assistance. One of the reasons given is the lack of educational preparation for such use. Another reason alluded to in the article may be lack of strategic alliances between educators, researchers and practitioners that would favor the development and use of practical and effective computer simulations and expert systems.

Another area in which computers are likely to impact performance is in the area of assessment and testing. Increasingly they are becoming an affordable, convenient, viable option for professional examinations geared to credentialling, licensing an/or registering eligible candidates. The Commission of Dietetic Registration has decided to implement computer-based testing for the entry level dietitian examinations by 1999. The format for the computer-based testing will range from conventional multiple choice questions to virtual reality simulations. Such an approach also offers the possibility of domain sampling and computer adaptive testing for ability estimation and classification. The American Dietetic Association has also prepared an informational diskette "Computer Adaptive Testing: A New World of Options in Assessment of Dietetics Professionals" for distribution to dietetics education program directors and licensure boards.

Even though computer-based testing is geared to the entry level practitioner seeking registration, anyone with foresight can envision a day when such tools may be used to recertify professionals in areas of practice as a means of assuring competence and quality of care. In the published proceedings of the Future Search Conference sponsored by ADA, there are several recommendations regarding technology: to use technology to provide an individualized prescriptive focus to designing continuing professional education programs and to use technologically advanced assessment mechanisms to ensure continued competency. If such is the case, continuing educators will have a golden opportunity to teach computer literacy skills to the pre-computer, computer-adverse or computer illiterate populations of practitioners. Finn and Rinke (1989) state that "we must go beyond computer literacy to computer savvy. After all, computers in dietetics have become an essential tool without which we cannot prosper" (p. 1442).

Introduction of this technology as a means of screening and certifying candidates for professional practice is also likely to raise issues of access, cost, skill in a profession that is faced with problems of low minority representation, salary inequities and disparities relative to other health care professions and increasing demands and competing forces for time, energy and resources available for skills upgrading.

Standards of Practice

Finn and Renke (1989) states that "A standard of practice is a statement of the dietetics practitioner's responsibility for providing quality nutrition care. These standards are our values—our professional mindset" (p. 1442). They indicate preferred practice patterns. With increasing emphasis being placed on performance affecting patient outcomes and less emphasis on structural requirements, continuing education is a natural mechanism to orient the practitioners' thinking towards the Standards of Practice.

In 1987, The ADA House of Delegates approved the implementation of the six Standards of Practice published by the Council on Practice in 1986. National dietetics practice groups were then charged to develop criteria sets for their specific areas for their areas of practice as members of the health care of food service team. In essence, the Association sought feedback from practitioners as to practical and effective means for implementing the Standards.

A survey of consultant dietitians in health care facilities (Gilmore, Niedert, Leif, & Nichols, 1993) indicated that for the standard of practice regarding lifelong self development to improve knowledge and skills, dietitians showed good correlation between agreement in theory and frequency of completion, although the frequency of completion was slightly lower. Dietitians agreed to have a written, specific plan for professional development with completion dates but rarely did so. They were also not completing some of the self-assessments documentations for Standard I. Unfortunately, different analytical methods used in compiling the data prevent practitioners for comparing data from one practice group to another.

One interesting variation is the description of the standards of practice for nutrition support dietitians. The standards as determined by the American Society for Parenteral and Enteral Nutrition (Winkler, 1993) were approved for use by the American Dietetic Association yet the standards include no criteria for continuing education or lifelong learning, a surprising finding in a field that is so technical and increasingly complex. Of note is the finding that a majority of the group considered the provision of home nutrition support and patient/family education as very important and participation in local, regional and educational programs as less important. It is perhaps the patient focus of the standards of practice that precluded the inclusion of a standard for personal and professional growth. Nevertheless, for ethical and quality of care reasons, some standard regarding an obligation to remain current with treatment and intervention modalities should be included in the Standards fee practice that govern practitioners.

Even though dietetics practice groups have themselves taken a lead in formulating and implementing standards of practice to promote the delivery of quality nutrition care, their effectiveness remains untested. Reddout (1991) noted that little research had been done on the use of standards in dietetic practice or on the usefulness of continuing education in maintaining these standards. "To date, no empirical determination of use of standards in dietetic practice has been made" (p. 931).

A key area for continuing education presently would appear to be working with dietitians on adopting the practice standards, guidelines and clinical indicators. Reddout (1991) found that dietitians failed to use the professional standards promulgated by ADA which calls into question the dissemination and implementation of their existence. She concludes that "Designing continuing education to aid in the implementation of standards in practice could help bridge the gap between education and practice" (p. 932).

Self Assessment Modules

Klevans, Smutz, Shuman, and Bershad (1992) ask a critical question: "How do professionals discover what they do not know and cannot do?" This question is consistent with the evidence that practitioners are less likely to identify, and presumably ameliorate, areas of deficiency and/or weaknesses in their present realm of practice. They are more apt to be comfortable with pursuing continuing education in areas outside their presumed areas of expertise.

Self-assessment offer one means to enable the practitioner to examine their knowledge and skills. By self-assessment, Klevans et al. mean the "systematic approach to the challenge of staying current while leaving individual learners in control of their own professional development" (p. 17). Their form of self-assessment is not one of determining self-perceived learning needs but rather one of a practitioners' determination of their own capabilities in comparison with a self-administered test which is based on external, profession-defined criteria, such as the Standards of Practice. Such a process is confidential, private and self-paced.

The American Dietetic Association was one of the first professional groups to work with this group of researchers to develop self-assessment modules as a means for practitioners to improve competence. In 1989, the Association contracted with the researchers at The Pennsylvania State University, Office of Program Planning to develop self-assessment modules for dietetics practitioners. The first self-assessment module in management became available in 1992. Based on the survey results, CDR proceeded to develop self-assessment modules in other areas: Nutrition Assessment, Nutrition Counseling, Nutrition Evaluation and Nutrition Programs for Consumers. A total of 21 self assessment modules are planned.

These modules offer the practitioner a systematic approach to identifying areas within a particular realm of practice that demonstrate their competence and areas of weakness. They were designed to be economical, assessable, practice oriented, individualized and confidential. The purpose was not to test and rectify knowledge but rather to provide a tool for practitioners to gauge their competency in a given area. Practitioners were surveyed for preferred topics. A side benefit of the assessment process is that frequently the self-assessment stimulates the professional to reflect on his or her practice, to gain new knowledge and to seek additional routes to enhancing the knowledge and skills base. As technology advances, it is possible that practitioners will use a computer assisted format to self-assess.

Two potential objections to the method that were addressed by the developers concerned issues of philosophical and perspective differences in approaches to treatment and intervention among advanced practitioners and concerns that poor performance on a self-assessment module might be used in malpractice cases or presumably as a basis for termination due to incompetence. Developers have addressed these concerns by clearly stating that the modules do not imply a standard of care and are intended for assessment purposes only. Legal counsel also reviewed and approved the modules.

Nontraditional Areas of Practice

A 1991 ADA Role Delineation Survey of entry level practitioners indicated that almost 50% of entry level practitioners worked in acute-care, in-patient settings. With health care reform and the increasing emphasis on wellness and health promotion, the traditional fields of practice are changing. Entrepreneurship is on the rise and was identified as an area of skills focus by the 1991 ADA Council on Education and the DPG Dietetics Educators of Practitioners group. Such an area of practice requires a set of skills not presently taught in formal pre-practitioner programs. One practitioner in this area, Kathy King Helm notes that practitioners in this area need to be self-confident and self-motivated. "Often the skill that distinguishes a person the most is her or his ability for self-promotion because in the nontraditional job arena, communication skills are less formal and structured (Helm, 1991, p. 411).

Parks et al. (1995) acknowledged some of the shortcomings of the present system of education when they write:

> education for health care professionals today is commonly characterized by a disconnection of liberal education components from professional components; a narrow focus on current practice issues rather than on a continuum of lifetime education; and domination by isolated, independant departments. A curriculum that teaches students (possibly practitioners—my own emphasis) how to obtain, evaluate, and use information and that instills a sense of inquiry is needed to prepare broadly educated, creative, critically thinking persons who are capable of change and professional growth. (p. 601)

Another change in the paradigm of traditional practice roles involves the possibility that integrated health care systems will be licensed rather than the individual practitioner and that professionals within these systems will be cross-trained. In order to maintain confidence that such an individual is competent to practice within a given area, organizations will need to explore the option of cross-credentialing and the educational programs in support of this. The major continuing education activities and training will be provided by the individual systems.

Nontraditional Approaches to Continuing Education for Dietitians

The Commission on Dietetic Registration recognizes the need for guidance on the part of dietetics practitioners in developing continuing education plans and selecting appropriate learning activities. In addition to its self-assessment modules, it is considering another option for restructuring the continuing education requirement to include alternative methods such as program-specific comprehensive examinations and portfolio evaluations. Other plans may offer dietitians substantial opportunities to expand their learning into non-traditional areas and to initiate continuing education projects rather than be dependant on local, district, state and national offerings. They become more actively responsible for determining the direction of their professional growth and for the documentation of its effectiveness and/or contribution to practice.

Also, the literature is starting to report continuing education efforts that are based on a collaborative model with opportunities for reflection, connection and interaction that supports "relatedness" in a manner that may be more grounded in womens' traditions of knowing. Helm (1991) describes a peer mentoring project in which three or four entrepreneurial dietitians get together monthly to discuss projects and share advice. She has found the group to be extremely supportive and has acquired valuable information. She notes that just hearing about someone else's experience helps her to do her job better the next time.

Darling and Schatz (1991) propose a model for a mentoring self-management model that includes educational workshops as a component.

Tu, Guzik, Ricketts-Byrne, and Weddle (1995) report on a project in which members of a local dietetics association decided that they wanted to become knowledgeable, skilled and more confident in their ability to do clinical research. None of the participants had participated in or conducted a research project prior to the initiation of the district sponsored project. The clinical dietitians indicated that their highest need was to learn how to conduct research. The District Clinical Dietetics and Research Committee facilitated the development of a multisite project involving those R.D.s wanting to learn how to do research, and recruited a mentor with clinical research experience from academia. The group met, formulated a research question and then conducted hands-on clinical research. The group achieved consensus on a research project, developed the research design and conducted the research according to established protocols and procedures. RD participants reported a positive experience resulting in increased skills, confidence and an expanded network—a type of connectedness and relatedness referred to by Loughlin and Mott (1992). Clinical dietitians were challenged to become involved in clinical research and evaluated the experience positively. Most assuredly, the dietitian participants learned from the hands-on experience and overcame their fears about conducting clinical research.

Whereas the above project involved an academic faculty member in an informal way, the following continuing education project involves a more formal delivery system in an academic setting. The actual delivery of the program was more consistent with adult education guidelines and produced a positive effect. The Effective Patient Teaching Course was designed for practitioners (mean years of experience = 12 years). Poor patient compliance with dietary regimes and dietetic practitioners' own responses to needs assessment surveys highlighted the need for improved nutrition intervention skills. Roach et al. (1992) noted that "Registered dietitians and other health professionals spend substantial time teaching. Unfortunately most have not had formal instruction in teaching and many do not routinely use teaching skills known to enhance instructional effectiveness" (p. 1468). The course used role modeling, practice and supportive feedback in their teaching sessions, along with videotapes and patient feedback questionnaires. Effective strategies for learning such skills might be to help the practitioners identify their weaknesses against a set of established criteria. The optimal skills for performance such as those established by the Standards of Practice can help the individual self-diagnose. Practitioners, through varying modes of continuing education may also involve peers in evaluating skill use (for example through videotapes, role playing and interactive sessions)

Evidence that dietitians desire personal development, recognition and career advancement is seen in the description by Watkins et al (1994) of a Professional Growth Program (PGP) at one University Medical Center. Dietitians were given the option to participate in the program which was a three level clinical ladder program. Participants selected written proposals for projects which they then completed within a contracted time period in order to receive points and a financial reward. Each project involved a new learning venture for the participant. A committee of supervisory personnel and peer dietitians reviewed and approved the proposals, monitored quality, and performed an evaluation at the conclusion of the project. Projects and activities included teaching and education, professional development, research, publications, cross training, and special projects. A survey of all clinical staff reported positive results both personally and for the department and a lower staff turnover rate.

CONCLUSION

The challenges of the 21st century facing continuing education professionals within the allied health professions are great. The half-life of scientific knowledge is now estimated to be between three to five years guarantees that the entry-level practitioner will need to learn how to become a lifelong learner and the practicing professional will need to assiduously maintain a continuing educational program that is customized to meet his or her individual needs. As Derelian, Babjak and Fitz (1995) note "the myth that once licensed means forever competent is no longer acceptable" (p. 924). The National Organization for Competency Assurance noted:

Health care technology is advancing too fast for a certificate of competence earned at the beginning of one's career to constitute proof of competence many years later. Demonstrations of continuing competence are as reasonable and necessary as are required demonstrations of entry-level competence. (p. 924)

Continuing professional education is an exciting and challenging endeavor. It encompasses the delivery of an effective approach, the motivation of members to accept newer, nontraditional formats and use of quality assurance techniques and evaluation methodologies to assure that the goal of professional competence and the highest standard of performance are met.

REFERENCES

Anderson, R. M., Arnold, M. S., Donnelly, M. B., Funnell, M. M., & Johnson, P. D. (1992). Continuing education needs of dietitians who are diabetes educators. *Journal of the American Dietetic Association, 92* (5): 607–608.

Belenky, M. F., Clinchy, B. M., Goldberger, N. R., & Tarule, J. M. (1986). *Women's ways of knowing: The development of self, voice, and mind.* New York: Basic Books.

Bogle, M. L., Balogun, L. Cassell, J., Catakis, A., Holler, H. J., & Flynn, C. (1993). Achieving excellence in dietetics practice: Certification of specialists and advanced-level practitioners. *Journal of the American Dietetic Association, 93* (2): 149–150.

Code of Ethics for the Profession. (1988). *Journal of the American Dietetic Association, 88:* (12): 1592–1593.

Commission on Dietetic Registration. (1991). Continuing professional education: Guidelines for the registered dietitian. Chicago: The American Dietetic Association.

Commission on Dietetic Registration Addresses Competency Assurance Challenge: Assessing the Learning Needs of Dietetic Practitioners. (1989). Chicago: The American Dietetic Association.

Commission on Dietetic Registration. Competency Assurance Panel Meeting. (Notes from presentation of January 14–15, 1995.)

Commission On Dietetic Registration. (1995). Setting the Standard for 25 years. Chicago: The American Dietetic Association.

Council on Practice Continuing Education Committee. The American Dietetic Association. (1988). Continuing education: Keeping pace with the changing scene. *Journal of the American Dietetic Association, 88* (10): 1224–1225.

Cross, N., Van Horn, L., Olson, R., & Kamath, S. (1984). Assessment of continuing education preferences in Illinois. *Journal of the American Dietetic Association, 84* (2): 181–186.

Darling, L. A. W., & Schatz, P. E. (1991). Mentoring needs of dietitians: The mentoring self-management program model. *Journal of the American Dietetic Association, 91* (4): 454–458.

Derelian, D., Babjak, P., & Fitz, P. (1995). President's Page: ADA leadership in regulatory reform to reengineer credentialing competency standards." *Journal of the American Dietetic Association, 95* (8): 924.

Dougherty, D. A., & Tower, J. B. (1989). President's Page: New Project to help practitioner competence. *Journal of the American Dietetic Association, 89* (7): 977.

Dwyer, J. T. (1991). Bringing ADA's strategic plan to life: Choice, caring, compassion, collaboration and compensation. *Journal of the American Dietetic Association, 91* (9): 1961–1064.

Eraut, M. (1994). *Developing professional knowledge and competence.* London: The Falmer Press.

Finn, S. C., & Rinke, W. (1989). Probing the envelope of dietetics by transforming challenges into opportunities. *Journal of the American Dietetic Association, 89* (10): 1441–1443.

Gilligan, C. (1982). *In a different voice: Psychological theory and women's development.* Cambridge, MA: Harvard University Press.

Gilmore, S. A., Niedert, K. G., Leif, E., & Nichols, P. (1993). Standards of practice criteria: Consultant dietitians in health care facilities. *Journal of the American Dietetic Association, 93* (3): 305–308.

Gregoire M. B., & Nettles M. F. (1994). Is it time for computer-assisted decision making to improve the quality of food and nutrition services? *Journal of the American Dietetic Association, 94* (12): 1371–1373.

Haughton, B., & Shaw, J. (1992). Functional roles of today's public health nutritionist. *Journal of the American Dietetic Association, 92* (10): 1218–1222.

Heiss, C., & Lopez, L. (1991). Survey clocks RDs' educational activities. *Journal of the American Dietetic Association, 91* (4): 418.

Helm, K. K. (1991). Finding nontraditional jobs in dietetics. *Journal of the American Dietetic Association. 91* (4): 410–420.

Holli, B. B. (1982). Continuing professional learning: Involvement and opinions of dietitians. *Journal of the American Dietetic Association, 81* (1): 53–57.

Insull, W. (1992). Dietitians as intervention specialists: A continuing challenge for the 1990s. *Journal of the American Dietetic Association, 92* (5): 551–552.

Kaufman, M. (1989). Are dietitians prepared to work with handicapped infants: PL 99–457 offers new opportunities. *Journal of the American Dietetic Association, 89* (11): 1602-1605.

Klevans, D. R., Smutz, W. D., Shuman, S. B., & Bershad, C. (1992). Self assessment: helping professionals discover what they do not know. In Baskett, H. K. M., & Marsick, V. *Professionals' ways of knowing: New findings on how to improve professional education.* San Francisco: Jossey-Bass, *55:* 17–27.

Loughlin, K. A., & Mott, V. W. (1992). Models of women's learning: Implications for continuing professional education. In Baskett, H. K. M., & Marsick, V. *Professionals' ways of knowing: New findings on how to improve professional education.* San Francisco: Jossey-Bass *55:* 79–87.

Mutch, P. B., & Wenberg, B. G. (1986). Continuing learning needs assessment for Michigan practitioners. *Journal of the American Dietetic Association, 86* (2): 247–249.

Olmstead-Schafer, M., Story, M., & Haughton, B. (1996). Future training needs in public health nutrition: Results of a national Delphi survey. *Journal of the American Dietetic Association, 96* (3): 282–283.

Parks, S. C. (1994). Anticipating the future by identifying and tracking today's trends. *Journal of the American Dietetic Association, 94* (8): 843–845.

Parks, S. C., Fitz, P. A., O'Sullivan-Maillet, J., Babjak, P., & Mitchell B. (1995). Challenging the future of dietetics education and credentialing—dialogue, discovery and directions: A summary of the 1994 Future Search Conference. *Journal of the American Dietetic Association, 95* (5): 598–606.

President's Page: Investment in our future—The role of science and scholarship in developing knowledge for dietetics practice (1994). *Journal of the American Dietetic Association, 94* (10): 1159–1161.

President's Page: Standards, guidelines, and indicators position dietitians for competitive advantage. (1993). *Journal of the American Dietetic Association, 93* (10): 1173–1174.

Proceedings: Challenging the future of dietetic education and credentialing. (1994). Dialogue, discovery, directions. Chicago: The American Dietetic Association and the Commission on Dietetic Registration.

Reddout, M. (1991). Perceptions of clinical dietetic practice: Continuing education and standards. *Journal of the American Dietetic Association, 91* (8): 926–932.

Roach, R. R., Pichert, J. W., Stetson, B. A., Lorenz, R. A., Boswell, E. J., & Schlundt, D. G. (1992). Improving dietitians' teaching skills. *Journal of the American Dietetic Association, 92* (12): 1466–1470.

Ruiz, B., Fitz, P. Lewis, C., & Reidy, C. (1995). Computer-adaptive testing: A new breed of assessment. *Journal of the American Dietetic Association, 95* (11): 1326–1327.

Schiller, M. R., Foltz, M. B., & Campbell, S. M. Dietitians' self-perceptions: Implications for leadership. *Journal of the American Dietetic Association, 93* (8): 868–874.

Schön, D. A. (1983). *The reflective practitioner: How professionals think in action,* New York: Basic Books.

Shoaf, L. R., & Bishirjian, K. O. (1995). Standards of practice for gerontological nutritionists: A mandate for action. *Journal of the American Dietetic Association, 95* (12): 1433–1438.

Slaughter, S. P., Kleypas, R. K., & Teague, O. E. (1991). A comparison of actual daily activities with preferred daily activities among registered dietitians. Caring and sharing—abstracts. *Journal of the American Dietetic Association,* Supplement *91* (9): A-28.

Sneed, J., Burwell, E. C., & Anderson, M. (1992). Development of financial management competencies for entry-level and advanced-level dietitians. *Journal of the American Dietetic Association, 92* (10): 1223–1229.

The American Dietetic Association Council on Practice Quality Assurance Committee. (1986). Standards of practice: A practitioner's guide to implementation. Chicago: *The American Dietetics Association.*

Tu, N. S., Guzik, C. J., Ricketts-Byrne, J. L., & Weddle, D. O. (1995). Local dietetic associations can facilitate collaborative clinical practice research. *Journal of the American Dietetic Association, 95* (93): 357–358.

Vickery, C. E., & Cotunga, N. (1992). Journal reading habits of dietitians. *Journal of the American Dietetic Association, 92* (12): 1510–1512.

Watkins, L, Blue, L, Cator, K, Miller, S, Roberts, S., & Suneson, J. (1994). Dietitians and a clinical ladder program: A successful combination. *Journal of the American Dietetic Association, 94* (9): 1038–39.

Winkler, M. F. (1993). Standards of practice for the nutrition support dietitian: Importance and value to practitioners. *Journal of the American Dietetic Association , 93* (10): 1113–1118.

14

The Ministry: A Concert of Concerns

Monty L. Winters

THE MINISTRY

Overture

It is easy to argue that the last quarter of the 20th century has not been kind to the office or profession of the clergy. Tele-evangelist scandals, molestation suits against priests, political activist ministers from first the left and then the right, government clashes with cultic leaders, and a perceived irrelevance of the church to a high-tech, information-driven society seem to have brought opinions of the clergy to a low point. The term "reverend" has become outdated, because ministers are rarely "revered," except by a few of their faithful adherents. As increasingly greater parts of the ministry are shared with (and demanded by) laypersons, pastors, and ministers themselves are confused about their professional purpose.

The directions and viability of continuing professional education (CPE) for the ministry will lie not only in updating or enhancing the profession, but also will require transforming that education to fit with a changing church in an uncertain society. Some of the challenges that planners, providers, and participants in clergy continuing education face are common to CPE in similar professions. Others are unique to the heritage, goals, and focus of the minister; these latter concerns are the substance of this chapter. Often the concerns are intertwined, and linked to one another. As a metaphor, think of musical groups singing close harmony. Each part is distinct, and yet related to the others. Changing or repositioning any one part can bring transformation, sometimes subtle and occasionally glaring, to the whole sound. Simply getting one part "on key" will not by itself bring resolution. So, *for your consideration,* here is a concert of concerns.

229

A DUET OF CRISES

The first crisis in continuing education of the clergy grows out of its unique history. Wilson (1985), traced the history of clergy continuing education from 1960–1985. Definitions of continuing education in the early years of this period focused on "systematic study" and "lifelong learning." But by 1985, it had been refined to include what Wilson called "five essential elements." The second of the five elements, was "The initial responsibility should rest with the minister-learner to begin individual planning for continuing education."(Wilson, 1985, p. 18) This optimistic definition of the autonomous, self-directed minister initiating continuing education according to his or her own goals, timing, and desired outcomes provided an aura of maturity, professionalism, and independence. It also contributed to low rates of participation in group CPE events, and the self-reporting by many ministers of sermon-preparation reading as their most common continuing education activity.

Unlike many other professions which are governed or supervised by a single national or statewide association/organization, ministers have traditionally belonged to one of a variety of denominations, associations, or orders. Their licensing is generally through those bodies, or one of its subunits, such as a district or bishopric. Their ordination (which in most groups functions as a form of professional certification) has recognition across these lines, but is weakened by its near-irrevocability. Thus, no overarching governing body administers continuing education for clergy.

Denominations and associations vary in their emphasis and provision of continuing education, but few have requirements. Those that do have requirements rarely enforce them. Most denominational offices serve a brokering, rather than a providing function, relying on their seminaries and some outside agencies to supply courses and events.

A few attempts have been made to develop a cross-denominational agency. The Society for the Advancement of Continuing Education in Ministry (S.A.C.E.M.), an organization composed mostly of mainline Protestant and a few Catholic members, was formed in the early 1960s to meet this need. It's annual conferences are usually gatherings of those responsible in their own associations for encouraging continuing education, tied into planning times for each denomination. The Association of Continuing Christian Education Schools and Seminaries (ACCESS), a consortium of evangelical institutions and individuals, focuses primarily on distance education issues.

Accompanying the focus on individually planned continuing education and a lack of overarching governance is a new, third trend. It may, in fact, be a consequence of the other two trends. This trend is the specialization of denominations and other agencies into areas that formerly were considered the "domain" of ministry continuing education. These competitors include field education, career guidance, ministry assessment, nontraditional entry routes to the profession, and distance education. They (and others) vie with continuing education departments in seminaries and denomination offices for visibility, funding, and leadership.

The crisis of defining and developing the unique character and identity of continuing education harmonizes with another crisis of identity. This crisis is discovering (some would say *rediscovering*) the uniqueness of the minister's call and professional purpose. Clergy seem confused about their role in the contemporary church. The emphasis on a return of ministry to the laity has reduced the scope of many traditional ministerial roles. The church growth emphasis shifted focus to leadership issues. Seminars on "vision" attract thousands to hear successful mega-church pastors tell them "how-to-make-it-happen-in-your-church." Almost every seminary offers degrees in pastoral counseling. Churches are demanding that pastors work harder, more effectively, and with frequent evaluations. At the same time, ministers hear persistent voices reminding them they are curates, not psychological counselors or corporate CEOs, and that their job is "curing souls." Although continuing education seminars on "Developing a Philosophy of Ministry" seem to abound, and books on purpose and "intentional ministry" are growing in popularity, ministers appear more paralyzed than emancipated. Continuing education may even be a factor in furthering this uncertainty. Klimoski (1989), in his study of 171 Roman Catholic priests, found that higher role conflict scores were associated with higher CPE scores.[1]

This second crisis, while certainly not limited to continuing education, is intimately linked to it. Without a clear understanding of their individual roles, professionals are tempted to feed their personal development through "quick-fix" techniques and "dessert-plate" menus of CPE offerings.

A QUARTET OF QUESTIONS

Question #1: Will providers, governing agencies, and clergy participants accept a larger role for continuing education in training and education?

Despite repeated claims for the greater efficacy of continuing education in ministerial development, the lion's share of resources (faculty, funding, facilities, and time) are still being invested in pretraining for clergy. Some church-based training programs focus almost exclusively on in-service training, with apparent success. But whether the denominations and associations that control entry to ministry (and the clergy participants themselves) will accept these new models is uncertain.

Question #2: Can denominations and associations assert a more pro-active role for themselves in continuing education?

Most of these governing/supervising bodies have a vital stake in the success of continuing education. But their efforts to promote, provide, or oversee CPE for their clergy are limited. In the last decade, most seminaries have made their contribution through Doctor of Ministry programs, while outside agencies have offered seminars, study and tour programs, retreats, and books. A few denominations, such as the Southern Baptists, have developed materials that assist clergy in personal planning (McCarty, 1991). But leaders in most denominations are uncertain about how and where to intervene in the current predicament.

Question #3: What are the cycles or developmental stages of clergy ministry, if any?

The assumption behind the question is that by discovering the ministry development stage of a minister, continuing education stakeholders (including the minister) will better understand if, when, and what type of CPE is needed. Cook and Moorehead (1990) attempted a brief outline based on personal experience, but few studies have explored this question. Note that the answer to this question has broad ramifications for the two questions above.

Question #4: Can distance education systems of CPE move beyond content delivery?

Distance education offers hope for overcoming the isolated nature of pastoral ministry, as well as providing convenience and timeliness. But most current distance education systems focus on delivery of cognitive materials. Ministers are still waiting for integrated systems that combine socialization, mentoring, behavior modeling, and attitude change, and yet are practical and affordable.

A TRIO OF TENSIONS

Three related tensions affect continuing education of the clergy today. The first of these is the tension between the *educative* aims of CPE and their *mutual care-giving* purposes. Support-group functions and personal reflection are stated objectives of most denominational programs. Yet these often conflict with competency development or skill updating. Peer groups vary in the emphasis they give to each of these functions. Likewise, stakeholders differ in the value they assign to each function.

A second tension is that between credit-bearing CPE (usually reflected in Doctor of Ministry and related graduate programs) and noncredit types. This tension is neither new nor unique to clergy continuing education. But the dichotomy between the two seems more pronounced here than in related professions. Seminaries are convinced that pastors will not participate unless CPE entails credit. This was confirmed in several interviews for this chapter. Yet, as Kitonga (1989) found in a study of United Methodist Church ministers, academic credit was not an important factor in their participation in CPE. Factors such as leadership quality, personal goals, congregational needs and reasonable cost were more influential in these ministers' decisions to participate.

A final tension grows out of the societal changes impacting ministry. Spouses of clergy were once seen as "lesser-partners" in a joint ministry. Today, they are confronted by a host of other models for their relationships. (Seater, 1982) Continuing education planners are especially torn between including tracks and specialization for spouses who carry on a "team-ministry" with their partners, while at the same time retaining sensitivity to spouses who choose to distance themselves from their partners' career. The unique nature of this problem can be puzzling to other professions, where the professional's personal life has traditionally been a private matter. Barbour's (1990) study found the most significant source of stress in clergy marital relationships is the triangle of the pastor-spouse-church. The ministers (and their spouses) believed they were often forced to choose between the church and their spouses. Field's (1988) study of 271 pastors in seven denominations in the western United States found that nearly one-fourth of the clergy felt their wives would rather not be married to a minister.

. . . AND A CHORUS OF ISSUES

Several individual issues also bear promise of significantly impacting clergy continuing education in the next few years:

An Aging Population.

Adult educators are well aware of the need to provide information and transform attitudes of professionals concerning older persons in our society. Clergy have a vital concern in this area, since studies reveal an increased spiritual interest accompanies aging (Lewis, 1991). Payne and Brewer (1988) reported on a nationwide survey of 113 seminaries, in conjunction with the Gerontology in Theological Education (GITE) project developed at the Gerontology Center of Georgia State University. They found that the greatest involvement of seminaries (82.3%) in programs dealing with older persons was in the areas of field education, internships, and other forms of contextual education; the least involvement (26.5%) was in continuing education.

Multicultural Congregants and Churches

The pendulum, which in the seventies swung away from integrated churches toward those based on homogenous unit principles, seems to be swinging back. However, the largest immigrant groups in the United States and Canada now arrive with backgrounds in non-Judeo-Christian religions and cultures. In addition, clergy working with their own first-generation immigrant groups experienced aggravated problems with the second- and third-generations. Meanwhile, long-term nonassimilationist groups, such as Native Americans, demand greater sensitivity and attention to their own needs. Continuing educators are challenged at the checkpoints of cultural barriers in areas such as content, delivery systems, and purpose.

Diversity of Clergy

Added to a growing number of clergy from cross-cultural backgrounds are two other factors: the dramatic growth in the number of female clergy over the last two decades, and the reemergence of a significant number of lay pastors. In their efforts to provide identical continuing education opportunities for women in professional ministry, planners may overlook the unique needs and experiences of this group. A special area of need is becoming apparent as clergywomen move into leadership positions in their denominations and associations. Lay pastors (and related groups, such as bivocational pastors and "church-planters") were a significant feature of most denominations and associations less than 100 years ago. Now, due to financial realities of small churches, redirected priorities of denominations, and an increased emphasis on lay involvement, these pastors are once again emerging as a major issue for continuing education.

Church-Seminary Cooperation

The renewed emphasis on large churches in the last two decades brought about a number of church-based training programs to prepare clergy from within those congregations. These "home grown" leaders have special needs, and large churches today are creating cooperative agreements with seminaries and other agencies to meet their continuing education needs. The changes and challenges these agreements may bring to both the churches and the seminaries may be an indication of future directions for both institutions.

Servant Leadership

The 1990s may well be the "decade of leadership" in North American churches. Leadership seemed to be the most over-used word in seminars, books, and training programs in the first half of the decade. Interestingly, many of the philosophies, techniques and results that are advocated to clergy are contrary to the tenets of their own religious faith! Discovering leadership styles, approaches, and goals that are consistent with their own moral beliefs will likely occupy a great deal of ministers' energy and reflection in the next decade.

Personal Spiritual Development

Because religious professionals deal with spiritual ministry as their stock-in-trade, they may turn a jaundiced or neglectful eye toward their own needs in this area. Interestingly, most continuing education providers seem to neglect that need or assume that professionals can treat themselves in this area.

POSTLUDE

The reader may wonder that technological issues were not listed as a concern or issue for clergy in this chapter. New technologies will undoubtedly affect the lives of clergy, and some will become immersed or involved in areas related to them. Yet the majority of crises, questions, tensions, and issues unique to continuing education of ministers in the next decade will likely be found in the areas listed above. If continuing education participants and providers are sensitive to these concerns, then perhaps, like Longfellow's Hiawatha, we will hear "sounds of music, words of wonder."

ENDNOTE

[1]Note that Klimoski explained this association by suggesting that increased role conflict causes priests to seek out continuing education. However, the alternative explanation (that increased participation in CPE results in role conflict) is also a viable interpretation.

REFERENCES

Barbour, J. H. (1990). Sources of marital stress in the clergy. *Dissertation Abstracts International, 51/08,* 2678A. (University Microfilms No. 91–02,891)

Cook, J. K., & Moorehead, L. C. (1990). *Six stages of a pastor's life.* Nashville: Abingdon Press.

Field, J. A. (1988). Career satisfaction, adult development, academic preparation, and other demographic characteristics of pastors of churches affiliated with Western Evangelical Seminary. *Dissertation Abstracts International, 50/06,* 1693A. (University Microfilms No. 89–14, 734)

Kitonga, D. M. (1989). An investigation of ministers' profession-related self-directed learning activities. *Dissertation Abstracts International, 51/02,* 381A. (University Microfilms No. 90–18, 706)

Klimoski, V. J. (1989). The relationship between participation in continuing professional education for clergy and perceived role stress and role satisfaction. Unpublished doctoral dissertation, University of Minnesota, Minneapolis/St. Paul.

Lewis, A. M. (1991). The middle aging of America: Spiritual and educational dilemmas for clergy education. *Journal of Religious Gerontology, 7,* 47–53.

McCarty, D. C. (1991). *LifeAudit: A planning guide for ministry and per-*

sonal growth. Nashville: Seminary Extension of the Southern Baptist Seminaries.

Payne, B., & Brewer, E. D. C. (1988). *Introducing aging content into the academic professional training of ministerial students*. Atlanta, GA: Georgia State University, Gerontology Center. (ERIC Document Reproduction Service No. ED 374 709)

Seater, B. B. (1982). Two Person Career: The Pastor and His Wife. *Free Inquiry in Creative Sociology,* 10, 75–79, 84.

Wilson, Fred R. (1985). Continuing Education and the religious professional: 1960 to 1985. *Lifelong Learning,* 9, n2, 17–19.

15

Continuing Professional Education for Teachers

Daniel J. Cavallini

Staff development has significantly changed from supplemental (and perhaps remedial) teacher training to an important vehicle for change in the modern school. This chapter discusses some aspects of continuing professional education for teachers, including a brief description of past practice, and staff development as it relates to organizational development and adult education. Some examples of current school issues or problems that might have staff development as part of the solution set are given. Also discussed are means for improving staff development, how developing the professionals also develops the profession, and suggestions for further study.

PAST PRACTICE IN STAFF DEVELOPMENT

Many years ago the training of teachers was limited and postemployment training was remedial. Teacher in-service training concentrated on dealing with a changing society, on the influx of non-English speaking immigrants, and on the educational theories of John Dewey and others. The post-World War I era brought a concentration on efficiency and on the training of teachers toward producing the caliber of workers needed for an industrialized America (Rivera, 1991). Additional changes in views of staff development reflected the societal and political changes from the Great Depression to the Cold War. While staff development has been and still is a district function, the federal government made teacher in-service training a national defense-related issue with categorical funding of staff development activities through the National Science Foundation, and later, the National Defense and Education Act of 1958 (Alkin, 1992). Summer institutes, concentrating on subject matter, were often located on university campuses and did little to address the site-based culture or needs of the common schools. Gray stated that such institutes were "much less successful in helping teachers to actually change the methods of their teaching, or to use different materials or media" (Gray, 1970, in Alkin, 1992). The growing professionalization of teachers led to questions about school leadership, supervision of teachers, and staff development. The study of group dynamics and the acknowledgment of the benefit of including teachers in staff development changed the remedial view of inservice training (Alkin, 1992).

STAFF AND ORGANIZATIONAL DEVELOPMENT AND ADULT EDUCATION

Although staff development is most often seen as a means to achieve a number of school and student-centered goals, it is also adult continuing education. Staff development programs not only provide professional knowledge but also play a role in the intellectual development of the individual person. The *American Educator's Encyclopedia* (1982) defines staff development as

> a program of activities that, in education, is most commonly designed to promote the professional growth of teachers. Staff development does not assume a deficiency in the teacher. Rather, it is predicated on the assumption that all employees have a need to grow on the job. (p. 492)

Staff development designers are urged to consider the foundation stones of modern adult learning theory offered by Malcolm Knowles (Bents & Howey, 1981). Various other aspects of traditional adult education are found in staff development literature. Joyce (1981) talks about the need to rebuild the school into a *lifelong learning* laboratory not only for children but for teachers as well. He also states that *learning how to learn* should be a major aspect of staff development.

Staff development is also closely related to other concerns and problems that, while considered in the contexts of adult education, are usually addressed from a business perspective. Organizational development has been a topic in business for many years. Roark and Davis consider organizational development concepts and skills as the substance of staff development programs:

> . . . staff development and OD both work to improve schools and ultimately education, but from somewhat different perspectives. Staff development attempts to achieve its goals primarily through an increase in individual competence while OD concentrates on organizational

competence. Both strive to improve the lot of both teachers and students and to improve the quality of education as a whole. (Roark & Davis, 1981, p. 56)

While a comparison between organizational development and staff development may show important similarities, some school reformers use this relation to business topics to illustrate the dire condition of current staff development practice. Joyce points out that successful enterprises invest in their personnel. He cites the armed services as training constantly; sales people and middle managers in business for 30 to 50 days annually; bank personnel for 3 days per month; and his barber for 10 days each year. Too many teachers get staff development training from their districts for 3 or 4 days each year and then work in isolation without time to consult with colleagues. Finally, Joyce compares teachers to actors who must give six performances daily without rehearsal, and offers this as a reason many repeat the same act too often (Joyce, 1986).

Many business and other organizations have been used as models by those interested in improving schools. Terms such as human resource development, organizational reform, and total quality management, more commonly associated with the business aspect of adult education, have been applied to schools in a positive way. Conversely, traditional school paradigms such as "teachers teach by telling," "learners learn by listening," and "competence and productivity are measured by courses taken and material covered," are cited as roadblocks to school improvement (Shanker, 1990). Other writers have criticized past (and to some extent current) staff development practices as being inadequate (Day, 1981), a waste of time (Roark & Davis, 1981), unlinked to classroom practice (Dillon-Peterson, 1981) and in conflict with other school goals (Shanker, 1990). Other persons may see staff development as a cure for most school ills. While hardly a panacea, staff development should definitely be considered part of the solution for many school problems.

SOME CURRENT SCHOOL ISSUES AND STAFF DEVELOPMENT

There are several current school issues that seem to be excellent arenas for staff development. Consider for example the current debate on appropriate special education placement, required by law to be the least restrictive environment. Advocates of inclusion believe that the child with special needs has a right to be educated in the same classroom as his nondisabled twin. It is no matter that one child may come to class bed-ridden with oxygen, catheter, and a health aide or nurse. For some students, inclusion is the optimal placement; for others, a separate venue is most appropriate. To properly serve individual needs, both ends of the continuum should be available, and the appropriate placement for most special students lies somewhere toward the middle, often in a regular class with additional assistance.

It would be very difficult for the child with special needs to derive the optimal benefit of placement in a regular education classroom without providing additional training to the regular education teacher. Compound this situation with the array of deficits the nondisabled students bring to the average public school classroom, and it should be clear that teachers need more staff development activities that are tailored to local needs and not just an occasional lecture by the director of special education. Educating the student with special needs in the regular classroom calls for the very best staff development available, requiring careful planning, close collaboration, guided practice, and nonthreatening evaluation. Staff development in special education requires a continuous effort to provide benefit to both student and teacher.

Another topic currently demanding attention in the schools is student violence and the related issues of drugs, gangs, and crime. There is probably no other concern that so demands all members of the school community to reason and work together. These are not the kinds of problems that are solved in 40 minutes after school on Tuesday. These are also not the kind of problems that are solved with meetings that do not include bus drivers, custodians, the cafeteria staff and members of the local school community. In this case the best staff development goes beyond the teaching staff.

Staff development should also be an important component of school reform and restructuring efforts. The primary focus of such activities should center on how one group within the school community plans and delivers service to another group. Would an English department or the eighth grade staff implement a program of collaborative learning, authentic assessment, or any other curriculum change without meeting to discuss the wide implications of such a change? Does any professional educator believe that such change can be accomplished with benefit to students if it has not been proven valuable to the teachers of those very students? How will the proposed changes be packaged and marketed to the local taxpayers? The best intentions of school boards and administrators to effect change in a school will be minimalized if all the stakeholders cannot be convinced that the change is needed and possible. Indeed changes on a large scale may not be possible if a comprehensive staff development program is not an integral part of the process.

IMPROVING STAFF DEVELOPMENT

Not to be confused with the continuing accumulation of graduate credit which is used for salary schedule movement, staff development at its best is a vehicle for personal and professional growth, the improvement of instructional practice, and, therefore, of educational service to students. At its worst, it is a divisive, morale-depleting exercise in authoritarian administration. Staff development in many districts is too often just another staff meeting.

Better staff development is considered not only a necessary vehicle for reform but also a probable product of reform and as a guarantee of lasting improvement. Hirsh and Ponder (1991) claim that the entire school culture will need to change before any improvements can be considered permanent. They state that the critical attributes of change theory (readiness, training, follow-up, and maintenance) must be addressed by effective staff development, and that this can only be accomplished when teachers are viewed as professionals and partners in staff development.

Researchers have closely linked teacher staff development with school improvement. House (1972, in Alkin, 1992) identified three points of view: (1) the techniques of teaching; (2) the political context, which has focused on the organization and its effects on change; and (3) the cultural context which has focused on the interaction of staff and students in schools with innovation and change. Various studies link staff development to school change, decision making and school improvement (Goodlad, 1975), peer-coaching and social support to facilitating transfer of in-service learning to classroom practice (Showers et al., 1987), and staff development as culture building (Lieberman & Miller, 1990).

In fact, staff development has also been linked in research to coaching (Neubert & Bratton, 1987), student achievement (Cavallaro et al., 1980 in Hendrickson et al., 1993), and to personal growth (Bonstingl, 1992). Staff development is also endorsed as a preventative for the serious decline in educational quality vis-a-vis the expected teacher shortages of the 1990s (Harris, 1989). A well-constructed program of staff development will provide the knowledge, skills, and attitudes needed for valuable curriculum development (Killion, 1993), help the school realize its potential as a learning organization (Senge, 1990), and improve student learning (Sparks & Loucks-Horsley, 1987).

Staff development is often cited as the only viable method available to keep teacher knowledge and skills in step with the changing needs of students. While preservice training has improved it should be noted that

> Few educators have had sufficient training in the individualized instruction, behavior management, teaching social skills, group instructional strategies, consultation, collaboration, and team teaching to meet the day-to-day needs of challenging students. (Hendrickson, et al., 1993, p. 31)

In discussing the need for continuing professional education, Schön (1987) states that the need to teach professionals to deal with the "indeterminate zones of practice" and "to make decisions under conditions of uncertainty" is not being met in preservice programs and must therefore be a subject of continuing professional development for the reflective practitioner. "Conditions of uncertainty" and "indeterminate zones of practice," however accurate, are not confined to public education. Cervero (1988, p. 31) points out that other professionals [also]

> conduct most of their practice in the swamp of the real world where problems do not present themselves as well-formed and unambiguous, but rather as messy and indeterminate.

Because so many different types of homegrown and packaged staff development programs have been tried over the years, teachers are more critical of activities they consider not worth their time. Among teachers studied, there is a very strong aversion to the "silver bullet" type of staff development that purports to cure all ills with one dose. Teachers reported preferences for "challenging experiences and opportunities to collaborate seriously with their peers who have good ideas and are excited about what they are doing" (Lewis, 1994). The desired professional environment for teachers would include "smaller classes, flexible grouping and scheduling, networking, and . . . new technologies" (Lewis, 1994, p. 508). Such experiences must be worthwhile and meaningful to their teaching before teachers will give up any substantial amount of time with their students. (Cutler & Ruopp, 1993)

For whatever immediate reason staff development is used, the underlying reason is a desire for change. Expression of this desire for change may come from the community, from the administration, because of some present problem being experienced by a significant number of students, from the teachers, or other staff members in need. Different groups have incorporated staff development into their specific change agendas and/or have shown how staff development will initiate, sustain, or maintain the group's ideal school.

DEVELOPING THE PROFESSIONALS DEVELOPS THE PROFESSION

One of the more often stated complaints by teachers is that they are not treated as professionals. Teachers do not set their own compensation or entry standards, nor do teachers police their own ranks as do other professionals. In *A Nation Prepared: Teachers in the 21st Century,* the status of teachers is very unfavorably compared to that of other professionals in the workplace.

> Professionals are presumed to know what they are doing, and are paid to exercise their judgement. Schools on the other hand operate as if consultants, school district experts, textbook authors, trainers, and distant officials possess more relevant expertise than the teachers in the schools. Properly staffed schools can only succeed if they operate on the principle that the essential resource is already inside the school: determined, intelligent, and capable teachers. (Carnegie Forum on Education and the Economy, 1986, p. 57)

This same need for professionalization and participation in leadership within the school structure has brought staff development to its premier position as a means of career-long learning. The changing demands of practice over a 20- or 30-year professional career have become so profound that staff development may be the only reliable method of keeping a teaching staff able to meet the challenge of such change.

Schools are urged to use the talents and potential of their professional personnel as the only sure way to improve the entire system. Effective organizations recognize that their greatest assets are the individuals within them, and so they make human resource development the linchpin for all improvement efforts. In contrast, much educational reform has tended to deal with the peripheral issues of schooling. School improvement is not always achieved by buying new programs; rather, genuine school improvement comes from changes made by the people involved. Significant changes cannot occur unless there is a willingness to invest in and support professional educators. Unfortunately, an extensive study of schooling practices across the nation found that programs to assist educators in professional development are generally fragmented and unfocused, with no clear setting of priorities or in-depth attacks on schoolwide problems (Goodlad, 1984, in DuFour, 1992). DuFour further states that this haphazard approach to the development of human assets would not be permitted in leading business and industries.

Staff development activities are seen by many as an essential requirement for instructional staff. Orlich (1989) emphatically states that the university or other preservice education of teachers is inadequate to sustain the knowledge and skill needs of the professional teacher throughout a career. In fact, he claims sufficient reason to question whether the preparation is even adequate for a successful *first* year without additional in-service training. While preservice education may be inadequate in some areas, a carefully tailored collaboration between a college or university and a school district might facilitate an excellent staff development program. Such a collaboration must focus on issues, strengths, and weaknesses of current staff and use the expertise of both college and district personnel. Simply employing an outside expert is unlikely to produce the lasting improvement that is the goal of staff development.

Many persons interested in the study of teaching as a profession view staff development as essential. If teaching is viewed as labor, little is required of the individual except to follow instructions. Teaching viewed as craft or art requires different applications of standards in relation to natural gifts. However, teaching viewed as a profession focuses on the deliberative teacher who makes choices based on student need. Staff development programs should also reflect the need for teachers to make decisions based on student need and their own professional needs. However, some staff development activities tend to increase rigidity and regulation. There is often little difference in treatment between new and veteran teachers by an administration except that novice teachers often get the worst assignments—what veterans avoid with seniority. Therefore, the students most in need of an experienced teacher—those in poor, problem-ridden areas—get the newest recruits (Darling-Hammond & Goodwin, 1993). Staff development needs are variable within a district, a school, among a faculty, and even over a teaching career. While staff development will not cure all the ills of the modern school, it is difficult to state a problem for which a good staff development plan cannot contribute to a solution. Staff development is a dynamic entity that should be part of the permanent composition of a school building.

School issues are too often unique to time and place to allow anyone to believe that there is a staff development model that works everywhere. The best staff development models have several factors in common: support and improvement is the motivation; planning, execution, and evaluation are collaborative; staff development is a continuing activity; effective staff development models good instructional behavior; evaluation is humanistic rather than bureaucratic; and the whole school community is involved on some level.

SUGGESTIONS FOR FURTHER STUDY

There is no shortage of issues to bedevil the educational practitioner in these times. The challenge is to keep current on the ones that have the highest potential personal impact and reasonably aware of many others. The following suggestions for further reading are not intended to be comprehensive for all issues and levels. The educator interested in staff development is advised to become accquainted with the National Staff Development Council, its journal, and other publications. Several frequent contributors including current director Dennis Sparks, Bruce Joyce, Susan Loucks-Horsley, Linda Darling-Hammond, and Bruce Showers, offer a wide range of ideas and suggestions to staff developers in particular and educators in general. The ability to use the Educational Resources Information Center (ERIC) K-12 school related clearinghouses will lead to many researchers with much to offer: Thomas Sergiovanni on leadership and supervision; Howard Gardner on multiple intelligences; Alfie Kohn, his supporters and detractors, on assessment; Michael Fullan and Richard DuFour on educational change and reform; John Jay Bonsingl on total quality and the impact of the thinking of W. Edwards Deming on school improvement. The journals and publications of the Association for Supervision and Curriculum Development and Phi Delta Kappa among others offer a wealth of information for those interested in the improvement of schools and teaching. Current education topics are also discussed in *Education Week,* and the publications of the American Federation of Teachers and the National Education Association and their many state and local affiliates. Many state offices issue regular bulletins that are routinely distributed to district offices, though further internal distribution may be very limited. The development of a network of colleagues who might be enlisted in the search for relevant articles should not be overlooked.

REFERENCES

Alkin, M. C. (Ed.). (1992). *Encyclopedia of educational research* (6th ed.). New York: Macmillan.

Bents, R. H., & Howey, K. R. (1981). Staff development-change in the individual. In B. Dillon-Peterson (Ed.), *Staff development/organizational development*. Alexandria, VA: Association for Supervision and Curriculum Development.

Bonstingl, J. J. (1992). *Schools of quality*. Alexandria, VA: Association for Supervision and Curriculum Development.

Carnegie Forum on Education and the Economy. (1986). *A nation prepared: Teachers for the 21st century* (Report of the Task Force on Teaching as a Profession). New York: The Carnegie Corporation.

Cervero, R. M. (1988). *Effective continuing education for professionals*. San Francisco: Jossey-Bass.

Cutler, A. B., & Ruopp, F. N. (1993). Buying time for teachers' professional development. *Educational Leadership, 50*(6), 34–37.

Darling-Hammond, L., & Goodwin, A. L. (1993). Progress toward professionalism in teaching. In G. Cawelti (Ed.) *Challenges and achievements of American education*. Alexandria, VA: Association for Supervision and Curriculum Development.

Day, B. (1981). In B. Dillon-Peterson (Ed.), *Staff development/organizational development* [Foreword]. Alexandria, VA: Association for Supervision and Curriculum Development.

Dejnozka, E. L., & Kapec, D. E. (1982). *American educator's encyclopedia*. Westport, CT: Greenwood Press.

Dillon-Peterson, B. (Ed.) (1981). *Staff development/organizational development*. Alexandria, VA: Association for Supervision and Curriculum Development.

DuFour, R., & Eaker, R. (1992). *Creating the new American school*. Bloomington, IN: National Educational Service.

Goodlad, J. (1975). *The dynamics of educational change: Toward responsive schools*. New York: McGraw-Hill.

Harris, B. M. (1989). *In-service education for staff development*. Boston: Allyn and Bacon.

Hendrickson, J., O'Shea, D., Gable, R., Hettman, S., & Sealander, K. (1993). Putting a new face on an old strategy: Inservice preparation for the 21st century. *Preventing School Failure, 37*(2), 31–35.

Hirsh, S., & Ponder, G. (1991). New plots, new heroes in staff development. *Educational Leadership, 49*(3), 43–48.

Joyce, B. (1981). A memorandum for the future. In B. Dillon-Peterson (Ed.), *Staff development/organizational development*. Alexandria, VA: Association for Supervision and Curriculum Development.

Joyce, B. (1986). *Improving America's schools*. New York: Longman.

Killion, J. P. (1993). Staff development and curriculum development: Two sides of the same coin. *Journal of Staff Development, 14*(1), 38–41.

Lewis, A. C. (1994). Developing good staff development. *Phi Delta Kappan, 75*(7), 508–509.

Lieberman, A., & Miller, L. (1990). The Professional development of teachers. In *Encyclopedia of educational research.* American Educational Research Association.

Neubert, G. A., & Bratton, E. G. (1987). Team coaching: Staff development side by side. *Educational Leadership, 44*(5), 29–32.

Orlich, D. C. (1989). *Staff development: Enhancing human potential.* Boston: Allyn and Bacon.

Rivera, J. A. (1991). *A critical analysis of the effects of packaged staff development programs on the professionalization of teachers.* Unpublished doctoral dissertation, Northern Illinois University, DeKalb, IL.

Roark, A. E., & Davis, W. E. (1981). Staff development and organizational development. In B. Dillon-Peterson (Ed.), *Staff development/organizational development.* Alexandria, VA: Association for Supervision and Curriculum Development.

Schön, D. A. (1987). *The reflective practitioner.* New York: Basic Books.

Senge, P. M. (1990). *The fifth discipline.* New York: Doubleday.

Shanker, A. (1990). Staff development and the restructured school. In B. Joyce (Ed.), *Changing school culture through staff development.* Alexandria, VA: Association for Supervision and Curriculum Development.

Showers, B., Joyce, B., & Bennett, B. (1987). Synthesis of research on staff development: A framework for future study and the state of the art analysis. *Educational Leadership, 45*(3), 77–87.

Sparks, D., & Loucks-Horsley, S. (1987). Models of staff development. *Educator's handbook: A research perspective.* New York: Longman.

16

Current Issues in Continuing Legal Education

Patrick J. S. Waring

INTRODUCTION

This chapter will examine two interrelated issues surrounding continuing legal education today contained in the MacCrate report (ABA, 1992). The MacCrate report is officially titled Legal Education and Professional Development—An Educational Continuum: Report of the Task Force on *Law Schools and the Profession: Narrowing the Gap*. While officially charged with examining law schools and legal education, this nationwide and influential committee made two continuing professional education recommendations. The first issue is recommending mandatory continuing legal education for the practicing bar. The second is the issue of increasing the involvement of law schools in continuing legal education. To allow the reader to appreciate the observations made in the final sections of the chapter, I will briefly review the history of continuing legal education (CLE), the current status of CLE in the 50 states and United States jurisdictions, the influence of The American Law Institute (ALI) and The American Bar Association (ABA), and other influences such as law schools, private corporations, state and local bar associations, and the judiciary.

In the second section, I will look at the contributions that professional adult educators have to offer continuing legal education. In the third section, I will examine some current issues in continuing legal education, including the MacCrate report's recommendations of involving law schools in the lifelong learning of lawyers and its call to mandate continuing legal education. In the final section, I will integrate the critiques made on the imposition of mandatory continuing legal education and the observations drawn on the involvement of law schools in continuing legal education.

THE LEGAL PROFESSION AND
CONTINUING EDUCATION

While it is hard in such a brief exploration to describe every permutation connected with continuing legal education, identification of trends, themes, and ideas that run through the literature will be highlighted.

Because legal education in America is a relatively recent phenomenon, formal requirements by the bars of most states for a professional law school-based education developed between 1880 and 1940 (ABA, 1992). Consequently, continuing legal education as an organized endeavor is a relatively recent development. The MacCrate reporters found it a phenomenon of the past 30 years. The first organized provider of continuing legal education was the Practicing Law Institute, and it incorporated in 1938. The Practicing Law Institute had the express purpose of helping law school graduates to "bridge the gap between law school and legal practice. Bridge-the-gap programs were the initial focus of the Practicing Law institute (PLI, 1983).

Because lawyers traditionally prepared for practice by "reading law" in a practitioner's office, there was little need to bridge the gap. Now, however, lawyers are trained in attending law schools. Therefore, the Practicing Law Institute proposed to meet the needs of new attorneys going into practice.

Over time, the Practicing Law Institute increased its focus to include the dissemination of new information. As the law began to change rapidly and technology entered the realms of the law, practitioners began to see a need for specialization and increasingly complex legal and technical education (Paterson, 1986). Bar associations, law schools, the ALI and the ABA, began to expand into the area of disseminating new information to practitioners. Some examples of these kinds of endeavors include tax preparation seminars, law office technology issues, factually based seminars in areas of substantive practice like silicon chip seminars for attorneys.

In addition to information dissemination, continuing education has historically been seen as a panacea for dealing with incompetence in the professions. Law has been no different. In one survey of federal judges, 48.3% of 83% of the federal bar felt that lawyers appearing before them did not perform to an acceptable level (Carter, 1984). Startling statistics like these permeate popular media culture and the professional literature.

Although competency was often a concern mentioned in the pre-Vietnam era literature, it was the 1960s and 1970s that saw a dramatic increase in the concerns for increasing lawyer competence through continuing legal education. The call for mandating continuing education in law was heard most clearly in the late 1970s and early 1980s. The first mandatory continuing legal education statutes were passed in 1975 in Iowa and Minnesota. By 1984, eight states had mandated continuing legal education for members of the bar (ABA, 1992).

Today 39 states now require some form of continuing legal education (ABA, 1992; Eveleth, 1995). In the wake of the lawyer boom of the eighties, followed by the scandals and critiques of the nineties, many state legislatures have sought to increase lawyer competence by mandating continuing legal education.

The Call for Mandatory Continuing Legal Education

The reputation of the legal profession is at an all time low (Paterson, 1986). The public cries out to the media, the legislatures, and whomsoever else will listen, for competent lawyers. One strong response to these issues has been the mandating of continuing education for attorneys. While rules and recquirements vary, typically they include 12 to 15 hours of continuing education activities. Often self-directed study or reading on legal issues is a part of these activities. Some require that continuing legal education offerings be approved by state sponsoring agencies. Teaching a continuing legal education course, teaching at an ABA approved law school, and writing a published law article in an ABA approved law school journal are other accepted forms.

Some states have mandatory bridge-the-gap programs for their new admittees. For example, in South Carolina, an attorney must use a state-run bar review for exam preparation. Then the attorney must attend a special introductory class in South Carolina practice. Last, the new attorney must observe several hours of actual trials. Most states have few requirements, or none at all, of continuing legal education for all practicing members of their bars.

Major Influential Organizations

Law Schools

Law schools are commonly the providers of continuing legal education. Law schools have the resources available at little or reduced costs. Classrooms are in abundance. Catering is often available right on campus. Reputation of law schools is often beyond question by continuing legal education agencies because of the ABA accreditation. Law professors may have both reputations and connections with leaders of the practicing bar. Law schools frequently are able to secure student help by tying the seminar to some student group or law journal. Therefore, law schools can provide continuing legal education at a substantially lower cost than other providers. However, those savings may not be passed onto practitioners but instead could be added to the school's budget.

Law schools are motivated to provide continuing legal education because of two factors. One is good publicity to the legal community as a whole and the second is repatriating alumni of the school. Continuing legal education seminars at law schools rely on alumni goodwill to fill chairs. The ability to come and rekindle relationships with one's classmates and former professors is an attractive option. Moreover, law professors are not above marketing their skills to a practicing bar that may require consultants at some future date.

Private Companies

Some private corporations exist for the sole purpose of delivering continuing education. Often these groups are able to hire national experts to present programs in various metropolitan areas. The private company secures accreditation from the appropriate agencies, secures locations in conference facilities, and coordinates registration.

Another private corporation approach is in Colorado. A company there markets lawyers within that jurisdiction. It makes its market by cultivating a loyal following among the bar and firms in Colorado. It will serve that market not only with regular offerings, but with special requests as well.

A third service in the private arena is in technology delivery. Lexus-Nexus offers a service called Counsel Connect in which lawyers participate in electronic forums on specific topics of interest. Legal associations offer internet news groups so that members may exchange information, ideas, and assist each other with tough problems. Electronic games are available to hone objection skills. Computer Assisted Legal Instruction (CALI) is available at many law schools for tutoring in the basics of a subject area. The list goes on and on. Considering the push in most firms for increasing billable hours and lawyer productivity, one may predict that technologies that allow lawyers to complete continuing legal education while in the office may become the wave of the future. If the information superhighway becomes a reality for lawyers, lawyers could subscribe to the continuing legal education channel.

Bar Associations

Bar associations will also use continuing legal education as a way to encourage attendance at bar functions, as a service to its general membership, and as a method of fund-raising. Bar associations often include continuing legal education within their mission. In states that have an integrated bar, the bar association is often the accrediting and administrative agency for maintaining continuing legal education hours and records. Therefore, all levels of bar associations are involved in the delivery of continuing legal education.

Judicial education

One area of the bar that has an extensive continuing educational program is the judiciary (Riches, 1990). Judges have requested that their employers, governments, and professional associations provide them with continuing legal education. Judges need extensive assistance in preparing for the bench (Arredondo et al., 1988; Catlin, 1982; Catlin, 1986; Hauptly, 1993; Li, 1995; Markey, 1994; Riches, 1990; Stein, 1986). The National Judicial Conference offers continuous and ongoing continuing education programs for all the federal judiciary. Although some authors have questioned the ethical implications of "educating" judges about the law, judges have insisted that they require this continuing education (Weinstein, 1994).

The literature of judicial education is filled with testimony about judges who feel the need to keep abreast, not only of new legal issues, but also of general knowledge issues. Frequently, judges are the factfinders in very complex cases and involved litigation. Some examples of unusual continuing education paths for judges include a federal judge who enrolled in medical school to study toxicology. Another federal judge went to Texas to study petroleum engineering to solve a case tried before him.

Most judicial commentators argue that CLE educational experiences are necessary. Moreover, they point out that there is little difference between a judge attending a practicing law institute lecture and a judge reading of a new approach in a law review opinion.

POSSIBLE CONTRIBUTIONS OF ADULT EDUCATION IN CONTINUING LEGAL EDUCATION

Continuing professional education has emerged as a discipline within adult continuing education. Several professors now hold tenured appointments on university faculties of education in the specialty of continuing professional education. This book and the need it hopes to address is another example of this emerging discipline. The field includes everything from the bare-bones of how-to-do conference planning through the actual curriculum development, assessment measures, and philosophical and ethical issues associated with providing continuing professional education. Writing separately, and with very little cross-fertilization, however, the discipline of continuing professional education tends to focus on the same three issues that continuing legal educators write about, namely, bridging the gap from university to the real world, professional competence, and new information dissemination (Merriam & Cunningham, 1989).

In the former instance, practitioners, acting as continuing legal educators, are frequently seen as being too focused on their specialty and unskilled in educational techniques. There is a difference between a good educational experience and an entertaining performer. Too often, continuing professional educators have found that famous or well-known practitioners tend to be better entertainers than educators. Therefore, the continuing professional educator sees his or her role as one of facilitating education with the assistance or guidance of a professional. For example, it is not uncommon for an accountant to secure additional training in continuing education in order to become a provider of continuing accounting education. In another example, a continuing educator could work closely with a practicing accountant to develop a curriculum and program that will be entertaining, educational, and contribute to the independent practitioner's knowledge. In either case, it is important that educational content be a part of the analysis.

CURRENT ISSUES IN CONTINUING LEGAL EDUCATION

This chapter promised to focus on two intertwined issues in continuing education of lawyers, namely mandatory continuing legal education and the recommendations of the MacCrate report.

Mandatory Continuing Legal Education

The literature is filled with calls for ensuring quality through mandatory and voluntary continuing education. The ALI-ABA has supported these trends. The MacCrate report also echoes the need for mandatory continuing legal education (ABA, 1992). The majority of lawyers are now required to report their continuing educational activities.

The typical statute for continuing education requires a mere 12 to 15 hours of continuing education each year. It also includes the definitions for approved continuing education. This may be education sponsored by a law school, bar association, state office of lawyer continuing education, and the ALI and ABA. It often details how breaks and lunches are to be deducted from the hours' requirement. It details alternatives to seminar participation like teaching, reading, writing, or attending classes for credit at an ABA accredited law school. It specifies penalties for failure to comply, usually suspension. And it generally includes provisions for going inactive so as to be exempt from the act. Usually, it provides for dual credit for attorneys licensed in more than one state.

Law School involvement in Continuing Legal Education

The MacCrate report is officially titled Legal Education and Professional Development—An Educational Continuum: Report of the Task Force on *Law Schools and the Profession: Narrowing the Gap*. It has specifically recommended that law schools become involved with the practicing bar to ensure that the development of lawyering skills and values continues throughout lawyers' professional lives. Law schools are currently involved in many aspects of practitioners' lives. In no other profession, except perhaps medicine, are professors so heavily involved in every aspect of practice. Law professors are expected to teach entry skills, certify character, provide job references, research, write and develop broad authoritative explanations of the current state of the law, explore and advocate new trends and approaches to law, consult on individual cases within their specialty, determine continuing education requirements, be skilled in a practice area and share that skill, be professional educators skilled in analyzing educational processes at the entry and continuing level, and capture and disseminate the spirit of ethical practice on every practitioner that they can.

Some law professors may argue that they and their colleagues have a negligible impact on the practicing bar. They may hold that teaching several hundred new and impressionable students each year and publishing occasionally is hardly a pervasive influence. Moreover, the professoriat is less likely to be respected in the debate, say these professors. However, it seems unlikely that these arguments are persuasive given the effect that professors do indeed have on the profession at every level. Now, unsatisfied with their "limited lot," the MacCrate report argues for an expansion of the role of the professor to include an official involvement with practitioners throughout their professional lives (ABA, 1992).

ANALYSIS

Mandatory Continuing Legal Education

The debate over whether to mandate continuing legal education for licensed attorneys is dominated exclusively by calls for increasing the competence of the practicing bar. Competency is the first assumption of the need for mandating continuing legal education.

Competence seems to be less important in "bridging the gap" or in dispensing new technologies. This view is somewhat common sense. Bridging the gap is something all new attorneys must go through. Whether they are individual practitioners and, therefore, must have the assistance of a formal program like a bridge the gap, or whether they practice in a firm and are mentored by older partners or, in a large firm, a formal "welcome to the practice of law" seminar, most attorneys find a way to acquire this valuable knowledge. Otherwise the results would eventually be negligence suits against them or disbarment if they failed to be informed.

People who are interested in new technology are often not learning in order to overcome incompetence, but because they need to stay competitive within their practice area. This segment of the market is for the people practicing on the leading edge of the law. Therefore, motivated people tend to enroll in these new technology, new ideas, new law, seminars.

Consequently, it is the issue of competency that is described most often as a vital element to the continued success of the profession as a whole. Competency and mandatory legal education are seen as intrinsically linked. The whole purpose behind having mandatory continuing legal education is to increase lawyer competence.

Several problems arise with these sets of assumptions. First is the issue of whether mandating continuing legal education would have any impact on competence at all. Although states can mandate attendance, they cannot mandate learning. There is always a major question about whether nonmotivated or incompetent attorneys would benefit at all from having to attend seminars. Learning is a much more difficult thing; it is intrinsically tied to motivation. Here, one assumes that because of intellectual deficit, emotional issues or burn-out (lack of motivation), incompetent lawyers would not benefit very much from continuing legal education.

The second assumption inherent in this theme in the literature between competency and mandatory continuing legal education is a preference for formal group learning as being more beneficial to incompetents. It strikes me as strange that lawyers need to be mandated to attend formal group learning experiences. The very nature of being a lawyer is that one must explore the law regularly on an independent basis. That to me is the definition of competent law practice. Each case provides a reason and a necessity for self-directed learning. Motivated lawyers, who are concerned about representing clients effectively, should be forced to continue their legal education daily. Every case necessitates that competent lawyers read cases, law books, case reporters, statutes and annotations, and procedural statutes. Also, they should write a pleading, write a summary of law, brief and synthesize information, include new information, access reference materials, and actively perform other educational activities. The essence of being a competent practicing lawyer is to continue one's education for life. Law, by necessity, is a scholarly profession. Therefore, the need for "mandating" continuing education seems questionable.

Last, are lawyers incompetent? In a profession where 50% of lawyers at trial lose, where compromise and settlement are the current solutions for heavy dockets, and where negotiation has entered an all time aggressiveness, many clients are likely to be unhappy with lawyer performance. Perhaps some of the public furor and legislative response in the form of mandatory continuing legal education is fueled by public misperception. Moreover, in a profession that deals with people from all social and educational levels, it is likely that differing understandings of the lawyer's role abound. If lawyers are to be constrained by public perceptions of competence, then mandatory continuing legal education will certainly not help.

Let me be clear here, and admittedly I may be naive, but I cannot imagine how any lawyer could escape continuing learning on a daily basis during practice. Incompetence to me is when the lawyer fails to perform his or her scholarly duty. How mandating attendance at continuing legal education would cure this is unclear. One suggestion is to add quality control measures such as peer review to the process. This proviso would allow for greater assurance of lawyer competence (Carter, 1984).

Moreover, there is a trend, due to the competitive nature of law in the 1990s, for other lawyers to second-guess lawyers tactics. Rather than ask the negligence standard of whether a given act was within the realm of competent practice, lawyers tend to assert that a given approach was wrong and that they would have done it differently. Lawyers have the unique ability to criticize freely without a true understanding of the validity of the choices of other lawyers. This policy surely increases the public dissatisfaction with lawyers as a group.

One example, among many, is the criticism that criminal defense teams have leveled against high-profile-case lawyers. I rarely hear statements like (1) They are just doing their job; (2) They are allowed to do that under the rules; and (3) They are being zealous advocates. Rather, comments were made about the acceptability of a given tactic, the effect it may have on the jury, or more likely, if the expert in the television studio would have done it the same way. Considering the public debate of lawyers, it is clear how the general public may become confused.

The Role of Law Schools in Mandatory Continuing Legal Education

The MacCrate report argues that the role of law schools should be to provide educational services for the life of the practitioner (ABA, 1992). The authors of the report reason that, because legal educators are both lawyers and educators, they are in the ideal position to provide continuing legal education and professional development. The report states further that because professors are constantly involved in scholarly pursuits they are best able to provide the information needed by legal practitioners. As one may imagine, several issues about this recommendation come to mind.

First, and foremost, is the theory correct that law professors are educators? Often law professors have had little or no formal training in educating students. Second, the Socratic method is typically touted as the mainstay of legal pedagogical approaches. Although the Socratic method may be the premiere method to prepare laypersons for entry into the profession, it is *not* appropriate for continuing legal education endeavors. Therefore, the assumption that law professors are skilled at educating practicing lawyers is questionable.

Third, it is questionable whether people who have dedicated their lives to scholarly pursuit are best able to communicate effectively with practitioners. Often, students remember law professors as difficult to understand. When they were entering the profession, pedagogical tradition allowed most students to tolerate the educational methodologies of law schools.

CONCLUSION

I am not convinced about the need for mandatory continuing legal education or the increased involvement of law schools in it. I cannot understand the necessity for formal education in a profession that requires daily education of all its members. The emphasis on formal requirements and required attendance fails to make intuitive or rational sense.

Moreover, the involvement of law schools in the process again seems less than ideal. Too much of the debate is focused on the value of law professors as legal educators. Yet law schools are geared to a very different venture. Professional entry education and training core values in law schools is very different from the concept of maintaining and expanding competence and performece via lifelong learning. I firmly believe that pedagogy in law schools including the core culture in these institiutions will begin to embrace methodologies that contribute to and catalyze lifelong learning in the legal profession. For now, the laying of an additional framework on the professoriat and the inculcation of continuing legal education into the core values associated with higher legal education is not incompatible with the needs of a competent or incompetent member of that profession in increasing his or her practice performance.

Moreover, the vast economic issues and vast revenue associated with mandatory continuing legal education indicate that law schools may be more interested in their piece of the pie rather than improving the profession. One may argue that if we do not start improving professional competence somehow, we cannot ever improve. Moreover, the literature does not demonstrate that competence is improved by mandated continuing education. The real problem is one of motivating lawyers to be watchdogs of their own competence.

A sense of vocation may be the real way to inculcate lawyer competence. Perhaps law schools, the guardians of the profession, should be more concerned with commitment to producing good lawyers than with grade point averages, law school admissions tests, and the age and prestige of the undergraduate institutions in admissions. Placing energies into the traditional role as gatekeeper will do a thousandfold more to improve the profession than mandatory continuing legal education or law schools' involvement with mandatory continuing legal education will ever do.

REFERENCES

(ABA) American Bar Association-Section on Legal Education and Admissions to the Bar (1992). *Legal education and professional development— An educational continuum: Report of the task force on law schools and the profession: Narrowing the gap* : American Bar Association.

Arredondo, L. A., Collier, H. V., & Scrimgeour, G. J. (1988, Fall). To make a good decision. *The Judges' Journal, 27,* 23–5+.

Carter, R. E. (1984). Improving the quality of trial advocacy in civil litigation in the federal courts. *Federal Bar journal & News, 28,* 291–4.

Catlin, D. W. (1982, Summer). An empirical study of judges' reasons for participating in. *The Justice System Journal, 7,* 236–56.

Catlin, D. W. (1986, Fall). Michigan's magic touch in educating judges. *The Judges' Journal, 25,* 32–5+.

Eveleth, J. S. (1995, May/June). Minimum CLE requirement approved. *The Maryland Bar Journal, 28,* 36–8.

Hauptly, D. J. (1993, December). The future of judicial education. *New York State Bar Journal, 65,* 22–5.

Li, P. M. (1995, Winter). How our judicial schools compare to the rest of the world. *The Judges' Journal, 34,* 17–19+.

Markey, H. T. (1994, Winter). A need for continuing education in judicial ethics. *Valparaiso University Law Review, 28,* 647–56.

Merriam, S., & Cunningham, P. (Eds.) (1989). *Handbook of adult and continuing education.* San Francisco: Jossey-Bass.

Paterson, A. A. (1986 July 25). Specialization and the legal profession. *New Law Journal, 136,* 697–9.

(PLI) Practicing Law Institute (1983). *1933–1983 PLI, the first 50 years.* New York: Practicing Law Institute

Riches, A. L. N. (1990, April). Judicial education—a look at the overseas experience. *Australian Law Journal, 64,* 189–202.

Stein, M. A. (1986, Fall). Judicial education: how does your state measure up? *The Judges' Journal, 25,* 28–31+.

Weinstein, J. B. (1994, Fall). Limits on judges learning, speaking and acting. *Arizona Law Review, 36,* 539–65.

17

Continuing Professional Education and Policing: A Vision for the Future

Thomas Arnold
and
Gene Scaramella

INTRODUCTION

The purpose of this chapter is to provide the reader with a brief overview regarding the professionalization of the field of law enforcement. As such, we have chosen to offer a rationale for determining whether policing can be viewed as a profession; describe the current state of continuing professional education (CPE) relevant to policing; identify what we believe to be the major obstacles to effective CPE in policing; present an informed opinion as to whether a policy of mandatory CPE activities should be implemented; and finally, make recommendations for more effective CPE in the field.

POLICING: OCCUPATION VS. PROFESSION

We must start by attempting to define not only what a profession is, but perhaps more important, attempting to distinguish professional groups from vocations by focusing on the various characteristics which have been associated with these professions.

Although defining what a profession is may appear to be an easy task, rest assured it is not! As a matter of fact, this issue has been the subject of much debate among educators in the field of continuing professional education. The most basic definition of a profession is ". . . . an occupation requiring advanced academic training, as medicine, law etc. . . . " (Kister, 1990, p. 470). Most CPE authorities attempt to define a profession in terms of the individual professional.

The earliest attempt at defining a profession or to suggest a framework to distinguish a profession from a vocation was described by Abraham Flexner in his article entitled "Is Social Work a Profession?" (1915, p. 901–15). We believe that Flexner's approach is too restrictive. Although all the attributes he mentions are admirable qualities, to exclude an occupation from enjoying "professional" status based on symbolic characteristics is too restricting and consequently does not accurately portray what a profession really is.

Another popular attempt at defining a profession was offered by M. S. Larson in her work entitled *The Rise of Professionalism: A Sociological Analysis* (1977). In sharp contrast to Flexner, Larson defines what a profession is not by identifying a list of objective criteria which characterize professional behaviors, but by examining the relationship between a profession and society.

As was the case with Flexner's approach, we feel that this point of view is too restrictive and demanding as well, unnecessarily preventing groups from attempting to professionalize.

The last method for attempting to define what a profession is was offered by Cyril Houle (1980). The question is not whether a particular occupation is professional, rather it is to what extent is it professional? The significant aspects of this assumption are that it allows virtually all occupations to proceed through a series of steps to achieve professional status; there is nothing which clearly separates professions from other occupations; and its underlying belief that no occupation ever reaches a point where it is perceived as an ideal model, thus allowing for perpetual improvement.

Houle identifies several characteristics or qualities which occupations should strive for in their journey along the continuum of professionalization. Very briefly, they include having a central mission; mastery of theoretical knowledge; self-enhancement; formal training; provisions for credentialing; creation of a subculture; legal reinforcement; public acceptance; ethical practice; establishment and enforcement of penalties; maintaining close relationship with related occupations; and a well defined provider-client relationship (Houle, 1980, p. 31–751).

If we examine the law enforcement occupation using the aforementioned approaches, two of the three immediately exclude policing as a profession. From Flexners's point of view, the criteria which are used to characterize professional behavior do not seem to match law enforcement practices currently employed.

Similarly, Larson's approach excludes policing as well. To our knowledge, there has never been a period in our nation's history when policing has either been valued socially or rewarded economically. More often than not, most historical accounts involving the police as a whole depict it as an occupation consistently exhibiting unprofessional characteristics, such as corruption, brutality, and incompetence.

The context in which this chapter is written utilizes the "process" approach to understanding the professionalization of policing. Therefore, if we view the law enforcement occupation as existing on a continuum of professionalization, the question to be addressed becomes "how professional is the field of policing?"

Based upon current conditions in practice and comparing those current conditions to literature sources that describe professions, it is our belief that policing is an emerging profession gaining momentum to reach full professional status in the not too distant future.

THE STRUCTURE OF POLICE TRAINING

A search of the literature concerning continuing law enforcement education reveals a paucity of data on the subject. Although there are numerous articles on training techniques, there is little information regarding the structure of continuing professional education in the field of policing. Anecdotal information allows us to conclude that there is little or no consistency in continuing education programs for police officers on national, state, or local levels. Some states have addressed police training issues by mandating a specific number of training hours that police officers must complete on an annual basis (Minnesota, Indiana, Wisconsin). Other states have yet to address the issue of mandatory CPE in the police service (Illinois). Our comparative analysis concerning those states that have mandated CPE for police officers shows some similarities but no uniformity in structure, content, or frequency of continuing education programs.

The absence of uniform standards of continuing professional education for police officers seems to be consistent with the overall state of affairs regarding police training and education. For example, according to a National Institute of Justice, Bureau of Justice Statistics survey, only a handful of police agencies, nationally, require a four-year college degree for employment as a police officer (Bureau of Justice Statistics 1993, p. 49–59). Employment qualifications for other agencies range from a GED to an associate's degree. As to the number of hours police recruits must spend in police academy training, we found even greater disparity. The number of training hours required for preparation to be a police officer varied from 176 hours to over 3,000 (BJS, 1993, p. 49–59). This absence of well-defined standards for training and education of police officers supports our position that police work, as an occupation, has yet to be recognized as a profession. Rather it seems that it is an occupation in transition capable of emerging as a recognized profession at some point in the future.

In order to continue to move toward acceptance as a profession, the police, as an instrument of government, must examine the way recruits and veteran officers are trained. This process will require an examination of the development of police training as well as the political and economic forces that may impede the process of professionalization. In understanding the impact that history, politics, and economics has had on American policing, we will be better able to create a vision for the future of education and training in the police service that will allow progression on a continuum of professionalization.

The formation of American police forces, as we know them today, began in the mid-19th century (Schmalleger, 1995, p. 151). Comparatively speaking policing is a fairly new occupation, especially in the United States. The history of American police training and education is even more recent. Most scholars of police history credit August Vollmer as being the "father" of American policing and with creating the first police training standards in the United States (Johnson & Wolfe, 1996, p. 225). Vollmer served as chief of police of the Berkeley, California, Police Department in the early 1900s and as the first professor of Police Studies at the University of California at Berkeley. As Chief of Police, Vollmer recruited new police officers from the ranks of college students and later established one of the first police training academies in the United States. Vollmer also helped to create the first curriculum in police science at the University of California at Berkeley (Johnson & Wolfe, 1996, p. 225). Prior to these efforts there was little, if any formal training for police officers, at all.

According to Schmalleger (1995), police training academies were being established in the 1920s in California and New York mandated preparatory training did not become common place until the 1950s and later. Today each state has established minimum standards for police training under the auspices of a state training board often referred to as Police Officer Training and Standards (POST) (Schmalleger, 1995, p. 225). These boards are granted the authority and responsibility of setting and regulating minimum police training standards, including mandatory continuing professional education, in states where it exists.

The fact that each state regulates its own police training standards may be a contributing factor to the disparity of training hours and standards found across the country. Although inefficient and confusing, it is not surprising that state regulation of police training has been the model for over one hundred years. Since the architects of our system of government were wary of a strong, and potentially oppressive, federal government, they reserved certain rights for the states. Among these rights is the right to organize police forces. From this right it is only reasonable that the states should also have the right to regulate all aspects of criminal law enforcement including the training of local and state police.

An understanding of the history and development of policing and police training is critical to the adult educator working in this field. Perhaps, even more important, is a need to analyze and understand contemporary political and economic issues that impact upon police training and education. Chief among these is the economic climate within which the police operate. Tax caps and taxpayer revolts have caused cutbacks in local government funding for the police. Like most other agencies of local government, police find themselves having to provide the same or more services with less money. Unfortunately training funds are the first victims of budget cuts. Private business and industry are able to measure the costs and benefits of up-to-date training in a competitive and technologically advanced marketplace. The police are less able to measure results. Unlike business and industry, the police are not able to accurately measure success and failure. Measures such as crime rates or number of arrests are unreliable as benchmarks for success. The number of crimes not committed because of the presence or intervention of the police is also unmeasurable. Because police administrators cannot directly link training to the fulfillment of the mission of the organization, in any quantifiable way, they are also hesitant to spend limited funds on such an intangible enterprise. Often police executives simply focus the expenditure of training dollars on those areas mandated by state governments and on programs to maintain a minimum level of proficiency among their officers.

A final consideration, which may impede the development of continuing professional education in the police service, is the absence of competition in the marketplace served by the police. The police are a government sanctioned monopoly. Citizens, generally, do not have a choice of police agencies that they can call for service. A call to 911 summons the local police, inside towns and cities, and the sheriff or state police in unincorporated areas. This monopoly may serve to diminish concerns, among police administrators, for accountability which, in turn, may lead to maintenance of the status quo rather than to a meaningful desire to advance the organization and its members through quality training and education. Some states have dealt with this problem by mandating continuing education and training for all police officers in their jurisdiction.

PARTICIPATION IN CONTINUING PROFESSIONAL EDUCATION

During the past 25 years, there has been a growing concern among consumer groups, various governmental agencies, and professional regulatory boards with respect to the competency of practitioners in several professions and occupations. Dramatic advances in technology and the "information explosion" our society has been experiencing have caused many to question whether initial professional licensure or certification ensures competency throughout the span of an individual's career.

Mandatory continuing education (MCE) has been implemented in a number of different ways. The most common methods are through direct government regulation of licensure laws, indirect regulation through employer and professional organization membership requirements, and through the use of informal social and peer pressure (Rockhill, 1983).

Either through state statute or enabling legislation, the government has succeeded in requiring professionals to participate in any given number of continuing educational activities (Rockhill, 1983, p. 108). Regardless of how MCE is implemented, the effect is essentially the same—professional adults are required to participate in a prescribed amount of educational activity to either maintain their licenses, work for and be associated with a reputable employer and organization, or to advance their careers.

As professionals, the ideal situation would be for all parties concerned to engage in voluntary continuing educational pursuits. With the possible exception of the health sciences, a significant number of professions have yet to demonstrate such a interest. For example, since the 1960s, a period in our history overshadowed by an alarming increase in crime and civil unrest, there has been a cry, not only for more police but for more professional police officers and related services (Cox & Moore, 1992, pp. 240–241). In response the Law Enforcement Assistance Administration (LEAA) provided federal funding to state and local governments for the purpose of educating and training police officers. It was only during that period that the law enforcement community began to give serious thought to training requirements and standards.

Though today every state has some form of statutory requirement pertaining to entry level police training, it is more important to note that law enforcement and related standards reveal that those requirements serve only as a prerequisite for certification or intital licensure (Scuro & Scuro 1983, p. 37). Even more alarming is that according to the National Law Enforcement Training Survey, as of 1992, while there is an indication of

> Movement toward enhancing minimum entry level requirements and boosting in-service requirements for law enforcement officers, only one state has mandated a combination of education and training. (Cox & Moore, 1992 p. 252)

In addition, characteristics such as developing, maintaining and enforcing standards and ethical practices are missing from initial police training. Possessing an internal commitment for continuing education past the initial licensure is not fostered either. This is evidenced by the fact that the majority of post-initial training relates to areas associated with civil liability, such as the use of firearms, the use of physical force, and high speed vehicle pursuits (Cox & Moore, 1992, p. 246). Because liability is almost always directed towards the employer, such training programs are generally the result of some court order or malpractice insurance requirement. For the most part, however, the fact remains that

> Unlike many other American professions, or unlike policing in some other countries, such as Germany,there are often no continuing education requirements for American police officers. (Schwartz & Yonkers 1991, p. 50)

The training that is being conducted seems to have fallen victim to many of the same criticisms of MCE in other professions. For example, vendors supplying the majority of police training programs fail to incorporate principles of adult education in their delivery of information. Research is seldom used to identify training needs, and not enough emphasis is placed on developing skills and putting new knowledge into practice. Perhaps vendors should follow England's philosophy:

> Teaching methods include facilitated learning in small groups to encourage depth of understanding; didactic teaching is usually reserved for those occasions when the principal aim is to impart knowledge. (Bunyard, 1991, p. 13)

Another problem police programs have encountered is their lack of emphasis on research pertaining to evaluation of the relevance and applicability of the training. In contrast, many other professions utilize sophisticated evaluation techniques designed to assess program effectiveness and relevancy. In addition, most professions emphasize research which attempts to link training to job performance. Unfortunately, this is not true for law enforcement training programs (Holmes, et al., 1992, p. 51).

Finally, in addition to the need for effective training requirements, many experts feel that the education level of police officers must be increased. Various studies with respect to the relationship between higher education and police job performance are mixed. However, the bulk of the evidence points to a positive relationship between education and job performance. Benefits associated with higher education include more effective communications skills, better problem-solving and analytical skills, an increase in public perception of police competence, fewer citizen complaints of verbal and physical abuse, and fewer disciplinary actions against college educated police officers (Cox & Moore, 1992, p. 250–53).

We believe the evidence is clear—if the field of law enforcement intends to move along the continuum of professionalization, participation in continuing professional edudation activities should be mandatory. Thus far, most state training boards leave the issue of education requirements and participation in these educational activities up to the individual police agencies. Unfortunately, while some departments emphasize post-entry training and education, the vast majority do not.

Therefore, when occupations and professions do not voluntarily move forward direct regulation by professional or governmental agencies and organizations seems to be a viable alternative.

VISIONS OF THE FUTURE

Having briefly discussed some historical and contemporary issues relative to continuing professional education in policing, we now wish to address the direction continuing professional education is or should be taking for the future in the police service. The police play an important, even indispensable, role in modern society. Created as an institution of formal social control, the police are charged with the responsibility of enforcing laws and maintaining order. At the same time, however, the police are also required to protect the rights of individual citizens and maintain the fundamental qualities of a free society. These sometimes divergent and conflicting tasks place the police officer in situations that require tact, diplomacy, and a keen understanding of complex political and social issues.

In response to an increasingly complex society, an endless array of new laws based on changing philosophies continue to be enacted. The dynamic nature of our legal system places a tremendous burden on the working police officer to maintain a thorough knowledge and understanding of a very complex legal system. Add to this the need to understand and utilize ever-advancing technology and the public's expectation that the police respond to and address an ever-widening range of community and social problems, it becomes clear that a new vision for police training and education is needed.

We have a great respect for the power of words. As symbols, words not only communicate, they also serve to inspire and define. It is for this reason that the terms "law enforcement" and "law enforcement officer" are, in our view, problematic. The message that these terms convey is that the primary and even exclusive function of the police is to enforce laws. This is an extremely narrow view of policing and one that is entirely inaccurate. Hess and Wrobleski (1993) estimated that only 10 to 20% of calls for police services dealt with matters related to crimes or criminal activity. If, however, the perception of the police is that of crime fighters and law enforcers and this perception is allowed to guide or influence decision making, particularly regarding police training, the police will fail to progress toward a higher degree of professionalism and will be unable to meet the challenges of policing in the 21st century.

The police have a long and distinguished history as providers of social services and as community activists. Before social work was a recognized profession, the police were responsible for providing communities with a wide range of social services. These services included managing soup kitchens, maintaining orphanages, unemployment services, youth athletic leagues, and rendering medical care to the poor (Miller & Hess, 1994, p. 7). For nearly a century the police embraced their role as social service providers. In the fifties and sixties social strife, an increase in the use of narcotics, the Vietnam War, and widespread allegations of police corruption in many major cities prompted a movement to reform the police, as an institution. This reform movement, referred to as the "professional era of policing" altered and limited the role of the police in our society (Miller & Hess, 1994). This initiative changed the role of the police from service providers to crime fighters. As part of the reformation of the police the introduction of advanced communications technology and an increased use of the police car as a primary means of police patrol allowed reformers to separate the police from the close ties it has had with the community, which was thought by some to promote corruption, and increase the efficiency of the working patrol officer. Police officers in cars could now cover a larger area than foot patrolmen creating a more cost effective and efficient use of manpower. Although there was a greater amount of manpower efficiency, these changes served to isolate the police from the people they served. Police officers no longer walked a beat, knowing the residents, business people, and ne'er-do-wells. Instead they were wrapped in a cocoon of metal, glass, and plastic speeding by on the way to the next call as dictated by the patrol car radio.

It has been over 30 years since attempts were made to "professionalize" the police. It appears, now, that we have come full circle in our guiding philosophy as to how police services should be delivered. Although many police administrators and line officers cling tenaciously to the "professional crime fighter model" of policing, there is a growing movement to reacquaint the police with the people they serve and to reestablish them as agents of social change in our communities. This new/old philosophy is called "community policing."

At the heart of this philosophy is the belief that the police cannot deal effectively with gang violence, drugs, domestic violence, and other social problems, without the help of the community. This philosophy is predicated on the notion that the police need to be more involved in the life of the community they serve. Community policing calls for a more holistic approach to crime control and encourages the police to once again become problem solvers rather than law enforcers. Communities are asking the police to take a leadership role in dealing with the underlying causes of crime and neighborhood deterioration. Rather than focusing on a reactive operational style, the police are being encouraged to take a more proactive approach in crime prevention. This new/old philosophy will require a major restructuring of both philosophical and operational goals and methods regarding the delivery of police services of which training will be an essential component.

If the concept of community policing is to be effective, the line officer will need to be granted more autonomy and more authority in dealing with community problems. With this policy will come a greater degree of accountability, not only to police command, but to the community in general. In order to deal with complex social issues and problems the police of the 21st century will need to possess ad-

vanced analytical, social, and communication skills along with critical thinking. To be effective, the police must understand and be able
to use new technology. It is doubtful that the current structure of police education and training will be able to prepare police officers for
these new challenges. Basic educational requirements, standardization of police training, and participation in meaningful and effective
continuing professional education will be necessary if the police, as
individuals and as an institution, are to meet the demands and challenges of this society in the next century.

REFERENCES

Bureau of Justice Statistics (BJS). (1993). Law enforcement management
and administrative statistics, 1993. (NCJ-148825). Washington, DC:
United States Department of Justice.

Bunyard, R. (1991, November-December). Police higher training in England
and Wales. *CJ International, 7,* 6.

Cox, B.,& Moore, R. (1992, August). Toward the twenty first century: Law
enforcement training now and then. *Journal of Contemporary Criminal
Justice, 8,* 3, 235–236.

Flexner, A. (1915). Is social work a profession? School and society. 1, 901–911

Hess, K., & Wrobleski, H. (1993). *Police operations.* St. Paul: West.

Holmes, G., Cole, E., & Hicks, L. (1992, November). Curriculum development: Relevancy and innovation. *The Police Chief,* 51–52.

Houle, C. (1980). *Continuing learning in the professions.* San Francisco:
Jossey-Bass.

Johnson, H., & Wolfe, N. (1996). *History of criminal justice* (2nd ed.) Cincin-
nati: Anderson.

Kister, K. (1990). *Webster's new world dictionary* (3rd ed.). New York: Simon
& Schuster.

Larson, M. S. (1977). *The rise of professionalism: A Sociological Analysis.*
Los Angeles: University of California Press.

Miller, L., & Hess, K. (1994). *Community policing: Theory and practice.* St.
Paul: West

Rockhill, K. (1983, Winter). Mandatory continuing education for professionals: Trends and issues. *Adult Education, 33,* 2, 106–116.

Schmalleger, F. (1995). *Criminal Justice Today.* Englewood Cliffs, NJ: Pren-
tice Hall.

Schwartz, M., & Yonkers, S. (1991). Officer satisfaction with police in-
service training: An exploratory evaluation. *American Journal of Police,
10,* 4, 49–63.

Scuro, G., & Scuro, L. (1983, March). The civil liability consequences of Department Rules and Regulations. *The Police Chief,* 36–38.

18

Continuing Professional Military Education: Present Programs and Current Issues

Tony Latham

INTRODUCTION

The United States Department of Defense is the cabinet level federal agency which has the responsibility for resourcing and directing the armed forces of our nation, Army, Navy, Marine Corps, and Air Force. The armed forces are populated by adults, young and older, who have volunteered to serve our nation as directed by our civilian leaders and military commanders according to applicable laws and regulations. The individuals in our nation's military units are recruited, trained and continually educated, assigned duties, and complete their service obligation by returning to citizen pursuits through separation from service or retirement (Department of the Army Pamphlet 600-3, 1986).

The individuals who serve in our armed forces are linked by one theme which characterizes their service: They participate in continuing professional education related to their individual military jobs and duties, to their part as a members of a team, and to the mission of their unit and branch of the service. The theme of continuing professional education in our nation's armed forces is the subject of this chapter. The programs of continuing professional education for the armed forces are similar. I have experienced the Army continuing professional education program and will use its model to describe continuing professional military education.

CURRENT ARMY PROGRAM
Enlisted Soldiers

The Army uses the term Officer and/or Enlisted Professional Development in place of continuing professional education. *Professional Development for each soldier and soldier leader is a process of meritorious selection for continued service.* One aspect of this process is initial training for a soldier's job or specialty (i.e., rifleman, cook, medic, truck driver). The training for entry level skills in the Army is conducted on military installations by Army instructors. Civilian teachers contracted for specific subjects are also involved with the soldiers' initial training. Successful completion of this initial training qualifies soldiers for assignment. During the second aspect of the development process the soldiers are members of units. They are educated (trained) daily in the skills, attitudes, and physical capabilities needed to do their job as effective members of the team helping to accomplish the unit's mission. The third aspect of development is counseling. At intervals during the soldiers' assignment to the unit, their job or duty performance is evaluated and they are counseled as to how to improve their performance. Counseling includes recommendations for future duty assignments to continue progressive job skill development.

The process of professional development is characterized by initial skill training; assignment to duties which allow application of the learned skills along with improvement and refinement of the skills, evaluation and counseling of job performance and help to improve capabilities. Planned and progressive rotation of duties and assignments to provide opportunities for professional growth is part of the process.

Professional development for enlisted soldiers is a daily function of Army units. This is a formal, mandatory program. It is low cost in money, time, and other resources as an overlay to fixed expenses necessary for essential unit operation.

Enlisted leaders (noncommissioned officers) are prepared for leading squads, sections, detachments and small units through a process of meritorious job performance, selection for promotion, and attendance at formal, centralized courses of instruction emphasizing relevant equipment, job, and leader skills. Most of the instructors for the noncommissioned officer courses are Army personnel. A few civilian instructors are contracted for special subjects and programs. Once newly prepared noncommissioned officers are leading soldiers, they will be continually educated and counseled, evaluated, and assigned to planned and progressive rotation of assignments. These opportunities to apply the learned skills help them enhance their capabilities as leaders.

Enlisted leaders who successfully apply the skills they learn to become leaders are recommended for basic and advanced noncommissioned officer centralized programs of instruction in the specialty. These formal leader development courses, coupled with earned promotions, prepare the noncommissioned officers to serve as platoon sergeants and assist with staff functions in personnel, operations and training, intelligence, and supply and maintenance. The on-the-job professional development continues for platoon sergeants and staff specialists: daily training, counseling, evaluation, and planned job rotations to help the leader grow professional capabilities.

A few very capable noncommissioned officers will be selected to attend the centralized First Sergeant Course and Sergeant Major Academy. Graduation from these programs will prepare these soldier leaders for service as first sergeants and staff sergeant majors and command sergeant majors. These senior enlisted leaders will assist commanders in the professional development of individual soldiers and the training, counseling, evaluation, assignment and selection of enlisted leaders.

Officers

The program for professional development of Army officers was the forerunner of the enlisted system outlined in preceding paragraphs. The program for officers has been refined as a result of reflection and investigation of methods which appear to contribute to the development of effective leaders.

Professional development is, again, one aspect of a personnel management system designed to produce officers with the needed skills to meet Army requirements; develop the competencies of officers through planned schooling and progressive assignments; assign officers to satisfy Army requirements; and to return officers to civilian life or retirement. (DA Pam 600–3, 1986)

The process of developing officers professionally is identical to the enlisted program with emphasis on technical competence in a specialty (i.e., infantry, transportation, administration); professional development education courses and schools, on-the-job training, individual study; planned and progressive rotation of duties to different job assignments; and counseling and evaluation by commanders.

There are five phases of professional development which are related to Army officer ranks. These phases are adapted to each officer in accordance with the requirements of the Army, the officers' capabilities and the officers' demonstrated performance of their assigned duties (DA Pam 600–3, 1986; Crocker, 1990).

The phases of professional development are as follows:

Lieutenant Phase

The lieutenant phase begins when the individual is sworn into the Army as an officer. The new officer attends the officer basic course in his or her branch (i.e. infantry, armor, finance). The course curriculum includes instruction on the branch mission and function along with the technical knowledge necessary to understand the duties and responsibilities of lieutenants in the branch.

The officer's assignment to Army unit and organization after this schooling allows the officer to apply the school training and develop leadership skills as a platoon leader.

Captain Phase

The objectives of the captain phase are to gain additional branch experience, grow in more general knowledge of other Army branches, and continue to develop practical leadership experience. All captains will attend their branch officer advanced course. This course qualifies officers completely in their branch and provides a broader understanding of command and staff operations, administration and logistics, and tactics.

Assignment for an officer graduating from the advanced course is focused on utilizing the officer's gained abilities in staff and command positions.

All captains will also attend the Combined Arms and Staff School. They must complete a nonresident phase of this program before they are scheduled for the resident portion. Completion of the Combined Arms and Staff School will prepare the officer to serve in staff positions.

Lieutenants and captains are encouraged to volunteer for optional courses which would allow them to learn additional skills and help broaden their knowledge of people, the Army and tactical operations. Most of these elective courses are offered at Army service school locations. When the need exists, some specialized professional development opportunities are offered at civilian colleges, universities, institutes, and companies which have the expertise the Army wants selected leaders to develop.

Major Phase

The objective of the major phase is for an officer to continue learning about his or her branch while helping to train and counsel captains, lieutenants, and noncommissioned officers. Majors will be assigned to positions of greater responsibility which will require the application of all of their previously learned competencies.

Some officers, about 40%, will be selected to attend the Command and General Staff College while in the grade of major. Graduation from this school will prepare officers to serve as battalion commanders and staff officers. This course helps qualify an officer for promotion to lieutenant colonel.

Lieutenant Colonel Phase

The objectives for the lieutenant colonel phase are to continue officer attainment of branch technical skills, understanding tactical applications of competencies, and application of their capabilities in demanding jobs as senior staff officers and for some officers, command of a battalion.

A few lieutenant colonels, 10 to 12% will be selected to attend the Army War College. The purpose of the course of instruction at this school is to prepare officers for high level command and staff assignments by stressing an understanding of senior leadership skills and techniques. Officers graduating from this program are ready for promotion to colonel.

Colonel Phase

The professional development objective of the colonel phase is to realize the maximum use of the officers' technical skills, executive talents, and leadership capabilities in assignments requiring the best leaders in the Army.

Colonels are assigned to positions as commanders of units; directors of programs, schools, installations; and principal staff officers of general officer commands. Colonels are responsible for running the day-to-day operations of the Army. They are custodians of the ongoing professional development programs throughout the vast Army operation.

Colonels are also developed professionally at discussions, seminars, and demonstrations related to Army plans, organizations, and training. The opportunities for development of colonels are sponsored by major military commands, civilian organizations, and gatherings of civilian professionals concerned about trends in personnel management, finance, logistics, maintenance management, engineering, aviation, environmental protections, safety, medicine, petroleum storage, and food storage and preparation.

In addition to the professional development courses and assignments included in each of the five phases, officers are counseled in detail about their current job performance and implied potential for promotion and therefore opportunity for future service. Officers, ultimately, are responsible for their professional development with the concerned assistance of their commander.

General officers are not formally included in the phases of officer professional development. Because general officers plan, direct, and evaluate all activities of the Army, they are intimately involved in creating the environment in which professional training of all soldiers and soldier leaders is planned, developed, conducted, and evaluated. The future readiness of the Army is in part based on the success of professional development programs the general officers support with time, resources, and their presence as mentors and models for all Army leaders.

CONCLUSION

Issues for Professional Development

All our armed forces have well planned and resourced continuing professional military education programs. The Army model is an example of how one service addresses and follows through on the concept of continuing education. These service programs are currently well defined and develop the best technical and operational leaders for our armed forces on a sustained basis.

Continuing professional education in our armed forces is evolving. A transitional period is forming in which the number of members in all armed services is being reduced dramatically. Fewer people to educate does not pose a problem unless the balance of personnel in units, on ships, in air wings to those service personnel in schools as faculty, and supporting education administratively are disporportionally reduced. The reduction of personnel dedicated to continuing professional education could be seen as the way to accomplish the same missions as in years past with fewer, but fully manned units, ships, air wings, and task forces.

Along with a possible disproportional reduction of people involved in professional development, the resources in equipment and available training locations might also be reduced. If the money for these educational support aspects were reprioritized to maintain equipment and operations in fewer Army, Navy, Marine, and Air Force units, then professional development will lose not only resources, but also status.

Money and what it buys are only one concern. Time to develop the service personnel and young leaders needed by our armed forces could become an issue. The necessity for full manning of the force to accomplish current operations could begin to delay educational opportunities. Approval for abbreviated training opportunities to keep units full could eventually evolve to denial of continuing professional development altogether.

The opportunity for experiential learning as a proving ground for professional development programs and their graduates could be a casualty of maintaining high unit readiness with our "best" people all the time.

Future Continuing Professional Military Education

Continuing professional military education programs have developed over the past decades to support the never-ending need for competent and ready leaders and service members to defend our national interests. *These well-developed and necessary programs of continuing education are currently threatened by fewer units, operational unit priorities for remaining units, potential loss of status for continuing education, and possible loss of education resources.*

Budgets and more personnel of the past allowed the services to keep many service schools full and units fully manned. The current environment dictates a need to adopt other approaches to gaining and maintaining professional competence through continuing education.

One approach to making professional enrichment opportunities available to all services and most phases of their professional development programs is to investigate the applicability of distance education principles and techniques (Meriam & Cunningham, 1989). *Where appropriate, continuing professional education could be centrally produced and remotely delivered to support individual and organizational needs.* This approach could reduce the necessity for costly single location lesson delivery, and the potential for cost saving consolidation of educational resources could be seriously investigated. For development activities requiring live, experiential reinforcement of learning, practicum sponsored by operational units could be planned, budgeted, and produced as needed.

The environment of continuing professional military education has changed. However, the commitment to leader and service member development through continuing professional military education could endure by adopting techniques of distance education to a proven continuing military education approach.

REFERENCES

The armed forces officer. (1988). DoD GEN-36A. Washington, DC: U.S. Government Printing Office.

Crocker, L. P. (1990). Army officer's guide. Harrisburg, PA: Stackpole Books.

Department of the Army Pamphlet 600–3 (1986). Officer personnel management system. Washington, DC: U.S. Government Printing Office.

Merriam, S. B., & Cunningham, P. M., (Eds.). (1989). *Handbook of adult and continuing education*. San Francisco: Jossey-Bass.

19

Continuing Professional Education in Real Estate

Margot B. Weinstein

INTRODUCTION

Real estate is a complex business that generates billions of dollars in transactions each year. It requires the services of millions of highly trained individuals, and it affects peoples' lives in a multitude of ways. "Real estate is the most basic resource in the world. It touches the lives of more people than any other single commodity," (Dasso, Ring, & McFall, 1977, p. 5). Real estate transactions dictate where people live, work, shop, and play. For many people, the purchase of a home, will be the largest investment in their lives. For this reason, since the early 1900s, everyone has been interested in regulating the real estate business in order to protect public interests. Because of the complexity and diversity of the real estate business, it was difficult to pass laws to control each transaction. Therefore, specific procedures were passed in order to ensure that professionalism and ethical standards were observed by practitioners in real estate. Today, the real estate professional has to follow procedures for prelicensing, licensing, and postlicencing education requirements. Furthermore, strict guidelines are set up as disciplinary measures in the event of infractions committed by professionals who do not follow these laws.

Real estate professionals are asked to make socially responsible decisions that assist in solving regional problems. In order to deal with the rapid pace of change in their workplaces, communities, and social structures, real estate professionals are pursuing lifelong education in professional associations, colleges, universities, and employing agencies. In order for these programs to meet the needs of their participants as well as the demands made by society, leadership in continuing professional education will need to develop innovative strategies to deliver programs and services. This chapter defines key terminology, discusses history of real estate professionals in America, and talks about the controversies, critical issues, trends, and visions in real estate continuing professional education for the 21st century.

The critical terms used in this chapter are defined as follows:

Real Estate: Land and improvements in a physical sense as well as the rights to own or use them, Harwood, 1979, p. 509).

Real Estate Broker: any person who, for another and for compensation or promise of compensation, performs an interest therein:(1) sells (2) lists (3) buys (4) rents or leases (5) collects rents (6) exchanges (7) deals in options (8) offers to perform or negotiate one of these activities (9) represents that he or she engages in any of these activities, (Pajor, 1985, p. 9).

Real estate sales person: any person who performs any of the previously listed activities while employed by or associated with a real estate broker. (Galaty, Selway, & Kyle, 1978, p. 14–2.)

REALTOR®: is a registered collective membership mark which may be used only by real estate professionals who are members of the NATIONAL ASSOCIATION OF REALTORS® and subscribe to its strict Code of Ethics, (NAR Membership, 1995, p. x).

HISTORICAL PERSPECTIVE

Prior to the 19th century, anyone could practice real estate. The real estate industry wanted to enhance its public image as a profession; therefore, in the early 20th century, there were several developments to ensure that people were trained to perform real estate transactions, were receiving adequate education, and, once educated, were performing their tasks well. Pajor (1985) stated that because of the unique nature of each real estate transaction, there is a significant lack of standardization within the industry. Rather than attempting the complex task of controlling the quality of each transaction there is, instead, control of practitioners through licensure. The first attempt to license people was in 1917 in California. Harwood (1979) argued

> this attempt was ruled unlawful because opponents claimed
> that this law was an unreasonable interference with the right
> of every citizen to engage in a useful and legitimate occupation

and were successful in having the law declared unconstitutional by courts. (p. 1)

Two years later, in 1919, the California legislature passed a second real estate licensing act; this time it was upheld by the Supreme Court. Other states followed, and soon persons who offered their services as real estate agents needed to be licensed. Today, all 50 states and the District of Columbia have enacted legislation providing for licensing and regulation of persons engaged in real estate business. Warner (1979) stated that the main reason for real estate practitioners to be licensed is to protect the public from unscrupulous and/or incompetent operators and to establish minimum qualifying standards for offering services.

Pajor (1985) stated that the public made several assumptions about the role of continuing education and continued competence in regard to licensure. Pajor (1985) cited the reasons expressed by Shimberg (1978):

(a) the possession of a license is evidence that a state agency has checked the applicant's qualifications and administered appropriate tests to ensure that he or she is fully competent; and (b) licensing boards monitor their licensees to insure that licensees have maintained their competence and are still fit to practice. (p. 215)

According to Pajor (1985)

consumers did not recognize the real estate practitioner as being a professional. Wooten (in Pajor) offered several possible reasons for this lack of recognition: (a) education in an institution of higher learning; (b) experience needed to be under the guidance of others in the same profession; and (c) rigid controls were needed of professional standards through licensing and self-policing. (p. 17)

Furthermore, the courts regarded real estate as a trade until recently: In the case *United States v. National Association of Real Estate Boards* (339 U.S. 485, 1950), the court stated that real estate brokerage is a trade. "Whenever any occupation, employment or business is carried on for the purpose of profit, a gain or a livelihood not in the liberal arts or in the learned professions, it is constantly called a trade" (339 U.S. 485).

Before the late 1970s, Wright (1976) stated that real estate professionalization had not occurred for several reasons: (a) there were very few restrictions to enter into the business; (b) because of these lax entrance requirements the public felt that they could perform the services themselves; (c) most practitioners stated that their main reason for entering the field was for personal economic opportunities rather than the opportunity to serve others; (d) the public felt that there was little correlation between commission fees and effort expended; (e) real estate practitioners did not have solid relations between universities and real estate practitioners; and (f) many licensees have no higher aspirations than to be successful technicians, and (g) most successful professions are better able to exploit the legitimization of their monopoly power over certain resources (knowledge) which are required by a large segment of the society.

BEGINNINGS OF PROFESSIONAL IDENTITY

The first professional real estate organizations were formed before laws required real estate agents to have licenses. These real estate boards, joined agents within a city or county on a voluntary basis. The push to organize came from real estate people who saw the need for some sort of controlling organization that could supervise the activities of individual agents and elevate the status to that of a profession in the public's mind. Next, came the gradual grouping of local boards into state associations, and finally, in 1908, the National Association of Real Estate Boards (NAREB) was formed. In 1914, the NAREB developed a model license law that became the basis for real estate laws in many states.

Local boards are still the fundamental units of the National Association of Realtors (NAR; the name was changed from NAREB on January 1, 1974). Local board membership is open to anyone holding a real estate license. These boards promote fair dealings among their members and with the public. They protect members from dishonest and irresponsible licensees. They also promote legislation that protects property rights, offer short seminars to keep members up to date with current laws and practices, and, in general do whatever is necessary to build the dignity, stability, and professionalization of the industry.

The National Association of Realtors (NAR) is the largest professional association in the world. NAR is made up of local boards and state associations in the United States. NAR developed a strict code of ethics in 1913 which the members agreed to abide by in order to help generate public confidence and attract business to members. This code of ethics has been revised several times to parallel existing laws. The adherence to the Code by members, provided an important assurance to the public of the integrity and professionalism of licensees in the field.

NAR develops and provides continuing education and certification for members to receive and maintain several professional designations. The professional designations are as follows: the General Accredited Appraiser (GAA) and Residential Accredited Appraiser (RAA), the Certified International Property Specialist (CIPS); the American Society of Real Estate Counselors (CRE); Commercial Investment Member (CCIM); Institute of Real Estate Management (IREM, ARM) and the Accredited Management Organization (AMO), REALTORS® Land Institute (RLI); Accredited Land Consultant (ALC); REALTORS® National Marketing Institute RNMI); the Certified Real Estate Brokerage Manager (CRB); and Certified Residential Specialist (CRS); Society of Industrial and Office REALTORS® (SIOR); and the Women's Council of REALTORS® (LTG). All these designations provide the opportunity for service, education, and professional designation representing advanced professional status.

NAR participates actively as a spokesperson for the real estate industry and maintains a full-time staff, headquartered in Washington, D.C., to provide testimony on important real-estate-related issues before Congress and various regulatory agencies. NAR also provides extensive educational programs and some leads to real estate special educational degrees such as "Graduate of Real Estate Institute," (GRI).

Today's real estate industry employs millions of specialists such as brokers, salespeople, appraisers, property, managers, financiers, developers, counselors, and educators. The real estate industry can generally be classified into four types: residential, commercial, industrial, or agricultural.

According to Case (1970), today real estate is a profession:

> Real Estate is viewed as a profession because clearly, there is a body of specialized knowledge which all who sell real estate must master if they are to succeed. Continuing success and survival in the business would appear to depend upon continuing education relating to many specialized types of real estate operations. (p. 7)

LAWS AND REGULATORY BOARDS CREATED
TO "PROTECT PUBLIC INTEREST"

Since 1917, states have passed real estate license laws intended to evaluate the competency of persons engaged in the real estate business and to regulate such businesses for the protection of the public. States usually follow a three-tiered legal system to help license and maintain professional designations. All states follow the national, state, and local laws governing real estate transactions. In addition, by the 1980s many states passed laws that made education mandatory. License laws are established throughout the country. Almost every state license law authorizes a board or commission to promulgate rules and regulations to implement the statutory provisions. Each state is controlled by a department of professional license regulations that oversees licenses. Some states, such as Illinois, were able to force the state government to enact a separate department of professional license regulations that deals only with real estate administration, education, guidance, and disciplinary action needed by licencees. The director of the department of professional regulation appoints a licensed broker to the position of commissioner of real estate. This person acts as the direct liaison among the department, the professional, and the real estate organizations and associations; prepares and circulates educational material for licensees; appoints committees to assist the department in carrying out its duties; and supervises the real estate unit of the department, subject to the administrative approval of the director, to whom the commissioner reports.

There is a real estate administration and disciplinary board that participates in the disciplinary process and provides guidance to the director of the department of professional regulation regarding standards of professional conduct, discipline and examination under the state's current license acts. In addition to its advisory functions, the board conducts hearings on disciplinary actions against persons accused of violating license laws of that state.

Furthermore, most states have a real estate education advisory council which approves and regulates schools, instructors, curricula, sponsors, and programs. Only sponsors approved by the advisory council may provide real estate continuing education courses. Each sponsor must provide participants with a certificate of completion and have a course exam with a 70% passing grade to earn the certificate.

In 1930, The Association of Real Estate License Law Officials (Arello) was established as a federation of real estate license law officials to assist each other in the administration and enforcement of license laws in the United States and Canada. Today, it has 57 member jurisdictions in United States, Canada and the Netherlands. Arello's mission is stated

> better administration and enforcement of real estate license and regulatory laws in the member jurisdictions. This distinctive task of the Association is to help equip its members to fulfill their roles as regulators. That role is to protect the public interest in real estate brokerage transactions. Protecting the public interest does not mean advocating an industry or a consumer position. Instead, it means assuring each individual's right to justice and equal opportunity under the law. There, the public interest demands the regulator's best effort to achieve impartial administration of the law. (Francis, 1995, p. ii)

In order to accomplish its mission, Arello dispenses research and communication on license law matters; provides educational development for personal and professional improvement; encourages and develops cooperation with other organizations of similar nature; and shares expertise, information, and networking techniques.

Furthermore, most states have a real estate research and education fund to finance the operation of the office of real estate and research that is usually located in a college or university in that state. There are over 100 such real estate research centers in the United States. These centers employ educators, researchers, students, and administrative staff for the purpose of real estate research. Most of the research that is gathered is on the real estate business. Very little research is done on the subject of real estate education.

The complexity and diversity of the real estate field have forced most real estate professionals to embrace the concept of lifelong professional education. Practitioners cite this increase in educational programs as due to the following: (1) the desire of real estate practitioners for higher status within the eyes of the general public; (2) the need to keep abreast of rapid changes in laws; (3) the necessity of keeping up with advances in technology; and (4) the availability of education of real estate practitioners in different formats. According to NAR (1981) sources of real estate education include The National Association of Realtors and its institutes, societies, and councils; state associations of realtors; local real estate boards; state licensing commissions; universities and colleges; franchise organizations; independent firms; and proprietary schools.

Sirmans et al. (1992) explained that several studies exist which have concluded that education and experiences have positive effects on earnings of real estate professionals. Real estate agents and brokers earn a positive return from educational investments undertaken through formal schooling and professional training.

In order to meet the demands of real estate professionals for more educational opportunities, in the last 10 years there has been a tremendous increase in undergraduate, graduate, and continuing education programs throughout United States.

WHO PROVIDES THE BEST EDUCATION FOR PROFESSIONALS?

One of the current controversies in the field has been over who can provide better real estate education in order to keep the professional up to date and upgrade status? Because professionals in real estate have continued to pursue their education both in formal degree programs as well as informal programs offered by professional organizations or by companies in which they work, there has been a controversy over which of these providers can best educate real estate professionals.

Until the 1980s, most college or university degrees received by real estate people were issued through departments which offered only a major or concentration in the real estate field. These degrees were usually given by the business, architectural, or law departments. Because real estate professionals have continued to pursue their education both in formal degree programs as well as informal programs offered by other professional organizations or by companies in which they work.

With the emergence in the late 1980s of a handful of master's degree programs directed specifically at producing real estate developers, Weinberg (1988), asked the question that has provoked the debate in both real estate development and academic circles, "Can colleges and universities effectively teach real estate development?" These new programs were offered at New York University's Real Estate Institute, University of Wisconsin at Madison, Texas A & M, Massachusetts Institute of Technology (MIT), the University of Southern California (USC), and elsewhere. He explained that these graduate programs should be distinguished from the large number of M.B.A. graduate programs with "concentrations" or "majors" in real estate.

Weinberg (1988) explained that the new graduate programs are trying to deal with most of the criticisms. The litany of criticisms of traditional graduate programs accuses them of training number crunchers and turning out graduates without true real estate understanding. He stated further that most programs are based in business schools and concentrate on finance to the exclusion of other needed subjects, those based in architectural schools concentrate too heavily on design, and those in planning schools are criticized for emphasis on urban planning.

Weinberg (1988) argued

> the best of these programs solicit candidates with two to five years of experience. The admissions policies are designed to attract students who already are possessed of some of the attributes needed by successful developers: judgment,entrepreneurial temperament, and interpersonal skills. These schools are blends of education and professionals and adjuncts who can balance the reticle principles with pragmatism.
>
> The programs offer large and varied curricula. (p. 2)

The success of these programs was further evidence that real estate was becoming a profession which deserved attention in colleges and universities across the country. These programs have helped other schools initiate more programs to help the real estate professional attain higher-level degrees in education.

THE MANDATORY CONTINUING PROFESSIONAL EDUCATION CONTROVERSY

In the last 10 years, the main controversy in real estate education has been whether mandatory continuing educations requirements should be tied to relicensing. Proponents for mandatory continuing education give arguments suggested by Lowenthal (1981):

> (a) initial licensure is not a guarantee of continued competence; (b) formal education does not provide all the information, skills and attitudes needed for effective and successful practice; and (c) in order to provide the best service to the public, individuals must keep current in their fields of practice. (pp. 519–535)

In recent years, the public has criticized licensure as a quality assurance mechanism, and many professional groups (including real estate) have proposed legal mandatory continuing education. Shimberg (1978) stated that continuing education has been cited as the mechanism through which practitioners can continually become more competent and remain qualified to engage in activities for which they are licensed.

The implication is that continuing competency may require formal education experiences (continuing education) of varying duration which may or may not provide academic credit. Quatrano and Conant (1981) explained that equally important to continuing competence is informal educational and/or work experience which contributes to mastery of basic competencies necessary for satisfactory performance.

Pajor (1985) stated

> the solution to the problem of continued competency in licensed professions is complicated by professional, legal, and emotional arguments for and against continuing education. He states that it is easier to legislate classroom time requirements than it is to define and measure competency and implement competency based activities. Because of this, many states are considering adopting legislative sanctions of continuing education. It is believed that the only way to require individuals to pursue education programs would be to make that pursuit a condition of license renewal. The reason for mandatory education is founded on the belief that it will: protect the public from professionals who are too lazy, uninterested or egotistical to participate in continuing education; remove from the roll those persons who are no longer practicing and interested in keeping up professionally; and result in better-informed practitioners. (p. 3)

Blackshear (1980) explained the critics' viewpoint of mandatory continuing education to include

(a) such requirements are not mandatory for all professionals;
(b) material may be too elementary for sophisticated brokers and salesperson who have already obtained specialized knowledge;
(c) the costs of the courses, materials, and loss of working time may be a burden to some licensees; and,
(d) such requirements may serve only as a profit vehicle to school operators. (p. 14)

Phillips (1987) argued

> mandatory continuing education has a positive impact on professionals: (1) most licensees in states with mandatory continuing education requirements approve of such regulations, (2) a large number of professional "laggards" are finding renewed interest in their professions

and in professional activities because of involvement in mandatory continuing education activities, (3) mandatory continuing education requirements lead to an increased number of participants in available programs, and (4) mandatory continuing education helps professions to examine new ways of improving performance." (p. 59)

Furthermore, in the last 10 years most states have passed mandatory continuing education as a condition for license renewal in the field of real estate. Cervero (1988) stated that these visions reflect the increasing amount of attention given to continuing education in the professions. Many professions have a system of accreditation for providers of continuing education (Kenny, 1985). Cervero (1988) explained that all 50 states use participation in continuing education as a basis for relicensing members of certain professions. Phillips (1987) lists 16 professions that are regulated that way.

The California Department of Real Estate (Wiley, Piaazza, & Smith 1981) funded three studies to understand this complicated issue: The first study was conducted in 1980, the study attempted to define the criteria for adequate performance by a real estate agent. The second study conducted in 1981 assessed the relationship between the educational and experiential characteristics of licensees through consumer evaluations of performance in transactions. The third study, also conducted in 1981, was a statistical profile of licensees whose licenses were suspended or revoked.

Pajor (1985) stated

authors found a significant relationship between consumer satisfaction and agent training. He further explained that some agents provide better service than others, but it does not seem to make much difference whether or not an agent has taken any particular kind of course. Non-required courses, also, seemed to have the most positive effect, reflecting the motivation of the individual licensee rather than the content of the courses. (p. 48)

However, the previous arguments do not articulate the fact that mandatory programs are big business, and administrators, educators, and researchers in these programs reap the financial benefits of mandatory continuing education. Mandatory education has become standard in most professions. Current literature confirms that the requirements have increased the quantity and quality of programs for real estate professionals.

In a survey focusing on whether the California real estate mandatory continuing education licensure requirement should be continued, active and nonactive licensees reported different benefits of continuing. education (Young & Company, 1987).

An important part of this legislation is that it required licensees to pass a test to prove competency of knowledge and license skills. Sixty-one percent of the real estate professionals opposed the elimination of the testing-evaluation requirements of individual courses. On the other hand, the nonactive licensees did not agree with the benefits of the continuing education licensure requirement. According to Phillips (1987), the nonactive licensees believed that the findings substantiate that they do little more than the minimum to maintain their status, and that perhaps for the least competent participants, it does nothing to either disengage or stimulate a renewed interest in learning.

> At a minimum, continuing professional education appears to be a complex of instructional systems, many of them heavily didactic, in which people who know something teach it to those who do not know it. The central aim of such teaching, which is offered by many providers, is to keep professionals up to date in their practice. (Houle, 1980, p. 254)

CRITICAL ISSUES IN MANDATORY CONTINUING EDUCATION

Presently in real estate, there are several major providers of mandatory continuing education: universities, professional schools, professional associations, employing agencies, and independent providers.

Since the real estate professional has mandated continuing education, thousands of members are not renewing their licenses. Although the leaders in the field realized that new mandatory continuing education laws would force many people out of the field who could not make a commitment of time and money to the field, no one predicted that thousands of memberships would not be renewed. If this trend continues, many predict that by the 21st century, there will be half as many real estate professionals as there are today. If this happens, there will be too many programs vying for the same participants to take courses. This will force schools to close, and many educators and researchers will not continue to be funded by the professionals that they now serve. As a result, leaders need to work with professionals to discuss the future of professionals and the role of mandatory continuing education in the field. Presently, they should make changes that will enable professionals to stay in the field by designing educational programs that meet the needs of participants, sponsoring organizations, and the public.

Leaders in continuing real estate education need to address seven critical areas to meet the challenges of educating real estate professionals for complexities in their field of practice in the 21st century.

The first critical issue is that leaders in the profession should recommend legislation that will allow participants choices for how, when, where, what, they can learn. Presently, most states have laws that require that continuing education be delivered by a set number of hours of classroom attendance, which is usually lecture format. At the end of time of class, participants must pass a test by 70% in order to retain their license.

The second critical issue is that administrators, educators, and researchers need training in developing, planning, administrating, and evaluating mandatory continuing education programs. Most people in the field, have been chosen because they have a real estate background, but few of them have come from outside the field in which they have learned strategies that could improve their educational practices. Real estate continuing education programs are usually directed by its own members.

Real estate programs could improve their professional development by referring to excellent program-planning methods discussed in books by Houle (1972), Knowles (1980), and Simerly and Associates (1987); resources emphasizing teaching and learning aspects of planning Brookfield (1986), Knox (1986), or Stubblefield's (1981) four-phase learning-project model. Many program planners try to improve practice by rigorously applying principles in their practice. Apps (1979) explained that the principles are usually a familiar five-step structure:

(1) Assessing learners' needs, (2) defining objectives based on these needs, (3) identifying learning experiences to meet those objectives, (4) organizing learning experiences, and (5) evaluating the program in terms of the objectives. (p. 3)

The third critical issue for providers of mandatory continuing education is to ensure that educators have training in teaching adults. Interviews with administrators in several states throughout United States, discussed the lack of training that most of their teachers had in teaching. Most of the teachers were chosen because they were active members in the real estate industry and the real estate associations. Because of lack of training in teaching, most educators taught

only in lecture format. In the future, providers of mandatory continuing education programs will need to either hire teachers with teaching background or provide training for their educators.

Cervero (1988) argued

> Learners are at the center of every continuing professional education-
> program. While learners are the key actors in this drama, the script
> has been crafted ahead of time by educators. Like playwrights, educa-
> tors stage an educational drama on the basis of their model of profes-
> sionals as learners. This model is rooted in what they believe about
> how professionals know, how professional incorporate knowledge into
> practice, under what conditions professionals learn best, and what role
> prior experience plays in learning. These models of learning are so
> deeply embedded in educators' psyches that they tend to act on them
> implicitly. Occasionally, these private beliefs become public concerns
> when debates occur in professional education literature about the best
> way to teach or plan programs for professionals. (p. 38)

As stated by Freire (1973)

> teachers must respect the consciousness and culture of their students
> and create the pedagogical situation in which students can articulate
> their understanding of the world. At the same time, teachers must be
> self-reflective and seek to understand their own presuppositions and
> assumptions, the ideological prism through which external reality is
> sorted and understood. (p. 56)

Leadership in mandatory continuing professional education must
look at how real estate professionals learn and how they transfer
learning from theory into daily practice.

The fourth critical issue is that participants in mandatory continuing education should be allowed to take courses in a variety of educational settings such colleges, university graduate programs,
large real estate firms, or community colleges. As long as instructors
and curriculum are approved by the state, professionals should be allowed to take courses in a school that will provide them the education at their level of expertise. For example, many real estate people
who have been in business for many years, may choose to go to a university and take an advanced course in real estate for their option.
Others may choose to go to schools or businesses that have computers available in order to learn the latest in online computer technology, and still others may want to take a language course to work with
business people in other countries.

The fifth critical issue suggests that leaders in the field of mandatory continuing education should consider offering some programming through partnerships. Cervero and Young (1987) suggested a topology of organizational interdependence among continuing professional education providers that includes six qualitatively different orientations or action strategies. These six types are (1) monopoly, (2) parallelism, (3) competition, (4) cooperation, (5) coordination, and (6) collaboration. Presently, most providers of real estate continuing education operate competitively. Given the changing nature of the field, providers may be able to stay in business and provide better services for both real estate professionals if they exchange ideas and provide different types of programs. Although Cervero (1988) argued that presently there is no evidence that such relationships work any better than competitive relationship in producing more desirable outcomes, such as higher quality, more accessible, or more effective continuing education (Cervero, 1988, p. 110).

The sixth critical issue is that educators must offer more variation in modes of delivery for instruction. Arello reported in its 1995 white paper report on "Alternative Methods of Continuing Education." Arello stated that in order to improve the quality and availability of real estate continuing education, many jurisdictions of education providers have developed alternative methods delivering continuing education beyond the standard classroom/lecture delivery. They learned that high-tech delivery methods are now offered in 12 jurisdictions, and many other jurisdictions are moving forward with high-tech course offerings. However, they explained that many jurisdictions reported that a law change is required in order to offer nonstandard courses, and that such legislation is being considered to provide more options for learners.

The seventh critical issue is that schools should provide more variation in subjects for courses in order to have professionals deal with the important issues, stay up to date on current issues, and add courses to meet constant changes in the field. Most providers of mandatory continuing education offer the same courses such as Changes in Local Laws, Ethics, Contracts, Trusts, Fair Housing, and specified mandated subjects that may include: Broker Courses, Preparatory and Agent Supervision, Consumer Protection, Anti-Trust, Civil Rights, Finance, Escrows, Condominium Reserves, Property Management and Landlord Tenant Laws.

The following are some of the important issues in the real estate field that should be added to current topics in mandatory continuing education.

First, several courses should taught on uses of technology. Technology changes implemented in November of 1995 at the National Real Estate Convention will revolutionize the way professionals do business in the future. Technology advances and computer software have aroused fear in many real estate professionals that if sellers can communicate directly with home buyers in some cyberspace arena such as the Internet, then real estate agents will lose their customers. In November at the Realtors National Convention, the Realtors fought back by launching the Realtors Information Network (RIN), an on-line system. RIN, a subsidiary of the Realtor group, is designed to keep the Realtors in control of the multiple listing service (MLS) property information. Allen (1995) stated

> the network does this through divided private and public operations. In the private section, accessible only by Realtors who have paid to join RIN, full MLS listings, sales transactions information, tax records and an array of geographical environmental and demographic dates will be available. (p. 4)

According to NAR (1995), RIN's aim was to keep Realtors the primary providers and distributors of the information consumers need in a real estate transaction, and since real estate went on the Internet and NAR offers two software programs, this will give the real estate professionals more opportunities to talk with people and banks immediately.

Allen explained (1995) that technology has already helped shrink the number of real estate agents. "In the last few years, thousands of offices have gone out of business as the need for computer equipment has raised overhead" (Allen, 1995, p. 4).

Allen further explained that Klein posed the question most real estate agents won't ask in public. "Do you think if people could get around paying for what we do, you think they'd do it?" (Allen, 1995, p. 4).

"To many of the 18,000 attendees at the National Association of Realtors convention in Atlanta in November, the survival of their jobs was in question" (Klein, 1995, p. 4).

This author agrees with Goldberg (1995) who stated

> when you hear rumblings among consumers and industry critics that REALTORS® are going to be replaced, you have to stop and think, in reality just how many buyers and sellers will try to transact a real estate deal without someone to facilitate it—-and who better qualified than the   REALTORS®. That because the consumer is more educated today than ever; it is critical now for REALTORS® to provide more in-

formation and services to consumers than they've ever had to before. This will enable them to make more intelligent real estate decisions. (p. 15)

Second, a course should be taught on "What it means to professionals to be socially responsible." Because of the profound effect real estate professionals have upon people's lives, they must be socially responsible. This responsibility is the core of the "credo" of all definitions of the real estate professional. As stated in the Preamble of NAR 1995

> Under all is the land. Upon its wise utilization and widely allocated ownership depend the survival and growth of free institutions and of our civilization. REALTORS® should recognize that the interests of the nation and its citizens require the highest and best use of the land and the widest distribution of land ownership. They require the creation of adequate housing, the building of functioning cities, the development of productive industries and farms, and the preservation of healthful environments. Such interest impose obligations beyond those of ordinary commerce. They impose grave social responsibility and a patriotic duty to which REALTORS®, therefore, are zealous to maintain and improve the standards of their calling and share with their fellow REALTORS® a common responsibility for its integrity and honor. (p. 8)

A third course should be designed on "Understanding and Evaluating future Environmental Problems, and how to solve them." Real estate people must be concerned with the importance of saving our environment. In the last 10 years, environmental concerns have been of increasing importance to policy makers as well as the general public. Real estate professionals must deal with problems such as toxic waste disposal and asbestos. Lasch (1992) stated that "the real question today is whether progress has built-in limitations. Environmentalists argue that the earth will not support indefinite economic expansion along the old lines. If professionals do not stay at the forefront of this issue before laws are passed, then it will cost them in the courts and with status as professionals.

The fourth new course should be designed around, "Transportation Issues." Peiser and Schwanke (1992) argued

> Transportation has always been one of the major sources of real estate value because of its impact on location, but solving the problem of overburdened roads promises to be one of the industry's principal concerns in the 1990's." (p. 356)

Location has always played a central role in real estate transactions. Real estate professionals must work with government to alleviate transportation issues that are created because of their developments.

The fifth course should be titled," "Understanding Laws." This course would focus on changes of the laws that affect real estate professionals in their particular work setting. There are mandatory courses that teach basic facts to real estate professionals each year. However, the field of real estate is very diverse. Therefore, these courses should be designed to address issues related to specialized areas in real estate. In this way, professionals will be able to understand and apply their knowledge more easily to their work setting.

Furthermore, this course should address how real estate people could use arbitration to settle disputes outside of court and how to use their professional organization to understand and work with government. As long as the society continues to force real estate professionals to meet more and more laws in order to avoid lawsuits, professionals must be up to date on the latest legal issues and laws. They must satisfy many constituencies such as local residents, city officials, public agency officials, preservation groups, fair housing laws, and disclosure laws. Real estate professionals must deal with constant changes in legal issues and citizen opposition. As members of a local association, professionals are provided the benefit of governmental liaison with governmental staff persons located in their state. In addition, they are encouraged to get together to meet on national issues. Professionals in real estate also should be aware of the arbitration committees that have jurisdiction over any controversy between members relating to a commission or any other financial matter arising out of their business as brokers or agents. These procedures comply with appropriate state laws and the committees are organized to represent the area of specialization involved such as residential, multifamily, commercial, sales, leasing, or industrial to ensure that each controversy is evaluated by members from the same area of business specialization.

Furthermore, this course should introduce professional to governmental communication provided by NAR because these contacts are maintained in the interest of keeping members informed and to help professionals in real estate communicate their viewpoint and concerns. The Association seeks to maintain an "open door" relationship with government officials and the many departments of state, county and local government whose activities affect different phases on the real estate business. Among these are the County Recorder's Office,

Assessor's Office, City Council, Mayor's Office, Zoning Board, Department of Development and Planning, Commission on Human Relations, and the Department of Professional Regulation.

The sixth course should be designed to look at how to improve education and business in "International Real Estate." This course would discuss effective communication, and teach business and educational strategies to work successfully in real estate with other countries. This is the second biggest change in the real estate field since the November 1995 national convention. We are quickly becoming a "Global Marketplace," and programs need to be created to address the special problems and training issues surrounding this subject. During the IREM's (Institute of Real Estate Management) Annual convention in Atlanta in November of 1995, the Institute signed a landmark protocol agreement with the Russian guild of RE-ALTORS® to establish ongoing educational cooperation in Russia to further the profession of real estate management in that country. The Russian Guild of Realtors represents 243 of the largest and best real estate firms throughout Russia. Van Huyck (1995) commented, "While our progress in developing property management as a competent profession has been good, the challenge and unmet needs is huge". This will force real estate professionals to speak different languages, learn cultural and customs differences, and laws relating to transactions in order to communicate effectively for satisfactory working relationships.

The seventh course should be titled, "Responding to Diversity in America." The changes in America's diversity in culture, language, people with disabilities, more women, and more older people force real estate professionals to adopt a policy for dealing with special populations both as members and as customers. Leaders need to have courses that deal with the sensitive nature and importance for professionals to respond and communicate more effectively both with colleagues and with customers. Changes in society forces programs to deal with the sensitive issue surrounding communication in a diverse society.

VISIONS FOR THE FUTURE OF REAL ESTATE CONTINUING PROFESSIONAL EDUCATION

Real estate professionals will continue to value lifelong learning in order to deal with the rapid pace of change in workplaces, communities, and social structures. Professionals will be increasingly expected to make socially responsible decisions that can assist in solving problems. In order to promote active learning and reflection among adults, today's leaders of continued professional education must possess vision and tools. Often, political, personal, and economic concerns are at odds. In the future, visionary leadership is needed to enable administrators, researches, and educators to design and implement programs for real estate professionals that will allow them to utilize effectively the knowledge they acquire in continuing education programs in their daily practice.

In the future, in order for administrators, researchers, and educators to address the problems discussed in this chapter through education, they will have to change how they develop educational programs to be more responsive to the needs of their learners as well as the needs of members of the society, and the purpose and mission of their sponsoring organization. The following are the 10 most important areas that I believe will guide the future in the real estate continuing professional education:

First, sponsors of continuing education programs must learn to be more entrepreneurial. Educational leaders need to remember that their members are business people. Prorgam development personnel will have to adopt business tactics in designing, presenting, promoting, marketing, budgeting, and evaluating programs and services. These programs and services will need to be cost effective and innovative.

Second, because technology is changing the way people work, administrators, researchers, and educators must offer the most up-to-date and latest methods both in continuing education programs and in the services they provide to their members.

Third, issues surrounding certification will become very important. Presently, states have very different standards for acquiring and maintaining licenses. Leaders ought to look at how they can make national standards for licensure.

Fourth, there will be more competition among providers of continuing education programs for clients. Providers should form relationships that allow them to work together.

Fifth, educators must improve mandatory continuing educational programs.

Sixth, international real estate research and investments will continue to flourish.

Seventh, it will continue to be important for real estate professionals to keep abreast of all changes in the laws that affect their work.

Eighth, protecting the environment will continue to be a top priority for professionals in real estate.

Ninth, leaders of organizations will need to focus on learning skills that will enable them to effectively train their employees on rapid changes in the field.

And last, because our population is becoming more diverse, leaders must deal with specific issues that relate to a multicultural society.

In conclusion, the field of real estate will continue to become more complex. Because of the rapid pace of changes in the business, real estate professionals will persist in pursuing lifelong education.

REFERENCES

Allen, Linn. (1995, November 16). Realtors develop cyberspace fears. On-line consumers could make contacts, deals, brokers countering with new system. *Chicago Tribune,* 4–11.

Apps, G. W. (1979). *Problems in continuing education.* New York: McGraw-Hill.

Blackshear, C. D. (1980). Real estate license laws: Ensuring professionalism. *Real Estate Today, 13,* (2) 11–14.

Brookfield, S. D. (1986). *Understanding and facilitating adult learning.* San Francisco: Jossey-Bass.

Case, F.E. (1970, June). Is professionalization necessary for real estate brokerage success? *California Real Estate Masgazine,* 6–7.

Cervero, R. M., (1988). *Effective continuing education for professionals.* San Francisco: Jossey-Bass.

Cervero, R. M., & Young, W. H. (1987). The organization and provision of continuing professional education: A critical review and synthesis. In J.C. Smard (Ed.) *Higher education: Handbook of theory and research. 3.* New York: Agathon Press.

Dasso, J. Ring A. A., & McFall, D. (1977). *Fundamentals of real estate* Englewood Cliffs, NJ: Prentice-Hall.

Francis, S. J. (1995). *The association of real estate license law officials (ARELLO) 1995 digest of real estate license laws in the United States and Canada.* Bountiful, UT.

Freire, P. (1973). *Education for critical consciousness.* New York: Continuum.

Galaty, F., & Allaway, W. J., & Kyle, R. C. (1978). *Modern real estate practice* (8th ed.). Chicago: Real Estate Education Company.

Goldberg, R. A., (1995). Clear understanding of realtors assists in marketing RIN. *RIN Update,* Washinton, DC 4, 15.

Harwood, B. (1979). *Real estate: An introduction to the profession* (2nd ed.) Reston, Virginia: Reston.

Houle, C. O. (1980). *Continuing learning in the professions.* San Francisco: Jossey-Bass.

Houle, C. O. (1972). *The design of education.* San Francisco: Jossey-Bass.

Kenny, W. R., (1985). Progress planning and accreditation. In R. M. Cervero & C. L. Scanlan, *Problems and Prospects in Continuing Professional Education*. New Directions for Continuing Education. Number 27: San Francisco: Jossey-Bass.

Klein, S. (1995, November 16). Realtors develop cyberspace fears, on-line consumers could make contacts, deals; brokers countering with new system. *Chicago Tribune*, Section 3, pp. 1–11.

Knowles, M. (1980). *The modern practice of adult education: From pedagogy to androgogy* (2nd ed.). New York: Cambridge Books.

Knox, A.B. (1986). *Helping adults learn*. San Francisco: Jossey-Bass.

Lasch, C. (1992, Fall). Is progresss obsolete? A noted historian argues that the dream has become far too exclusive. *Time Special Issue Beyond 2000*. NY: Elizabeth P. Valk.

Lowenthal, W. (1981). Continuing education for professionals: voluntary or mandatory? *Journal of Higher Education, 52* (5), 519–535.

National Association of Realtors (NAR). (1981). *Membership profile 1981*. Washington, D.C.: The Economics and Research Division.

National Association of Realtors (NAR). (1995). *New membership packet 1995*. Chicago.

Pajor, Michael (1985). Comparative analysis of licensee attitude toward continuing eduation in real Estate. (Doctoral Dissertation, Northern Illinois University, 1985) Department of Learning, Development and Special Education. LD2411.6.P1511985.

Peiser, R. B., & Schwanke, D. (1992). *Professional real estate development*. Washington, DC: Dearborn Financial Publishing.

Phillips, L. E. (1987). Is Mandatory Continuing Education Working? *Mobius, 7* (1), 57–64.

Quatrano, L. A., & Conant, R. M. (1981). Continuing Competency for Health Professionals: Caveat Emptor. *Journal of Environmental Health, 44* (3), 125–130.

Shimberg, B. (1978, Autumn). *Mandatory continuing education: Some questions to ask state government*. 215–219.

Simerly, R. G. (1987). Achieving success in strategic planning. In R. G. Simerly & Associates, *Strategic planning and leadership in continuing education:* enchancing organizational vitality, responsivemenss, and identity. San Francisco: Jossey-Bass.

Sirmans, S. G., & Sirmans, C.F. (1992, January/February). The value of professional asset management. *Journal of Property Management*, 52–53.

Stubblefield, H. W., (1981). A learning project model for adults. *Lifelong Learning: The Adult Years, 4* (7), 24–26.

Van Huyck, (1995, November–December). "IREM Russia agreement=opportunity for members". *CPM ASPECTS-IREM'S newsletter for CPM members and CPM candidates, XXVII.* (6) Institute of Real Estate Management, Chicago, Illinois, 5.

Warner, A.F. (1979). *Continuing education in real estate: A survey of current status and evaluation of future needs*. Columbia, South Carolina: Center for Real Estate and Urban Economic Studies, University of South Carolina.

Weinberg, N. (1988). The new master's degrees in real estate development. *Real Estate Review*. Stoughton, Massachusetts: Warren, Gorham & Lamont, 8–9.

Wiley, J. A., Piaazza, P. & Smith W. (1981, August) Characteristics of licensees who were disciplined or against whom complaints were filed in fiscal year 1979–80: A record linkage study. (A report from the California Department of Real Estate contract number 80-329). Berkeley, CA: Survey Research Centers. University of California.

Wright, A.L. (76, Nov/Dec) Professionalization in real estate. *Real Estate Today*, 36–39.

Young, A., & Company. (1987). *Review of california's continuing education program*. Sacramento: California Department of Real Estate.

20

Critical Issues Facing Engineering

Richard Eugene Clehouse

Reengineering the engineer, engineering, and engineering education—the critical issues are complex—the formidable tasks are numerous. What role will continuing education and educators assume in resolving the critical issues that face the engineering field? Will continuing education and educators be agents of change? How will continuing education retrofit the present workforce and sculpt the future for the workplace 2005?

The following simplistic ads represent a limited historical perspective of the changes in the field of engineering and the opportunities that lie ahead:

1970

WANTED: Engineer with above-average specialized technical knowledge, with the ability to design. Company offers many career advancement opportunities and fringe benefits.

1980

WANTED: Engineer with a strong technical knowledge base in communications jamming equipment. This is a two-year defense contract. Must have government clearance.

1990–2005

WANTED: Engineer with technical expertise, exceptional communication, and problem-solving skills. Will be required to work in a cross-functional environment as a team player with leadership capability. Can handle continuous change with a strong career focus.

NEW CHALLENGES AND NEW DIRECTIONS

We live in a time of revolutionary change. "We are, right now, in the very early stages of a new economy, one whose core is . . . fundamentally different from its predecessor's" (Huey, 1994, p. 36). The world is relying increasingly on technology for economic growth and job development, but the nation is making the difficult transition of refocusing a significant amount of its technology investment from national security to international economic competitiveness. At the same time, we view technology as important in helping solve many difficult social problems, from creating environmentally sustainable development and improving communications, to devising more effective and cost-efficient health care systems. Communications developments alone are leading to profound redefinition of such concepts as "community," "library," "corporation/workplace environments," and even "University" (American Society of Engineering Educators, 1994).

Within this technology context, engineers play an increasingly significant role. They develop new manufacturing processes and products; create and manage energy, transportation and communications systems; prevent new and redress old environmental problems; create pioneering health care devices; and, in general, make technology work. Through these activities, engineers create a huge potential for the private sector to develop national wealth. As noted by Richard Morrow, past chairman of the National Academy of Engineering, "The nation with the best engineering talent is in possession of the core ingredient of comparative economic and industrial advantage" (ASEE, 1994).

FRAMING THE ISSUES

Critical Junctures

The tried and true no longer guarantee the future. No longer can an engineer count on having a job with the same company for a lifetime. The "cradle-to-grave" security is gone and probably will never return. Volatile economic conditions, coupled with rapid technological change, call for a flexible engineering workforce to achieve competitiveness. The importance of diversifying our multicultural and multiethnic workforce, of regulating the environmental impact of chemicals and toxic waste, of husbanding our natural resources, and of retraining our industrial workforce, exerts powerful pressure on leaders and followers alike. The need to make the right decisions about how time, money, and people are utilized requires a flexible, informed, and technically competent engineering workforce. (Institute of Electrical and Electronics Engineers, 1994a). What are the symptomatic forces that are influencing and shaping the engineer, engineering, and engineering education? What are the opportunities, promises, demands, and challenges that can be expected?

SETTING THE STAGE

The following diagram sets the stage. It attempts to illustrate the relationship between the paradigms and the paradigm shifters in the multifaceted realm of engineering:

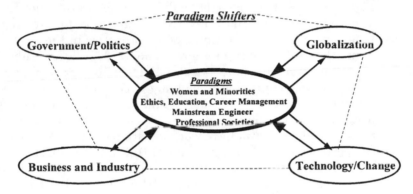

Diagram 1
Paradigms and Paradigm Shifters

The outside ellipses represent the "paradigm shifters" that impact engineering education, engineers, and the engineering profession. Careful examination of the diagram indicates the paradigm shifters, at present, are exerting a greater influence (larger arrows) on the paradigms than the paradigms (smaller arrows) are on the paradigm shifters. The diagram elucidates the present posturing of engineering education, the engineer, and the engineering profession. The professional societies are the most active agents in shifting influence and setting markers for the other paradigms. Professional organizations are waging a hard battle against being adversely affected by these paradigm shifters, but they lack a fervent constituency to effect control on the agents acting *in* the paradigm shifters. Educational institutions, continuing educational professionals, and the members of the professional societies must position themselves to be the effectors of change rather than being affected by change. All people at all levels in the paradigms in Diagram 1 need to be proactive rather than reactive to the changes that are critical to the engineering profession. The rest of the chapter offers further insight into the composition of the paradigm shifters and the paradigms that encompass the engineering profession.

PARADIGM SHIFTERS

Government and Politics

There exists, more than ever before, the necessity for engineers to keep a watchful eye on what the politicians and the federal government are doing to effect changes that will impact their profession. No longer can engineers, and those involved in the education of engineers, hide from the responsibility of being proactive in the politics that become the underpinning for governmental legislation. Albert D. Rosenheck pointed out that, "Science and technology are playing an increasingly important role in shaping national policy, but few congressional members or their staffs possess extensive scientific/technical knowledge." He went on to say, "While many of us in industry and academia have worked with federal agencies, we have no experience in dealing with Capitol Hill" (1994 p. 3). It is not always conventional wisdom that prevails with issues of government spending as Marvin Hammond, chair of IEEE-USA's R&D Policy Committee decreed. Congressional cuts on key technology programs ". . . have been made with a lot of misunderstandings, and it's been more of an emotional issue" (Reppert, 1995a pp. 1–2). Arvid G. Larson, former IEEE-USA board chair and current head of ASEE (American Society of Engineering Educators) task force on Technological Competitiveness said, "The overall outlook for federal supported R&D is *bleak*." Larson observed that "engineering education will suffer greatly, because much of it is federal government." He added, "It is difficult to predict how many engineering jobs could be lost as a result of current and projected R&D cuts . . . but the impact could be substantial" (1995, p. 2). A report recently released by the AAAS (American Association for the Advancement of Science) cited a congressional budget resolution with "sweeping reductions in nondefense R&D programs" . . . the resolutions assume program cuts of 33% in nondefense R&D by FY 2002 after adjusting for expected inflation (Reppert, 1995b p. 2). Rep. Robert S. Walker, R-PA, chair of the House Science Committee, emphasized that "we have, in fact, kept our word about funding basic science . . ." adding that the 33% R&D cutback amounted to "reductions from wish-list spending." According to Walker, "The strongest thing we can do for technology in this country is to reduce regulation, reduce the amount of litigation, and develop a more responsible taxation system" (Reppert, 1995c p. 2). These examples represent the political climate and culture of this decade and show the power of government in declaring what the future may hold for engineering and technology.

Globalization—Impact on the Engineering Workplace

Without a doubt, we are in the midst of a global trade revolution that has given rise to a breadth and intensity of competition without parallel or precedent in human history. There is an ever-growing number of increasingly capable global competitors who are producing world-class, innovative products; achieving phenomenal design, production and decision speeds; and meeting customer expectations for product quality, performance, reliability, and availability. In some cases they are subsidized by their own governments and are basically unencumbered by burdensome rules and regulations that businesses face in the United States. These competitors value flexible teams with multitalented members and have little use for multiple tiers of management. Their educations are excellent and they're as smart as we are, as well as tougher than ever to compete with (Black, 1994). What are U.S. businesses doing to compete in this global market, and how will this change the engineering workplace? The implications for change are these: (1) the traditional hierarchical organization will give way to a flatter organization; (2) the vertical division of labor (in which authority and expertise increase at higher levels) will be replaced by a horizontal division of labor in which expertise is vested in individuals with specialties, not in positions (collaboration among autonomous teams will replace chain-of-command management); (3) mass production will be replaced by customized manufacturing; (4) more companies will shift some in-house functions or services to "outsources," smaller firms will increase in importance; and, (5) highly educated generalists termed "gold-collar workers" who act as "integrators" adding value to products and services. The emerging pattern has been termed the "freelance economy" (Kiechel, 1993) in which multiskilled, flexible, entrepreneurial workers will replace the concept of job with "meaningful, market-driven work assignments in post-job organizations." (Huey, 1994 p. 44).

Now that business is attuned to the challenges, the resolution will be achieved through continuous emphasis on total quality management (TQM), continuous process improvement (CPI), and cycle time reductions. These goals can be actualized by reducing layers of management/staff, and moving toward self-managed work teams. For engineers, what is technically possible is no longer the key. They are now members of product teams, using quality function deployment (QFD) to match customer desires to possible designs. The engineers participate in cross-functional teamwork and lifelong learning— "learning a living" as futurist Marshall McLuhan once put it (Black, 1994 p. 27).

Technology and Change

The workplace of the 21st century is taking shape now. It is still an ameba as it changes to meet the new technologies and the needs that this changing paradigm produces, but one thing is sure: change and the technology that has helped to bring it about will impact everyone, whether they embrace it or not. The trends that are rising to the surface are these: (1) there will be no typical workplace— the workplace will be defined by tasks, not by location; (2) traditional management styles of general and troops will give way to educated workers making more decisions about job priorities and schedules, thereby creating an erosion of middle managers/engineers; (3) continuing education/lifelong learning will be conducted throughout one's career; (4) the "good old boy" network will yield to the growing influx of women and minorities, creating more parity in hiring, wages, training, and advancement; and, (5) flextime and flexible benefits will become a necessity due to the demographic "crunch" and the high cost of recruiting and training qualified employees (Kleiman, 1994). The engineer must not only understand the roots of these cultural changes but learn to manage them in ways that will contribute to the holistic nature of business and industry.

Technology is in such a state of flux that to predict what specific technologies will be available in the 21st century would be impossible if not ludicrous to try. For sure we know that we will continue to depend on people with advanced scientific and technological knowledge to reduce environmental pollution, combat disease and hunger, and develop new sources of energy and energy conservation, which will bring with it new challenges and opportunities for science and engineering.

BUSINESS AND INDUSTRY
Redefining

Business is being driven not only by the technology but also by TQM, CPI, and QFD, which are the underpinnings of the modern engineering process. Business and industry will need engineers with new and applied skill sets, who will be able to function in the following process environment through (1) product or system requirements that address customers' real needs, reflect customer values, are competitive in cost, value, and reliability, as well as environmentally friendly; (2) effective time management across the whole business team and within each team segment that eliminates non-value-added process steps; and, (3) integrated product development and concurrent engineering employing a team approach to product definition, design, manufacturing, marketing, and support. Team goals, team contributions, and team rewards supersede individual goals and contributions (Black, 1994 p. 27).

Restructuring

Restructuring businesses want a "Renaissance Engineer" who can function under a business strategy that, through its dynamic process, has identified the following core competencies as necessary to efficient and effective engineering practices: (1) teamwork—this requires team skills. There is an overwhelming belief that technical skills are all that is needed for success, which is just not true anymore (Ferrell, 1996). This model of interaction requires effective inter/intrapersonal communications skills. Manchester Partners Inc., a human resources and management consulting firm in Atlanta, estimated that as many as 40% of recently promoted managers in all industries quit or are demoted within 12 months. Manchester said the largest factor contributing to failures by technical managers is that they don't possess the people skills needed to manage others effectively; (2) a sense of the total business—understanding the business equation such as profit and loss, and balance sheet issues. Companies use engineering personnel on product development teams, in customer support, and sales, which requires a broad skill set. (3) a systems perspective—a holistic sense of the operations (Katz, 1993). Joe Bordogna at the National Science Foundation, "believes the job of the engineer is to integrate all knowledge to some purpose. *Integrate* is the key word here. Engineers don't take things apart; they put things together to make things that haven't been around before. To accomplish this they must work with people, resources, and policies, and they must consider social needs. In short, engineering is an integrative process . . ." (Staff, 1995); (4) a thorough knowledge of the current design tools—incorporating software basics, CAE (Computer Aided Engineering), simulation/ modeling, and analysis tools (Black, 1994 p. 27). These are powerful computer tools that engineers must use in order to optimize the "idea to product" equation.

EDUCATION
Ties That Bind

There appears to be a continuous theme a . . . "tie that binds" . . . that cries out at all levels of engineering education "CHANGE IS IM-MINENT-CHANGE IS NECESSARY." The following transitions in the continuum of engineering education or what may be referred to as "pivotal points" are critical to producing, advancing, and maintaining the engineering workforce for the 21st century.

Adjusting to New Roles

Traditionally, instructors have provided the entrance to information. They surely are the gatekeepers of academe. They have had control over the input, throughput, and output relating to the content of the subject matter (Grana & Rutherford, 1995 p.82). Traditional pedagogical methods are authoritarian when the power is in the control of the teacher who predetermines what subject matter is important and how it will be transmitted. In this construct, learning is synonymous with books, lectures, note taking, recitation, and passivity. This activity is centered around the teacher because the teacher is the controlling factor in this scenario. This method of approach has been termed "teacher-centered learning." This method of instruction produces "knowers" (who remember information and systematically repeat skills) versus "learners" (who can create, apply, modify, and adapt concepts) to the evolutionary nature of each day. In contrast to teacher-centered learning, "student-centered learning" promotes active learning where the student is engaged in the process through collaborative/cooperative learning strategies and problem-based learning, which encourages the student to practice higher level cognitive skills. This approach gives new roles to both the teacher and the student. The teacher changes from authoritarian and dominant figure to mentor, collaborator, and coach—a facilitator in the education process. Students in this process must take more responsibility for their own learning by being proactive in the exploration of knowledge processing and acquisition and coauthoring methods of instant assessment and active learning techniques (Laszlo & Castro, 1995) (Mehta, 1995) (Rogers & Stemkoski, 1995) (Wagner & Combs, 1995).

A Fused Versus Fractured Curriculum

Engineering education at all levels must fuse its curriculum with other courses to create a broad academic perspective. The narrowly focused traditional college engineering curriculum which embodies the concept of teaching courses in isolation will not survive. Mating the nontechnical courses with the technical subjects supports the transition to the business environment. Individuals with graduate training cutting across areas of engineering, management, and business will turn into better candidates for employment than more narrowly educated specialists. A highly trained scientist or engineer cannot be very effective if she or he has no knowledge of how and why a company is organized, lacks understanding about the principal staff and the operating functions, is ignorant of the rudiments of accounting and finance, and is unaware of product liability issues that directly affect product development. The message is clear—there needs to be a convergence of skill sets across the curriculum that provides the future engineer with a holistic, contiguous perceptual approach to the practice of engineering.

SYNCHRONOUS AND ASYNCHRONOUS LEARNING ENVIRONMENTS
Synchronous Learning Environment

The synchronous learning environment is typified by traditional classrooms where the transmission and reception of information is in real time. Both the giver and receiver experience information exchanges that rely on both parties sharing in the same time and place constraints. Distance learning via video/audioconferencing or computer "chat areas" expanded the synchronous environment by eliminating the same space constraints. Although an improvement over the traditional classroom, distance learning requires real-time interaction in order to work. The modality of distance learning does offer engineering education an alternative to its dilemma of limited capital, human, and monetary resource allocations that are endangering the rudiments of its existence. Engineering students are facing much the same encompassing boundaries as engineering education with time as an added restrictive element. Alternative delivery mechanism(s) are needed that will improve undergraduate, graduate, and continuing education of engineers.

Asynchronous Learning Environment

The asynchronous learning environment is typified by its independence from time and space requirements facilitating the concept of any time, anywhere learning using information technology. It is a form of distributed learning using the World Wide Web (WWW) which, by its very nature, can distribute resources and information in a "virtual" world. The word "virtual" in modern discourse is mostly associated with virtual reality, "the electronic construction of images that are indistinguishable from the nominal realities they purport to represent" (Sorkin, 1992). In an asynchronous environment, the teacher and learner are not interacting in the same space and time domains. How then have faculty and institutions chosen to use this virtual world called the WWW? It appears there are two fundamental approaches to the use of information technology: (1) as an information delivery tool where lecture notes, assignments, calendars, course syllabi, and other course-related materials are made available through the WWW; and (2) where courses and entire degree programs are delivered in whole, or in part, over the WWW (Polyson & Saltzberg, 1995). The Sloan Center for Asynchronous Learning Environments (SCALE) project sponsored by the SLOAN Foundation at the University of Illinois Urbana-Champaign and approximately 21 other universities is an excellent example of using the WWW as an information delivery and lecture supplement tool (Mayadas, 1994). Predominantly used in the undergraduate curriculum, its success to date indicates it is worth expanding to the graduate and continuing education arenas. The preliminary results of the SCALE project have shown that students are actively engaged in this new learning process resulting in increased retention, improved test performance, positive student feedback, positive student evaluations, and increased "transaction density" with faculty and teaching assistance (Oakley, 1995). The SLOAN Foundation, which is supporting the SCALE project, is interested in determining the effect the ALN

(Asynchronous Learning Network) has on self-paced learning, re-tention, time-to-degree, lowering the cost of education, and the ability to earn a degree at home (Mayadas, 1994).

The second use of the WWW for educators and learning institutions has been to create courses and entire degree programs in a "Virtual Curriculum Model" (Leitzel & Vogler, 1995) (Goodman, 1995) (Acker, 1995) (Rossman, 1993). National Technological University (NTU) is one of several educational institutions offering virtual degrees on the WWW. Headquartered in Fort Collins, Colorado, NTU operates one of the largest one-way digital distance learning networks in the world. NTU annually delivers more than 800 graduate courses and 400 noncredit classes over 44 satellite up-links and 300 compressed digital down-links to over 100,000 technical professionals at *Fortune* 500 companies and government agencies across North America (Walsh & Reese, 1995 p. 61). Participants in WWW and the distributed learning models say that it inherently supports and offers many benefits to the educators, institutions, and students they serve through (1) student-centered, (2) collaborative learning, (3) convenience, (4) ease of use and accessibility, (5) development is relatively quick and easy, (6) updating and disseminating information, (7) creation of interactive textbooks and supplementary material that integrates images, video, sound, and, (8) the luxury of having additional resources that the educator and the learner can access by linking to other web sources (Polyson & Saltzberg, 1995 p. 10). What does the future hold for this new conglomerate of educational virtues and the WWW? No one knows for sure . . . but what is known is that technology changes much more rapidly than human behavior. So, it is incumbent upon all of education and its constituents to envision education as a process where the learning is efficient, effective, and interactive so that the functional aspects of learning support the praxis of the learner as "knowledge accessor."

THE MAINSTREAM ENGINEER

The mainstream engineer is predominantly a white, middle to upper-middle class male protected by legacy and the "good old boy" network embodying all that is right and all that is wrong with the practice of engineering. The paradigm shifters, as illustrated in Diagram 1, are presenting new challenges and opportunities to the mainstream engineer. As businesses and industries continue to reorganize their structures in order to accommodate a flatter organization, jobs not only become more scarce but are functionally redefined.

Government and the politics that produce the policies, which are a result of this paradigm shifting, mandate changes in the "what" and "how" engineering is practiced. Globalization and the resulting competition challenge the engineer not only to create new and better products and processes that are cheaper and faster to market but also to experience diversity and multiculturalism. Technology and change are synonymous with transformation and suggest that the mainstream engineer can no longer continue with "business as usual." The mainstream engineer who is conscious of a proactive approach toward these paradigm shifters will continue to be successful; the engineer who is not will face the same fate as yesterday's technology.

WOMEN AND MINORITIES

Although it is dangerous to generalize the issues between women and minorities, the limitations of this chapter necessitates bringing forth the common barriers rather than the differences associated with the challenges women and minorities encounter in education and the workplace.

The Gender Gap

In 1992, women accounted for 15% of B.S. degrees, 14% of M.S. degrees, and 9.7% of Ph.D. degrees in engineering. The gender gap in the engineering profession is even more dramatic; women make up roughly 50% of the population and 44% of the United States workforce, but, as of recently, they represent only about 4% of practicing engineers (Dietz, G. Felder, R. Felder, Hamrin & Mauney, 1995).

Minorities

African Americans, Hispanics, and Native Americans also continue to be significantly underrepresented in the engineering community. African Americans, for instance, represent about 12% of the general population but are estimated to make up only 2–3% of the total engineering workforce. Although minority enrollments in total have increased in recent years, African Americans, Hispanics, and Native Americans collectively still received less than 8% of all B.S. degrees awarded in 1992. Together, these three groups account for 27.5% of our college population (Morrow, 1994).

For a variety of practical and moral reasons, steps must be taken to attract and retain more women and minorities in engineering curricula. The obstacles to doing so are formidable. From an early age, women and minorities are told, subtly or overtly, that science and mathematics are not for them. Some get this message at home, most get it at school from classmates and, occasionally, from teachers, and many accept it. Males, for example, are likely to ascribe the problems they encounter with mathematics to the difficulty of the subject; females and minorities are more likely to attribute failure to their lack of ability (Dietz, G. Felder, R. Felder, Hamrin & Mauney, 1995).

Generalizations extracted from the literature point to these common issues faced in both education and business.

Barriers in Education

The lack of self-confidence.

A well-documented phenomenon called the "impostor syndrome" accompanied by a fear of being "found out" is exhibited in higher percentages among women and minority students. A major reason for these feelings is the lack of role models. White males have a number of successful men with whom they can identify . . . they benefit from the self-reinforcing concept that they "belong." On the other hand, women and minorities have few role models who have been successful before them, and they often feel like outsiders (Levenson, 1990).

Oppression in the classroom.

Oppression in academia is very subtle, and the women and minorities who experience it have little power to do anything about it. Call it the transparency factor. This is typified by the following example: a suggestion for a math proof is offered by a female student in class and gets no response or recognition from the professor only to have one of the male students nearby suggest the same thing a few minutes later and be congratulated for a good suggestion (Rosser, 1993).

Traditional instructional modes.

Traditional forms of teaching stress individual work and competitive grading. This is a significant deterrent, especially for women who prefer an atmosphere of "collaborative behavior" that is so necessary in scientific investigation. The singular approach to content ignores the differences in learning styles and perceptions of a diversified classroom. This is reflected in the poor retention rate of minorities. African Americans and Native Americans retention rate is 35% and for Hispanics it is 45% compared to 70% for all freshman and close to 100% for Asians (Morrow, 1994 p. 17) (Brush, 1991).

Barriers Faced in Business

The same but different.

Women and minorities start off at relatively equal pay when beginning their careers; however, as they get into their thirties, men pull ahead in their base salaries. This is a trend that continues for the rest of their careers. Young women engineers are irritated by attempts to "off load secretarial type work" (Society of Women Engineers, 1993) (Geppert, 1995). Women of color are often viewed as having gained a position because of affirmative action and not through competent work. If a woman of color makes a mistake, it is often blamed on her gender and race (Betters-Reed & Moore, 1993).

The glass ceiling.

Ragins and Sundstrom (1989) proposed a model which explains how gender affects promotion to powerful positions in organizations. They propose that women are less likely to be promoted to power than men because they have disadvantageous organizational, interpersonal, and individual equivalent factors. The organizational factors include selection, tracking, and training practices. The interpersonal factors include mentors, networks, and gender ratios of managerial hierarchies. The individual factors are those of personality (e.g., self-confidence, success attributions), nonwork roles (home demands and associated career interruptions), and early background (e.g., parents' employment). The model indicates that interpersonal processes are most associated with women CEOs' status. They also suggest that interpersonal and organizational situational factors are more associated with women CEOs' status than are personal factors. Moreover, interpersonal, organizational, and nonwork variables differ most for men and women CEOs (Tharenou, 1995 pp. 201–212) (Bailyn, 1986).

The mainstream engineer who continues to practice the hegemonic doctrines of the "old guard" (where women and minorities are more tolerated than accepted in the engineering profession) dooms not only himself but the organization that employs him. Much has changed in this century, except the recognition and acceptance of those who are not of the dominant culture. It has been observed that members of the dominant culture frequently are suspicious of gatherings of people who are in the minority. They do not recognize that they have the privilege of doing this everyday without question.

Questions Remain

Have the universities in engineering education provided the kind of supportive atmosphere, including mentoring, that many studies have found essential for encouraging minorities to enter and remain in the field? Have the universities been sensitive enough to the need for remedial work in some areas in order to encourage and support minorities so they can participate fully? Has business worked closely enough with historically African American colleges and universities, and has business encouraged the hiring of minorities and women engineers and helped them advance (Marrow, 1994)?

ETHICS—RHETORIC OR CREDO FOR A NEW AGE?

A profession comes into being on the basis of a special body of knowledge, then builds itself with institutionalized education, accreditation, and self-regulation. Eventually, the public grants to the specialists a sort of franchise. In exchange, however, society requires that the experts demonstrate concern for the commonwealth. The professionals, for their part, are sensitive to the expectations of the public and respond to their own consciences. Engineering societies have traditionally treated questions of professional obligation under the rubric of "engineering ethics." The topic receives far less attention than technical and economic concerns, but it makes up in passion what it lacks in priority. Can morality be mandated through standards of ethical practice? Wherein lies the responsibility of establishing and regulating ethical standards . . . with education, companies, engineers, government, or the public? What power does ethical rhetoric have over the engineering profession? Is establishing ethical standards an act of academic futility where conferences, publications, and courses are platforms in which everything gets discussed and nothing gets decided . . . a kind of dialectic circle (Florman, 1987)?

Practically speaking, people who start out to do a good job and people who start out to do good often end up in the same vicinity. Many different journeys can end at the same shrine. Engineering societies have long recognized an obligation to commission studies, issue reports, set standards, schedule seminars, warn, lobby, and placate. They have a respectable history of calling attention to technological problems: overexploited resources, polluted air and water, deteriorating infrastructure, and so on. At present, only the codes of the Institute of Electrical and Electronics Engineers (IEEE) and the American Society of Civil Engineers (ASCE) mention the environment in their code of ethics. Will the professional societies have the same effect on their members' moral and ethical dilemmas as they do with the technical issues?

Credo for a New Age

Not until recently has engineering education emphasized the importance of including ethics as a part of the engineering curriculum. Taking on this challenge is the Accreditation Board of Engineering and Technology (ABET) that requires accredited engineering programs to introduce students to ethical concerns. ABET is advocating a kind of preventive ethics, which is geared toward the education of the engineering student in order to promote an understanding of the ethical attributes of the engineering profession and practice. Undergraduate engineering students study ethical situations to be able to anticipate possible consequences of actions to avoid serious on-the-job consequences. Preventive ethics through education can stimulate the moral imagination, heighten the ability to recognize ethical issues, develop essential analytical skills, eliciting in engineers a sense of responsibility for their actions when the time comes for them to practice their profession (Harris, Pritchard, & Rabins, 1995). Who then must actuate the best ethical practices? It is the character and competence of individual engineers that will, in the end, make all the difference. Once this is realized, professional societies will devote less energy to composing codes of ethics and more to figuring out how best to educate the engineers of the future. For poets, clerics, politicians, and educators, there are a variety of moral roads to be followed and much can be said in favor of each. For engineers, however, the one true road must pass the litmus test of conscience, an ideal starting, continuing, and ending test for individual ethical actions (Florman, 1987).

Professional Societies

Professional societies offer their members a smorgasbord of opportunities and benefits as an enticement to join and participate. For example, the IEEE (Institute of Electrical Electronics Engineers) is the world's largest technical professional society. Benefits to members include insurance, annuities, credit cards, mutual funds, loans, special car rental and motel rates, as well as job listing services and career planning. Opportunities include the regional and national meetings and seminars and conferences that publicize, educate, inform, and unite its membership to address issues that face their profession. Special professional societies, such as SHPE (Society of Hispanic Professional Engineers), SEA (Science and Engineering), and SWOE (Society of Women Engineers) are examples of smaller societies that can't offer a large benefit package to belong but, instead, offer a narrower focus and the professional nurturing often forgotten in larger societies. Because these are not-for-profit organizations, they must rely, for the most part, on volunteers to run them. Those members who choose to participate can learn to lead, function in a team environment, do public speaking, and can fail in an atmosphere that will not threaten their careers. Those society members who do not participate are susceptible to early obsolescence. The ASEE (American Society of Engineering Educators) is an excellent example of an organization that is making progress in promoting new andragogical methods and alternative delivery mechanisms in engineering education. Continuing professionals have an obligation to link with these societies in order to facilitate the education and training in new and emerging technical domains and nontechnical skill sets.

CAREER MANAGEMENT
Vicissitudes of Life

As unpredictable as life is, one thing is for sure—"*change*" is the operative word in organizational structure, technology, globalization, and government policies. This suggests that engineering professionals must be proactive in managing their careers in order to best manage and envision the future. It is not a matter of survival; surviving means something unexpected has happened, and one makes it through the situation the best one knows how. Organized, contiguous, proactive career planning for the engineer is the concept of the day. The "cradle-to-grave" security is gone and with it the complacency that it fostered. Planning for "change," as opposed to reacting to change, requires a new perspective and improved procedures to effectively navigate through turbulent times. What are some of the fatal design flaws engineers incorporate into their career planning model?

Having fussy targets. Fussy targets will slow down efforts to stay

ahead of the pack. Many professionals adopt such unclear goals because they think that this will keep their options open.

Eclecticism. This scenario uses the convenience approach to learning. Course titles are chosen from catalogs because they sound good
or happen to fit this time and location constraints. Training must not
be an isolated event but rather a sequence of learning activities that
fits one's career plans and promotes present work performance.

Too narrowly focused. Engineers need to be diverse in their basal
structure. (Youst & Lipsett, 1994). It is as important to be business
smart as it is to be technically aware of what business is about and
the infrastructures that are in place. Engineers need to read and
think outside of the box, and, at the same time, to be in sync with
their company's changing focus and shifting priorities. Lifelong
learning is no longer an option; it is a necessity. It is the only way to
avoid obsolescence today.

Career Asset Manager

The career asset manager plan (CAMplan) is a result of the IEEE's
(Institute of Electrical and Electronics Engineers) realization that engineers do not know how to manage their careers. CAMplan is divided
into three sections: (1) information, (2) database/record keeping, and
(3) a customized career planning guide. Each section of CAMplan has
subunits that guide while allowing the engineer the opportunity to develop an individual career management tool that can be used to facilitate career mobility (Institute of Electrical and Electronic Engineers,
1996). Diagram 2 on the following page traces the CAMplan process in
a circular mode to illustrate the continuous nature of career planning.

SUMMATIVE HIGHLIGHTS

The world is changing. Globalization and the resulting work environment will have a tremendous effect on the composition of the
workforce. Those who want to be ready must start now. The demands
of a fluid, global economy powered by technological development and
innovation have improved the job performance and knowledge requirements in the spectrum of engineering. The days of labor intensive capitalization are gone. As real contributors everyone will be responsible for the success of an enterprise. There has been a
persistent perception that science and technology are independent of
culture and society. The expansion of trade among nations and
changes in the international political order have been creating a

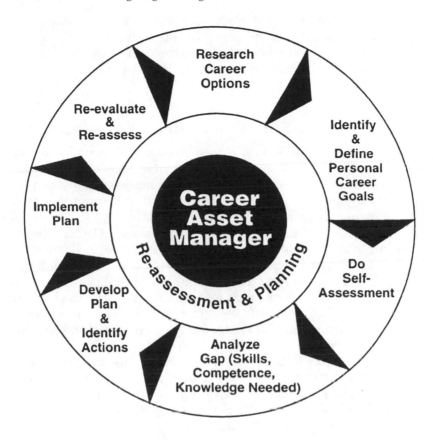

Diagram 2

world of growing interdependence. These emerging global cross-linkages pose new challenges for citizens in general and, in particular, engineers as they are increasingly confronted with problems whose analysis and solutions require an understanding of cultures and people beyond their native borders.

Knowledge, powered by information technology, will be the source of wealth as we continue to migrate from an industrial, technological era to a knowledge-information technology era. The "knowledge economy" will influence policy, education, armed forces, religion, and how women and minorities participate in the workforce. The distribution of knowledge will become more important than the distribution of products, a trend already visible in the application of intellectual property. In this world of knowledge, innovation and new approaches will require "out-of-the-box" thinking, combined with problem-solving skills to exploit knowledge in the marketplace.

Reengineering Continuing Education

The changing domains of time, space, cost, and accessibility to continuing professional education demand new tenets. Information technology via the Internet is offering continuing education an opportunity to envision a new future for itself and those it serves. Reengineering, as promoted by Hammer and Champy (1993), is not significantly different from Davidow and Malone's (1992) concept. According to Hammer and Champy (1993), reengineering is "the fundamental rethinking and radical redesign of business (educational) processes to achieve dramatic improvements in critical, contemporary measures of performance, such as cost, quality, service, and speed" (p. 46). The concept of reengineering involves a process orientation, ambition, rule-breaking, and creative use of information technology.

The enabling role of information technology makes asynchronous learning and virtual curricula possible. Asynchronous learning and virtual curricula provide a fresh coupling between education as "ideation" and application. Mastering the integration of ideas and technology in an information technology rich environment will be the clarion call of continuing education professionals for the 21st century. It will mean a new synergy for the development and delivery of professional education curricula, resulting in a broader educational content and multidisciplinary perspectives. The implication is clear. Continuing professional education must be "customized on demand education" to meet the knowledge seekers of the 21st century. One important question remains—will continuing education reengineer itself for the 21st century, or will it continue with business as usual?

REFERENCES

Acker, S. (1995). Space, collaboration, and the credible city: Academic work in the virtual university. Internet page @ URL *http://cwis.use.edu/dept/annenberg/vollissue1/acker/ACKTEX.html*

American Society of Engineering Educators (ASEE). (1994, October). Engineering education for a changing world; A Joint Project Report by the Engineering Deans Council and Corporate Rountable. 1111 195th St., N.W., Suite 608 Washington, DC 20036-3690

Bailyn, L. (1986). Experiencing technical work: A comparison of male and female engineers. MIT Industrial Liaison Program Report. Internet page @ URL *http://web.mit.edu/afs . . . acts/Bailyn-study.html*

Betters-Reed, B., & Moore, L. (1993). The technicolor workplace. U.S. Women Engineer Magazine of the Society of Women Engineers. (Abstract for ECSEL: Internet page @ URL *http://web.mit.edu/afs . . . stracts/womeneng2.html*

Black, K. (1994). An industry view of engineering education. *Journal of Engineering Education, 83* (1), 26–28.

Brush, S. (1991). Women in science and engineering. *American Scientist, 79,* 404–419.

Davidow, W., & Malone, M. (1992). The virtual corporation: Structuring and revitalizing the corporation for the 21st century. New York: HarperCollins.

Dietz, J., Felder, G., Felder, R., Hamrin, C., & Mauney, M. (1995). A longitudinal study of engineering student performance and retention. III Gender differences in student performance and attitudes. *Journal of Engineering Education, 84* (2), 151–163.

Ferrell, T. (1996). Preparing for the workplace 2000: Engineering. *Peterson's Job Opportunities in Engineering and Technology, 2–9,* Princeton, NJ: Peterson's Guides.

Florman, S. (1987). *The civilized engineer.* New York: St. Martin's Press.

Geppert, L. (1995, May). The uphill struggle: No rose garden for women in engineering. *Spectrum,* 40–50.

Goodman, D. (1995). Education and the internet: The coming challenge to internet culture. *Syallabus,* 10–12.

Grana, S. J., & Rutherford, L. H. (1995). Retrofitting academe: adapting faculty attitudes and practices to technology. *T.H.E. Journal,* 82–86.

Hummer, M., & Champy, J. (1993). Regineering the corporation: A manifesto for business revolution. New York: Harper Collins.

Harris, C., Pritchard, M., & Rabins, M. (1995). Engineering ethics: Concepts and cases. Albany New York: Wadsworth.

Huey, J. (1994). Waking up to the new economy. *Fortune,* 36–100.

Institute of Electrical Electronics Engineers (IEEE). (1996 January). [Newsrelease educational activities department], P.O. Box 1331, 445 Hoes Lane, Piscataway, NJ 08855-1331.

Institute of Electrical and Electronics Engineers (IEEE). (1994a, May). Industry 2000: technical vitality through continuing education. *Executive summary.* P.O. Box 1331, 445 Hoes Lane, Piscataway NJ 08855-1331.

Katz, S. (1993). The entry-level engineer: Problems in transition from student to professional. *Journal of Engineering Education, 82* (3) 171–174.

Kiechel, W. (1993). How we will work in the year 2000. *Fortune,* 38–40, 44, 46, 48, 52.

Kleiman, C. (1994). *The 100 best jobs for the 1990s and beyond.* New York: Berkley Publishing.

Larson, A. (1995). Cuts will affect engineering education. Internet WWW page @ URL *http://www.ieee.org:80 . . . /perspective.menu.html.*

Laszlo, A., & Castro, K. (1995, March-April). Technology and values: Interactive learning environments for future generations. *Educational Technology,* 7–13.

Leitzel, T., & Vogler, D. (1995). The virtual curriculum: Outcome-based/ customized course development. *Journal of Studies in TechnicalCareers, XV* (1), 11–19.

Levenson, N. (1990). Educational pipeline issues for women. Internet WWW page @ URL *http://www.ai.mit.edu/ . . . s/Gender/pipeline.html.*

Mayadas, F. (1994). Asychronous learning networks: Alfred p. Sloan foundation's program in learning outside the classroom. Internet page @ URL *http//W3.scale.uiuc.edu/education/ALN.new.html*

Mehta, S. (1995). A method for instant assessment and active learning. *Journal of Engineering Education,* 295–298.

Morrow, R. (1994). Issues facing engineering education. *Journal of Engineering Education, 83* (1), 15–18.

Oakley, B. (1995). The Sloan center for asynchronous learning environments. [speech at the national communications forum October]. Chicago, IL.

Polyson, S., & Saltzberg, S. (1995, September). Distributed learning on the world wide web. *Syllabus,* pp. 10–12.

Ragins, B. R. & Sundstrom, E. (1989). Gender and power in organizations. *Psychological Bulletin,* 105, 51–88.

Reppert, B. (1995a). Engineers brace for tough 1996 in wake of R&D program cutbacks, pp. 1–2. Internet WWW page @ URL *http://www.ieee.org: 80 . . . /perspective.menu.html*

Reppert, B. (1995b). AAAS report offers dismal outlook, p. 2. Internet WWW *http://www.ieee.org:80 . . . /perspective.menu.html*

Reppert, B. (1995c). Republicans aim to rescue regulation, cut costs, p. 2. Internet page @ URL *http://www.ieee.org:80. . . /perspective.menu.html*

Rogers, R., & Stemkoski, M. (1995). Reality-based learning and interdisciplinary teams: An interactive approach. *Journal of Engineering Technology, 12* (2) 44–48.

Rosenheck, A. (1994). My capitol hill diary as a congressional fellow, p. 3. Internet WWW page @ URL *http://www.ieee.org:80 . . . /perspective. menu.html*

Rosser, S. (1993). Female friendly science: Including women in curricular content and pedagogy in science. *Journal of General Education, 42* (3), pp. 191–220.

Rossman, P. (1993). The emerging worldwide electronic university. Westport, Connecticut: Praeger. Internet page @ URL *http://www. cms.dmu.ac.uk/People/cph/VR/whatsur.html*

Sorkin, M. (1992). Scenes from the electronic city: Impact of virtual reality on lifestyle and social relations. *I.D., 39* (3), 70–78.

Society of Women Engineers. (1993). A national survey of women and men engineers: A study of the members of 22 engineering societies. 120 Wall Street, 11th Floor New York, New York 10005-3902.

Staff. (1995, May/June). Educating tomorrow's engineers. *ASEE Prism*, pp. 10–17.

Tharenou, P. (1995). Correlates of women's chief executive status: Comparisons with men chief executives and women top managers. *Journal of Career Development, 21* (3), 201–212.

Walsh, J., & Reese, B. (1995). Distance learning's growing reach. *T.H.E. Journal: Technology Horizons in Education.* 58–66.

Wagner, E., & McCombs, B. (1995). Learner centered psychological principles in practice: Designs for distance education. *Educational Technology,* 32–35.

Youst, D., & Lipsett, L. (1994). Survival of the fittest. *Spectrum,* 67–69.

21

Continuing Education for Information Systems Professionals

David D. Branigan

INTRODUCTION

In this chapter, I will address information systems employees as a discrete profession, the need for content-related continuing professional education, applicable certification, and continuing professional education that goes beyond the specific content-related material applied directly to the improvement of computer technology skills. Information systems has not always been looked upon as a profession. Curry, Wergin and Associates (1993) include three brief references to computer science as a profession. It requires collegial education and it has a base in special knowledge. It serves the social good.

Members of this profession have special educational requirements. The primary need is for education that goes further than the formal university curriculum. Computer science an ever-changing, ever-demanding profession. As technology changes so do the needs of its users. Computer science professionals are beginning to sort out the matter of certification and licensing. In the United States this is an evolving process and has been developing for some time.

Beyond the functional aspects of the profession, beyond the technical needs of its members, there are other educational needs. As the profession changes, the skills of its members are changing to encompass what have come to be known as "soft" skills. These are primarily the skills of teamwork, communications, and ethics.

Educators of information systems professionals should examine these notions carefully and seek to understand the profession. The needs of its members must be understood. Only then can educators hope to serve those members well.

THE INFORMATION SYSTEMS PROFESSION

When I first began my career, I was a high school math and computer science teacher seeking to get out of teaching and into practice. I was hired to do customer training on mainframe database management systems. My audience consisted of highly technical professionals, predominantly programmers. The environment was almost totally mainframe computers.

Since then the field has gone from data processing (DP) to management information systems (MIS or IS) to information technology (IT), and it is often referred to as computer science. The basic career path has stayed much the same. Programmers, who write programs, progress to analysts, who design them. Analysts progress to project leaders. Project leaders become systems managers. Programmers who do not wish to progress to management remain programmers or become database administrators or systems programmers. Several new positions have entered the field during the past 10 years. Chief among them is the local area network administrator.

These are the people who keep the large computer systems of business running. They write the software programs that make data into usable information. If information is the life blood of the corporation and the computers are the heart pumping that blood throughout the system, then the IS professionals are the physicians who keep that heart pumping and define how that information will flow.

Qualifications for the profession have changed also. Engineers developed and operated the early computers. Early data-processing employees came from the engineering field or from other positions, not necessarily professional, within the company. Today a degree in information systems or information technology is a requirement for most starting positions within the profession although degrees in associated fields (mathematics, accounting, engineering) are occasionally accepted.

THE NEED FOR CONTINUING
PROFESSIONAL EDUCATION

Woodard (1990) explained the need for continuing education as follows:

> For IS employees vulnerable to technical obsolescence, the need to explore ongoing educational opportunities is particularly crucial. Many

IS professionals have to realize, perhaps for the first time in their careers, that doing the same thing for 15 years has made them obsolete and overpriced. (p. 75)

Computer technology is expanding at lightening speed. Personal computers (PCs) came out in the late 1970s and early 1980s. We are already on our fifth generation of PCs and about to go into our sixth. With this expansion has come a switch from systems that reside only on large mainframe computers to systems that exist on a combination of mainframes and microcomputers. With this explosion of hardware technology has come a parallel explosion of software, the programs that make the computers work.

Once, only corporations had access to computers. Programmers gave them that access by developing software. Now, programs that allow end users access to micro computers can be purchased off the shelf. This does not mean an end to the IS professional. Someone has to integrate those user-designed, off-the-shelf systems into the company's information system.

With the explosion of off-the-shelf products for end users, there has also been an explosion of products for the IS professional. These products are designed to make more sophisticated systems easier and faster to design and implement. There is also the transference to client/server technology. These systems run on networks of microcomputers and other mid-sized computers referred to as minis and often interface with the mainframe systems. The products to create these client/server systems are often significantly different from the products on the mainframe. These new products must be learned.

Meanwhile, the old systems must still be maintained with the older technology until they can be translated into client/server technology. Many colleges and universities have made the transition from teaching mainframe skills to teaching client/server skills. This changeover has sometimes left a void in the skills of new employees. As older employees battle to learn and shift to the new technologies, newer employees are being trained in the old technologies. Menkus (1992) said, "No longer will it be possible for one to rely throughout one's career primarily on knowledge acquired while pursuing a degree." Mernard-Watt (1993) stated that, "Many of these software workers have technical knowledge which is rapidly becoming obsolete . . ." (page 23).

These conditions have caused a booming business for continuing professional education. There are two primary sources of technical computer training for professionals. Vendors like Oracle Corporation, developer of a database management system of the same name, have customer training departments to provide training on their products for their customers. Training and consulting companies like Automated Concepts Inc. sell courses to companies on a variety of mainframe and micro technologies. Most major software vendors have training staffs. There are probably thousands of training companies in the United States alone.

Most of these companies offer standard, stand-up, platform training. Courses range from 1 to 5 days. Many include hands-on exercises. Evaluation consists of a "feel good" evaluation asking questions like, "Did you like the class?" "Was the instructor good?" "Was the atmosphere conducive to learning?" and so on.

CERTIFICATION

Certification of inforamtion systems professionals has never been of great importance in the United States. The Institute of Certification of Computer Professionals has been offering a voluntary certification and recertification program since the 1970s (Norcini & Shea, 1993). Patton (1994) stated

> Not once in over 20 years has anyone ever asked if I'm certified to perform a job. My point is this. Are you going to take tax advice from a CPA or your brother-in-law Fred? We have too many Freds. Perhaps we should even take this one step further and go for licensing.

Recently several vendors have been offering certification programs and companies have been paying attention. Oracle offers certification to database administrators and application developers. One takes a prescribed curriculum of Oracle classes and then must pass a test. Novell, vendor of the world's most popular network operating system, has been certifying network administrators and network engineers for years. One takes courses from a certified Novell instructor and then must pass a test.

Microsoft has recently entered the certification arena. One can become certified in Microsoft's NT operating system, application development, or one of several Microsoft products. Again classes are given by Microsoft certified instructors and then a test must be taken. If one looks at the help wanted ads in any large metropolitan newspaper the value of this certification can be seen. Most ads for these types of positions require certification.

BEYOND THE FUNCTIONAL

In reading through what little literature exists on continuing education for information systems professionals, three topics stand out that need to be addressed by educators: (1) critical thinking skills, (2) teamwork, and (3) ethics. Often students are taught what information systems is about, what the tools are, and how to use them. Seldom are they taught how to think critically. The hope is that by the time they have worked on enough systems and are ready to progress to the analyst level, they will have developed these skills through the process. I have seen enough professionals in my classes to know that it just does not happen.

There was a time when being an excellent technocrat was qualification enough to build a career in information systems. This is no longer true. I have observed many IS professionals who languish in the same position year after year because they lack the soft skills necessary to progress. They came out of college thinking that technical skills were all they needed. Now they are passed over for promotion.

The old notion of the computer nerd sitting mysteriously in his cubical listening to some acid rock group and becoming one with his computer while those in awe stand idly by as he performs his magic is no more. Today teams of IS professionals and professionals from other departments within the company work together to produce a system. The IS professional may know the computer but the accountant knows the accounting system and what has to be done with the data. Menard-Watt (1993) said, "IS professionals will be working less as individuals and more as a member of workgroups and business teams." Misic and Graf (1993) in a study of Systems Analysts found their role to be, " . . . interwoven with the most important activity of maintaining good human relations between all individuals involved in the system development process." (page 13).

More and more corporations are turning to systems integrators and outsourcers to handle their information systems work. This policy means more work is being performed by nonemployees of the company. This work needs to be managed by someone on the IS staff. Menkus (1992) saw the IS professional as being, "less of a technician and more of a facilitator" as this happens.

In a study of IS graduates on the job, Licker and Miller (1989) made an amazing discovery. They asked their subjects to rank the traits necessary to advance in programming. Programming skills ranked ninth closer to important than very important or essential. The skills that topped the list were solving logical problems, aptitude for precision and detail, and ability to work in groups.

Mizock (1986) considered ethics as a more prevalent issue as the use of computers becomes more important. He noted, ". . . an increased awareness by DP professionals that they must get involved with computer ethics education by developing classes and explaining what should be taught." Couger (1989) pointed out that "Both the ACM and DPMA curriculum committees include ethical issues in the recommended curriculum for IS majors" (page 211).

Armour and Fuhrman (1993) discussed the role of liberal learning in continuing professional education. Liberal learning has three components: (1) It teaches critical thinking skills, (2) establishes the kind of context in which thinking is most valuable (ethics), (3) and stresses communications. All three are very important skills for IS professionals. They also observed that, "faculty in the professions must assume responsibility" for conveying this knowledge to the professionals they serve.

CONCLUSION

What I have attempted to accomplish in this chapter is to provide a brief description of the continuing education of information systems professionals. I have described the profession itself. I have explained the necessity of technical continuing education. I have uncovered some nontechnical subjects that should be approached.

The study of continuing education for the information systems professional needs researching. There has been very little work done in the field. I was able to discover two dissertations on the topic. One is a study of the *Learning Styles of Software Engineers* (Banks, 1992), the other a study of *How Programmers Learn* (Sacks, 1992). More should be done.

What is the best way to teach technical topics? Nontechnical topics? Does this teaching differ by function within the profession? Is there a best way to teach the soft skills such as teamwork, ethics, and communications? Are there other skills that require the attention of professional educators?

There is one topic obviously missing from this chapter. What of evaluation? How are programs of professional IS education evaluated? Have there been any studies of evaluation in the field? Have there been follow-up studies to see if those evaluations were effective?

How do members of the profession choose the subjects they will study? How much study is formal, informal, or self-directed? How do corporations decide what courses to offer the members of the profession?

I am sure there are other questions as well. As more attention is paid to the field answers will be found. Now it is up to us to begin the inquiry.

REFERENCES

Armour, R., & Fuhrman, B. (1993). Confirming the centrality of liberal learning. In Curry, L., Wergin, J. (Ed.), *Educating professionals* (147). San Francisco: Jossey-Bass .

Banks, D. (1992). *Learning styles of software engineers.* Unpublished Doctoral Dissertation.

Couger, J. (1989, June). Preparing IS students to deal with ethical issues. *MIS Quarterly,* 211–217.

Curry, L., Wergin, J, & Associates (Eds.). (1993). *Educating professionals.* San Francisco: Jossey-Bass.

Licker, P., & Miller, M. (1989). How are DP/MIS graduates doing? *Journal of Systems Management, 40,* 25–32.

Menard-Watt, L. (1993). Changing role of IS professionals, *Journal of Systems Management, 44,* 23–24.

Menkus, B. (1992). How to continue professional growth. *Journal of Systems Management, 43,* 19.

Misic, M., & Graf, D. (1993). The interpersonal environments of the systems analyst. *Journal of Systems Management, 44,* 12–16.

Mizock, M. (1986, August). Ethics—the Guiding Light of professionalism. *Data Management, 221,* 16–18.

Norcini, J., & Shea, J. (1993). Increasing pressures for recerticfication and relicensure. In L. Curry, Wergin, & Associates (Eds.), *Educating professionals* (p. 81). San Francisco: Jossey-Bass.

Patton, M. (1994). Professionalism. *Journal of Systems Management, 45,* 40–41.

Sacks, M. (1992). *How programmers learn systems. A study of adult learning in a professional setting.* Unpublished Doctoral dissertation.

Woodard, W. (1990, July). Learning to cure technical obsolescence. *Datamation, 36,* 75–76.

22

A National Board Certification Process for K–12 Educators: A Model for Professional Development

Rita E. Clehouse

INTRODUCTION

In his State of the Union address, February 5, 1997, President Bill Clinton charged the nation to become "shapers of events, not observers. . . to rise to a new test of leadership. . . [and] to ensure that all Americans have the best education in the world." To achieve these goals, President Clinton proposed a national crusade for education standards that would represent "what our students must know to achieve in the knowledge economy of the 21st century." To have the best schools, America must have the best teachers. An organization mentioned by President Clinton that has been developing a national certification process for K–12 educators is the National Board for Professional Teaching Standards. With federal support for the next four years, the National Board Teacher Certification process will be under scrutiny. Many questions concerning this organization have arisen.

- What is the foundation of the National Board Certification Process for K–12 Educators?
- Who/what is the National Board for Professional Teaching Standards?
- Just what is the National Board Certification process?
- Is National Board Certification another attempt to interfere with state's rights? Will the National Board Certification process be forced upon state boards of education?
- I'm already "certified" in my state to teach certain subjects. Why would I want National Board Certification?

339

• Does this mean that National Board Certified Teachers can teach in any state and don't need state licensure?
• I've seen a teacher in my district preparing her portfolio for National Board Certification, and, frankly, it scares me to death! Why would anyone want to apply for National Board Certification?
• What impact might this National Certification process have upon Higher Education?

All these questions and many more are on the lips of teachers, superintendents, board members, and the public as the work of the National Board for Professional Teaching Standards continues to appear in professional journals and local newspapers. Much fear accompanies these queries, clouding judgment and eliciting emotional responses. As usual, it is a lack of understanding that is causing unnecessary concerns. Let's examine this organization and dissolve the myths.

What is the foundation of the National Board Certification Process for K–12 Educators?

In 1983, the President's National Commission on Excellence in Education's report, *A Nation at Risk: The Imperative for Educational Reform,* horrified Americans with phrases like, "If an unfriendly foreign power had attempted to impose on America the mediocre educational performance that exists today, we might well have viewed it as an act of war." Education, business, parents, and legislators, reflecting upon effective improvement strategies, closely reexamined the lagging American education system. In 1986, the Carnegie Task Force on Teaching as a Profession responded to *A Nation at Risk* with a call for the teaching profession to establish standards and certify teachers who would meet these standards in an attempt to create "a profession of well-educated teachers prepared to assume new powers and responsibilities to redesign schools for the future." In its report, *A Nation Prepared: Teachers for the 21st Century,* the Carnegie Task Force suggested that the key to the reform of American schools lies in the teachers themselves. Thus, in 1987, began the first teacher-led national education reform organization, the National Board for Professional Teaching Standards (NBPTS).

Who/what is the National Board for Professional Teaching Standards?

The National Board for Professional Teaching Standards is a nonprofit, nonpartisan, nongovernmental, independent organization led by a 63-member board of directors, which includes a majority of classroom teachers (those noted for excellence in the classroom, plus leaders of teacher unions, teacher educators, representatives of discipline areas and teaching specialty associations), as well as school administrators, local and state school board members, governors, state legislators, higher education officials, and business and community leaders. The organization receives its funding from grants by the nation's major private foundations and corporations and from federal sources (NBPTS Candidate Guide, 1993). Once the whole national certification system is in place and operating, the fees paid by or on the behalf of National Board Certification candidates will be used to run the organization.

Mission of the National Board for Professional Teaching Standards

The mission of the National Board for Professional Teaching Standards is to establish high and rigorous standards for what accomplished teachers should know and be able to do, to develop and operate a national voluntary system to assess and certify teachers who meet these standards, and to advance related education reforms for the purpose of improving student learning in American schools.

"What Teachers Should Know and Be Able to Do" evolved from this mission statement with five core propositions upon which the National Board Certification process is based: (1) effective teachers are committed to students and their learning; (2) effective teachers possess in-depth knowledge of subject matter, delivery techniques, and students (they know their students as individuals); (3) effective teachers competently manage and monitor student learning; (4) effective teachers systematically reflect upon their teaching experiences and learn from that experience (they are reflective, lifelong learners); (5) effective teachers are members of the learning community (they share their learning/teaching experiences with others—colleagues, parents, etc.). Currently, the National Board is developing advanced standards structured around student developmental levels and discipline areas in more than 30 certification fields. Each set of standards mirrors professional unanimity of the critical aspects of teaching in that area with committees of classroom teachers, teacher educators, disciplinary field experts, and authorities in human development extensively working together on a national level. The National Board for Professional Teaching Standards scrutinizes the standards again before they are accepted.

Just what is the National Board Certification process?

National Board Certification is a display of teachers' ability to measure themselves against high and rigorous National Board standards that have been established by their peers. Multipart standard-based assessments are used to measure the principled, professional judgment of National Board Certification candidate in various situations. These performance-based exercises reinforce and encourage the candidates' continuing professional growth as they demonstrate their talents, skills, and knowledge through on-site portfolio exercises (involving videotaping classes, analyzing student work, reflecting upon teaching practices, sharing examples of school and community involvement, etc.) and an off-site one-day series of intensive assessment exercises. Though the exercises vary from discipline area to discipline area, similarities do exist.

In every discipline, emphasis is upon the accomplished teacher's knowledge of subject matter, the teacher's knowledge of the student as a person-learner, the teacher's pedagogical knowledge, the teacher's resultant improved knowledge of self as learner-teacher

Typical Portfolio Exercises		
Subject	Typical Exercises	Typical Requirements
ENGLISH/LANGUAGE ARTS	Instructional Analysis Whole Class	Videotape Reflective Writings
	Instructional Analysis Small Group	Videotape Reflective Writings
	Analysis of Student Response to Literature	Student Work Teacher Reflection
	Analysis of Student Writing	Student Work Teacher Reflection
	Documented Accomplishments (Professional Development)	Teacher Involvement with Families, Colleagues, and the Community

through the reflective components of the portfolio, and the teacher's professional development as a member of a learning community, which includes fellow teachers, parents, and the community. Teachers reflect upon their self-made classroom videos and examples of student work as they create profiles of effective instruction and professional judgment. It is a learning adventure, a growing experience, and an opportunity to look at one's teaching and decide how to improve it.

After completing the portfolio assessment process, teachers attend an off-site assessment center for a day of further assessment designed for teachers to further demonstrate their knowledge, skills, and abilities in another setting. At the assessment site, teachers participate in various exercises which assess their expertise in the areas based on the five propositions which form the core of the National Board Certification process: (1) commitment to students and their learning, (2) knowledge of subject area and how to teach it, (3) responsibility for monitoring and managing student time, (4) reflective thinking, and (5) learning from experience, and membership in a learning community. One of the Early Adolescence/English Language Arts assessment exercises asks the candidates to read several books and write about how to include them in their curriculum (Pearlman, 1995).

Is National Board Certification another attempt to interfere with states' rights? Will the National Board Certification process be forced upon state boards of education?

The National Board for Professional Teaching Standards does not seek to override current states' licensing policies, although various states are now becoming interested in the National Board Certification process. Because North Carolina's governor, James B. Hunt, Jr.,

Assessment Center Activities English-Language Arts
Areas of Assessment
Teaching Literature
Reading Literature
Teaching Writing
Language Study
Prior to arriving at the assessment site, candidates will receive a reading list and professional articles to read in preparation.

is current chair of the National Board of Professional Teaching Standards' Board of Directors and is convinced that the work of the National Board for Professional Teaching Standards is essential for the continued growth of education, his state is one of the most active supporters of the work of NBPTS. In North Carolina, the state legislature has appropriated $475,582 for the 1995–96 school fiscal year to provide funds to pay fees for teachers who complete the National Board Certification process and to help them in that process by granting them 3 days' release time to work on their portfolios (Current National Board Certified Teachers report spending approximately 120 out-of-class hours preparing their portfolios) and prepare for the assessment center activities. North Carolina also provides an annual bonus of 4% of the teachers' state-paid salary to those who achieve and retain National Board Certification. (At this time, the expiration date of the National Board Certificate is undetermined.) North Carolina, which further grants a North Carolina teaching license to relocating National Board Certified Teachers, also is creating NBPTS-based staff development training programs and plans to incorporate the National Board's standards into institutions of higher education programs.

Like North Carolina, other states are expressing support for National Board Certification in a variety of ways. Alabama's legislators have established that Alabama shall acknowledge national reciprocity when the National Board Certification process has been completed for all areas. In the state of Colorado, the State Board of Education has determined that professionally licensed teachers who achieve National Board Certification will be eligible for Colorado "master teacher" certification and all professional development activities associated with National Board Certification may be submitted for license renewal. In Iowa, legislation has established that an individual who receives National Board Certification shall receive an Iowa endorsement when the State Board of Examiners determines that National Board standards meet or exceed the Iowa requirements. Iowa also allocates funds that may be used for district teachers who wish to participate in the assessment activities leading to National Board Certification (State Action, March 1995).

In addition, Ohio legislators have earmarked funds to pay certification fees for up to 250 teachers seeking National Board Certification in the 1995–96 school year and fees for up to 400 teachers in the 1996–97 school year. Also, a teacher achieving National Board Certification will receive an annual award of $2,500 for the life of the certificate. In addition, Ohio's Office of Teacher Education and Certification has determined that any Ohio teacher who completes the National Board Certification process will receive enough equivalent continuing education credits (CEUs) to have his or her license renewed (*Teacher to Teacher, 3,* 1995, p. 3). In Oklahoma, legislation has instituted the Oklahoma Commission for Teacher Preparation to address issues associated with NBPTS, as well as the design, development, and implementation of a competency-based teacher preparation system. Out-of-state teachers who have achieved National Board Certification and are relocating to Oklahoma can receive Oklahoma licensure without having to fulfill additional requirements normally needed for relocating teachers. It was further established that the SBE (State Board of Education) modify teacher licensing categories to be compatible with National Board Certification categories and develop an incentive program to encourage teachers to achieve National Board Certification (State Action, March 1995).

Other states are hopping onto the National Board Certification bandwagon. This year the Illinois State Board of Education contacted its five National Board Certified Teachers to ask their assistance in mentoring 16 candidates for whom the State Board of Education is funding the assessment fee, plus furnishing 3 days of release time to help the candidates prepare their portfolios. The mentoring process furthers the sense of community among the participants and furnishes them with another opportunity to share, reflect, and grow as teaching professionals.

State involvement in the National Board Certification process often is initiated at a local level. In Broward County, Florida, Nova University presented a National Board Certified Teacher with a $25,000 scholarship to pursue graduate studies. Candidates who weren't certified were granted $1,000 scholarships in recognition of their lifelong commitment to learning. National Board Certified teachers in Broward County receive a $2,000 yearly supplement for the term of their certification. In addition, they receive in-service points that can be applied toward state license renewal. In New Orleans, Louisiana, teachers who hold valid National Board Certification receive a 5% annual supplement to their salary if the teachers are serving in the area in which they are certified. In Boston, Massachusetts, the Boston public schools will reimburse teachers for the cost of National Board Certification fees and will then consider that teacher for "lead teacher" status, which includes a 10% to 20% salary increase. In Corpus Christi, Texas, the school district has agreed to pay $1,250 more each year to any National Board Certified Teachers for the length of the certificate. More and more states, schools, and districts are becoming involved as the mission of the National Board for Professional Teaching Standards becomes more well-known and understood.

I'm already "certified" in my state to teach certain subjects. Why would I want Nationally Board Certification?

Though the terms certification and licensure are used interchangeably, they are, in fact, two very different procedures. In most professions, states are responsible for licensure while professional organizations grant certification. Until the National Board for Professional Teaching Standards was established, there was no such professional organization for teaching (Bradley, 1995). National Board Certification is neither a replacement for current state teaching licenses, nor is it mandatory or for everyone. In fact, National Board Certification is very different from most current state licensing processes. A simple look at the requirements for each will provide verification of this fact.

What National Board Certification Is Not
☑ a replacement for current state teaching
☑ mandatory
☑ for everyone

In the state of Illinois, the general education requirements consist of courses in American government, American history, anthropology, biological science, communication skills, cultural geography, economics, English, fine arts, foreign language, health, history, humanities, language arts, linguistics, literature, mathematics, Third World culture, philosophy, physical development, physical science, political science, psychology, social science, and sociology. Varying numbers of semester hours are required in each of these, depending upon the teaching license being sought. In addition to these courses, professional education courses are required, which include methods courses and student teaching experience. After one has completed these courses successfully, it is necessary to pass a basic skills test and a subject matter knowledge test. Then a person can receive an Illinois teaching certificate/license. State licensing is mandatory and designed to ensure that beginning teachers meet certain *basic* criteria.

National Board Certification is *not* mandatory, nor is it intended to become mandatory. Its purpose is to improve education by drawing upon the strengths of those who are exemplary educators and teaching others their techniques. Too often those who are excellent teachers find no motivation to remain within the classroom. Their strengths are not recognized, and others who could learn from them are not given the opportunity. National Board Certification is an attempt to keep exemplary teachers in their classrooms while encouraging them to serve as mentors and leaders in the continuing professionalization of teaching. Because National Board Certification is voluntary, it complements but does not replace mandatory state licensing. It is a continuation of professional growth and a recognition of accomplished teaching.

Furthermore, National Board Certification is *not* for everyone, but then again, few things are. Beginning teachers do not meet the 3-year teaching experience prerequisite. Many excellent, experienced teachers have situations which do not allow them the time or opportunity to meet the professional development standards. They are so busy being mothers, fathers, aunts, uncles, grandparents, etc., that they do not have the time or desire to pursue the National Board Certification process. That does not mean that these individuals are not accomplished teachers, only that their current priorities are elsewhere.

In contrast to the Illinois teaching certification/licensing process, the National Board Certification process is voluntary, rigorous, and intended for accomplished teachers who have taught for a minimum

Comparison of National Board Certification Process and Teaching Certificate from the State of Illinois	
National Board Certification	Illinois Teaching Certification
• voluntary	• mandatory
• high and rigorous standards for experienced teachers	• entry-level standards for novice teachers
• analysis, synthesis, and evaluation assessment	• knowledge and comprehension assessment
• professional development opportunity	• process
• a time for verification, reflection, validation, and improvement	• a time for verification, validation
• confirming, affirming	• conforming
• assessment in natural classroom environment	• assessment in an artificial environment

of three years. It involves three elements: (1) standards of what an accomplished teacher should know and be able to do, (2) assessment of the skills needed to meet those standards, and (3) professional development wherein a teacher grows through the National Board Certification process. Being multidimensional ("learner-centeredness, cultural awareness, content knowledge, integrated curriculum, and coherent pedagogy"), the assessment process involves the candidates' creating "multi-layered responses to the exercises using videotapes, teaching artifacts, commentaries, and self-reflective essays" (Flannigan, 1994). The latter is an essential part of the National Board Certification process, which validates the roles of reflection and lifelong learning as integral to the teaching profession.

Does this mean that National Board Certified Teachers can teach in any state and don't need state licensure?

The idea of state reciprocity is appealing to many teachers, especially those who find themselves frequently moving from one state to another; however, this is a state issue that needs to be decided individually. At this point, only Oklahoma has taken steps in that direction. Iowa has decided that National Board Certified Teachers will be eligible for an Iowa license once the State Board of Examiners determines that the National Board's standards meet or exceed their own. It remains to be seen what other states may decide.

I've seen a teacher in my district preparing her portfolio for National Board Certification, and, frankly, it scares me to death! Why would anyone want to apply for National Board Certification?

Those teachers who have become involved with the National Board Certification process all seem to agree that it was one of the "best-worse" professional development activities of their teaching careers. Jon-Paul Roden , an early adolescence/generalist candidate felt that "participation in the project . . . compelled [him] to reassess all of [his] training and experience as a veteran educator" (Shapiro, 1994). The self-reflective element via observation and commentaries on the videotapes, as well as student work, was a definite "improvement enabler" for many of the teachers. One of the teachers, Kathleen Reeves, upon viewing her videotape, said she noticed several specific positive and negative student-teacher interactions that she would not have realized had she not observed the tape. She shared these insights with her students, "I am doing this because I really want to be a good teacher, and this is going to help me become a better teacher. Here are some things I learned from watching the tape last night" (Shapiro, 1994). When students can see teachers learning from their mistakes, then students feel it's okay to make mistakes and to learn from those mistakes—to take the risk of learning. In fact, the message of the need for self-reflection as an outgrowth of the National Board Certification process is often repeated by the National Certified Teachers.

Claire Ratfield of Lincoln Elementary School in Corona del Mar, California, claims, "It was the best of times . . . it was the worst of times . . . [but] . . . the addition of 'reflective practice' to my daily practice has turned my otherwise good teaching into extraordinary teaching; analyzing setbacks has now become critical for continual self-improvement" both for herself and her students.

Many teachers were quiet about their involvement in the National Board Certification for fear of failure—failure to achieve national certification—but, as they became more involved in the process, they realized that they could not fail if they improved their teaching as a result of the National Board Certification. They could not fail if they grew in their profession through reflecting and learning about themselves as a learners-teachers-professionals. As National Board Certified Teacher Patsy Dean Wallin remarked, "The portfolio and the assessment center forced me to step back and reflect on what I do and why . . . I'll never go through anything with my students again without that reflection" (Needham, 1994).

Mary-Dean Barringer, Vice President for the Advancement of Teaching, echoed that sentiment when she spoke to two Indiana teachers who had been part of the first field test.

> My passion for the National Board is rooted in my belief that it is the best opportunity for teachers to strengthen their voice, and be heard, on matters of teaching and learning, and on policies governing the profession. I am convinced that a powerful transformation results from involvement with the National Board, through its standards-setting process, assessment development activities, focus groups, pilot groups, field test groups, or as certification candidates. And I am convinced that this transformation lasts forever . . . like the story of the Velveteen Rabbit . . . Once you are real, you can't become unreal again. It lasts for always . . . You have made a real impact in your classrooms, in your school district, in the national educational awareness/conversation, in

the work of the National Board . . . You are "real" teachers, and like the growth you've experienced, the teacher-leaders you've become, and the impact you've made, it lasts for always. (1995, Spring, p. 5)

What impact might this National Board Certification process have upon Higher Education?

National Board Certification already is affecting higher education institutions' teacher preparation and professional development programs as colleges and universities work in conjunction with state boards of education. Emporia State University in Kansas offered a satellite graduate credit workshop in November, 1995, to acquaint teachers with the National Board for Professional Teaching Standards. In Maine, exploratory conversations were held with the Chief State School Officer and the Southern Maine Partnership (higher education/school district initiative). The Indiana Professional Standards Board is studying the best strategy to incorporate National Board Certification into its teacher education programs, as well as its continuing professional development courses. The University of Minnesota is working with the Minnesota Federation of Teachers to design and implement professional support programs for National Board Certification candidates. The Dade-Monroe Teacher Education Center in collaboration with the University of Miami has been awarded a Goals 2000 Preservice/Inservice Grant for professional development, support, and assistance for potential National Board candidates. In New Mexico, legislation has been established requesting the State Board of Education to work with state universities' teacher preparation programs to examine teacher education competencies to ensure that they are compatible and consistent with National Board standards (State and Local Action, October, 1995). As time continues, it is probable that other state legislatures and institutions of higher education will form partnerships for the betterment of education.

LINGERING REFLECTIONS

The National Board for Professional Teaching Standards, although still in its infancy, is drawing the respect and attention of public and private sectors alike as they recognize the cogency of its message of improvement of education from within the teaching profession itself. From its initial "call to arms" as a response to the 1983 *A Nation at Risk: The Imperative for Educational Reform,* educators, businessmen, parents, community leaders, industry, and legislators worked together to reexamine the lagging American educational system. Within 3 years, the Carnegie Task Force on Teaching as a Profession appealed to the teaching profession to "heal itself." In 1987, the National Board for Professional Teaching Standards was born as a teacher-led national education reform organization. Using the combined strength of teachers, community, business, and legislators, this organization sought to "establish high and rigorous standards for what accomplished teachers should know and be able to do" through a voluntary assessment and certification system, which could promote improved student learning. They decided that accomplished teachers were committed to their students and learning and were very knowledgeable about their subject matter and pedagogy. Also, they were reflective, lifelong learners who shared their knowledge with others. From the first group of 145 National Board Certified Teachers in 1995, the ranks are expected to swell as current National Board Certified Teachers continue to mentor candidates. Various legislatures and universities are becoming involved as liaison-enablers in the National Board of Professional Teaching Standard's battle to improve learning in America's schools.

REFERENCES

Barringer, M. (1995, Spring). Becoming a real teacher. *Teacher to Teacher, 3,* 5.

Bradley, A. (1995, August). Building a profession. *Teacher Magazine,* 12–13.

Bradley, A. (1994, April 20). Pioneers in professionalism. *Education Week,* 18–27.

Flannigan, A. (1994, June). First field test of teacher certification system nearing end. *The Council Chronicle, 3* (5), 2.

Clinton, B. "We must be shapers of events, not observers. We must rise to a new test of leadership." State of the Union Address. Washington, D.C., 5 Feb. 1997.

Incentives, Supports and Professional Acknowledgments for National Board Certification

Kogan Krell, J. (Ed.). (1995, Spring). Administrators and policymakers honor the nation's first national board certified teachers. *Portfolio, 2,* 1–3.

Koprowicz, C. L. (1994, January). What state legislators need to know about the national board for professional teaching standards. *State Legislative Report, 19* (1).

National Board for Professional Teaching Standards. (1995, August). *An Invitation to National Board Certification Q & A.*

National Board for Professional Teaching Standards. (1995, March). *State Action Supporting National Board Certification.*

National Board for Professional Teaching Standard. (1995, October). *State and Local Action Supporting National Board Certification.*

National Board for Professional Teaching Standards. The Vision of the National Board.

National School Board Association. (1995). What school boards should know about the national board for professional teaching standards.

Needham, N. R. (1994, December). Waiting for the call. *NEA Today, 13* (5).

Pearlman, M. A. (Ed.). (1995, December). The redesigned assessment looks like this! *the envoy, 1* (1), 2.

Shapiro, B. (1994, Spring). Field test participants advance toward national board. *Teacher to Teacher, 1,* 1–3.

Staff. (1995–1996, Winter). State and local incentives and supports encourage teachers to reach highest standards. *Teacher to Teacher, 4,* 3.

Staff. (1995–1996, Winter). The standards development process. *Teacher to Teacher, 4,* 4–5.

U.S. National Commission on Excellence in Education. A nation at risk: The imperative for educational reform: A report to the nation and the secretary of education. Washington, D.C.: GPO, 1983.

Conclusion
William H. Young

I would like to conclude this book with a summary of thoughts I use when I provide a career planning session that is part of a general education course to help future professionals ready themselves for both the private and public sectors of the workforce.

Usually I start the session by providing examples of how a great positive first impression is a tremendous asset to any professional, from the first minute of the job interview, to the last moment of the retirement party. That first impression is based upon several factors including a good physical image, warmth, proper dress and accessories, a great handshake, a genuine interest attitude, and adherence to deadlines and timelines. It is very difficult to change a bad first impression and it is very easy to build upon a great first impression. Continuing professional education personnel working with displaced workers and other professionals looking for success should consider basic programming dealing with something as simple as first impression strategies for success for targeted professional groups.

Second, I talk about change using the K-12 classroom and travel as examples. The K-12 classroom has always had its problems; however, those problems have changed over the past several decades. When I was in school, primarily in the 1950s, running in the halls, making loud body noises, getting out of turn in line, and gum chewing were considered problems. For the past several years, problems such as alcohol abuse, drug abuse, suicide, and murder have become major problems. What a difference! If we look at changes in travel over the past 150 years, we see monumental changes in both time and comfort. In the mid-1850s wagon trains took at least 150 days to cross the United States. By 1981 the space shuttle crossed the United States in nine minutes. Retired spy planes have set transcontinental speed records in less than 70 minutes. Many of the chapter authors discuss change and provide strategies for the involvement of continuing professional education in planning for and coping with change in professional practice. Futurists continue to tell us that future porfessionals will change jobs at least 10 times and will change careers at least three times. Change and its manifestations will continue to grow in importance as a major topic in continuing professional education.

Third, I spend some time talking about the general conditions that exist in business, industry, and education today. When I was a future professional (1961–65), professional life was relatively simple, straightforward, bureaucratic, rather rigid (yes/no and right/wrong) and one was expected to excel as an individual. The world of professional practice has changed dramatically. Today the environment is very complex—ambiguous, not straightforward, flexible, not rigid— and is becoming more ad hoc and less bureaucratic. Individual accomplishment is giving ground to team productivity. People are expected to have experiences working in teams before they are hired. An ambiguous, complex, flexible, team-oriented, and ad hoc work environment makes wellness, empowerment, critical thinking, entrepreneurship, technological sophistication, and the ability to work in many diverse learning organizations necessities for professional success in the coming years.

Finally, I discuss with the students the need for them to have two or more professional skills. Organizations will continue to flatten and professionals will be asked to do more with fewer colleagues and more technology. As an accounting graduate in 1965, I planned for a 40-year career in accounting with a "Big Eight" accounting firm or the government. It was certain that if I were good, I would find my second and possibly my last career move with one of my client organizations. Accounting is not enough for tomorrow's professional. This future professional will also need to have a second and possibly a third language to work at home in urban environments and in the global village. When worldwide standards for excellence move into the service arena, professionals will have to perform at a mistake free level to maintain credibility in the workplace.

In order to provide professionals with the education needed to assist them in their quest for lifelong learning, it will be necessary for educators to change their focus dramatically very soon. The idea of counting credits for preplanned accredited activity must give way to learner centered, just-in-time educational activity that improves professional practice.

We hope this book has helped! Continued success!

INDEX